Reader in Comedy

Magda Romanska is Associate Professor of Theatre Studies and Dramaturgy at Emerson College, USA, and Visiting Associate Professor in Dramaturgy and Dramatic Criticism at the Yale School of Drama, USA. She is the co-founder and co-Executive Director of the *Theatre Times* website (www.thetheatretimes.com), author of *The Post-traumatic Theatre of Grotowski and Kantor* and editor of *The Routledge Companion to Dramaturgy*.

Alan Ackerman is a Professor of English at the University of Toronto, Canada. From 2005 to 2015, he served as Editor of the journal *Modern Drama*. His books include *Just Words: Lillian Hellman, Mary McCarthy, and the Failure of Public Conversation in America* and *Seeing Things, from Shakespeare to Pixar*.

Reader in Comedy: An Anthology of Theory and Criticism

Magda Romanska

and

Alan Ackerman

Bloomsbury Methuen Drama
An imprint of Bloomsbury Publishing Plc

B L O O M S B U R Y
LONDON · OXFORD · NEW YORK · NEW DELHI · SYDNEY

Bloomsbury Methuen Drama

An imprint of Bloomsbury Publishing Plc

Imprint previously known as Methuen Drama

50 Bedford Square	1385 Broadway
London	New York
WC1B 3DP	NY 10018
UK	USA

www.bloomsbury.com

BLOOMSBURY, METHUEN DRAMA and the Diana logo are trademarks of Bloomsbury Publishing Plc

First published 2017

British Library Cataloguing-in-Publication Data
A catalogue record for this book is available from the British Library.

ISBN:	HB:	978-14742-4789-4
	PB:	978-1-4742-4788-7
	ePDF:	978-1-4742-4791-7
	ePub:	978-1-4742-4790-0

Library of Congress Cataloging-in-Publication Data
A catalog record for this book is available from the Library of Congress.

Cover design: Eleanor Rose
Cover design shows a detail from *Stanczyk during a ball at the court of Queen Bona in the face of the loss of Smolensk* by Jan Mateyko, 1862. Courtesy of the Warsaw National Museum, Poland.

Typeset by Fakenham Prepress Solutions, Fakenham, Norfolk NR21 8NN
Printed and bound in India

To Lawrence Switzky

Contents

Acknowledgements

We would like to express our gratitude foremost to Robert Sabal, Dean of the School of the Arts at Emerson College for his financial support of this project. It would not have been possible without his foresight and patronage.

For such a wide-ranging project, we depended on the generosity of gifted colleagues and experts in the diverse periods this work covers to read and critique our introductions and make suggestions for the anthology's content. Each of the following people read drafts of particular sections and provided indispensable input in their areas of expertise: Brian Corman, Suzanne Akbari, Alex Eric Hernandez, Melba Cuddy-Keane, Jeannie Miller, Victoria Wohl, Rachel McArthur, and Jeremy Lopez. We also would like to thank the following colleagues for their insights and support: Elinor Fuchs, Sara Warner, David Krasner, Harvey Young, Catherine Sheehy, Laurence Senelick, and Martie Cook.

Andrea Most read every chapter and, as always, provided support in innumerable ways. We wish to offer a special acknowledgement of Jeffrey Rusten for his mentorship and for allowing us to use his outstanding translations of the Greeks. Many thanks are also due to our superb editorial assistants Emma Futhey, Andie Anderson, and Hanife Shulte.

We gratefully acknowledge those at Bloomsbury Methuen Drama who have contributed to this project along the way. Mark Dudgeon shepherded this project with enthusiasm even when we stalled. Thanks also to Emily Hockley, our excellent copyeditor Rosemary Morlin and indexer Agata Dabek.

Finally, we wish to take this opportunity to express our deep gratitude to our colleague and dear friend Lawrence Switzky, who made our collaboration possible, read each introduction, provided vital and unstinting feedback, and to whom we dedicate this book.

General Introduction

Comedy is difficult to define, though the word has been in active use for thousands of years. In ancient Greek, *komoidia* and, in classical Latin, *comoedia* referred to amusing stage-plays. In fourteenth-century French, there was *comedie*, and the first recorded use of 'comedye' in English dates to Chaucer's poem *Troilus and Criseyde* in 1374. Today, if you go to 'Genres' on any movie database, you will find 'Comedy'. But if you click on 'Subgenres', you will discover more than a dozen options, including 'Dark Comedies', 'Mockumentaries', 'Romantic Comedy', 'Satires', 'Slapstick', 'Stand-up Comedy', and more. Send-ups of politicians, jokes about sex, love stories that end in marriage, and old people making themselves ridiculous by pretending to be young are all forms of comedy that have a long history. Political humour, satire, farce, burlesque, sketch comedy, comedy of character, and comedy of manners – these many kinds of comedy employ different styles and make fun of diverse targets. Is it possible to generalize across this diversity?

Common themes, structural principles, aims and characters do appear. But critics often return to the problem of pinning comedy down, as if its resistance to definition (to *define* means to limit) is paradoxically a key characteristic. The difficulty of defining comedy, which includes debates about where the word came from in the first place, does not let critics off the hook. On the contrary, both the difficulty and the necessity of defining critical terms are central to comic theory. This problem also indicates a common notion about comedy itself, namely that it mocks conventions and offers a (temporary) liberation from routine restrictions. When contemporary theorists of comedy and postmodernism remark that what defines it is its very resistance to definition, they further the conversation by suggesting that the dialectic of freedom and form, novelty and tradition, is central to comic theory and practice. After describing the provenance of our key terms, this introduction will (1) briefly outline debates about the importance of comedy's historical contexts, (2) consider comedy as a narrative structure and sketch some exemplary comic plots, (3) examine well-known comic character-types, and (4) conclude with a synopsis of relevant theories of humour and of laughter. Each of these topics will attract significant attention in the chapters that follow.

Formal dramatic comedy originated in Athens in the fifth century BCE. The philosopher Aristotle refers to it in his *Poetics* (335 BCE), though even then comedy was changing from the so-called 'Old Comedy' of Aristophanes to the 'New Comedy' of Menander, and Aristotle traces 'comic plots' to an earlier period in Sicily. Furthermore, Aristotle appears to enter a debate about the definition of comedy that was already underway in ancient Greece. The *kōmos*, a drunken procession of revellers, which occurs at the end of many of Aristophanes' plays, is still often supposed to be an important source of comedy, but Aristotle says that '*kômôdoi* (comedians) acquired their name, not from *kômazein* (to revel), but from the fact that, being expelled in disgrace from the city, they wandered from village to village'. This comment has proved a valuable historical reference, but it settled nothing. Aristotle does not indicate what exactly comedy has to do with village life, and the spirit of revelry – letting loose with sex, wine, and music – continues to be a key subject of comic performance, theory, and criticism. Festivals celebrating rebirth in spring, such as those honouring Dionysus, the god of fertility in ancient Greece, have been linked to comedy by anthropologists, sparked in the twentieth century by Cambridge classicist Francis Macdonald Cornford's *Origin of Attic Comedy* (1914).

In the medieval period, when formal dramatic comedy virtually disappeared due to the antitheatrical bias of the Church, the communal, profane, and scatological impulse of ancient comedy found its way into the marketplace. Russian theorist Mikhail Bakhtin coined the term *carnivalesque* (1968) to describe how this liberating spirit, which he traces to the medieval Feast of Fools, shapes other kinds of comic literature and language as well. Carnival and similar marketplace festivals celebrated a temporary liberation from the established order. Social hierarchies, norms, and prohibitions were suspended or inverted. Carnival was a release valve for the lower classes. Bakhtin also explains the importance of clowns and fools in the medieval culture of humour and the 'misrule' that characterized carnival festivities and the comic rituals connected with them. His work has had an enormous influence on subsequent criticism, particularly on late twentieth-century Marxist and New Historicist scholars of Renaissance comedy and the network of materialist practices and social structures that shaped and was shaped by it.

Comedy is a feature of many different cultural forms and aspects of life. In addition to comic stage-plays, we also speak of people in everyday life acting comically or having a comical experience. When a prankster plays a joke, someone may say, 'He's such a comedian!' In *The Republic*, Plato warns against taking too much pleasure in 'comic representation', which he associated with irrationality and vulgarity, because it might lead 'you [to] become a comedian in your own life.' Scholars speak of comic novelists, poets, and even comic painters. Comic strips began appearing in newspapers in the nineteenth century. Diverging from Plato's critique of comedy, British author George Meredith describes comedy in his 1877 'Essay on Comedy' not as a particular genre at all but as a useful 'Spirit', a civilizing influence, a fountain of common sense: 'the Comic Spirit is a harmless wine, conducing to sobriety in the degree it enlivens. It enters you like fresh air into a study, as when one of the sudden contrasts of the comic idea floods the brain like reassuring daylight.'

Meredith's mixed metaphors and forced metaphysics point to two key features of comic theory: first, although we can identify generic conventions of dramatic comedy, it is also possible to speak of 'the comic' as a spirit, mode, sensibility, or attitude. Second, insofar as Meredith's *theory* grounds itself in 'common sense' or, in paradoxical 'solid minds', his contradictions indicate a key strain in comic theory, its resistance to abstraction. Reacting against the drabness of a bourgeois society that privileged science over art, Meredith's essay is pragmatic. The 'Comic Spirit', in his view, can rejuvenate a humanity crushed by modern mass culture. The subject of comedy tends to be ordinary experience, not the sublime, the lofty, or metaphysical. Plato objected to comedy's vulgarity and believed it represented a degraded (rather than ideal) form of truth. As literary theorist Kenneth Burke commented, 'Comedy deals with *man in society*, tragedy with the *cosmic man*' (original emphasis). Comedy often seems to privilege the life of the body over that of the mind (though the relative importance of body and mind in comedy is contested). It can be irrational, and contradictory. Comic theory too has a curiously anti-theoretical quality, returning continually to the empirical and the local. This is not to say that comedy is opposed to thinking; on the contrary, comedies are inherently self-reflexive. Burke refers to comedy's 'forensic complexity,' the way comedy refuses to accept any experience as final, subjecting social life to examination, finding importance in the seemingly trivial or mundane. Faced with the fact that there is no essential aspect that defines comedy, even Meredith must deduce its features from concrete instances. From Plato to the present, theorists have asked what comedy can teach us, if anything, about lived human experience. This Reader will offer a wide range of theories of comedy and humour and how they are interrelated.

Comedy and humour change from one period or culture to another. Roman dramatic comedy was deeply influenced by the Greek (often translating and adapting Greek originals). But it was also shaped, closer to home, by the improvised musical performances of the Etruscans (of ancient Tuscany) and by Atellan farce, which featured clowns and stock characters such as the braggart soldier (*miles gloriosus*). Roman audiences attended *ludi scaenici* or theatrical games, which included gladiator fights, chariot races and animal baiting, unlike Greek audiences who witnessed comedies in dramatic competitions at festivals for the god Dionysus. In the 1590s, writing *The Comedy of Errors*, Shakespeare drew from the Roman playwright Plautus, but Elizabethan comedy is also informed by medieval theatrical practices, Christian theology, the growth of the modern city, and the rise of capitalism. Shakespeare's 'festive' comedies were not only joyful but also linked to actual festivals, such as May Day and Christmas. *Twelfth Night* (1601–2), for instance, was written for the Christmas celebration of the Feast of the Epiphany. Modern comedy and comic theory reflect the impact of new technologies and the conditions of a mass industrial society.

This Reader is arranged chronologically to reflect the fact that comedy and theories of comedy are historically contingent. Comic theorists wrote in specific historical contexts that both shaped and were shaped by their work. The final section of this book includes selections from modern theorists, from Virginia Woolf and Constance Rourke to Michael North, who argue that modes of comedy, specific character-types and forms of humour are culturally specific. Comic authors have also responded to critics of their day. In 1579, Stephen Gosson's moralistic critique of Elizabethan comedy and theatre, *Schoole of Abuse, containing a pleasant invective against Poets, Pipers, Plaiers, Jesters and such like Caterpillars of the Commonwealth*, prompted Sir Philip Sidney to defend not only comedy but also poetry in general, in *An Apology for Poetry*. Authors developed theories in response to particular comedies. Sometimes playwrights, such as Ben Jonson and John Dryden, were theorists themselves. However, the breadth of this Reader will also show that comic structures and characters have displayed a remarkable consistency from ancient times to the present. While comedies have taken diverse forms, antique comic plots and characters have proved resilient and remain popular today in diverse media (although they have evolved: from the clever slave in Roman comedy, for example, to the clever servant in the Renaissance to the witty friend in contemporary sit-coms). In organizing selections to indicate both their historical specificity and elements of trans-historical continuity, this Reader also aims to highlight a methodological debate between historicists and formalists that has evolved into a more dialectical approach that historicizes form. Great comic authors and performers manipulate comic structures in historically significant ways, generating laughter in part from their irreverence toward forms, both social and dramatic. Thus, form becomes content (and vice versa).

This Reader does not confine itself to theories of theatre, but, as the selections indicate, comic novels, poems, and even TV sit-coms trace their roots to dramatic comedy. The *eirôn,* from which we derive the word 'irony,' was a central stock character in ancient Greek comedy. Aristotle describes the theatrical *eirôn* as a 'self-deprecator.' The word also appears in Plato's *Republic*, where it refers to a way of taking people in. Socrates assumes this role in Plato's dialogues. He pretends to be foolish, though he is very clever. Socrates as *eirôn* asks naïve questions in order to undermine the self-assured assertions of others, though it is important to note that Plato and Socrates did not regard this philosophical irony as comical. On the contrary, they are among the first critics of the comic, lamenting that people laugh when they feel superior to others or take pleasure in others' misfortunes. For Plato, comedy was vulgar and irrational, whereas for Meredith, in the nineteenth century, it was 'civilizing.' In these antithetical ideas, we can see the contours of an ancient debate.

Our modern sense of *irony*, which refers to a tension between what people say and what they actually mean or between what we expect and what really happens, is also linked to satire and parody, two more terms we trace to the Greeks. These forms of humorous imitation make light of weightier subjects. The playwright Aristophanes imitated the styles of tragedians Aeschylus and Euripides in *The Frogs*, making them ridiculous. Mel Brooks parodied the suspense films of Alfred Hitchcock in *High Anxiety* (1977). Theorists of comedy over the centuries, therefore, have engaged in a conversation about the definitions of irony, parody, and satire, debated their effects and how those effects are achieved. Wit punctures boastful self-seriousness in the comedy of Aristophanes, of the Marx Brothers and of Mel Brooks. The tricky slave and braggart soldier are comic types that make their way from the plays of Plautus to the prose fiction of Cervantes, Henry Fielding, and Mark Twain, and on to television sitcoms such as *The Honeymooners* in the 1950s and *30 Rock*. As comic forms evolve, they do not entirely change. Similarly, theorists of comedy participate in an ongoing dialogue.

The plot structure of Greek New Comedy is the basis of many films today, even when variations are taken into account: boy/girl falls for boy/girl; an obstacle (often parental) intervenes; a twist of the plot allows the lovers to unite in marriage, sexual consummation, or perhaps some less defined form of happiness. Youth is rewarded; old is made new. Rebirth is a common comic trope and structural principle. While sex is central to comedy, harking back to the fertility rites and phallic processions of antiquity, gender and comic attitudes towards women have become vital subjects of recent feminist critique. In ancient Greece and Elizabethan England women onstage were played by men. Commonly viewed as virgins or whores, women were sexual objects, and sexual violence is a frequent feature of comedy from Rome to the Restoration. Wives, on the other hand, were constant subjects of ridicule, often associated with unruly passions and needing to be tamed, as in *The Taming of the Shrew*. Cross-dressing, usually men playing women (or, in Shakespeare, men playing women playing men), both reflected on the construction of existing gender roles in performance and generated a frisson of homoeroticism. Critics debate whether the sexual politics of comedy in diverse periods has been progressive or conservative, but at the end of a standard comic plot, whether in a wedding or a chorus line, characters realize a new social compact, which the audience recognizes as desirable. Such audience expectations have proved extremely durable, despite local differences, including changing attitudes about gender. Blocking characters, who want to prevent the happiness of others, may be kicked out, like Malvolio from *Twelfth Night* or Jud Fry from *Oklahoma!* On the other hand, often they embrace the match they had obstructed, as do the fathers in Plautus or Lady Bracknell (a caricature of Victorian womanhood occasionally played by a man) at the conclusion of Oscar Wilde's *Importance of Being Earnest*. At the end of Molière's *Misanthrope*, the un-laughing Alceste decides to leave the world of lovers, which he disdains, though a joyful couple plans to follow him and hopes to change his mind. Generosity trumps disapproval. The *agelast*, derived from the Greek for one who refuses to laugh, is also a longstanding comic type dealt with in comic plots and theories. Of course, not all comedies conclude with marriage, and some non-comedies, such as D. W. Griffith's *Birth of a Nation*, a historical film about the American Civil War and Reconstruction, do – returning us to the difficulty of defining comedy.

Broadly speaking, comedies are characterized by happy endings, often figured in a movement from bondage to freedom (or in a marriage bond that suggests a new kind of freedom). Of course, the happiness achieved at the end of a comedy may be imperfect, and, though common, the happy end is not invariable. In some comic plots, characters' fortunes change not from bad to good but good to bad. Nonetheless, the exceptions tend to prove the rule. For instance, Ben Jonson's cruel, yet hilarious satire, *Volpone, or The Fox* (1606), moves not from bondage to freedom but from freedom to bondage. 'Though my catastrophe may, in the strict rigour of the comic law, meet with censure', Jonson writes in the Prologue, 'I desire the learned and charitable critic to have so much faith in me to think it was done of industry.' In other words, he *intended* to turn comedy on its head in order to teach the audience a lesson. At the end of Jonson's play, the title-character, Volpone, who has gained wealth by fraud and attempted to rape a young woman, is condemned to 'lie in prison, cramped with irons,' until he is 'sick and lame indeed.' But before he is hauled off to jail, the fox invites the audience to 'fare jovially, and clap your hands.' Jonson, a careful scholar of Greek and Latin sources, explains that he took liberties because 'even in the ancients themselves … comedies are not always joyful.' The 'office of a comic poet', he says, is not simply to make us laugh, though it is that too, 'but to imitate justice and instruct to life, as well as purity of language or stir up gentle affections.' This justification of a comedy that does not end happily indicates the association of comedy with joy and happy endings that people presume. To write his form of comedy, Jonson must write against the other, paradoxically reinforcing it. 'The good ended happily, and the bad unhappily. That is what Fiction means', Oscar Wilde writes parodically in *The Importance of Being Earnest*, indicating the force of this central tradition of comic theory, while mocking it. Jonson's assertion that comedy need not be joyful raises more questions than it answers. In doing so, it represents a crucial debate in comic theory. The function of comedy may be both to amuse and to instruct, but how much amusement and how much instruction ought to go into the comic pot? How 'moral' should comedy be? What does it even mean to *be* moral? Isn't it possible that too much instruction will make a work unamusing and, thus, uncomical? Stand-up comedians can be brutal, yet funny too. In challenging the definition of funny, they draw, like Ben Jonson, on this tradition in comic performance and theory.

As Wilde's joke about Fiction suggests, happy endings please people not because they are true but because they represent a wish fulfilment. They are achieved by fictional or conventional means – in short, by a manipulation of form. Life, which concludes with death, rarely ends happily, whereas comedy often involves a form of resurrection – a character presumed dead comes back to life, figuratively if not literally – a structure informed at least since the Middle Ages by the Christian myth. In Wilde's self-declared 'Trivial Comedy for Serious People,' a subtitle that raises theoretical questions about the *importance* of concepts such as triviality and seriousness, it turns out miraculously that Jack is named Ernest after all (and won't need to be re-baptized, though he is figuratively reborn), allowing him to marry Gwendolyn in conformity with the audience's desire and to exit happily. On the other hand, playing against form, Anton Chekhov also subtitled his plays of disappointment, *The Seagull* and *The Cherry Orchard*, 'comedies,' though one ends with an apparent suicide and one with the loss of the family home. In doing so, he emphasizes the treatment of his subject over the structure of the plot. Chekhov's letters suggest that the generic designation was a kind of stage direction – like the 'allegro' in a musical score – intended to encourage the actors to play their parts up-tempo, in a lively rather than lugubrious manner. Yet, by invoking comedy in such an uncomfortable way, he also intensifies the irony and deepens our sense of the absurdity of the society he depicts. These comedies don't conclude with a new social compact but with social disintegration. The seemingly un-comic conclusion gains power from playing against type.

Some comic plots place less emphasis on irony and more on romance. Canadian theorist Northrop Frye identifies a continuum of comic structures that runs from satire, at the most ironic end, to romance at the other. Romance is characterized not only by love – though *Eros* is both a driving force and a goal of these comic performances – but also by scenes of miraculous recognition and reconciliation, such as when long-lost siblings or separated parents and children are reunited. Romance tends to shift from the kind of realism that characterizes the deflating thrust of satire to idealism, though it tends to be an idealism balanced by earthy, quotidian, even domestic concerns, often related to marriage and household harmony. The romantic conclusion of social redemption combines idealism and materialism, as in the wondrous restoration of wealth and other material benefits to those who had temporarily lost everything (as in Molière's *Tartuffe,* for example). Characters resolve differences and return from a 'green world,' a natural or magical dream space, free from ordinary constraints, to a social reality of law and order (as in *A Midsummer Night's Dream*). The psychically sick become well. For Sigmund Freud, the function of the 'comic,' like that of jokes and humour, is to allow for the therapeutic release of repressed energy. Scholars and psychologists dispute Freud's theory today, but, in doing so, they participate in a conversation that developed in the eighteenth century about the relief comedy and humour could provide for the 'animal spirits' of citizens of Western societies, increasingly channelled by rationalism, capitalism and urban lifestyles.

The recognition scene in romantic comedy, when confusion is cleared up, relatives identified, and lovers united, has remained a central structuring feature, despite variations in custom and setting. In great comedies, the more complicated the plots, the more they draw attention to the artificiality of plotting, which thus appears comic. Whether in a satire that privileges irony or a romantic comedy centred on love, the outcome may run counter to the characters' expectations. However, there is a wide range of comic structures between satire, on the one hand, and romance, on the other. Frye suggests that in the most ironic phase of comedy a humorous society triumphs over a dull or pretentious one; whereas in less ironic cases the hero may not transform a society but runs away from it, as Huckleberry Finn flees 'sivilization' in Mark Twain's comic novel.

At the other end of this spectrum, which begins with the notion that satire serves as a social corrective, is the model of romance that represents the achievement of a redeemed society. Thus, at the conclusion of *The Tempest*, often called a 'romance' by critics, the major characters come together in harmony: Prospero forgives his brother, who had usurped his dukedom, and will marry his daughter Miranda to the son of the King of Naples. Before returning from his island to civilization, he will drown his book of magic and break his magic staff. He concludes the play by saying, uncomically, that his 'ending is despair, / Unless I be relieved by prayer', and addresses the audience: 'As you from crimes would pardon'd be, / Let your indulgence set me free.' The 'prayer' and 'indulgence' this aging man begs of the spectator in his final lines have theological overtones, and they tap into the deep ritual structure underlying comedy that is realized most explicitly in a work that is neither funny nor ironic, the *Divine Comedy* of Dante Alighieri, which details the poet's travels from Hell to Purgatory to Heaven. We would not call Dante's *Commedia* (as it was originally entitled) a comedy today. But the structure of the *Commedia*, with its theme of redemption, speaks to the potential seriousness of comedy and comic theory. While theorists acknowledge the limitations of the terms and their flexible usage, they continually insist on the importance of definitions.

It is difficult to isolate character from plot, both crucial subjects in any discussion of comedy. Different kinds of comic plots require different kinds of characters, and vice versa. In the spectrum from satire to romance, Frye identifies six types of comic plot. Film theorist Gerald Mast lists eight, from the plot of New Comedy (young lovers wed despite obstacles) to parody or burlesque to romance to the story of a person who discovers an error he or she has been committing for a lifetime. Humour generated by comic irony deflates the pretensions of those who block the happiness of others. Satirical comedy exposes affectation and aims, more or less overtly, to correct vice. It may challenge the cruelty of a pointless law. When theorists such as Meredith claim that comedy asserts common sense, they privilege realism, as opposed to an idealism that seems formal and rigid. Humour is as crucial to comic characterization as to plotting. *Commedia dell'arte*, an Italian form of comedy that evolved in the sixteenth century centred on stock characters, such as the miser Pantalone, the tricky servant Harlequin, and the lover Pulcinella (an ancestor of the British Punch-and-Judy puppet show). Actors, wearing masks depicting these social types improvised within various scenarios or comic sketches (this type of theatre was originally called *commedia dell'arte all'improvviso*), rather than acting out a scripted plot. This model anticipates more recent forms of sketch and situation comedy on television, which tend to privilege character over plot. Today, we also see classical stock characters in stand-up comedy unconstrained by traditional comic plots.

In the *Nicomachean Ethics*, Aristotle identifies four main comic types that have had great staying power: the *alazôn* (an impostor, e.g. the boastful soldier, angry father, or miser of New Comedy), the *eirôn* (a trickster, mocker, the self-deprecator or ironist), the *bomolochoi* (the buffoon), and the *agroikos* (a churlish, country bumpkin). Comic plots often involve a contest between the clever *eirôn* and the boastful *alazôn*. Usually, the former wins because the latter lacks self-knowledge. The *alazôn* declaims pompously, while the *eirôn* makes sarcastic asides. Comedy teams often combine these qualities: one might be a boaster, while the straight-man has elements of the ironist or the churl. Groucho, Chico, and Harpo Marx represent twentieth-century versions of the *eirôn*, the *agroikos*, and the *bomolochoi*, while their puffed-up antagonists derive from the *alazôn*.

Marx Brothers' performances tend to be chaotic, not contributing to but disrupting conventional plots. Drawing on what Henry Jenkins calls a 'vaudeville aesthetic,' they emphasize the brilliance and personality of the individual performers, rather than the coherence of the narrative. Critics often describe them as anarchic; as they turn society on its head in a way that harks back to the topsy-turvy, slapstick world of Aristophanes rather than that of the more predictable New Comedy. They are full of gags and musical performances that seem to have no relation to a particular story. They ridicule respectability. In the role of Rufus T. Firefly, Groucho Marx is a modern Lord of Misrule, an updated version of a central figure in medieval carnival. The topsy-turvy world of *Duck Soup* (1933) is unique to early twentieth-century America. It reflects the anxieties and the energy of a pluralistic society dealing with mass immigration and new models of social difference; other modern comedies deal with changing attitudes about race. Yet these comedies retain connections to comic devices of the distant past. Groucho, like Bugs Bunny, is a trickster with an ancient lineage in Western comedy, yet trickster figures appear in many cultures, from Old-Man Coyote in the Native American oral tradition to the Signifying Monkey in African American vernacular discourse. In his book, *The Signifying Monkey: A Theory of African-American Literary Criticism* (1988), Henry Louis Gates, Jr. shows how the Yoruba Esu-Elegbara, another phallic god of generation, a figure of indeterminacy and a guardian of the crossroads, was disseminated via the slave trade among black cultures in West Africa, South America, the Caribbean, and the United States. Signifying can be very funny, though Gates does not theorize its comic aspects. Western comedy also evolved in antiquity through cross-cultural pollination between the states around the Mediterranean, often through imperialism and war. The great Roman playwright Terence was himself a freed slave who had been brought to Rome from North Africa. As these comedies suggest, people often laugh at what makes them most uncomfortable, and as a way of coping with oppression.

Comic humour makes some characters within the plays, as well as spectators watching them, conscious of actions that are usually performed by rote. Thus, *Seinfeld* was supposedly a situation-comedy 'about nothing' – laughing at the habitual practices of everyday life, including the business practices of the television industry that contributed to the show's own making. *Seinfeld* is an instance of a kind of comedian-centred comedy in an age of celebrity, media, and mass culture. Some critics have described its metafictional, self-reflexive stance as postmodern, yet there are ample precedents for these performances-within-performances, as in the 'good fooling' of the 'witty' clown Feste in *Twelfth Night*, or of clowns and fools that speak earthy truth to power in Shakespeare's tragedies *Hamlet* and *King Lear*. These figures, in turn, trace their lineage to jesters hired to entertain the nobility in the Middle Ages, as well as to the *eirôn* of antiquity, of which the tricky slave Pseudolus, in Plautus's play of that name, is a famous example. Pseudolus, whose name indicates that he's a liar (*pseudo* means false), mocks social and dramatic conventions. Speaking to the audience, he compares his scheme to swindle his master to the plot of a playwright; he challenges everyone not to trust a word he says and refers to himself as both a playwright and an actor. Sit-coms in the twenty-first century often revolve around a stand-up comedian, who steps out of the plot of the comedy to deliver social commentary in his or her role as a *comic* in a comedy club. The metatheatricality, self-consciousness, or doubleness, the pose of the wit and the trickster, has often seemed an essential feature of comic performance, militating against the earnestness that Wilde associated with 'serious people'. This 'good fooling', as Feste calls it, continues to serve as a framing device in television shows.

Film historians identify another kind of comedian-centred comedy that revolves around a clown who does not or cannot integrate into normative society but instead disrupts it, from the work of Buster Keaton and Charlie Chaplin's tramp to that of the Marx Brothers, Bob Hope, and Jerry Lewis. These comic performers are also often metatheatrical, reflecting on the comic practices and frameworks within which they perform. In being self-conscious and puncturing the artificiality of their fictive world, they assume the mantle of the *eirôn*. Their comedies generate a tension between the comedic performance of the virtuoso comedian and the rest of the narrative, perhaps a standard romantic plot. So, sometimes films and stage-performances combine more than one type of comedy, bridging the spectrum from romance to irony, and the different comic forms and characters come into productive conflict with each other.

Drawing attention to the complexity of comic plots with a figurative (and sometimes literal) wink, comic characters from Pseudolus to Seinfeld to Tina Fey's Liz Lemon in *30 Rock* and Amy Schumer's character in *Inside Amy Schumer*, the *eirôn* often assumes the role of author in his or her own work. Comic authors create problems in order to remove them. This Reader offers a range of theories for how and why comedy generates self-awareness. Jokes can seem like mini-comedies or microcosms of the larger work. Many theorists link jokes and comedy, or speak of them in the same essays without making an explicit connection. Like dramatic comedy, jokes have structure. Anthropologist Mary Douglas suggests that jokes are rites that play with the symbolic forms of society, and scholars have made similar arguments about comedy, linking its origins to ritual. A joke, like a comic plot, creates an expectation in its listener, and it has been argued that humour results from an incongruity between expectation and result. The so-called 'incongruity theory' (in contrast to Plato's 'superiority theory' and Freud's 'relief theory') developed in the work of eighteenth-century thinkers such as Francis Hutcheson and Immanuel Kant. According to Kant, the punchline of a joke, like the comic twist of a plot, is the evaporation of expectation into nothing. The eighteenth century also gave rise to other competing theories, sparking a conversation that has continued for more than 400 years. For instance, the relief theory, first articulated by Lord Shaftesbury in his 1709 'Essay on the Freedom of Wit and Humour,' held that laughter allowed the release of 'animal spirits' built up in the human nervous system, and subsequent theorists of humour, like theorists of comedy, describe a process that moves from expressing the fears or anxieties of their audience to a release. Jokes like comic plots start with discomfort, generating tension, and leading to the release of laughter, which is a form of liberation. Philosopher Simon Critchley calls this experience 'structured fun' and says that 'most humour' is both subversive and conservative. It offers an escape from routine, often making fun of those higher up the social ladder, then returns us to a common world of shared practices, even reinforcing the hierarchy it had temporarily undermined.

One product of comedy, and a crucial goal of jokes, is a physical reaction, namely laughter. Thinking about the importance of comedy has prompted theorists to ask, what is the good of laughter? If characters tell jokes or audiences laugh in tragedies, does that mean that comedy is not constrained by genre or dramatic form, or what is comic relief? The point of laughter and the goal of comic plots, according to some theories, is to effect a transition from habitual behaviour, arbitrary laws, obsession, hypocrisy, and fixed social arrangements to a state that is self-aware, more fluid, honest and creative. Politically speaking, comedy has been regarded as being both conservative and progressive. The authors collected in this Reader ask, how so? French philosopher Henri Bergson believed that laughter corrects men's manners by mocking extreme, yet habitual, behaviours and character traits. Such correction tends to involve some punishment, and Bergson notices that laughter is the foe of emotion: 'To produce the whole effect, then, the comic demands something like a momentary anesthesia of the heart. Its appeal is to intelligence, pure and simple.' Whether or not it is simple, this theory of comedy participates in an important conversation about comedy and affect: how and why are the emotions engaged, if at all, by comedy? For Bergson, the intellectual work of comedy restores our humanity and our capacity to feel. Many conservative theorists and performers still believe that comedy has a normalizing or didactic function, revealing what is ridiculous about our actions so that we can fix what is wrong and return to what is right. In this sense comedy appears to be conservative. Liberals observe that comedy privileges youth over age and leads to a new, more positive social order; in this sense, it's progressive. By ridiculing extreme, outdated, habitual and pointless behaviours, comedy captures essential qualities of each epoch, illuminating the present in concrete terms. In short, comedy touches on big subjects ranging from ethics and education to how we know what's 'true' about ourselves and the world around us. But *theorizing* about comedy can be deadly dull, and the mismatch between comedy and theory is another problem that thinkers have grappled with for millennia.

One problem in tracing a tradition of theories of comedy is that there isn't one. Rather, there are many. Aristotle's *Poetics* is the foundational text of Western literary and dramatic theory, but it centres on tragedy. Although Aristotle writes a little bit about comedy in *Poetics*, allegedly he wrote more in another treatise called *Tractatus Coislinianus*, which was lost and resurfaced in tenth-century Paris. *The Name of the Rose*, a historical novel by Umberto Eco, imagines a conspiracy by the Roman Catholic Church to suppress Aristotle's treatise on comedy in the Middle Ages. Ancient comedy emphasized the body, not the spirit. It celebrated drinking and sex, aspects of life Christianity opposed. Comedy is about *this* world, here-and-now, erotic pleasure, money, and politics, not metaphysics or the hereafter. Articulating a version of the superiority theory of humour, Aristotle said that comedy was 'an imitation of inferior people,' a notion that has been taken in various directions: comic characters may seem inferior in social class, inferior in morality, inferior in intelligence. He says that comedy deals in ugliness and notes that the comic mask is distorted; prompting questions about what is ugly and leading to theories today about comedy and disability.

Two thousand years after Aristotle, Oscar Wilde challenges us to reconsider our definitions of seriousness and triviality. When comedy presents supposedly great thinkers, especially those who boast about how great they are, the *eirôn* deflates them, making comedy markedly different from tragedies such as *Oedipus, the King* or *The Tragedy of Hamlet, Prince of Denmark*, which honour that kind of grand intellectual ambition. Comic thinkers, like Shakespeare's Falstaff, poke holes in abstract concepts such as 'honour'. So, comedy has long been peripheral to intellectual culture. It may seem that serious people think about tragic suffering, while those interested in comedy just want to have fun. However, from Plato and Aristotle to Henri Bergson and Sigmund Freud, comedy *has* attracted the attention of serious thinkers. This Reader brings together diverse theories of comedy across the ages, centring on a tradition in which theorists have engaged in conversation with each other, to show that, far from being peripheral, comedy speaks to the most pragmatic aspects of human life.

Bibliography

Aristotle. *Nicomachean Ethics*. Trans. Terence Irwin. Indianapolis: Hackett Publishing Company, 1985.

Aristotle. *Poetics*. Trans. James Hutton. New York: W. W. Norton, 1982.

Bakhtin, Mikhail. *Rabelais and His World*. Trans. Helene Iswolsky. Bloomington: Indiana University Press, 1984.

Bergson, Henri. 'Laughter.' *Comedy*, ed. Wylie Sypher. Baltimore: Johns Hopkins University Press, 1980.

Burke, Kenneth. *Attitudes Toward History* (1937). 3rd edn. Berkeley: University of California Press, 1984.

Critchley, Simon. *On Humour*. London: Routledge, 2002.

Freud, Sigmund. *Jokes and Their Relation to the Unconscious*. Trans. James Strachey. New York: W. W. Norton, 1960.

Frye, Northrop. *Anatomy of Criticism, Four Essays*. Princeton, NJ: Princeton University Press, 1957.

Garber, Marjorie. *Shakespeare after All*. New York: Anchor Books, 2004.

Gates, Henry Louis, Jr. *The Signifying Monkey: A Theory of African-American Literary Criticism*. New York: Oxford University Press, 1988.

Jenkins, Henry. *What Made Pistachio Nuts? Early Sound Comedy and the Vaudeville Aesthetic*. New York: Columbia University Press, 1992.

Jonson, Ben. *Volpone. Three Comedies*. London: Penguin, 1966.

Leggatt, Alexander. *English Stage Comedy 1490–1990*. London: Routledge, 1998.

Mast, Gerald. *The Comic Mind*. 2nd edn. Chicago: University of Chicago Press, 1979.

Meredith, George. 'An Essay on Comedy.' *Comedy*, ed. Wylie Sypher. Baltimore: Johns Hopkins University Press, 1980.

Olson, Kirby. *Comedy after Postmodernism: Rereading Comedy from Edward Lear to Charles Willeford*. Lubbock, TX: Texas Tech University Press, 2001.

Segal, Erich. *The Death of Comedy*. Cambridge, MA: Harvard University Press, 2001.

Shakespeare, William. *The Tempest, The Riverside Shakespeare*, ed. G. Blakemore Evans. Boston: Houghton Mifflin Company, 1974.

Stott, Andrew. *Comedy*. New York: Routledge, 2005.

Wilde, Oscar. *The Importance of Being Earnest. Complete Works of Oscar Wilde*. London: Collins, 2003.

1

Antiquity and the Middle Ages

INTRODUCTION

Greek comedy began with wild rejoicing. It was associated with revelry and, specifically, with civic festivals that honoured the god Dionysus and the rebirth of spring.
The Athenians celebrated a festival known as the City Dionysia. The Romans gave
their own twist to a similar holiday, the Saturnalia, honouring the god Saturn. Both
involved drinking to intoxication, feasting, and a celebration of the fertility of the
earth and of erotic love, which in Greece took the form not only of obscene speech
but also the display of large phallic symbols. People wore costumes. In Greek plays
men dressed as women, and there was a sense of liberation from ordinary rules of
social decorum. During the festival, regular legal business was suspended. Although
medieval Christian culture differed in profound ways from these ancient antecedents,
a comparable festive spirit informs medieval carnivals. Twentieth-century Russian
theorist Mikhail Bakhtin characterizes this spirit as 'the liberty to do what is as a rule
prohibited.' We can see elements of these traditions in Shakespeare's *Twelfth Night*, a
play characterized by drunkenness, cross-dressing, and servants acting out of place.
At the same time, it is vital to mark distinctions. Fifth-century comedy, for instance,
differed from medieval carnival and Roman Saturnalia in fostering participation in
Athenian democracy, holding prominent men responsible through comic ridicule and
criticism for what went wrong in public policy.

In ancient Greece, the City Dionysia included dramatic competitions. The first tragic
competition took place around 508 BCE, followed by the first competition devoted to
comedy in 486 BCE. Many comedies were produced for those competitions, but only

eleven relatively complete texts written by Aristophanes remain. From these few plays – which revolve around a central *agōn* or conflict (often between competing ideas, such as war and peace, or wealth and poverty), and a *parabasis* (in which the chorus 'comes forward' and delivers a message to the audience), and conclude with the singing, dancing, and invitation to drinking at the *kômos* – scholars and theorists have generalized about fifth-century comedy more broadly. Today most believe that the ancient Greek word for comedy derives from *kômos* (revel) and *ōidé* (singing). In Aristophanic comedy, actors wore large mock penises between their legs. The humour was bawdy. As with the limited archive of ancient comedic plays, few texts of ancient and medieval comic theory remain. Furthermore, in these few, such as Plato's *Philebus* and Aristotle's *Poetics* and *Ethics*, comedy often has a peripheral position. Nonetheless, these scattered remarks have proved influential. Generations of critics have extrapolated from Plato's brief comments on the function of the ridiculous, or from Aristotle's discussion of the means, the objects, and the manner of dramatic imitation, to formulate their own comic theories.

Ancient Greek playwrights did not generally mix tragedy and comedy in the same play. Separate playwriting competitions were held for comedy and tragedy. However, each year tragic playwrights submitted not only three tragedies but also a fourth work, a satyr play, which was performed after the tragedies and presented a comic take on a mythic theme. Satyr plays, from which we get the word satire, offered comic relief. Much theory since that time has investigated connections and differences between comedy and satire, though satyr plays were not, in the modern sense of the word, satirical. They were burlesques. Onstage satyrs played pranks. Ancient comedy and satyr plays differ in other ways too; for instance, the bestial plays little part in Greek comedy. Satyrs themselves were mythically divided creatures, half-beast and half-man, and some authors have theorized that comedy itself tends to represent a state of half-ness or self-division. Only one satyr play survives (Euripides's *Cyclops*), but according to an ancient hypothesis, Euripides presented his moving drama *Alcestis*, in which the heroine is rescued from death and restored to her husband by Hercules (who also gives a drunken speech and calls for dancing in the end), as the fourth of his contributions to the tragedy competition of 438 BCE – in other words, where the satyr play would typically go. Complicating the classification of *Alcestis* further is the fact that tragedies occasionally had a happy end. Aristotle says that tragic plots sometimes involve a change of fortune from bad to good, though he argues that an unhappy ending is more truly 'tragic,' and he singles out Euripides as the most *tragic* of playwrights. The dissonant *Alcestis* is a tragedy with humorous elements, but ancient comedy and tragedy were generically distinct.

Historians generally recognize three types of Greek comedy, which were written in different periods: Old, Middle, and New Comedy, a periodization first suggested by the ancient critic Aristophanes of Byzantium (c. 257–185/180 BCE). Old Comedy, as the plays of 486 to 400 BCE are called, was brash and bawdy. Our understanding of Old Comedy is derived from the surviving works of Aristophanes, the oldest of which, *Archarnians,* won first prize at the Lenaia festival in 425 BCE. The battles of ideas that characterized Old Comedy gradually gave way to more logically plotted dramas that centred on domestic life. Yet, from the *parabasis* of Old Comedy to the ironic commentary with which Roman comedy broke the conventional 'fourth wall,' much comic theory comes from the plays themselves. The best-known author of Middle Comedy, Antiphanes (408–334 BCE) argued that comic playwrights had a more difficult job than tragedians, who recycled the same few plots, because they had to be more inventive. Greek tragedy did not disrupt the theatrical illusion to comment on the play itself, whereas Greek comedy commonly did, giving it an air of vitality and immediacy.

New Comedy began around 336 BCE with Menander and continued with the Romans, Plautus (c. 254–184 BCE) and Terence (195/185–159 BCE). Old Comedy was episodic in structure and depicted political and historic figures, including living people who would have been in the audience. New Comedy focused on family affairs (parent-child conflicts, adultery, and jealousy), and featured stock characters (e.g. the clever slave and the greedy old man) and simple plots. Middle Comedy, of which only fragments remain, was a transitional genre that saw the elimination of the chorus and a shift from public or political topics to private ones; it was less sharp-edged than Old Comedy and often satirized mythological subjects. Many comedies from this era were based on fifth-century satyr plays. Middle Comedy flourished from roughly 400 to 320 BCE. Philiscus's *Birth of Hermes*, which portrays the mythic messenger of death, in satiric light, and Antiphanes's *Birth of Aphrodite* indicate how birth and rebirth quickly became one of comedy's major themes.

Little direct theoretical writing about comedy has come down to us from antiquity. For the most part, we have comments about aspects of comedy from works on other subjects, ranging from metaphysics to rhetoric. Plato (429–347 BCE), an Athenian philosopher considered the father of Western philosophy, was troubled by the fact that art could inflame people's passions, which has long been a complaint against comedy, associated as it is with laughter, drinking, and sex. Plato believed that the world we experience with our senses is a degraded reflection of an eternal world of Ideas (*eidê*), accessible not through the senses but through thought. The Platonic conception of the world would seem to rule out comedy. Yet Plato's works are written as dialogues, and they employ wit and irony. In *The Republic*, Plato establishes a dichotomy between the ideal and the real, laying the foundation in the Western tradition for our perception of our world. *The Republic* says little directly about comedy, but comic theorists have extrapolated from Platonic theory. Ideas are perfect, and objects are their embodiments or imperfect copies. The philosopher's profession is to seek the truth, but comedy distracts us from truth and goodness. Slapstick humour, not to mention parading around with a giant penis, draws attention to the body, and to the 'lowest' aspects of human experience. According to this view, comedy is far from a perfect, unchanging realm of Ideas. But what if comedy doesn't simply *reflect* a degraded reality? What if it *shapes* or even *creates* reality? Although he says only a few words about comedy in *The Republic*, Plato would provoke later thinkers to ask key questions about the potential of comedy as not only a mirror onto reality but also an art of persuasion and a social corrective. Comedy may have little to say about an ideal realm, but it can say much about the daily vicissitudes of commercial and family life.

Plato's *Symposium*, a dialogue on the nature of love (*Eros*), is literally a 'drinking party' thrown by the tragedian Agathon to celebrate his victory at a dramatic competition, the City Dionysia of 416 BCE. The comic playwright Aristophanes is also present as a character, and he narrates a famous creation myth, speculates about the origin of human sexuality, and posits a notion of human beings originally divided (looking for their 'better halves'). People feel 'whole' when they find a partner. In articulating his theory of love, Aristophanes indirectly fosters the notion that comedy represents a state of half-ness or self-division. Some scholars have read the speech itself as a comic interlude. Toward the end of the party another historical figure, Alcibiades, an Athenian general, comes in drunk and plops down between Agathon and Socrates. Alcibiades assumes a Dionysian role. He compares Socrates to Silenus, the mythical tutor of Dionysus, and to a satyr. The comic ending expands as a group of drunken revellers disrupts the banquet and compels everyone to drink more. Finally, only Agathon, Aristophanes, and Socrates remain awake, drinking together. Socrates theorizes that the genius of comedy is the same as that of tragedy, and that the writer of tragedy ought to be a writer of comedy also. 'To this they were compelled to assent,' Plato writes, 'being sleepy, and not quite understanding his meaning.' With this fine, humorous touch, Plato does not posit a thesis, but teases us with the open-endedness of comic theory.

Philebus, one of Plato's last dialogues, turns to the relationship between knowledge and pleasure. Following Greek ideals of balance and moderation, Socrates – the central character again – suggests that a good life is a balance of both. Through Socrates, Plato provides the first definition of what today we could call *schadenfreude,* arguing that although comedy brings pleasure, it is grounded in malice, because 'when we laugh at the ridiculous behaviour of our friends, mixing pleasure with malice, we are mixing pleasure and pain,' since malice is an affliction of the soul, and thus brings pain. The notion that comic pleasure involves the *soul* raises a question about how comedy affects us. For Socrates, laughing at others is a character flaw, a combination of hubris and foolishness. Only someone with an exaggerated self-image, that is, someone who lacks true knowledge of him- or herself, would laugh at someone who is being derided or ridiculed in public. Socrates also suggests that, because it combines the pleasure of laughter with the pain of malice, comedy restores the body to a tranquil, orderly state by balancing the feelings of pain with pleasure. Nonetheless, laughter becomes destructive when overindulged.

Plato's dislike of comedy has a personal story behind it. In *The Clouds,* the playwright Aristophanes portrays Socrates as a sophist who plants a lot of dangerous ideas in the heads of the young men of Athens. In *The Apology of Socrates,* Plato writes that Aristophanes' comic portrayal of Socrates led to his death sentence on charges of corrupting the Athenian youth. Plato seems to have considered humour to be potentially harmful. For that reason, contemporary theories of humour which emphasize its negative aspects often begin with Plato, whose writings have provided a framework for three branches of comic theory: (1) the superiority theory according to which laughter is a manifestation of one's unfounded sense of self-importance, (2) the ambivalence theory according to which laughter is a result of contradictory feelings, and (3) the aggression theory according to which laughter is a manifestation of hostility. But Plato doesn't regard humour in a completely negative light, as Socrates often uses humour as a didactic tool to advance philosophical inquiry. Plato seems to distinguish between laughter and humour. Here we can see how theories of comedy quickly move beyond a discussion of stage-plays. Unlike laughter, which is physiological, humour is an intellectual activity: it requires understanding and ability to discern when and why two things don't go together, where there's a verbal or visual mismatch. Plato sets the stage for debates not only about comedy but also about humour, particularly the sense that laughter is provoked by a sense of incongruity, a notion that would be developed in the eighteenth century by philosophers such as Frances Hutcheson and Immanuel Kant.

A student of Plato, Aristotle (384–322 BCE) wrote on a range of topics, including physics, politics, art, and theatre. Aristotle's *Poetics* is the foundational text of Western literary and dramatic theory, though it was composed as a collection of lecture notes.

With Aristotle, we get a shift from the metaphysical to the rhetorical. He privileges plot over character, thought, and spectacle, emphasizing logical causality in constructing stories. *Poetics* is also a historical resource. Aristotle traces the origins of comedy to 'the phallic processions which still remain customary in many cities,' as accompaniment to Dionysian rites. During the festivities, a group of young Athenian men paraded with torches and phalluses, singing racy songs to the sound of a flute. The group of revellers was commonly called a *kômos*. Their song was called *kōmōidía*. But, as we have seen in our General Introduction, Aristotle also contested this etymology, suggesting that, while comedy evolved from revelry, the word itself suggests a connection to the countryside. '*Kômôdoi* (comedians)', he writes, 'acquired their name, not from *kômazein* (to revel), but from the fact that, being expelled in disgrace from the city, they wandered from village to village.' From Aristotle, comic theory continues to investigate comedy's depiction of relations between the country and the city.

Aristotle also traces the roots of comic drama to a non-dramatic, though literary and ethical precedent in Homer, whose comic mock-epic *Margites* offered a model of comedy that avoids personal abuse. Aristotle argues that comedy is an imitation of buffoonish people who are not evil but flawed. Greek comic actors wore masks that might be ugly or distorted, but their comedy should not cause pain. The hero's badness is not destructive or depraved. A comic flaw is ultimately harmless, unlike a tragic flaw (*hamartia*) that crushes the protagonist. The precise nature of comic flaws, including how serious they may be, has been an important subject of comic theory ever since. Aristotle's *Nicomachean Ethics,* a broad inquiry into the good life, advances a theory of happiness, of pleasure, and an extension of his theory of comedy: 'Those who go to excess in raising laughs seem to be vulgar buffoons … Those who never say anything themselves to raise a laugh, and even object when other people do it, seem to be boorish and stiff.' Aristotle favours moderation, intelligence, and an 'intermediate state', inhabited by 'decent and civilized' persons: 'Those who joke in appropriate ways are called witty, or, in other words, agile witted.' A preference for 'suitable' manners leads Aristotle to prefer comedy of his own day (e.g. Menander) over that of fifth-century Athens (e.g. Aristophanes), 'for what people used to find funny was shameful abuse, but what they now find funny instead is innuendo, which is considerably more seemly'. Even comic characterization requires good taste, critiquing harmless vice through clever suggestion and innuendo. In a similar spirit, *Poetics* offers a philosophy of the middle path, as 'comedy prefers persons who are worse, tragedy persons who are better, than the present generation'. What exactly is *worse*? What is *extreme*? These questions became a touchstone for comic theory, as the answers evolved. Aristotle's language implies that comic characters are low on the ladder of social status but also that their behaviour is defective, whether excessively buffoonish or boorish. Yet Aristotle also insisted that comedy needed to be taken more seriously than it had been to his day, for it could serve a normalizing function, promoting the Greek virtue of moderation.

The rhetorical or pragmatic aspect of humour, rather than Plato's idealist critique of it, was taken up by Roman authors Horace and Quintilian. The Romans were practical people, and comedy was the best attended and most performed of Rome's drama. Cicero (103–43 BCE), the great Roman politician and orator, argued that generating laughter was an effective oratorical tactic, as 'merriment naturally wins goodwill for its author'. Just as Greek performances developed in connection with festivals, Roman plays became associated with games, the marketplace, and the middle class. Horace (Quintus Horatius Flaccus) was a satirist, born in Italy in 65 BCE and educated in Rome and Athens. In *Ars Poetica*, Horace outlines a distinction between tragedy and comedy, types of characters, the dramatic structure of comedy, and the best way to combine profit with pleasure. In his poems, he suggests that poetry is a way to deal with life, rather than a grand artistic pursuit. Horace's *Satires,* a collection of autobiographical poems exploring the nature of happiness and the art of poetry, merge poetic style with personal narrative, creating a portrait of the satirist as a commentator on everyday life. Satire is a type of comedy that uses ridicule to censure folly, the satirist being a kind of self-appointed guardian of standards. In his poems, Horace's father appears as a guiding force that shaped his moral character in the same way that Horace now shapes his poems. This form of comic writing has a didactic purpose. Horace's philosophy of life draws on Greek ideals of inner balance and moderation, with satire playing a corrective role. He argues that Greek comedic playwrights 'noted with great freedom the faults of any who deserved it.' Horace also makes himself and his poetry an object of his satire. He lists all the criticism made about his work by people whom he had earlier satirized, delving further into the discussion about the true nature of satire. For whom should satire be written: elites or the general populace? Would the satirist become vulgar if he tried to please too many people? What is the social and political role of satire? Assuming a moral role, Horace's satire aims to guide the elites in a quest for self-knowledge and political wisdom.

Roman poets such as Horace and the rhetorician Marcus Fabius Quintilianus (c. 35–100 CE) greatly influenced medieval and Renaissance thinkers. Quintilian's collection of writings, *Institutio Oratoria,* is a practical guide to rhetoric, providing advice on cradle-to-grave aspects of life, including politics, literature, and early education, including reading and writing, and the art of persuasion. The volume's main objective is to train a good man, *vir bonus,* who is 'skilled in speaking'. In doing so, it critiqued earlier Greek and Roman writers including Aristotle and particularly the indecent Aristophanes. Quintilian favoured Menander for subtle characterization – 'so rich is his power of invention and his gift of style, so perfectly does he adapt himself to every kind of circumstance, character and emotion' – and advises that comedy should not be vulgar or cause pain either to the audience or to the object of its jokes. One should rather give up a joke than lose a friend who might be offended by it. Comedy and jokes must be used in moderation but never to lower the dignity of the speaker and make him appear less serious. Quintilian praises improvisation over a prepared text, noting that an audience regards improvisation as more authentic and credible than the delivery of written remarks. Improvisation has a crucial place in the history of comedy and comic theory, from satyr plays to *commedia dell'arte,* to carnival perfor-mances. Improvisation draws attention to the here-and-now, the social context and the relation of spectator to performer. In discussing wit and laughter, Quintilian cautions that during a debate, one must be careful not to allow his wit to 'give the appearance of studied premeditation, or smell of the lamp'. Premeditation, however, is valued in a jester, as 'there are no jests so insipid as those which parade the fact that they are intended to be witty'.

Roman critics commonly compared Latin comedy to the Greek, of which it was both a translation and an adaption, developing a theory of adaptation (*vortere* in Latin) along with a theory of comedy. Horace had critiqued the Roman playwright Plautus for simply making a buck out of the Greek originals, but as many critics have since argued, Plautus was unique, transforming Athenian comedy into a complex and creative new form. Only in the late twentieth century have some of those originals come to light, and they reveal Plautus's innovations in heightened realism, irony, and characterization. Plautus's plays themselves are a major source of comic theory princi-pally because they are extraordinarily metatheatrical. They often feature characters, such as the clever slave Pseudolus, who serve as a mouthpiece for the author. Pseudolus explicitly compares himself to a playwright and compares his scheme to trick his master to a dramatist's plotting. Plautus also reflects on the process of adaptation in the self-reflexive prologue to his play *Trinummus* in which a character refers explicitly to the playwright Plautus, who translated the Greek original into 'barbarous language' (in Latin, *barbare*). These playful self-reflections illustrate ways in which Plautus's art was much more than translation. Some historians believe that he was the first professional playwright. Clearly, the fact that he needed to make a living from his comedy had implications for comic theory and practice in his broad humour and his characters' comments to the audience.

The first appearance of the word '*tragicomoedia*' or tragicomedy occurs in Plautus's *Amphitryon*. This play, in some ways like *Alcestis*, takes a mythological subject, in this case Jupiter's seduction of a virtuous married woman, which leads to the birth of half-god/half-man Hercules. Comedy literally and figuratively brings the Olympians down to earth. In the prologue, the trickster god Mercury, who is Jupiter's servant, says that he is going to present a tragedy, though he knows the audience is expecting a comedy. But then, responding to their apparent disappointment, he offers a compromise: 'I will make it a mixture: let it be a "tragicomedy." I don't think it would be appropriate to make it consistently a comedy, when there are kings and gods in it. What do you think? Since a slave also has a part in the play, I'll make it a tragicomedy.' Mercury's comment points to a few topics in comic theory, from Aristotle to the present: first, there is the question of decorum or the proper subject of comedy – not kings and gods but slaves and servants – the notion that comedy represents a lower social class or, as Aristotle ambiguously puts it, 'persons worse than average', and is less dignified in its themes and performance style than tragedy. Then, Mercury's speech draws attention to the characters' self-consciousness in comic performance, or meta-theatricality, and the interaction of comic performers and their audiences. Equally important, this prologue addresses the idea of comedy as a *genre*, and the notion that it may be important to discover key principles that operate not only in one work but across a number of works. As a spokesman for Plautus, Mercury prompts a theoretical consideration: to what degree can or should we generalize? It is vital to acknowledge that ancient comedy is not all the same in order to see how particular performances and texts not only derive from but also transform an existing set of expectations. Such a self-reflexive articulation of difference, acknowledging where comedy ends and where a new, possibly hybrid genre begins, helps to clarify what it is, if only by saying what it is not.

Terence, though less popular in his own day than Plautus, had a greater impact on readers' understanding of comedy into the Middle Ages, largely due to the elegance of his language and his oratorical quality. Unlike Plautus, Terence rarely breaks the theatrical illusion. His plots employ less broad, irreverent humour. Rather, he developed a model of comedy that heightened dramatic suspense, as well as the double-plot structure that Shakespeare would later exploit. Most important, however, he aimed for a fine, clear, and direct translation of Greek originals, which made his comedies important school-texts from the medieval to the modern period. Julius Caesar called him a 'lover of pure speech' (*puri sermonis amator*). The widespread appreciation of his language is evidenced by the fact that there are many medieval manuscripts of his plays. Church Fathers apparently found his works more acceptable than those of Plautus. Martin Luther quoted Terence often in his own writings and recommended his comedies for the instruction of schoolchildren. In his 'Epistle Dedicatory' to Shakespeare's works (1623), Ben Jonson refers to 'neat Terence'. Terence's comedy tends toward the sentimental, combining tears and laughter, which prompted the admiration of the eighteenth-century French critic Denis Diderot for his *comédies larmoyantes* (tearful comedies). Together, Terence and Plautus established models of comedy for centuries to come – sometimes one, sometimes the other having the greater influence. Yet when classical comedy moved from the theatres to the schoolrooms and monastic libraries of Europe, it was Terence who had the upper hand.

*

After the fall of Rome, theatre went underground. The teaching of Christianity, which privileged the life of the soul over that of the body, was hostile to comic performances. We know that mimes, acrobats, jugglers, illusionists, and dancers existed for centuries after the fall of Rome largely because the Church pronounced against them. After the fifth century CE, theatres were closing everywhere, and actors were not allowed to join the Church without repenting. Priests were forbidden to attend theatrical performances, and laymen were tacitly discouraged. Theatre was considered a pagan ritual, and the early Church considered laughter to be a sign of arrogance. Eventually, however, the Church distinguished between good and evil laughter, concluding that some forms of laughter were acceptable. Priests used jokes in their sermons to mock the wicked and reach out to their flocks. The Church even depicted Christ as a holy fool to illustrate, in the words of Paul, that God 'made foolish the wisdom of this world' (1 Cor. 1.18-25). What the Church Fathers feared, however, was satire, which often took priests as its objects. Since the early Church Fathers banned theatre as such, most criticism from the early modern period focused on ancient comedy. Despite its interdiction of theatre, the Church valued ancient writings. Terence was highly regarded, even though the Church Fathers didn't consider his work suitable for performance.

After centuries of repression, however, a late medieval rebirth of theatre originated in the Church itself as part of the liturgical ritual. Church Fathers wanted to make biblical stories accessible to illiterate audiences. With time, these performances became elaborate and began crossing over into the secular spaces of market squares and private courts. The performances would mingle religious narratives with troubadour songs and folktales. Eventually they evolved into cycle plays (or mysteries), performed outdoors by the entire community. Spokesmen for the Church recognized the difference between serious and comic representations of scripture in the twelfth century, yet they took what to modern readers may seem a counterintuitive view: the Fall of Lucifer and of Adam, which seems to correspond to Aristotle's definition of tragic reversal, were for them based on an error of judgement and thus ridiculous or absurd. Though tragic for Lucifer and Adam, their conduct appeared ludicrous in the eyes of the Church. So, the comical characters of early liturgical drama tend to be the evil ones. Spectators were invited to laugh at their vanity and pride, as well as at personifications of the Deadly Sins. The twelfth-century *Play of the Anti-Christ* explicitly ridicules unbelievers. Lucifer and his *diablerie*, a grotesque parody of the angels they once were, are the most famous group of medieval comic characters.

Since official attitudes toward comedy were severe, Hrotsvita of Gandersheim, a tenth-century German nun, and the first-known woman playwright, apologized in the preface to her comedies for their subject matter, claiming she had 'often blushed and been ashamed' when writing about illicit affairs, but as they can be used to warn others, she felt a moral obligation to depict them. It is difficult to say whether Hrotsvita genuinely felt such ambivalence toward her plays, or whether she felt compelled to justify her writing. She also claimed that she wrote her plays so that people would have a Christian alternative to reading the pagan plays of Terence, on which she modelled her Latin verse and realistic dialogue. *Dulcitius*, the second of her six plays, represents two important features of medieval comedy. The play is about the martyrdom of three virgins during Diocletian's persecution of Christians in Thessalonica at the hands of Governor Dulcitius. Despite what to modern eyes would seem a depressing topic, the play reflects important features of medieval comedy: first, the virgins' martyrdom is, in medieval terms, a happy ending. 'This is the greatest joy I can conceive', one of the girls declaims before she is slain, for she 'will enter the heavenly bridal chamber of the Eternal King'. Weakness triumphs over strength, faith over force. Second, the play employs broad farce when the lustful governor attempts to rape the girls but is miraculously struck by temporary insanity, embracing pots and pans instead of the girls themselves, and soiling himself in the process. Those possessed by the Devil thus become ridiculous. In the twelfth century, reflecting a similar spirit in a more public setting, the 'Puy', a set of seasonal dramatic competitions, began to take hold in northeastern France and Flanders. Jean Bodel's immensely popular *Jeu de saint Nicolas* (*Saint Nicholas play*, performed probably in 1202) centred on the saint and employed comedy to ridicule the demons that animated the pagan idol Tervagan.

At the same time, another form of comedy evolved with the Christian feasts of praise and thanksgiving, Easter and Christmas. Christ's resurrection and birth conformed to classical models of comedy, but it was only in the thirteenth century that they were represented dramatically. Comic sketches also developed with the founding of Europe's first universities (one of the earliest is in English, *The Interlude of the Student and the Maiden*, c. 1300), and they tended to feature farcical situations, satire and wit. Meanwhile, an unofficial theatre of mimes, singers, and acrobats took place throughout the Middle Ages as part of the daily market activities among the village and city dwellers. Medieval comedy flourished during Carnival, the Feast of Fools, and Shrovetide. Few written records remain, but these holidays, often presided over by a Lord of Misrule or the Boy Bishop, featured buffoonery and burlesque, and they trace aspects of their performance to similar festivities in ancient Rome. These purgative celebrations were anti-hierarchical, even anti-clerical, in spirit, and later came to dramatize, on the side of the poor, an anti-bourgeois spirit as well. The shows were performed in market squares and taverns. Medieval comic performances were episodic in structure and included sketches, songs, and physical humour. The subject matter often revolved around the lower classes, prostitutes, thieves, and seducers, giving a new spin on the 'vulgar.' The plots were simple and, as in New Comedy, included stock characters, such as the husband, the wife, and the wife's seducer.

In his book *Rabelais and his World* (written as a dissertation in Russian in the 1930s and published in English in 1968), Mikhail Bakhtin describes the transgressive role of comedy in medieval life as pivoting on the opposition between the 'official' culture of Church and State and that of ordinary people in the marketplace: 'Officially the palaces, churches, institutions, and private homes were dominated by hierarchy and etiquette, but in the marketplace a special kind of language was heard.' That language was 'natural' and coarse. Its humour celebrated sensuality, sex and the life of the 'lower' body – belly, bowels, genitals – which Bakhtin finds in the 'grotesque' comic fiction of French humanist François Rabelais (1483–1553). This indecorous comedy offered a relief from sober Christian didacticism, which denied earthly pleasure. Medieval humour resided on the margins of the official culture of piety as, in Bakhtin's words, 'laughter made its unofficial but almost legal nest under the shelter of almost every feast'. The feast offered a brief respite from the prohibitions and hierarchic barriers of the official system. 'For a short time', Bakhtin writes, 'life came out of its usual, legalized and consecrated furrows and entered the sphere of utopian freedom'. Medieval comedy satirized the rich and powerful, including the Church figures who generally banned it. Adam De La Halle's 1276 *Play of the Bower*, for example, makes fun of the monk who sells the 'bones of saints', claiming they'll perform all kinds of miracles and cure every possible disease.

Despite the prohibition of pagan performance, theorists after the fall of Rome continued to study ancient comic writing. Aelius Donatus, the mid-fourth century critic and grammarian, wrote a work entitled simply *De comedia* and a *Commentary on Terence,* which argued that 'in comedy the fortunes of men are ordinary, the onslaughts of difficulties minor, the outcomes of actions happy'. Donatus describes the origins of comedy, explaining the difference between New and Old Comedy, and tracing the development of comedy from Menander to Terence. Donatus's fellow grammarian Evanthius also offered a formal analysis of ancient comic genres, including the satyr play, in *De Fabula*. Both Donatus and Evanthius, with their emphasis on structural principles and moral themes, remained influential into the Middle Ages. In the sixteenth century, a preface to Donatus's commentaries, 'De Tragoedia et Comoedia', argued that while tragedy shows only negative models of behaviour, comedies also represent exemplary ways of acting. Juxtaposing positive and negative, comedy incorporates a practical, pedagogical function that tragedy lacks, and which links comedy to rhetoric. According to the essay, comedy is a 'mirror of everyday life … from which one may learn what is valuable and what is to be avoided'. The tenth-century *Tractatus coislinianus*, a fragment of uncertain provenance, widely considered to be a distillation of classical writings (perhaps by Aristotle) catalogues jokes and comic character-types, and adopts an Aristotelian approach to defining comedy as a form and genre. The Byzantine scholar John Tzetzes (c. 1110–80) also shows the continuing influence of Aristotle in his definition of comedy as 'an imitation of an action … purgative of emotions, constructive of life, moulded by laughter and pleasure'. Aristotle's distinction between tragedy and comedy in *Poetics* found new interpreters in the Islamic world as well; tragedy was understood in terms of praise poetry and comedy in terms of vituperation, two existing genres in Arabic classical literature.

Although it was not generally recognized as a dramatic genre in the Middle Ages, comedy was understood as a particular kind of literary narrative. In his Middle English *Troy Book*, the Benedictine monk John Lydgate wrote that comedy begins in 'a manner compleynyng, / And afterward endeth in gladness'. Lydgate's *Mumming at Hertford* (1425), a lighthearted entertainment for the young Henry VI, represented another medieval breakthrough, though it resembles classical precedents in structure and theme: a group of humble working-men have been upended by their shrewish wives, and they beg the king to restore them to mastery and correct this inversion of the normal hierarchy.

The most important poet of 'comedy' in the Middle Ages was Dante Alighieri (1265–1321). In his own definition of comedy in the treatise *De vulgari eloquentia,* Dante considers it to be inferior to tragedy in style, form, syntax, and diction – the 'vulgarity' of style qualifies the work as comic – yet elsewhere he also justifies the title of his epic *Divine Comedy* as it begins in adversity (*Inferno*) and ends in joy (*Paradiso*). Dante himself called the work *Commedia* (*Comedia* in the spelling of his day; he refers to *la mia comedìa* in *Inferno*, canto 21). The *Divine Comedy* is an allegorical representation of the poet's journey toward God. In short, Dante drew on the ancient classification of comedy, which dealt with 'low' subjects and ended happily. His poem, however, is not comical in our modern sense, but a serious meditation on life and death. In juxtaposing two seemingly contradictory notions – divinity and comedy – inverting the relationship between comic and tragic values in the cosmic order, the concept of 'divine comedy' raises crucial theoretical questions. Dante's work indirectly comments on features attributed to comedy in antiquity: the bodily, materialistic aspect of Greek and Roman comic drama, which was supposedly beneath the sublime conflicts of tragic heroes, not to mention Plato's idealized world of pure forms. After Dante, comedy entered a new era: comic pleasure was no longer regarded as necessarily opposed to the sacred. Giovanni Boccaccio was the first to apply the word *divina* to the work in lectures published as *Expositions* (1373). The combination of divinity and comedy, in other words, is part of the reception of the work, rather than explicitly formulated in those terms by Dante. Although comedy retained vital connections to folk festivals and bawdy humour, comedy could also represent divine spirit and higher truth. Theological reconciliation through love served as a prototype for romantic comedy.

The crisis of faith that followed the plague of the mid-fourteenth century and wiped out populations of Europe turned much medieval comedy in a morbid direction: death and dying were popular topics, as was the failure of religion to stave off the plague. Comedy was still bawdy and robust, but humour in some areas became darker and more sardonic. Woodblock prints of the era show allegorical and often grotesque images of Death positioned in humorous situations *vis-à-vis* human characters who try to either escape or outwit it. Such figures appear in wall paintings and were probably carried out as ritual performances as well. A far cry from Dante's 'divine' comedy, the dark humour of the Middle Ages also points to later developments in comic theory, though the term 'black humour' was not coined until the twentieth century.

Around the same time, comedy appeared in the figure of the court jester, a fool who was given leeway to tell the truth but also appeared as a kind of comic scapegoat.

Associated with the innocence of Christ, the fool served as a darkly humorous reflection on the folly of mankind. In 1511, the great Renaissance humanist Desiderius Erasmus published a bitter, satirical essay, *In Praise of Folly*. Speaking through the character of Folly herself, Erasmus critiqued the corruption of the Church in what would become a central work of the Protestant Reformation. Ultimately Folly asserts both the ideals of Christianity and the importance of foolishness to human happiness:

> And so at last I return to Paul. "Ye willingly," says he, "suffer my foolishness," and again, "Take me as a fool," […] and in another place, "We are fools for Christ's sake." You have heard from how great an author how great praises of folly; and to what other end, but that without doubt he looked upon it as that one thing both necessary and profitable. "If anyone among ye," says he, "seem to be wise, let him be a fool that he may be wise."

The job of fools was to mock human vices. In Europe, the court jester would be called *fool, buffoon, clown, jongleur, stultor, scurra, fou, histrio, morion,* among many other names. He was an essential fixture of the royal courts and master castles. Jesters came from a range of backgrounds, from nonconformist university dropouts to excommunicated monks. The jesters were also associated with the physically or mentally handicapped. Ostracized by society, the jesters' marginal position offered them an unparalleled vantage point from which to peer into its faults. Allowed to speak truth to power, they were granted 'comic dispensation' to say anything about anyone, including the king. The revered Polish jester Stańczyk (1480–1560) was considered the most politically astute man of his era, able to predict the unfavorable turn of Polish history. Shakespeare often employed the wise fool, both in tragedies such as *King Lear* and comedies such as *Twelfth Night*. Hamlet famously mourns his beloved childhood jester: 'Alas, poor Yorick!' He remembers this comic performer as 'a fellow of infinite jest, of most excellent fancy'. Today, political humourists commenting on corruption in government and social evils owe an important debt to their medieval forebears. When stage comedy again flourished in the Elizabethan theatre, Renaissance playwrights would recover a complicated double legacy, which reached back to both antiquity and the Middle Ages, classical and gothic precedents.

Bibliography

Bakhtin, Mikhail. (1965) *Rabelais and His World*, trans. Helene Iswolsky. Bloomington: Indiana University Press, 1984.

Carlson, Marvin. *Theories of the Theatre: A Historical and Critical Survey, from the Greeks to the Present.* Ithaca, NY: Cornell University Press, 1984.

Case, Sue-Ellen. 'Re-Viewing Hrotsvit'. *Theatre Journal* 35 (4), Ideology and Theatre (December 1983): 533–42.

Henderson, Jeffrey. 'The Dēmos and the Comic Competition', in *Nothing to Do with Dionysus?* ed. J. J. Winkler and Froma I. Zeitlin, 271–313. Princeton: Princeton University Press, 1990.

Hokenson, Jan. *The Idea of Comedy: History, Theory, Critique.* Madison, NJ: Fairleigh Dickinson University Press, 2006.

Janko, Richard. *Aristotle on Comedy: Towards a Reconstruction of Poetics II.* Berkeley: University of California Press, 1984.

Kove, V. A. 'God-Denying Fools: Tristan, Troilus, and the Medieval Religion of Love'. *Telling Images: Chaucer and the Imagery of Narrative II.* 223–56. Stanford, CA: Stanford University Press, 2009.

Mallette, Karla. 'Beyond Mimesis: Aristotle's *Poetics* in the Medieval Mediterranean'. *PMLA* 24 (2): 583–91, 2009.

Miller, Mitchell. 'The Pleasures of the Comic and of Socratic Inquiry: Aporetic Reflections on *Philebus* 48a–50b'. *Arethusa* 41 (2) (2008): 263–89.

Palmer, Jerry. 1993. *Taking Humour Seriously.* London: Routledge, 1994.

Revermann, Martin. *Comic Business: Theatricality, Dramatic Technique, and Performance Contexts of Aristophanic Comedy.* Oxford, New York: Oxford University Press, 2006.

Rossiter, William T. 'Comedy in Chaucer and Boccaccio'. *Studies in the Age of Chaucer* 32 (2010): 414–17.

Segal, Erich. *The Death of Comedy.* Cambridge, MA: Harvard University Press, 2001.

Shaw, Carl A. 'Middle Comedy and the "Satiric" Style'. *American Journal of Philology* 131 (1) (2010): 1–22.

Shelley, Cameron. 'Plato on the Psychology of Humor'. *Humor: International Journal of Humor Research* 16 (4) (2003): 351–67.

Stott, Andrew. *Comedy.* New York: Routledge, 2005.

Symes, Carol. *A Common Stage: Theater and Public Life in Medieval Arras.* Ithaca, NY: Cornell University Press, 2007.

Wickham, Glynne. 'Medieval Comic Traditions and the Beginnings of English Comedy', in *Comic Drama: The European Heritage*, ed. W. D. Howarth, 40–62. London: Methuen & Co., Ltd. 1978.

TEXTS

Ancient Views of Comedy

1. Plato, *Philebus* (360 BCE) 'The Basis of Comedy is Malice', translated by Jeffrey Rusten

Socrates and Protarchus have just discussed the sort of pleasure derived from tragedy, and now turn to comedy.

> *Socrates.* Now as to the disposition of our soul at comedies, are you aware that here to there is a mixture of pleasure and pain?
> As for the concept of malice, which we mentioned just now; would you consider that a pain of the soul, or what?
> *Prot.* Yes.
> *Soc.* Furthermore, the man with malice will turn out to be one who is happy at his neighbors' misfortunes. Now ignorance is a bad thing, as is the condition we call boorishness. It's from these premises that you can discern what nature the ridiculous has.
> *Prot.* Tell me.
> *Soc.* Generally speaking, it is a sort of wickedness, called by name after a sort of condition. And in turn the experience of this wickedness is the opposite of what is prescribed by the inscription at Delphi.
> *Prot.* You mean 'know yourself', Socrates?
> *Soc.* Yes. Clearly the opposite of that would be if the inscription said "do not know yourself at all."
> *Prot.* Of course.
> *Soc.* Now, Protarchus, you must try to split this very concept into three parts.
> All instances of those who 'do not know themselves' must necessarily be in one of these three categories.
> *Prot.* How?
> *Soc.* First, as regards money – imagining themselves richer than their wealth justifies. There are even more who imagine themselves to be taller and better-looking, and physically quite different from their true selves. Yet much the largest number are mistaken about the third type of things – i.e., those of the soul, since they imagine themselves better in virtue, when in

fact they are not. And furthermore, do we not find the majority of them fiercely making a claim, full of contention and false knowledge, about the virtue of wisdom?

Prot. Of course.

Soc. Would one be correct in calling every such situation bad?

Prot. Absolutely.

Soc. So then, Protarchus, this still has to be divided in two – if, that is, we are to develop this view of childishness of malice into a view of the strange mixture of pleasure and pain. How can we divide it in two, you may ask? Among all those who are so foolish as to have this false impression about themselves, some must have power and strength, others the opposite – just as with people in general.

Prot. It must be, yes.

Soc. Then you must divide them by this criterion: those whose ignorance is accompanied by weakness and the inability to retaliate if laughed at, then you would correctly call 'ridiculous'; whereas you will give the truest account of those who are powerful and able to retaliate if you call them 'frightening' and 'hostile.' That is because ignorance by the powerful, both itself and its imitations [on stage], is hostile and disgraceful, since it harms others; but weak ignorance is naturally classed as something ridiculous.

Prot. You are absolutely right. Yet it is not yet clear to me how this involves a mixture of pleasure and pain.

Soc. Well, consider first of all the potential for malice. Is there a sort of pleasure and pain that may be unjust? And it is not unjust or malicious to rejoice in our enemies' misfortunes?

Prot. Of course not.

Soc. And yet if we see our friends in trouble, as sometimes happens, isn't it unjust if we should feel joy rather than grief?

Prot. Of course.

Soc. Have we, then, stated that ignorance is always a bad thing?

Prot. Correct.

Soc. Then, since we said that our friends' imagined wisdom or good looks or our other examples must fall into three categories, and that the weak ones are ridiculous, the strong ones hateful, should we or should we not agree to what I just said, that this disposition on the part of our friends, if it is not harmful to others, is ridiculous?

Prot. Very much so.

Soc. Are we not agreed that, since it is ignorance, it is bad?

Prot. Absolutely.

Soc. And are we feeling joy or grief when we laugh at it?

Prot. Obviously we feel joy.

Soc. And have we not said that it is malice that makes us feel pleasure in our friends' misfortunes?

Prot. Necessarily.

Soc. The argument, then, amounts to this: when we laugh at the ridiculous behavior of our friends, mixing pleasure with malice, we are mixing pleasure with pain; since it was long ago agreed that malice is a pain of the soul, whereas laughter is a pleasure, and both occur together on these occasions.

Prot. That is true.

Soc. So our argument makes it plain that not only in dirges and tragedies, but in countless other things as well – not just in plays but also in the entire tragedy and comedy of real life – pleasures are mixed with pains.

2. Aristotle on the Origins and Function of Comedy

a. Aristotle, Poetics (350 BCE), translated by Jeffrey Rusten

Some people say they are called dramas (lit. "actions"), because they imitate people doing things. This is also why the Dorians[1] lay claim to both tragedy and comedy (the Megarians claim comedy, those here for the time when they had democracy, those in Sicily[2] because the poet Epicharmos, who was much older than Chionides and Magnes,[3] came from there, while some of those in the Peloponnese claim tragedy), considering the name significant; for they say that they used to call neighboring villages *komai*, but the Athenians called them *demes*, on the assumption that comic actors [*komodoi*] were named not from their reveling [*komazein*], but from the fact that they were expelled from the city and wandered around the villages [*komai*]. And that they call acting *dran*, while the Athenians call it *prattein* …

---

[1] I.e. Greeks from areas which spoke the Dorian dialect (mainly the Peloponnese), as opposed to Athenians.
[2] There was another Megara north of Syracuse in Sicily.
[3] Chionides and Magnes were famous early Athenian comic poets.

The genesis of tragic and comic poetry

Since to imitate is innate in us, and so are music and rhythm (for meters are obviously constituents of rhythms), the people who were most naturally talented at these things must have started from improvisations, then developed them little by little, to invent poetry.

But poetry diverged according to its different characters: the more serious people imitated good actions by good people, while the more trivial people imitated those of boors; they began by making poems of abuse, while the other composed hymns and poems of praise. Now we can't identify any such poems of abuse by a poet before Homer, but it is likely there were many, and we *can* name some once we reach this time, like his *Margites*[4] and similar ones. In these poems there appeared the *iambic* meter because it was suitable, which is why it is called *iambeion* now, since this was the meter in which people used to lampoon (*iambizon*) each other.

And among the oldest writers some were poets of epic, some of iambic verse. And just as Homer was the best poet on serious subjects (not only were they good poetry – they also employed dramatic imitation), in the same way he first outlined the shape of comedy, by dramatizing not abuse, but the ridiculous: *Margites* has the same relationship to comedy that the *Iliad* and *Odyssey* have to tragedy.

And when tragedy and comedy were developing, those who had been pursuing either epic or iambic poetry became either comic poets instead of iambic ones, or producers of tragedies instead of epic, according to their natural inclination because the forms of these genres were more grand and more in public favor than the earlier ones.

To examine whether tragedy has now reached perfection in its constituent parts, and to offer a critique of the genre itself and its reception, are things I must leave for another time. But once it had come into being from a beginning in improvisation – both tragedy and also comedy, the former from those who lead out the dithyramb,[5] the latter from the songs to the phallus[6] which even now continue to be customary in many cities – it expanded little by little as poets developed whatever features appeared. Finally, after undergoing many changes, tragedy ceased to change once it possessed its own unique nature.

---

[4] This poem is no longer preserved, but it seems to have told of an anti-hero who could do nothing right.

[5] A song sung to the lyre at festivals of Dionysus, of uncertain contents; no complete dithyramb is preserved.

[6] Men dressed as satyrs carried a large wooden model of a penis during the parade of Dionysus and sang obscene songs as they did so; Aristophanes' first preserved comedy, *Acharnians*, portrays such a procession. Its origins are obscure.

Characteristics and early history of comedy

[handwritten: never blame malace for what can be explained by foolishness]

As we said, comedy is an imitation of more buffoonish people – not characterized by complete evil, because in fact what is base[7] can sometimes be ridiculous, since the ridiculous consists of baseness which causes no pain and is not destructive, for example a comic mask which is ugly and distorted, but not painful. Now the transitions of tragedy and their sequence have been documented, but comedy, because it was taken less seriously at the start, was not. Indeed it was only late that the archon provided a chorus of comic actors, instead of volunteers. It was only after it possessed several of its forms that there is a record of those who are called its poets; and it is not known who introduced masks, or prologues, or more than one actor or the like. The composition of plots originally came from Sicily; at Athens, it was Krates [c. 450 B.C.] who began to depart from the form of the lampoon and compose general stories and plots.

b. Aristotle, 'On the Qualities of Character that Are Moderate (i.e., do not belong to one extreme or another),' *from* Nicomachean Ethics *(350 BCE) translated by Jeffrey Rusten (1999)*

A sense of good taste is also proper to a moderate character; good taste consists of saying and listening to the sort of things that befit a liberal and reasonable man. There are in fact certain things which are fitting for such a man to say and hear in jest, and the jokes of a liberal man will be different from those of a slavish one, and those of the educated from the uneducated. One can observe this difference in Old Comedy and New: the old considered obscene talk to be funny, whereas the new merely hints at such things for humor. They are very different in their respectability.

c. Aristotle, Tractatus Coislinianus *(350 BCE), translated by Jeffrey Rusten*

Tragedy removes the emotions of fear from the soul through pity and fright, and its aim is a due proportion of fear; its mother is grief.

Definition of comedy

Comedy is the imitation of an action which is funny and without magnitude, complete, with each of the parts separate in its forms, by an actor and not by narrative, bringing

---

[7] The Greek word *aischros* has a wide range of meaning, from physical ('ugly') to the moral ('base,' 'evil').

about through pleasure and laughter the purification of such emotions; its mother is laughter.

Techniques for producing laughter

Laughter comes about 1) through speech: by the use of homonyms, synonyms, repetition, wordplay, diminutives, alterations (through addition or subtraction), or a figure of speech (in a dialect or among some social group); 2) from situations: by comparison (to advantage or detriment) with the familiar, trickery, impossibility, the possible but illogical, events contrary to expectation, exaggeration of characters' stupidity, use of crude dancing, characters with the ability to be important choosing instead to be trivial, and disorganized plots without any sequence.

Random observations

Comedy differs from verbal abuse, in that abuse recounts the victim's actual faults quite openly, whereas comedy requires what is called *emphasis* (= 'implication').

The mocker desires to bring to light the faults of the body and the mind.

There is a correspondence between fear in tragedy and what is funny in comedy.

Parts of comedy

The constituents of a comedy are: plot, character, motivation, style, music and staging. A comic plot is one that is based on funny actions; the characters in comedy are the buffoon, the trickster and the braggart; of motivation there are two sorts, state of mind and methods of proof (oaths, contracts, testimony, refutations, legal precedents).[8] Comic style is universal and popular. The comic poet must make his characters use the dialect of his own homeland, [except to foreigners he will not give this one],[9] but the one native to each. Song is the province of music, so that considerable previous experience in music will be necessary. Staging is extremely useful for the drama, because it brings everything together. Plot, style and music are observable in all comedies; motives, character and staging in few.

The parts of a comedy are four: prologue, chorale, episode, and exodus. The prologue is the part of a comedy up to the entry of the chorus; the chorale is the song

---

[8] These methods of proving a case in court are well-known from Aristotle's *Rhetoric* I.15.1375a24–25, but they seem to have little application to comedy.

[9] The text is corrupt here; I follow the improvements suggested by Vahlen and H-G. Nesselrath (*Attische mittlere Komodie*, 137).

sung by the chorus, when it has sufficient grandeur. An episode is what is between two choral songs. The Exodus is what is spoken at the end by the chorus.

Ages of comedy

Old comedy tried to be funny; New comedy still aimed at being funny, but tried to make it more civilized; Middle comedy is a mixture of them both.

3. Horace, 'Remarks on Comedy', from *Epistles, Satires* (40–10 or 9 BCE), translated by Jeffrey Rusten

Epistles (The origins of comedy and subsequent censorship)
In the countryside long ago, when people were strong and content with the little they had, once the harvest had been stored and they wanted to relax the body and mind which had toiled so hard for this goal, the fellow workers, loyal wives and children joined in sacrificing a pig to Tellus, milk to Silvanus, and flowers and wine to the Spirit who guarded their short lives. It was in this way that 'Fescennine'[10] free speech was invented, which spewed out rough insults in poetic dialogues. This free speech was accepted for a series of years while it joked in a friendly way, until the mockery, which had already become fierce, switched to undisguised rage, and began to threaten families of the highest character. They were stung by these vicious attacks, and even those not yet affected became concerned about the general problem. A law was actually passed with a penalty, forbidding anyone to be pilloried in a song: so they changed their ways, forced by fear of beatings back to entertainment without insults.

Epistles (the so-called 'Art of Poetry')
After tragedy came Old Comedy
These were followed by Old Comedy, which won no small praise; but its free speech degenerated into crime, and a violence that deserved legal restraint. A law was passed, and the chorus, its right to inflict harm denied, grew silent.

Satires (realism in the New Comedy prevents it from being true poetry)
[T]hat is why some have asked whether comedy is poetry or not, since extreme feeling

---

[10] These were somewhat racy verses sung at Roman weddings, here used to mean 'obscene.' Despite the names of Roman gods, Horace appears to be talking about Greeks rather than Romans, as the next passage makes clear.

and force are absent from its language and content – it's merely talk, except that unlike talk, it's in a fixed meter. You may object, 'but the angry father speaks in a rage, because his son and heir is crazy about a girlfriend who's a whore, and rejects a wife with a big dowry and, even worse, walks around drunk carrying torches even before dark.' But would Pomponius hear anything less harsh, if his father were alive? So, it's not enough to stick together a verse with inoffensive words, which you could rearrange and have anyone rant just like the father does in a play.

Epistles (criticism of Plautus)

It's believed that comedy requires less effort, because it takes its subject matter from the everyday; but it's actually more of a chore, because you get less indulgence. Just look at how Plautus manages the part of a young boy in love, or of a worried father, or a dastardly pimp, what a buffoon he is in his hungry parasites, how he bounds across the stage with his socks down. He only cares about putting cash in his wallet, and once that's done he doesn't give a damn whether the play stands firm or falls.

Epistles (the state of the contemporary Roman theatre)

Often even a bold poet is routed and terrified away by the fact that those greater in number, though less in virtue and rank, uneducated and stupid but ready to fight it out if the upper class disagrees, interrupt the middle of a play to demand a bear-baiting or boxers. That's what the mob enjoys. In fact, the delight of all the upper class has also shifted from the ear to the flitting eye and its empty pleasures. The stage is open for more than four hours, while squadrons of cavalry and companies of infantry run away. Next, unlucky kings are dragged in, their hands tied behind them. Chariots rush by, wagons, carts, ships, captured ivory is carried past, even the conquered city of Corinth. Democritus,[11] if he were still alive, would laugh if a panther mixing his different species with a camel, or a white elephant, should turn the heads of the mob; he would watch the audience more intently than the contest itself, since it would provide with much more entertainment. He would tell you that the poets were telling their story to a deaf and dumb ass, because no speech could be heard over the noise that emanates from our theatres.

---

[11] A Greek philosopher said to have found humanity infinitely amusing.

4. Quintilian, *Institutio Oratoria* (CE 95), translated by John Selby Watson

Book 3, Chapter 8

It ought, indeed, to be a chief object with declaimers to consider what is suitable to different characters, for they speak on but few subjects of controversy as advocates, but generally harangue in the character of sons, fathers, rich men, old men, morose or good-natured persons, misers or superstitious people, cowards or jesters, so that actors in comedy have scarcely more parts to master on the stage than they have in the schools.

Book 6, Chapter 2

20. *Pathos*, or what we very properly call *affectus* or 'emotion', is quite different from that which is referred to as *ēthos*, and that I may mark, as exactly as I can, the diversity between them, I would say that the one is similar to comedy, the other to tragedy. This kind of eloquence is almost wholly engaged in exciting anger, hatred, fear, envy, or pity, and from what sources its topics are to be drawn is manifest to all and has been mentioned by me in speaking of the exordium and peroration.

Book 6, Chapter 3

27. What is said in jest, moreover, is either gay and cheerful, as most of the jokes of Aulus Galba, or malicious, as those of the late Junius Bassus, or bitter, as those of Cassius Severus, or inoffensive, as those of Domitius Afer. But it makes a great difference where we indulge in jests. At entertainments and in common conversation, a more free kind of speech is allowed to the humbler class of mankind, amusing discourse to all.

28. We should always be unwilling to offend, and the inclination to lose a friend rather than a joke should be far from us. In the very battles of the forum I should wish it to be in my power to use mild words, though it is allowed to speak against our opponents with contumely and bitterness, as it is permitted us to accuse openly, and to seek the life of another according to law. But in the forum, as in other places, to insult another's misfortune is thought inhuman, either because the insulted party may be free from blame or because similar misfortune may fall on him who offers the insult. Therefore, a speaker must first of all consider what his own character is, in what sort of cause he is to speak, before whom, against whom, and what he should say.

29. Distortion of features and gesture, such as is the object of laughter in buffoons,

is by no means suited to an orator. Scurrilous jests, too, and such as are used in low comedy, are utterly unbecoming his character. As for indecency, it should be so entirely banished from his language, that there should not be the slightest possible allusion to it, and if it should be imputable, on any occasion, to his adversary, it is not in jest that he should reproach him with it.

30. Though I should wish an orator, moreover, to speak with wit, I should certainly not wish him to seem to affect wit, and therefore he must not speak facetiously as often as he can, but must rather avoid a joke occasionally rather than lower his dignity.

31. No one will endure a prosecutor jesting in a cause of a horrible nature, or a defendant doing so in one of a pitiable nature. There are some judges, also, of too grave a disposition to yield willingly to laughter. It will sometimes occur, too, that reflections which we make on our adversary may apply to the judge or even to our own client.

32. Some orators have been found, indeed, who would not avoid a jest that might recoil even on themselves, as was the case with Sulpicius Longus, who, though he was himself an ugly man, remarked that a person, against whom he appeared on a trial for his right to freedom, had not even the face of a free man. In reply to him, Domitius Afer said, "On your conscience, Longus, do you think that he who has an ugly face cannot be a free man?"

Book 10, Chapter 1

8. On the contrary, our stock of words must be prepared by us with judgment, as we have a view to the proper force of oratory and not to the volubility of the charlatan. But this object we shall effect by reading and listening to the best language, for by such exercise, we shall not only learn words expressive of things, but shall learn for what place each word is best adapted.

9. Indeed, almost all words, except a few that are of indecent character, find a place in oratorical composition, and the writers of iambics, and of the old comedy, are often commended for the use of words of that description. But at present, it is sufficient for us to look to our own work. All sorts of words, then, except those to which I have alluded, may be excellently employed in some place or other, for we sometimes have occasion for low and coarse words, and those that would seem mean in the more elegant parts of a speech, are, when the subject requires them, adopted with propriety.

65. The old comedy retains, almost alone, the pure grace of Attic diction, and the

charm of a most eloquent freedom of language. Though it is chiefly employed in attacking follies, it has great force in other departments, for it is sublime, elegant, and graceful. Next to Homer's (whom it is always right to except, as he himself excepts Achilles), I know of no poetry that has either a greater resemblance to oratory or is better adapted for forming orators.

66. The authors of it are numerous, but Aristophanes, Eupolis, and Cratinus are the principal.

Book 12, Chapter 11

38. For if the Greeks succeed better than we in plainer and simpler subjects, so that we are beaten on such ground and accordingly, in comedy, do not even venture to compete with them, we must not altogether abandon this department of literature, but must cultivate it as far as we can. We can, at least, rival the Greeks in the temper and judgment with which we treat our subjects, while grace of style, which we have not among us by nature, must be sought from a foreign source.

39. Is not Cicero, in causes of an inferior character, acute and not inelegant, clear and not unduly elevated? Is not similar merit remarkable in Marcus Calidius? Were not Scipio, Laelius, and Cato, the Attics of the Romans, as it were, in eloquence? Surely, then, those must satisfy us in that sort of style, than whom none can be imagined more excellent in it.

5. Evanthius, 'On Drama' (c. CE 350) translated by S. G. Nugent

On the supremacy of Terence

Terence observed the rules concerning the appearance, age, duty and roles of characters more scrupulously than anyone else. And yet he dared, even against the traditions of comedy, since he sought the ring of truth in his fictional plots, to introduce from time to time prostitutes who were not wicked. In these cases, however, there was both a reason why they might be good and a pleasure in the thing itself.

Since Terence had done these things extremely skillfully, it is especially admirable that he upheld tradition, in that he did write comedy, and that he tempered the mood so that it would not pass over into tragedy. This is a quality that we find, along with other things, less successfully maintained by Plautus and Afranius and Appius, and for the most part by many comic playwrights. Also among Terence's strengths, it is remarkable that his plays are so well balanced that they neither swell to tragic heights nor sink to low farce.

Also, he brings in nothing arcane, nor is there anything which must be clarified by antiquarians. But Plautus does this more often and is more obscure in many places.

In addition, Terence is so carefully attentive to the plot and the style that he always either deletes or delicately handles anything that might get in the way. And he ties the central portion to the beginning and end so well that nothing seems added to anything else, but the whole play seems to be formed as one organic unit.

Another feature that is admirable in Terence is that in the beginning he does not mix four characters together in such a way that the distinction among them is unclear. And also he does not have an actor say anything to the audience as if he were outside the comedy, which is a very common fault of Plautus.

Also this quality of his, among other things, seems praiseworthy: he chose to create richer plots by doubling what goes on. For except for the *Mother in Law*, in which there is only the love affair of Pamphilus, the other five plays have two sets of lovers.

Definitions of comedy and tragedy

Although there are many differences between tragedy and comedy, these are chief distinguishing features: in comedy the fortunes of men are ordinary, the onslaughts of difficulties minor, the outcomes of actions happy. But in tragedy everything is the opposite: the characters are outstanding, the fears are great, the outcomes disastrous. Then again, in comedy the beginning is stormy, the end calm, but in tragedy the opposite holds true. In tragedy a life is portrayed a life which one must flee, in comedy a life which one ought to seek. Finally, all comedy deals with fictional plots, whereas tragedy is often sought in historical reality.

6. Donatus, 'On Comedy' (c. CE 350) translated by S. G. Nugent

A comedy is a play that presents various manners of life of private citizens, from which one may learn what is useful in life and what, on the other hand, is to be avoided. The Greeks defined comedy in this way: "comedy is a narrative of the acts of private individuals, which does not entail danger." Cicero said that comedy was an imitation of life, a mirror of experience, an image of truth [...]

Comedy, moreover, because it is a work composed to be an imitation of life and a faithful representation of characters, depends upon gesture and speech. Among the

Greeks it is doubtful who first devised comedy, but among the Romans it is certain: Livius Andronicus first devised comedy and tragedy and the *togatae* [comedies with Roman as opposed to Greek plots; of which none is preserved].

And he said, justifiably, that comedy is a mirror of daily life. For, just as we easily grasp the outlines of reality by means of the image when a mirror is held up to us, so through the reading of comedy we perceive the image of life and of daily habit without difficulty.

Medieval Views of Comedy

7. Hrotsvita of Gandersheim, 'Prologue to the Comedies' (c. 935–972), translated by Christopher St John

There are many Christians (and I am unable to exonerate myself entirely of this fault) who for the elegance of the cultural language prefer the frivolousness of pagan writings to the usefulness of the sacred scriptures. Still others, although attentive to scripture and scornful of the rest of pagan literature, nonetheless read again and again the fictions of Terence, and because of the pleasure they take in the writing are corrupted by the knowledge of things best kept hidden. Therefore I, the Strong Cry [Hrot-svita = 'strong in glory'] of Gandersheim, have not shrunk from the task of imitating him in writing (while others merely enjoy reading him) so that, as far as my poor talent allowed, the same genre used to present the promiscuity of lewd women might be turned to the praise of the glorious purity of holy maidens.

For all that, I have often blushed and been ashamed that writing in this vein has compelled me not only to study but even to dignify by copying things which shouldn't even be heard of – the disgusting folly of illicit lovers, and the sinful pleasures of their conversation. But if I had ignored these out of embarrassment, I could neither fulfill my task nor set forth in such detail as my abilities allow the praise of the innocents; for the more persuasive the temptations of the wicked, the more sublime the greatness of our heavenly defender is revealed to be, and the more glorious the victory of his triumphant forces. This is especially so when it is the weakness of a woman that conquers, and the strength of a man that suffers a shameful defeat.

I have no doubt that the objection will be made that these slight productions are much poorer and worse than their model, and totally unlike it in expression. This is of course true, but I deny strenuously that I can be justly faulted with pretending to a place among those whose higher knowledge far surpasses my own indolence; for I am not even bold enough to venture a comparison with the most remote of their pupils. I rely only on this: however meager my accomplishment, I am offering back with spiritual devotion and humility the talent I have received to Him who gave it. Thus I am not so vain as to seek to avoid criticism at the cost of neglecting to proclaim the virtue of Christ, who works through the saints, so far as He grants me the ability to do so.

If my devotion finds any favour I will be pleased; but if because of my ineptness or the lack of skill in my writing it finds none, I will still be happy with what I have done, because the pursuit of my humble task – expressed in the heroic meter in my other ignorant efforts, in dramatic narrative here – has kept me away from the pernicious temptations of the pagans.

8. Dante Alighieri, *De Vulgari Eloquentia* (On Eloquence in the Vernacular) (1302–1305), translated by Steven Botterill

Now that I have, not without difficulty, elucidated some tricky problems – who and what is worthy of the aulic vernacular, as well as which form I consider worthy of such honour as, alone, to be suited for the vernacular at its highest – I wish, before moving on to other matters, to enquire thoroughly into the canzone form, which many clearly employ more at random than according to the rules; and since, so far, all this has been taken for granted, I will now throw open the workshop of that art (leaving the forms of ballata and sonnet aside for the moment, since I plan to explain them in the fourth book of the present work, which will deal with the middle level of the vernacular). Looking back, then, at what was said above, I recall that I frequently called those who write verse in the vernacular 'poets;' and this presumptuous expression is beyond question justifiable, since they are most certainly poets, if we understand poetry aright: that is, as nothing other than a verbal invention composed according to the rules of rhetoric and music. Yet they differ from the great poets, that is, those who obey the rules, since those great ones wrote their poetry in a language, and with a technique, governed by rules, whereas these write at random, as I said above. Thus it comes about that, the more closely we try to imitate the great poets, the more correctly we write poetry. So, since I am trying to write a theoretical work about poetry, it behoves me to emulate their learned works of poetic doctrine. First of all I declare that anyone must adjust the weight of his material to suit his own shoulders, lest the excessive burden bearing down upon them overcome his strength and send him sprawling in the mud; and this is what our master Horace teaches at the beginning of his *Ars poetica*, where he says

'Choose your subject'. Then, when dealing with the various subjects that are suitable for poetry, we must know how to choose whether to treat them in tragic, comic, or elegiac style. By 'tragic' I mean the higher style, by 'comic' the lower, and by 'elegiac' that of the unhappy. If it seems appropriate to use the tragic style, then the illustrious vernacular must be employed, and so you will need to bind together a canzone. If, on the other hand, the comic style is called for, then sometimes the middle level of the vernacular can be used, and sometimes the lowly; and I shall explain the distinction in Book Four. If, though, you are writing elegy, you must only use the lowly. But let us leave the other styles aside and, as is appropriate, discuss only the tragic here. The tragic style is clearly to be used whenever both the magnificence of the verses and the lofty excellence of construction and vocabulary accord with the gravity of the subject-matter. Therefore, remembering well that (as has been proved above) whatever is highest is worthy of the highest, and seeing that the style we call 'tragic' is the highest kind of style, the subjects that we have defined as requiring to be treated in the highest style must be treated in that style alone. And those subjects are well-being, love, and virtue, and the thoughts that they inspire in us, as long as no accidental circumstance intervenes to defile them.

9. John of Garland (1234), Dante Alighieri (1319), John Lydgate (written c. 1412–1420, first published 1513), 'Definitions of Comedy'

a. John of Garland (c. 1180–c. 1252), On the arts of prose, meter and rhythm (1234)

The five necessary characters in a comedy are: 1) the husband; 2) the wife; 3) the wife's seducer; 4) the seducer's helper or critical friend; 5) the maid of the wife or servant of the husband.

b. Dante Alighieri (1265–1321), Letter to Can Grande della Scala (1319)

The title of the book is, 'here begins the *Comedy* of Dante Alighieri, a Florentine in birth but not in character' [...] Comedy is in truth a kind of poetic narrative different from all the others. It differs from a tragedy in its subject matter in that tragedy in its beginning is admirable and quiet, in its ending or catastrophe foul and horrible [...] Comedy, however, begins with some adverse circumstances, but its plot has a happy ending, as appears in the comedies of Terence. And hence certain writers were accustomed to say in their salutation in place of a greeting, 'a tragic beginning and a comic ending.' Likewise they differ in their style of language, for tragedy is lofty and sublime, comedy relaxed and humble [...] From which it is evident why the present work is called a comedy. For if we consider its theme, in the beginning it is horrible and foul, because it is Hell; in its ending, fortunate, desirable and joyful, because it is Paradise. And if we consider the style of language, the style is unstudied and humble, because it is the vulgar tongue in which even housewives speak.

c. John Lydgate (1370–c. 1450), Troy Book *(written c. 1412–1420, first published 1513)*

Comedy has in its beginning
at prime face, a manner of complaining,
and afterward endeth in gladness;
and it the deeds only doth express
of such as are in poverty plunged low.

10. John of Salisbury, Honorius of Autun, Liutprand of Cremona, 'Attitudes to the Comic Theater'

a. John of Salisbury, Policraticus (1159)

There can be no doubt that on the authority of the church fathers the grace of the holy sacrament is forbidden to mimes and actors, so long as they persist in their wicked occupations.

b. Honorius of Autun (c. 1080–c. 1159), Elucidarium (1098)

Pupil: Do players have any hope of salvation?
Master: None; for they are with their whole hearts the servants of Satan. About them it is said 'they have not known God.'

c. Liutprand of Cremona (888–949), Antapodosis

Unless I am mistaken, just as the vision is dulled if struck directly by the rays of the sun without any substance interposed to prevent their appearance in their pure state, so the mind is weakened by the study of the combination of Academic, Peripatetic and Stoic doctrines, unless it is refreshed either by the beneficial amusement from comedies or the diverting stories of heroes.

2

The Renaissance

INTRODUCTION

The Renaissance, an immensely rich cultural movement that spread across Europe from the mid-fourteenth to the mid-seventeenth centuries, looked in two directions. On the one hand, the term, meaning 'rebirth', conveys a sense of looking backward to the humanistic culture of antiquity. Renaissance artists and scholars literally dug up old books and rediscovered the Latin works of Lucretius, Plautus, Terence, Seneca, and others. The earliest French comic theory, from roughly 1501 to 1530, tended to appear in new editions of Terence. With references to Donatus, Diomedes, Horace, and other classical authors, these texts prescribed rules on such topics as the proper language for comedy, decorum, and propriety. On the other hand, the Renaissance was the beginning of modernity, the start of the world as we know it today. It represented not only a shift from a theological to a scientific worldview, but also a new embrace of beauty and pleasure in art, as opposed to the Church's privileging of spirituality over sensuality. The Renaissance saw a renewed investment in the lives of human beings, which corresponded to a rise in global commerce, exploration, and plunder, a scientific understanding of the material universe (illuminated by astronomers Copernicus, Kepler, and Galileo), attention to the physical body as anatomized by sculptors and painters, and a return to vernacular literatures and languages. Most important for our purposes was the resurrection of the theatre itself, in England between 1576 and 1642, in France, where some of the most intense theoretical debates occurred, and in Spain, where dramatists turned often to the *theatrum mundi* or idea that theatre provides a metaphor for life.

Rebirth itself is a comic trope, and these years were marked by extraordinary cultural flowering and renewal. Though marred horribly by religious warfare, Reformation and

Counterreformation, the Renaissance might be characterized as a comic epoch. The jarring cosmological conflicts gave rise to scepticism about transcendental verities, as evidenced most plainly in the works of Italian political philosophers, such as Niccolò Machiavelli (1469–1527) and Giambattista Vico (1668–1744), as well as in those of English playwrights, William Shakespeare (1564–1616) and Christopher Marlowe (1564–93). French writers of the seventeenth century were the first since antiquity to prioritize reason in the observance of aesthetic rules. A key figure in this development is René Descartes (1596–1650), a brilliant mathematician who aspired to apply the rigour of mathematical proof and scepticism to other subjects. He first attempted to improve the methodology of science in his 1637 *Discourse on the Method of Rightly Conducting One's Reason and of Seeking Truth in the Sciences*. Descartes did not, as is often supposed, discount the importance of passion or physical experience in the pursuit of knowledge, but reason (and its limitations) subsequently became a crucial concern of French dramatists and theorists in the construction of logical plots, the fashioning of characters, and imagining the cognitive experience of the spectator. Vico's great philosophy of history, *Scienza Nuova* (*New Science*) applied theories of rhetoric to history and treated religion as a poetic construct. Unlike Aristotle, whose *Poetics* focused on tragedy and privileged plot over character, Vico believed that 'poetic characters' were 'the essence of poetry itself', and so he drew examples from 'New Comedy [which] portrays our present human customs.'

The Renaissance was also distinguished by great tragedies, in life – from the burning of 'heretics' such as Jan Hus and Giordano Bruno to the St Bartholomew's Day Massacre in France – and onstage in Racine's neoclassical *Phèdre, Andromaque,* and *Athalie,* or Shakespeare's *Hamlet* and *King Lear*. Nor was everyone a rationalist and a sceptic. But Shakespeare never wrote pure tragedy like Sophocles; his darkest works make space for fools and clowns. Even people who seem to be in deep mourning may be only playing, as Hamlet says, for 'all forms, moods [and] shapes of grief' are merely 'actions that a man might play'. Thus, great English Renaissance tragedies often have a comic underpinning, as illustrated in an exchange between Hamlet and a joking grave-digger on the subject of death and the discovery of the skull of Yorick, the King's jester, whose 'flashes of merriment … were wont to set the table on a roar'. Commenting on early-modern English drama, literary historian Stephen Greenblatt says, 'The effect is … to challenge the habit of mind that looks to heaven for rewards and punishments.'

A period of violently contending forces and ideas, the Renaissance introduced the idea of *commedia grave* (serious comedy) and tragicomedy. Battista Guarini's 1601 *Compendium of Tragicomic Poetry* argues that mixing tragedy and comedy is 'reasonable'. 'Pity and laughter', he adds, are 'not inharmonious'. Thus, Renaissance comic theory raised new questions about genre. In *A Midsummer Night's Dream*, Duke Theseus remarks that the 'tragical mirth' of the play-within-the-play sounds paradoxically like 'hot ice', but Shakespeare commonly depicted the interpenetration of comedy and tragedy. *The Merchant of Venice* is a comedy, with three joyous marriages, that centres on the grievous suffering of Shylock, the Jewish money-lender. Shakespeare's late comedies, such *Measure for Measure*, take a very dark turn, while in *Macbeth*, the drunken Porter jokes about a devil immediately before the entrance of Macduff, who discovers Duncan's slaughtered body. As Shakespeare, Spanish dramatist Pedro Calderón de la Barca (1600–81), French playwright Pierre Corneille (1606–84), and numerous others showed, comedy, tragedy, and history all inform each other, and this period gives rise to debates, in theory and on stage, about boundaries not only between comedy and tragedy but also between theatre and reality. Corneille's metatheatrical *L'Illusion comique* (*The Comedy of Illusion*; 1635) blends humour with pity and terror, farce and fear of death. In the dedication to the play, Corneille called it a 'strange monster', claiming that the last act was a tragedy but that the whole work was a comedy.

In France, where dramatic rules were institutionalized by the Académie Française, founded in 1635 by the influential Cardinal de Richelieu, a major theoretical debate erupted in 1637 with the performance and publication of Corneille's *Le Cid*, which was subtitled a 'tragicomedy' and, again, intentionally defied the neoclassical tragedy/comedy distinction. The '*Querelle du Cid*' ('Quarrel of *Le Cid*'), centred on a rigid interpretation of Aristotle and other ancient sources regarding supposed rules of dramatic construction, including the question of drama's moral function. The Académie Française published a document condemning the popular *Le Cid* as 'dramatically implausible and morally defective'. A central complaint was that the subject, a young woman who marries the murderer of her father, was inappropriate for comedy. Following the performance, Georges de Scudéry, a rival dramatist who sought the favour of Richelieu, published an anonymous pamphlet, *Observations sur le Cid* (followed by a letter to the Académie) which argued that Corneille's subject was 'worthless'. Many others, including Corneille himself, joined the fight, and it shaped the rest of the playwright's career, prompting him to reflect deeply and often on the principles of his art. Corneille's work demonstrates most strikingly the dialectical relationship between comic theory and practice in the Renaissance, as practice contended with theory, the real with the ideal, in a constant and productive tension. In short, comic writing and theory became a vital mode of reflection for Western Europe in a time of radical and difficult social change.

In Italy and France, a form of comic theatre called *commedia dell'arte* centred on stock characters, played by actors in half-masks, who improvised performances based on sketches or scenarios. Improvisation became a crucial aspect of theatre because it was increasingly recognized to be a central aspect of social life, fundamentally connected to manners. Even the diabolical Iago in *Othello* is gifted with the art of improvisation; it is arguably his ability to improvise that makes him diabolical. The diabolism of such Renaissance villains derives from the medieval Vice, a figure of comedy not tragedy in Christian culture because devils and personifications of the Deadly Sins represented error and thus became subjects of parody not pathos. The idea that identity was not inherited but made, even manipulated via an artful process meant, as Shakespeare wrote in his comedy *As You Like It* (c. 1600), that 'all the world's a stage'. The French playwright Molière (1622–73), whose company initially resembled a *commedia dell'arte* troupe, developed the comedy of manners most brilliantly in the seventeenth century, as well as an increasingly naturalistic style of acting (*jeu naturel*), by which he theorized the audience 'cannot distinguish truth from mere appearance'. Affectation was commonly the target of his satire. The increasing awareness in the Renaissance that selves could be fashioned, as theatrical characters could be, indicated a new range of meanings for the sin of vanity and a dovetailing of comic and tragic tropes. This perception led to a radical, often dangerous, new sense of freedom, mobility, and change, an emphasis on the power of rhetoric over that of abstract truth. These ideas are central to writing of and about comedy.

Roman comedies, particularly New Comedy with its emphasis on middle-class social mores and decorum, became primary sources for Renaissance comedy, with Plautus and Terence as crucial sources of plots. In the literature of the sixteenth century, Old Comedy was considered a 'primitive form' compared to sophisticated New Comedy. Literary critics of the era distinguished between *comédie forte* and *comédie douce*, regular and irregular comedy, which partially paralleled the differences between Old and New Comedy. Renaissance debates around the relative influence of the two Latin authors focused on questions of comic form and different kinds of humour. For French playwrights, Terence's plays became the principal model, as they considered Plautus to be too vulgar, while Aristophanes' Old Comedy, with its bawdy jokes and lack of structure, violated every rule of Aristotelian and, by extension, neoclassical propriety and order. The 1502 prologue to Terence's comedies prepared by the French scholar Jodocus Badius (also known as Badius Ascensius), established the long-lasting interest in his writings. Badius was primarily interested in issues of decorum, which prescribed the principles governing characters and language. French stage comedy attended closely to rules of verisimilitude and decorum; in brief, characters ought to behave in a way appropriate to their sex, social position, and upbringing. Nicholas Udall (1504–56), in the prologue to his *Roister Doister* (c. 1538), regarded as the first English-language comedy, proclaimed that both Terence and Plautus used comedy as a model for moral life.

Renaissance comic theory centres on rhetoric or the art of persuasion, rather than trying to represent a notion of transcendent truth. Rhetorical texts, such as Regnaud Le Queux's *Instructif de la seconde rhétorique* (1501) offered advice on comic writing as a way to foster practical morality. Theoretical debates prompted by Plato and Aristotle in antiquity were resurrected in new forms. A Greek notion of transcendent truth can still be seen in the neo-Platonic idealism of Italian philosopher Marsilio Ficino (1433–99), which informs the language of Shakespeare's comedies. For instance, in *A Midsummer Night's Dream*, Theseus comments that 'The poet's eye, in fine frenzy rolling, / Doth glance from heaven to Earth, from Earth to heaven.' Yet he adds that the poet must give 'to airy nothing / A local habitation and a name', shaping reality here and now, and the rhetorical model proved more influential than the neo-Platonic among theorists who believed that comedy should be useful.

Most Renaissance theorists of comedy considered it a tool to correct improper behaviour through humour and derision. One of the earliest Renaissance critics to promote the rhetorical model was Gian Giorgio Trissino (1478–1550), an Italian poet, playwright, and grammarian, who achieved high position in the Church and the diplomatic service. A true Renaissance man, Trissino studied classical philosophy and drama and was central to the revival of Aristotelian criticism in Italy. He is best known for his tragedy, *Sofonisba* (1514–15), which was translated into French in 1553 and helped to establish his reputation as a playwright and expert on Aristotle's *Poetics*. In his theoretical writings, Trissino promoted Dante's argument for writing in the Italian vernacular rather than Latin. His *Poetica* (1529) emphasized the importance of the actor sticking to his character and the corrective nature of comedy. If tragedy educates its audience through fear and pity, comedy educates through ridicule and derision. On the nature of laughter, Trissino writes that laughter brings pleasure, but only by depicting 'small ills', as grand ills evoke fear and pity. We 'laugh at the ignorance, imprudence, and credulity of someone else', especially if we believe that we are free of the same characteristics. Laughter can be produced by deformities of body or mind, and from ambiguities, puns, sarcasm, allegory, hyperbole, and so forth, but in his view pain or death has no place in comedy.

Although Roman authors Horace and Quintilian were well known for their writings about character development, early Renaissance theorists of comedy were more strongly influenced by Donatus's commentary on Terence. Francesco Robortello (1516–67), who taught rhetoric at universities in Lucca, Pisa, Venice, Padua, for example, argued that comedy 'imitates human actions that are rather base and vile'. New Comedy especially 'imitates behaviour that is daily observed in the ordinary relations of men'. Robertollo's *On Comedy* (1548) borrows the concept of ordinary relations from Donatus. Donatus's commentary on Terence also influenced Erasmus, the Dutch Renaissance humanist from Rotterdam (1466–1536), and Philip Melanchthon (1497–1569). In *On the Method of Study* (1512), Erasmus remarks: '[A]mong Latin writers who is more valuable as a standard of language than Terence? He is pure, concise and closest to everyday speech and then, by the very nature of his subject-matter, is also congenial to the young.' Like Badius, Erasmus believed that comedy was important because of its power of characterization and its adherence to decorum, and therefore to the moral order. Though a Catholic priest, Erasmus was also a classical scholar and a critical thinker who sought to reform the Church. He used New Comedy as a model for education, writing that the teacher 'should show that decorum especially is studied, not only in its universal aspect', as in stock characters like the young lover, the old miser, the prostitute, or the tricky slave, 'but also in the particular delineation of individual characters as developed by the poet'. Following Donatus, Erasmus believed that Terence's comedies adhered to this premise. Melanchthon, a German reformer and colleague of Martin Luther, expanded Donatus's definition of comedy to incorporate pre-Christian comic devices into the teachings of Christianity. The mistakes of Roman comic heroes, particularly their extramarital affairs, were intended to instruct viewers in the rewards of a virtuous and God-fearing life. These Renaissance scholars were not men of the theatre, but their writings (disseminated by the recently invented printing press) brought new attention to the actions and agency of human beings and greatly influenced later playwrights.

Aristotle's *Poetics*, which had been practically unknown until 1500, gained new influence, but this important work provided few guidelines for stage practice before the seventeenth century. Instead early-modern comedy developed via Christian holiday rituals, carnival, medieval festivals such as the Feast of Fools, when the lesser clergy could ridicule their superiors, comic sketches in recently founded universities, and the incorporation of Roman comedy into the Latin curriculum in grammar schools. Like other schoolboys in Elizabethan England, Shakespeare would have encountered Plautus and Terence at his grammar school in Stratford-upon-Avon. Although in some cases the structure of Renaissance comedy followed the Aristotelian model, in many cases it did not. In Italy, lectures by Giovanni Giraldi Cinthio (1504–73) helped to systematize the *Poetics* as a guidebook for playwrights. However, a wide range of performances crossed the conventions. A central neoclassical ideal was that of verisimilitude, or, as Hamlet put it, to hold a mirror up to nature. But basic questions arise with this dictum: What exactly is nature or 'truth', and how does a dramatist 'mirror' it? Other theoretical questions follow: Does comedy (or art in general) copy truth or make it? Shakespeare did not adhere to the unities of time, place, and action, as most French playwrights aimed to do. Hamlet may advocate holding a mirror up to nature, but he also sees a ghost, while fairies, sprites, and other supernatural creatures populate Shakespeare's comedies. In *A Midsummer Night's Dream*, Theseus offers a counter-theory when he says that 'as imagination bodies forth / The forms of things unknown, the poet's pen / Turns them to shapes and gives to airy nothing / A local habitation and a name.'

Reflecting on the question of making-versus-copying, a central motif of Renaissance comedy was the idea of metamorphosis or transformation. The doubling of language and people in twin comedies, for example, was informed by a growing sense of enormous change and, therefore, a duality and tension between ideals (epitomized by Thomas More's *Utopia*) and reality. It became possible to imagine a self, divided between what one was and what one might become. For these reasons, Plautus's comedy *Menaechmi Twins* (in Latin simply *Menaechmi*) became the model for a number of twin-related plots as the co-presence of twins provoked questions about the neo-classical unities of time, space and action. With twins, it seemed that a character could be in two places at once, leading not only to comic confusion but also to deeper questions about the perception of time and space and even the possibility of achieving a unified identity. The most famous adaptation of Plautus's twin plot is Shakespeare's *Comedy of Errors*, which adds a second pair of twin brothers, who are servants to the first.

Renaissance comedies adapted the old plots of thwarted lovers to accommodate new ideals of romantic love that arose in the late medieval period, with a shift in emphasis from sex to emotional connection. Shakespeare's comedies, *Much Ado about Nothing* and *Twelfth Night*, do not simply revolve around sex and marriage, or overcoming the objections of a mean old father; rather, they focus on the question of personal affinity and a richer psychological conception of love. *As You Like It* is indebted to the literary tradition of pastoral romance that dates to antiquity. In Shakespeare's pastoral comedy, people leave the hierarchical world of the court for an idealized rural life among shepherds in the country where they raise questions about the conventions of romantic love and the injustices of supposedly civilized society. Renaissance comedy also satirized chivalric romance, most famously in Miguel de Cervantes's comic novel

Don Quixote (1605, 1615). Love was a central theme of Renaissance comedies, but in a culture in which marriage and betrothal were often arranged and, in England, where women were not allowed onstage, the very idea of love was evolving along with other social practices. Love served not just as an excellent device for complex intrigue but also as a philosophical problem that drew on Christian themes of spiritual redemption and reconciliation. Often the complicated romantic plots and subplots had nothing in common with Terence's tightly woven dramatic structure. New conceptions of romantic love contributed to new forms of romantic comedy.

Evolving conceptions of personal freedom shaped, and were shaped by, new comic stage performances. Roman comedy provided basic guidelines for the stock characters (Pantalone, Doctore, Harlequino, innamorati, and zannis) for the *commedia dell'arte* (improvised comedy), and plots for the *commedia erudita* (written or learned comedy). The *commedia dell'arte*, sometimes also called *commedia improvisa* or *commedia non scrita*, originated in Italy during the late fifteenth century, and blossomed during the sixteenth and seventeenth centuries. Bands of travelling troupes performed open-air spectacles, which included slapstick, jokes, short sketches, and *lazzi*, well-rehearsed bits of comic action. There was no script as such, only an outline of the story, which the performers used, along with *lazzi*, while improvising. These diverse forms of Italian comedy provoked basic theoretical questions about the relative importance of plot and character, which date back to Aristotle's *Poetics*. Comic authors would demonstrate their ingenuity by piling up complications that generic figures would have to overcome. On the other hand, in Shakespeare's *Henry IV* history plays, an extraordinarily rich comic character, the hard-drinking, cowardly yet eloquent barroom tutor of Prince Hal, named Sir John Falstaff emerges from, yet completely transcends, the *miles gloriosus* [boastful soldier] of Plautine comedy, the Lord of Misrule of the Feast of Fools, and the medieval Vice. Falstaff also owes a great deal to the brilliant improvisational clowning of two actors: Richard Tarlton (recently deceased in 1588), the most famous clown of the era, a favourite of Queen Elizabeth, best known for his impromptu doggerel verse, and William Kempe, the other great comic performer in Shakespeare's theatre company. Kempe probably originated the role of Falstaff in 1597. He died in 1603.

The political theorist and comic author, Niccolò Machiavelli is a crucial figure behind the evolution of characters such as Falstaff and notions of plotting, or intrigue. Machiavelli wrote the most famous book on politics ever, *The Prince* (1532). The essence of this politics is that a prince can literally get away with murder, and no divine sanction or twinge of conscience need ever punish him. Machiavelli took a radically modern, pragmatic view of the relationship between ethics and politics. He created a way of describing the world of human action that allows for personal freedom. His comedy *Mandragola* (c. 1518) is one of the best and earliest examples of the typical Italian Renaissance plot of *commedia erudita*, in which an enamoured lover, with the help of his servant, tricks a buffoonish husband into unknowingly letting him sleep with his wife. In *commedia erudita*, laughter at others' misfortunes became central to the very structure of the comic narrative, and it was often considered a didactic tool to hold up vice to ridicule.

Another key feature of this new kind of comedy was a profound ambivalence toward the notion of female agency. *Commedia erudita*, for instance, relied on men in drag and stock characters and negative stereotypes to deliver laughs. However, though a sexual object in *La Mandragola*, Machiavelli's Lucrezia is, in fact, a 'shrewd young woman' (*saviezza*), for she is able to turn all of the plotting of the men to her own advantage, or to allow herself to be deceived for her own pleasure. The place of women on the Elizabethan stage was far more complex, and Shakespeare's plays often reflect the paradox of a patriarchal society governed by a female monarch (Queen Elizabeth). So, while women (played by boys) appear to need taming, as in *The Taming of the Shrew* or *A Midsummer Night's Dream* in which the Amazonian Hippolyta has been conquered by Theseus, they also make space for female desire and agency, particularly in comedies of cross-dressing such as *Twelfth Night* and *As You Like It*. In both Plautus' and Terence's comedies, women were no more than property to be won, exchanged, or bought. Roman comedies were misogynistic, and none of the characters – male or female – were developed as they came to be in the early-modern era. Nonetheless, women gain social power in Renaissance comedies only in extraordinary circumstances, as when they are disguised as men, or everyday reality has been turned upside down, or in periods of carnival which may grant them temporary freedom of expression. Such comic inversions largely tended to reinforce the patriarchal status quo.

Misogyny (hatred of women) has been central to comedy since antiquity, but it has also changed dramatically across history, and there are crucial differences between cultures in the representation of women. Unlike Elizabethan companies, French travelling troupes of the Renaissance included women. The earliest records of French female actresses in a travelling company date to 1545. By 1630, in France, all young female parts were played by women and not boys, as was the custom in England, though in some instances men still played female leads. Italian women developed new female comic roles for the *commedia dell'arte*. Celebrated actress and skilled playwright

Isabella Andreini became known for playing the *prima donna inamorata* in the later sixteenth century. The first Columbina – a female trickster role that would evolve into the sassy maid, *intrigante*, and *fausse ingénue* – was Isabella Franchini, whose granddaughter, Caterina Biancolelli, turned Columbina into an important stock character.

A few European noblewomen had a vital impact on dramatic theory in the Renaissance as philosophical interlocutors. Two of the most important yet little recognized cases are those of Princess Elisabeth of Bohemia to whom René Descartes dedicated his late work, *The Passions of the Soul* (1649) and his pupil Queen Christina of Sweden for whom, it has been argued, the philosopher wrote the libretto of a ballet, *The Birth of Peace*, also in 1649, to celebrate the end of the Thirty Years' War. For Descartes the mind had no gender. Elisabeth, he claimed, understood his philosophy better than anyone else. In letters that only came to light in the nineteenth century, Elisabeth challenged him to reconsider his theory of mind-body dualism. As recent scholarship has shown, Descartes' late thought contributed to new conceptions of the embodied art of theatre, the emotion/reason opposition, the relation between comic and tragic stage practice, and acting theory. These new ideas about the relationship between human interiority and theatrical expression can be seen in Molière's emphasis on the mental agency of the comic performer, whom he began to designate an *acteur* (from Latin *agere*) rather than a *comédien* (from the Greek *komoidia*). The actor expresses her own personal agency, an idea represented most pointedly in rehearsal burlesques of the late seventeenth century, such as Molière's 1663 meta-theatrical *Versailles Impromptu*. Comic theory and stage practice thus reflected the importance of critical thinking, rather than acceptance of eternal verities, for humanists of the period and the role of what Descartes called 'methodological doubt' in the pursuit of knowledge. Renaissance comic writers were influenced by the rule of 'comic impartiality', the idea that no subject was sacred. Mikhail Bakhtin comments that Renaissance laughter 'has a deep philosophical meaning … It is a peculiar point of view relative to the world; the world is seen anew'.

Comic theory in the Renaissance is closely related to the many guidebooks for courtiers, as we have already seen with Machiavelli's *Prince*. Castiglione's *Book of the Courtier* is a dialogue. This genre is deeply connected to the history of comedy. English scholar and diplomat, Sir Thomas Elyot (1490–1546) published his *Boke named the Governour* (or *The Governor*) in 1531; this celebrated work also aimed to teach those in high positions moral principles that would guide them in their public duties. The book, dedicated to King Henry VIII and printed by Thomas Berthelet had a great influence on sixteenth-century moral philosophy. Since Elyot was primarily concerned with moral philosophy, he argued that comedy is 'a mirror of man's life, wherein evil is not taught but discouered'. In comedies, Elyot writes, 'good counsel is ministered,' as one remembers a moral lesson better and longer when it is shown in comedy. Oftentimes, the goal of comedy was 'dissuasion from vice:' simply to warn young men against foolishness and debauchery, and young girls against frivolity and idleness. To prove his point, Elyot cites Terence, Plautus, and Ovid.

George Gascoigne (1535–77), an English poet and soldier, is considered one of the most important poets of the early Elizabethan era. His most notable work is *The Supposes* (first performed in 1566). A translation of Ariosto's prose comedy *Gli-Suppositi*, its plot and characters served as the basis for *The Taming of the Shrew*. Gascoigne's *Glass of Government* (1575) was a tragicomedy, which represented the didacticism of the Courtesy-book model of Renaissance comedy, which aimed to demonstrate the rewards and punishments of virtues and vices. The prologue warns the reader not to expect the usual merriment and 'vain delight' typically expected of comedy, pointing out that this comedy is not like Terence's. Rather, it is intended to serve as a warning to 'rash youth', and to Lords who ought to 'see themselves in it'. The play itself tells the story of four young men, two of whom are guided by rash judgement that ends their careers in disgrace. The other two follow virtuous paths and are rewarded for doing so with honourable positions. *The Glass of Government* is a guide for young men and women as to proper behaviour; it includes generous quotations from the Scriptures and from Greek and Roman moral philosophers. As in a medieval morality play, the characters are allegorical, with names that represent their single dominant characteristic.

While many comic theorists considered comedy to be an appropriate venue for moral conduct, others feared that comedy could cause moral decay. Starting in 1530 in England, Puritan propagandists waged a rhetorical war against all kinds of theatre and condemned comedy as a vice-promoting genre, which stirred ungodly passions, mocked virtue, and promoted vice. Stephen Gosson's *The School of Abuse* is one of the best examples of a Puritan backlash against comedy. A failed actor and playwright, Gosson attacked the vulgar comedy (based on Old Comedy) that was being introduced in London. The pamphlet was dedicated to Sir Philip Sidney, who responded with his *Apology for Poetry* (1579, pub. 1595), in which he wrote that 'Comedy is an imitation of the common errors of our life, which he [the playwright] representeth in the most ridiculous and scornful sort that may be; so as it is impossible that any beholder can be content to be such a one.' Gosson's invective provoked other rebukes, including Thomas Lodge's *Defence of Playes* (1580). As Gosson disowned his own plays, calling them 'pigs' and his 'folly', the actors' revenge on the Puritan writer was to revive them. Many in the 1590s argued against the evils of comedy. Sidney (1554–86), whose prose romance *Arcadia*, is based on Terence's comedic structure, came to the defence of a kind of comedy that could delight rather than merely provoke vulgar laughter at the expense of others. In *The Apology*, Sidney writes, 'Comedy is an imitation of the common errors of our life', and he explains its pedagogical value. 'Comedy is an imitation of the common errors in our life', represented 'in the most ridiculous and scornful sort', he writes, 'which he [the playwright] representeth in the most ridiculous and scornful sort that may be; so as it is impossible that any beholder can be content to be such a one'. Comedy thus sheds light on our follies and serves as a social corrective.

Yet laughter at the expense of others also took a new turn. In Elizabethan England a comic genre emerged known as city or citizen comedy. These works, by authors such as Ben Jonson and Thomas Middleton, were set in a predominantly middle-class social milieu. Jonson, a major author of both comedy and comic theory, was proud of his classical learning, but he believed that comedy should not be tied to 'strict and regular forms', as neoclassicists argued. Rather comedy has to adapt to the society it ridiculed. Jonson's comedies focused on class and money. He was himself the stepson of a brick-layer to whom he was apprenticed, a former soldier, and was highly conscious of extremes of poverty and wealth. He came of age at the moment playwriting became a profession, and he was ambitious in both social and literary senses. In Jonson's *Volpone* (1606) and *The Alchemist* (1610), the main characters are unsympathetic manipulators, whose con games dupe equally unsympathetic naïfs. His 'comedies of humours' set a new standard for English comedies of manners, mocking people who are dominated by one peculiar character-trait or affect. Jonson often wrote critical prologues to his plays, which included literary criticism. Comedy, he suggests in *The Magnetic Lady* (1632), is 'the glass of custom' that reflects 'men's lives', and those lives are material-istic and often unpleasant. His early comedy *The Case Is Altered*, drew from Plautus's *Aulularia* (which centres on a miser) and *Captivi* (which is about prisoners of war), but his later comedies were influenced more by Terence. In the prologue to *Volpone*, Jonson notes that he follows only the 'needful rule[s]' of ancient playmaking, including the Aristotelian prescription of the unity of time, place, and persons. In his 1616 prologue to *Every Man in His Humor*, Jonson remarks that comedy reflects the 'Image of the times' and as such should follow the rules of verisimilitude, including the rule of three unities. Jonson could be a vicious satirist at a time of renewed interest in classical models of satire, as troubles beset the monarchy of Queen Elizabeth. City comedy represented early capitalism and the growth of the urban middle class. It satirized the reduction of human beings to commodities traded for money and property. In Middleton's *A Chaste Maid in Cheapside* (c. 1613), which centres on the marriage market, a country wench gets rid of an unwanted baby by pretending that it is a piece of meat. Jonson and Shakespeare represented two models of comedy, and Jonson's classical and corrective work arguably had more influence on subsequent playwrights than Shakespeare's often fantastical romantic and pastoral comedy.

The humanism of the Renaissance, the return to favour of pagan authors, the growth of secularism with the Reformation, the appreciation of worldly pleasures, and the assertion of personal independence, all contributed to the flowering not only of comedy but also of comic theory. However, efforts to accommodate ancients to early-modern theory and practice paled before the inventiveness of comic innovators. These authors reflect a trend across Western Europe perhaps best exemplified by the comic master of the Italian vernacular, Giovanni Boccaccio (1313–75). Boccaccio's father was not an aristocrat but a banker, but his son was determined to become a poet. The bawdy stories of Boccaccio's *Decameron* (1353), though borrowing from French *fabliaux*, exploded inherited forms of comic writing while paving the way for new ones. The *Decameron* emerges from suffering yet celebrates health, vitality, and sexual energy. Starting with the Black Death, the bubonic plague that devastated Europe in 1347–8, Boccaccio presents seven upper-class women, who are silent and depressed, when one suggests that they leave Florence (as young lovers would leave Shakespeare's cities for a green world) along with three young men; so they depart for the country, where they plan to have 'as much fun as possible, feasting and making merry, without ever overstepping the bounds of reason'. The pleasures of the flesh (*gli stimoli della carne*) stimulate Boccaccio's characters to break rules, which, in effect, serves as a kind of theory of comedy. Sixteenth-century Italian stage comedies drew from Terence; they are largely imitative and today seem unremarkable, yet they also drew a new worldly spirit from Boccaccio. In general, Renaissance comedy expresses a greater interest in the here-and-now than in the world to come. Ariosto (1474–1533), who allegedly coined the term 'humanism', wrote vernacular comedies that still amuse. But, as his prologues indicate, they suffer from a neoclassical anxiety of influence. Renaissance authors and performers expressed both disenchantment with old modes of thought and optimism about the human condition.

The burlesque element of parody that had persisted through the Middle Ages, often in conjunction with pageants and religious festivals, grew into new forms with the establishment of permanent, professional theatres that reflected the radical socio-economic changes of the times and contributed to a criticism not only of dramatic form but also of historical reality itself. Satirists such as John Heywood targeted a corrupt clergy, setting plays in towns and country parishes, representing daily life, tricksters, and the inversion of norms. In Heywood's 'merry interlude', *The Play of the Weather* (1533), Jupiter is dethroned and humanized. All the while, despite the official disapproval of the Church, the clergy themselves got into the act, as the earliest and earthiest English comedies were penned by figures such as the monk and poet John Lydgate of Bury (c. 1370–c. 1451) and John Still (1543–1607/08), the Bishop of Bath and Wells, whose *Gammer Gurton's Needle* first thrust the sort of rude mechanicals Shakespeare would depict in *A Midsummer Night's Dream* into a Latinized plot structure. In 1576, when James Burbage built England's first playhouse, called the Theatre, in a suburb of London, the ground had been seeded for a rebirth of comedy in theory often best expressed in wildly inventive new stories and plays.

Bibliography

Barton, Anne. *The Name of Comedy*. Toronto: University of Toronto Press, 1990.

Beecher, Donald, ed. *Renaissance Comedy: The Italian Masters*. Toronto: University of Toronto Press, 2009.

Brand, C. P. 'The Renaissance of Comedy: The Achievement of Italian *Comedia Erudita*'. *Modern Language Review* 90 (4) (October 1995): xxix–xlii.

Carlson, Marvin, *Theories of the Theatre: A Historical and Critical Survey, from the Greeks to the Present*, exp. edn. Ithaca, NY: Cornell University Press, 1993.

Giannetti, Laura. *Lelia's Kiss: Imagining Gender, Sex, and Marriage in Italian Renaissance comedy*. Toronto: University of Toronto Press, 2009.

Gobert, R. Darren. *The Mind-Body Stage: Passion and Interaction in the Cartesian Theater*. Stanford, CA: Stanford University Press, 2013.

Greenblatt, Stephen. *Renaissance Self-Fashioning from More to Shakespeare*. Chicago: University of Chicago Press, 1980.

Grund, Gary R., ed. *Humanist Comedies*. Cambridge, MA: Harvard University Press, 2005.

Hardin, Richard F. 'Encountering Plautus in the Renaissance: A Humanist Debate on Comedy'. *Renaissance Quarterly* 60 (3) (Fall 2007): 789–818.

Hart, Jonathan Locke. *Shakespeare and His Contemporaries*. New York: Palgrave Macmillan, 2011.

Herrick, Marvin T. *Comic Theory in the Sixteenth Century*. Urbana: University of Illinois Press, 1950.

Herrick, Marvin T. *Italian Comedy in the Renaissance*. Urbana: University of Illinois Press, 1966.

Hokenson, Jan. *The Idea of Comedy: History, Theory, Critique*. Madison, NJ: Fairleigh Dickinson University Press, 2006.

Leggatt, Alexander. *Introduction to English Renaissance Comedy*. Manchester: Manchester University Press, 1999.

Newman, Karen. *Shakespeare's Rhetoric of Comic Character: Dramatic Convention in Classical and Renaissance Comedy*. New York: Methuen, 1985.

Orr, David. *Italian Renaissance Drama in England Before 1625: The Influence of Erudita Tragedy,*

Comedy, and Pastoral on Elizabethan and Jacobean Drama. Chapel Hill: University of North Carolina Press, 1970.

Radcliff-Umstead, Douglas. *The Birth of Modern Comedy in Renaissance Italy.* Chicago: Chicago University Press, 1969.

Radulescu, Dominika. 'Caterina's Columbina: The Birth of Female Trickster in Seventeenth-Century France'. *Theatre Journal* 60 (1) (March 2008): 87–113.

Roston, Murray. *Tradition and Subversion in Renaissance Literature: Studies in Shakespeare, Spenser, Jonson, and Donne.* Pittsburgh, PA: Duquesne University Press, 2007.

Womack, Peter. 'The Comical Scene: Perspective and Civility on the Renaissance Stage'. *Representations* 101 (1) (Winter 2008): 32–56.

TEXTS

1. Erasmus, *Collected Works of Erasmus* (1512), edited by Craig R. Thompson, translated by Betty I. Knott and Brian McGregor

There are however individual characters within these general types. It is not enough to grasp what is consistent with the character of an old man, a young man, a slave, the head of a house, or a pimp. Otherwise representatives of the various types would all be indistinguishable from each other. The comic poets especially seem to have aimed at variety in characters belonging to the same general type. What could be more dissimilar than Demea and Micio in Terence? Micio is mild even when he is trying to reprimand his son severely, Demea is cross-patched even when he is doing his best to be pleasant. Yet they are both old men, and brothers at that. What could be a greater contrast than Chremes who is always easy-going and pleasant-spoken, and Simo who is vehement and suspicious? or Pamphilus, who is a young man of spirit, and Charinus who cares nothing for the consequences? There is a great difference between Davus who is determined to look on the bright side, and Byrria who has nothing to offer but despair, between the two parasites Gantho and Phormio, and between these and the sort of parasites depicted by Plautus. Likewise Plautus' courtesans are very different from Terence's, who for the most part depicts good courtesans, like Philotis and Bacchis in the *Hecyra*. Plautus makes his old men lecherous and cheerful, and old hands at deceiving their wives, though he does in one play invent a different sort of character in Euclio, who is unbelievably miserly and suspicious.

But it is foolish to give one or two examples when the whole of comedy is nothing but a picture of human life. I could have produced similar specimens from tragedy, pastoral poetry, and dialogues, but for a work on this scale I think I have sufficiently indicated to students of lively intelligence the way they should proceed.

In my opinion examples may be properly derived not only from the sources I have discussed but also from dumb beasts and even inanimate objects, though these possibly belong rather with ὁμοίωσις [simile or parallel case]. I mean things like holding up the industry of the ant as an encouragement to people to work hard to get what they want, or describing the social organization of the bees in order to promote respect for law and civil discipline. To discourage lack of respect for parents, one could cite the young of the stork who are said to feed and carry the old birds about in their turn when age has made them weak; or when exhorting an audience to show proper care for their children, one could bring in the she-ass which will go through a raging fire to rescue its foal; or if one wanted to hold up ingratitude to obloquy, one could use the story of the lion which Gellius quotes from Apion, or of the snake which, according to Pliny, saved its rescuer when he was beset by robbers; or to censure a man entirely without affection, neither loving anyone nor being the object of anyone's love, one could introduce the dolphin that loved a boy, or the eagle seized by a burning passion for a girl, or the magnet that draws metal to itself. I shall probably say more about such topics when I get to the section on fables. Meanwhile, to return to my subject.

Comedy will provide us with an example of female inconsistency when Sostrata in the *Adelphi* says 'Why man, you must be mad. / Do you consider this a thing to tell abroad?' and then a few lines later says 'Not for all the world will I do that. / I'll tell it out.' The inconstancy of lovers is demonstrated by Phaedria, who goes to the country and suddenly comes back, the inconstancy of youth by Antipho in the *Phormio*. It would however take too long to pursue this topic properly.

The poets are splendid at this. The more violent emotions, which the Greeks call πάθη [passions] are to be discovered in Homer's *Iliad* and in tragedy; the calmer ones, which are pleasant rather than disturbing, are supplied by Homer's *Odyssey* and by comedy. Yet ἤθη [disposition, feelings], which is what the Greeks call the emotions of comedy, are often interspersed in the *Iliad* and Greek tragedy. Latin tragedy makes rather sparing use of them.

Among the emotions we must include pleasure, though this should be incorporated throughout the speech wherever appropriate, not just in the peroration. What different people find pleasing is dealt with in detail by Aristotle in his sections on the emotions, and Cicero has written on jokes and Quintilian on laughter, discussing the theory of humour.

Now in approaching each work the teacher should indicate the nature of the argument in the particular genre, and what should be most closely observed in it. For instance, the essence of the epigram lay in its pointed brevity. Then he will deal with the theory of wit which Quintilian and Cicero present, pointing out that this literary form takes particular delight in rhetorical exclamations, cleverly thrown in at the end, and thereby startling the reader into remembering their point. In tragedy, he will point out that particular attention should be paid to the emotions aroused, and especially, indeed, to the more profound. He will show briefly how these effects are achieved. Then he will deal with the arguments of the speakers as if they were set pieces of rhetoric. Finally, he should deal with the representation of place, time, and sometimes action, and the occurrence of heated exchanges, which may be worked out in couplets, single lines, or half-lines. In comedy, he should show in particular that decorum and the portrayal of our common life must be observed, and that the emotions are more subdued: that is, engaging, rather than passionate. He should show that decorum especially is studied, not only in its universal aspect, I mean that youths should fall in love, that pimps should perjure themselves, that the prostitute should allure, the old man scold, the slave deceive, the soldier boast, and so on, but also in the particular delineation of different characters as developed by the poet. For example, in the *Andria* Terence introduces two old men of widely different temperament. Simo is forthright, rather irritable, yet not stupid or dishonest. On the other hand, Chremes is polite and always calm, self-controlled on every occasion, resolving all differences as far as he can, gentle but hardly simple-minded. Likewise he introduces two young men of divergent natures: Pamphilus, wise for his years, and very resourceful, but rather blunt, so that you recognize him as a true son of his father, Simo. Set against him is Charinus, who is childish, inept, and resourceless. Again, two slaves of different character: Davus, crafty, packed with guile, unshakably optimistic; Byrria is the exact opposite, totally lacking in initiative, a constant source of despair to his master. Likewise in the *Adelphi*: Micio is gentle and gay even when scolding, while even the sweetness of Demea has a touch of bitterness to it. Again, take Aeschinus who, because he is city-bred and has the trust of Micio, will attempt anything, but you still appreciate the basic decency of the man who is dutiful to his brother, faithful to his sweetheart. On the other hand, Ctesipho is rather boorish and timid because of his inexperience in those things. Syrus is wily and daring, constantly confounding truth and falsehood, so that in drunkenness alone is his deceit revealed; while Dromo is dull and obtuse. But it is not my purpose here to develop these points; it is sufficient for the present to have pointed that way. In the *Eclogues* the teacher should remind them that the setting is the Golden Age with its portrayal of the fabulous antique way of life. Consequently, he should point out that in such a context all aphorisms, similes and comparisons are drawn from pastoral life; that the characters' emotions are simple and they delight in songs, aphorisms, and proverbs, and are susceptible to signs and portents. In the same way he will be careful to remind pupils of the essential nature of epic poetry, history, the dialogue, the fable, satire, the ode, and the other literary genres. Then he will not shrink from pointing out the merits or even the faults of particular authors in particular passages, in order that the young may become accustomed, even at so early an age, to employing what is, in everything, of paramount importance – judgement. In this matter, apart from his own expertise and native wit, the teacher will obtain additional help in Cicero's short treatise *De claris oratoribus* and in the literary criticism of Quintilian, Seneca, and Antonio Campano, not forgetting the ancient interpreters; Donatus in particular was concerned with this.

2. Gian Giorgio Trissino, 'Division VI: Comedy', from *Poetica* (1529), edited by Allan H. Gilbert

Comedy

It remains, then, to treat the imitation of actions and traits less dignified and of a worse sort, which may be done by deriding and censuring them, and in that way teach men virtue, something usually done by comedies, in which the poet does not speak for himself but, in the same way as in a tragedy, always brings in persons to speak and act. So it is also in pastoral eclogues, though in these there is sometimes utterance by the poet, as is apparent in Theocritus and Vergil. Comedy, then, imitates worse actions with speech, rhythm and harmony, as does tragedy; and it imitates an action single, complete, and large, which has a beginning, a middle, and an end. But in this it differs from tragedy, that as tragedy carries on its teaching by means of pity and fear, comedy teaches by deriding and censuring things ugly and vile […] It suffices to know that comedy is an imitation of the wicked and the vicious, yet not in every extremity of the vices, but merely of that which is ugly, whence springs from the ridiculous, which is an ugly defect without pain and without deaths; of the ridiculous we shall treat at length in its place.

The comic plot

Comedy, then, has the same substantial parts as tragedy, that is, the fable, the human traits, the thought, the words, the stage presentation, and the melody, because to make a comedy that would be perfect it is necessary to represent it on the stage, where it needs the chorus of melody. The comic fable, then, is made up of actions diverse from those of tragedy, and as it were contrary to them, because tragedy produces the effect of its teaching with pity, with tears, and with fear, which are sad things, while comedy does it with jokes and with laughter, which are pleasant things; hence as for tragedy are sought out piteous acts of great and illustrious men, so in comedy it is necessary to use jocose acts of persons of low rank and unknown, and as in tragedy there come about sorrows and deaths and it almost always ends in unhappiness, so in comedy, though there are some disturbances, they do not involve wounds and deaths, and all terminate in good, as weddings, peaceful agreements, and tranquility, through which characters issue in peace from the scene […].

Comedy resembles tragedy

The moral type is that in which morals are most prominent, as the *Hecrya* of Terence, and the ridiculous is that in which jokes and ridiculous things prevail, as the *Menechmi* of Plautus, from which we have adapted the *Simillimi*. And nothing forbids that the same comedy should be made simple and moral, as is the *Adelphi,* and double and moral, as is the *Hecrya,* simple and ridiculous, as is the *Auluaria,* and double and ridiculous, as the *Simillimi.* But it cannot at the same time be simple and double, for they are contraries. So he who wishes to compose a comedy well should first arrange the fable, that is, find the action and write a summary of it, and put it before his eyes, and consider well the moral traits, and see what is fitting and what is contrary or repugnant, and then put in the names, and insert the episodes, and treat it with excellent sententious sayings, and with words familiar, ornate, and suitable, as we have said about tragedy.

Comedy differs from tragedy

But comedy will differ from tragedy in that while in tragedy the actions and names are true, either all or the greater part, in comedy the actions and names are all invented by the poet, though Plautus in his *Amphitryo* did not do it, whence it is called a tragi-comedy. Yet such a thing was not afterward imitated either by himself or by any other, but rather they have all abandoned true names, especially since Athens, to restrain the license of comedy, which unjustly blamed and derided worthy men, it was established by law that in comedies no one should be permitted to call anyone by name; thence was derived the custom of the new comedies, in which no real names are introduced, but all are invented by the poet. Such names are formed either from countries, as in *Mysis* from *Mysia, Syrus* from *Syria,* or from cities, as *Messenius* from *Messina,* or from mountains or rivers, as *Pachinus* and *Alesa,* or from qualities, as is *Phaedra* meaning *joyous, Sophrona* meaning *prudent, Chremes* meaning *avaricious,* and the like. The formation of such names from traits or qualities of men is the best way and the most suitable to comedies of all, and the plan of forming them from the Greek language is good, because they are formed more appropriately, although they are also appropriately derived from the Latin, *Mizio* from *mitis*[1] and from the vulgar tongue, as *Scovoletto* from *scovolo,*[2] and the like.

---

[1] Gentle.

[2] Sponge.

The ridiculous

In this place we shall especially treat of the ridiculous, which, as Aristotle says, pertains to comedy. Of the ridiculous Aristotle says in his *Rhetoric* that he has dealt with it in his *Poetics;* perhaps it was in the part dealing with comedy, which has been lost through the ravages of time, and with it the treatment of the ridiculous, which was included in it. So it is necessary to investigate it, which we shall do according to a method other than that used by Marcus Tullius and Fabius Quintilianus, because their method was rather oratorical than philosophical. The ridiculous then, as Aristotle says, is a mild form of the ugly, and is a defect and an ugliness that is neither deadly not painful. Tully then and Quintilian, who perhaps took their idea from Aristotle, say, not badly, that the place and seat of the ridiculous is in ugliness and deformity, but from what cause this ugliness moves laughter they do not say, and the part of Aristotle which perhaps gave it is lost. Hence we shall investigate it in the following manner.

Laughter

It is evident that laughter comes from the delight and pleasure of him who laughs, and this pleasure cannot come to him except through the senses, that is from seeing, hearing, touching, tasting and smelling, or from the memory of the pleasures that they have had from something, or from the hope that they are going to have them. Such pleasure does not come from every object that delights and pleases the sense but merely from those objects that have some share of the ugliness, for if a man sees a beautiful lady or a beautiful jewel or something similar that pleases him,[3] he does not laugh, nor does he laugh on hearing music in praise of him, nor on touching, tasting, and smelling things that to the touch, the taste, and the smell are pleasant and grateful; rather these together with pleasure bring admiration and not laughter. But if the object that is presented to the senses has some mixture of ugliness, it moves laughter, as an ugly and distorted face, an inept movement, a silly word, a mispronunciation, a rough hand, a wine of unpleasant taste, or a rose of unpleasant odor moves laughter at once, and those things especially cause laughter from which better qualities were hoped, because then not merely our senses but also our hopes are slightly offended, and such pleasure as this comes to us because man is by nature envious and malicious,[4] as is clearly seen in little children, for almost all of them are envious, and always delight to do evil, if they are able. It can be observed also that man never naturally delights in the

---

[3] Cf. Sidney, *Defense*, sect. 50, below.
[4] Cf. Dryden, *Of Dramatic Poesy,* sect. 59, below.

good of others, except through accident, that is, through some good which he hopes from it for himself, as Plautus says:

There is no one who would not envy the obtaining of something pleasant.

Hence if anyone sees that someone finds some money, he does not laugh or take pleasure, but rather is envious, but if he sees that someone falls into the mud and soils himself, he laughs, because that evil which does not come on ourselves, as Lucretius says, is always pleasant to observe in others. But if we have like sufferings, the sight of them in others does not move us to laughter, for no hunchback laughs at another hunchback nor a lame man at another lame man, unless he thinks that these ills are in him less ugly than in the other. If the evils, then, that we see in others are deadly and painful, as are wounds, fevers, and injuries, they do not move laughter, but rather pity through fear that similar ills may come to ourselves or to some of our circle, for we think those who belong to us parts of ourselves. The small ill, then, not painful or deadly, that we see or hear in others, as ugliness of body, and folly of mind, when it is not or we believe it is not in ourselves, is what pleases us or makes us laugh.

Laughter and deformity

As man is composed of mind and body, so ugliness in him is double, of the mind and the body, and the special deformities of the mind are ignorance, imprudence, credulity, and the like, which often depend one on the other, and therefore in jokes we laugh at the ignorance, imprudence, and credulity of someone else, and especially when we see them in persons who are thought substantial and of good intelligence, for in such as these many times opinion and hope are deceived. To such instances of ugliness may be reduced all the jokes and jibes written by Boccaccio and the Courtier, and likewise all the ridiculous stories and jokes and clever sayings gathered up by Tully, Quintilian, Boccaccio, Poggio, and the Courtier.[5] It is well to know that if the ugliness and deformity of mind we have spoke[n] of are great, such as betrayals and perjuries, they do not move laughter, but disdain, and are condemned and rebuked, as are lies, exhibitions of ignorance, and similar awkward things of mind or body. But if they are slight, they move laughter and are mocked at and delight is taken in them. All these ridiculous deformities are either pointed out, or narrated, or observed with some urbanity. Those which are pointed out are of the sort that Tully assigns to Crassus,

---

[5] Castiglione in the *Courtier*, Bk. II, secs. 42–89, discusses comedy, with illustrative examples. His discussion, like that of Trissino, owes much to Cicero's remarks in *De oratore* II, 54–71.

who, when speaking against Helvius Mancia, said: "Now I shall show you who you are." Mancia urgently answered: "Who will you show that I am?" Then Crassus, turning, pointed with his finger to a Cimbrian shield of Marius on a shop, on which was carved the face of a Frank, brutal and distorted, which certainly resembled the face of Mancia, at which everyone began to laugh.[6]

Comic stories

Deformities can also be shown in narrative only, as was that of Strepsiades in Aristophanes,[7] who was narrating the disagreements between himself and his wife; since he was a countryman and avaricious, and she a citizen and proud, they disagreed in many things, especially in the name they were going to give the son who was born to them; Strepsiades wished to give him the name of Pennysaver, and the proud mother the name of Horsemaster; in the end they agreed to give each half a name, to wit Savehorse or Phidippides. Such a story as this excited laughter everywhere, because it throughout makes plain the ignorance and avarice of the countryman, and the pride and imprudence of the lady, which are all of them deformities of the mind. Such deformities either of body or mind can be pointed out with some word, an action called urbanity;[8] an example appeared when someone indicated the deformity of body of Testio Pinaro, who twisted his chin in speaking as if he had a nut in his mouth, and his adversary said to him: "Say what you wish, when you have cracked the nut you have in your mouth." Similarly a buffoon pointed out a deformity in the face of the Emperor Vespasian of such a sort that it appeared to strain to get away from the body; the emperor asking him if he were going to say something, the buffoon replied: "I will speak when you have got away from your body." Also M. Bartolomeo Pagello noted the deformity of mind in M. Lionardo da Porto, who said it was easy to provide so that the hail would not injure Vicentio by placing some cannon in certain mountains above which the hail-bringing clouds were accustomed to come, and when those clouds were seen coming to discharge the cannon unto them so that they would burst and let out their water and the hail would not fall on the lower ground. Pagello then put his hand into his purse and took out two *marcelli* and gave them to M. Lionardo, saying: "Please take these, and say that it was I who have spoken so fine a remedy." At this everyone laughed, and so with urbanity he made plain the folly of such a remedy,

---

[6] The story is told by Cicero, *De oratore*, II, 66, but assigned to Crassus by Pliny, *Natural History*, xxxv, 8.
[7] In the *Clouds*.
[8] In the Latin sense of cleverness.

without answering at all. This urbanity is a thing brief, sharp, swift, and excellently fitted to keen and ridiculous sayings, and it appears in speaking and answering, and it is a good source for anything involving ridicule, such as ambiguity, deceiving the expectation, scoffing at the nature of another, comparison with something still more deformed, dissimulation, inept sayings, and rebuking the silly; and all of the aforesaid things have many parts that excite ridicule, either in denying or refuting or defending or diminishing; and these all move laughter because they point out some deformity either in oneself or in some other.

Ambiguity

An example of ambiguity is that sonnet of Antonio Alemani on Alemano Salviati. This Alemano was with other citizens on a committee which did not wish to please the said Antonio in something he wished; so Alemano to excuse himself said to Antonio: "It is not I, that is, I am not the one who did not wish to please you." Antonio, feigning to think that he said that he was not Alemano Salviati, wrote as follows:

> Alemano says to me, I am not I,
> And this is not true, because he is he.
> But when he denies that he is himself
> He wonders whether he will speak the truth of my action.

Here the ridiculous rises from the ambiguity of *I am not I*, with which he feigns ignorance of himself in a lie in Alemano, both of which are deformities of the mind. Much like this was that circumstance of Scipio Nasica and Ennius the poet that Tully tells. Nasica, going to the house of Ennius and asking if he were at home, heard Ennius answer the servant that he was not. A few days later, Ennius, going to the house of Nasica, asked if he were there, and Nasica answered in a loud voice that he was not, and Ennius said: "What, do I not know your voice?" Then Nasica said: "You are not very courteous, for the other day when your servant told me you were not at home I believed him, and now you are not willing to believe me when I tell you myself." Here are two defects of mind that produce the ridiculous, one the ignorance that Nasica feigns in himself in wishing that Ennius should believe he was not at home when he heard he was there; the other is the lie which is revealed in Ennius who when he was at home had his servant say he was not there. Similar humor was that in a reply of Pievano Arlotto, who, finding himself on a street in Florence and passing a beautiful and bold girl, said to his companion: "This is a beautiful lady." The bold girl turned toward him and said: "I cannot say as much for you." Pievano instantly answered: "Yes indeed, since you wish to tell a lie of me, as I have of you." Thus Pievano, by feigning in himself deformity of mind that led him to lie, discovered the deformity of an ungrateful spirit in the lady who censured a man who praised her, and at the same time he made a game of deformity of body in her. These two comic conditions are not very different from that above of Alemani, except that these do not come from ambiguity as does that.

The pun

Of this ambiguity there are many kinds, such as the changing of letters which by some is called a pun, as Garifilo to Garofolo, Luca Michiele to Licamelculo,[9] and the like; it is also done by means of some addition, as *moral* to *mortal*, as in that sonnet of Aretino as follows:

> Though you are, I confess it,
> Both poet and mortal philosopher
> Without a *sesino* and without natural.[10]

Here the ridiculous is produced not merely with ambiguity by saying *mortal* in place of *moral*, but also with irony, when he says, *Though you are, I confess it*, and with synecdoche, by saying *sesino*, which is a kind of money, in place of money, which is the genus, and then he turns again to ambiguity, saying *without natural*, in place of *without natural philosophy*, for ambiguity, as though always feigning ignorance in itself, reveals deformity in others, as equally irony does, with which Aretino and Bernia produced many ridiculous passages, and not merely with these but also with sarcasm, allegory, hyperbole, and the other things we have mentioned [...].

What is contrary to expectation

That which deceives expectation is the mode most appropriate to the ridiculous, because it reveals the imprudence of the one who waits, as in the jest of Giovanni Cannaccio with Prior Pandolfini, who believed for a certainty that Frate Girolamo Savonarola was a saint and that though then dead he should rise up; therefore he said one day to Cannaccio, who was one of those who sentenced the Frate to death: "What will you say, Giovanni, when you see Frate Girolamo raised from the dead?" Cannaccio

---

[9] *Garofolo* means *clove;* the English equivalent would be to call Mr. Clive, Mr. Clove. The modification of Luca Michiele seems to involve a diminutive camel.

[10] The pun on *natural* is obscene in both English and Italian.

responded, contrary to the expectation of Pandolfini: "I shall say that next time we ought to have him hanged." But here since the expectation is deceived in so grave a matter, it does not move so much laughter as if the thing were less serious, because every slight thing in which a man deceives himself moves laughter not only in others but also in the man himself, when he understands it, that is, when he sees he has uttered one word instead of another or has taken up one thing for another. Therefore the *Amphitryo* of Plautus and *I Simillimi* are very gay comedies because the persons in them many times deceive themselves, and because of resemblance take one person for another; thus they reveal that they themselves think they speak to another; thus they reveal that they themselves and the others are in some slight way ignorant, and frequent ridiculous situations arise […].

The acute response

A laugh is also roused by an acute response to some proverb that is uttered, such as was made by Maestro Gerardo Bolderico, a Veronese physician, to that lady of the Malaspini who asked from him a remedy for her only son. The physician answered nothing was wrong with the boy and she should not wish to have medicine given to him, but the lady still insisted that he should use some remedy, and wishing to excuse herself for such insistence, did it with a proverb, saying to him: "O sir, he who has but one eye often wipes it." The physician added: "And wipes it so much that he digs it out." The comedy sprang from the revelation of the imprudence of that lady, who believed that medicine would help one who was not sick.

Literary comedy

And finally all the comic passages in Aristophanes, Plautus, Terence, Apuleius, and others, and in some Italian authors, as Boccaccio, Burchiello, Poggio, Pulci, Ariosto, Aretino, Bernia, and Mauro, all show and point out little or ordinary deformities of body or of mind of some person, and with pointing out or otherwise revealing in different ways those deformities, produce ridicule, and pointed sayings, and jests. And what we have said will suffice for the ridiculous, so far as it pertains to comedy. It is manifest, then, that words in comedy should not attempt to be lofty and sounding and lordly, as do those of tragedy, but should aim to be low, clear, and urbane, and that the metaphors and other figures should be easy and such as are common in ordinary speech, which comedy especially imitates. Comedy therefore should not have diversity of foreign expressions or things that may make it appear foreign, nor should it show too much pains or too much ornament, because, as we have said, words very splendid and labored hide ideas and human traits; moreover expressions not in common use produce elevation, a thing not fitting to comedy.

3. Sir Thomas Elyot, 'XII: The second and third decay of learning' *The boke named the gouernour / deuised by Thomas Elyot knight* (1531)

[Comedy]

First, comedies, which they suppose to be a doctrinal of ribaldry, they be undoubtedly a picture or as it were a mirror of man's life, wherein evil is not taught but discouered; to the intent that men beholding the promptness of youth into vice, the snares of harlots and bawds laid for young minds, the deceit of seruants, the chance of fortune contrary to men's expectation, they being thereof warned may prepare themselves to resist or preuent occasion. Suitably remembering the wisdoms, aduertisements, counsels, dissuasion from vice, and other profitable sentences, most eloquently and familiarly showed in those comedies, undoubtedly there shall be no litle fruit out of them gathered. And if the vices in them expressed should be cause that minds of the readers should be corrupted: then by the same argument not only interludes in English, but also sermons, wherein some vice is declared, should be to the beholders and hearers like occasion to increase sinners. And that by comedies good counsel is ministered it appeareth by the sentence of Parmeno, in the second comedy of Terence:

> In this thing I triumph in my own conceit
> That I have found for all young men the way
> How they of harlots shall know the deceit,
> Their wits, their manners, that thereby they may
> Them perpetually hate; for so much as they
> Out of their own houses be fresh and delicate,
> Feeding curiously; at home all the day
> Living beggarly in most wretched estate.[11]

There be many more words spoken which I purposely omit to translate; notwithstanding the substance of the whole sentence is herein comprised. But now to come to other poets, what may be better said than is written by Plautus in his first comedy?

---

[11] *Eunuch*, v. 4, 8–18. Cf. Heywood, *Apology*, sect. 10, below.

Verily Virtue doth all things excel.

For if liberty, health, living and substance,

Our country, our parents and children do well,

It hapneth by virtue; she doth all advance,

And in whom of virtue is found great plenty,

Anything that is good may never be dainty.[12]

[Sentences in Ovid and Martial]

Also Ovid, that seemeth to be most of all poets lascivious, in his most wanton books hath right commendable and noble sentences; as for proof thereof I will recite some that I have taken at adventure:

Time is in medicine if it shall profit;

Wine given out of time may be annoyance.

A man shall irritate vice if he prohibit

When time is not met unto his utterance.

Therefore, if thou yet by council of art recuperable,

Flee thou from idleness and alway be stable.[13]

Martialis, which for his dissolute writing is most seldom read of men of much gravity, hath notwithstanding many commendable sentences[14] and right wise counsels, as among divers I will rehearse one which is first come to my remembrance:

If thou wilt eschew bitter adventure

And avoid the gnawing of a pensifull[15] heart,

Set in no one person all wholly thy pleasure,

The less joy shalt thou have but the less shalt thou smart.[16]

I could recite a great number of semblable good sentences out of these and other wanton poets, who in the Latin do express them incomparably with more grace and delectation to the reader than our English tongue may yet comprehend.

---

[12] *Amphitryo*, 648–52.

[13] *The Remedy of Love*, 131–6.

[14] See *sentences* in the index.

[15] Sorrowful, brooding.

[16] *Epigrams*, XII, 34.

[Reading is not to be censored]

Wherefore since good and wise matter may be picked out of these poets, it were no reason, for some little matter that is in their verses to abandon therefore all their works, no more than it were to forbear or to prohibit a man to come into a fair garden lest the redolent savors of sweet herbs and flowers shall move him to wanton courage, or lest in gathering good and wholesome herbs he may happen to be stung by a nettle. No wise man entereth into a garden but he soon espieth good herbs from nettles and treadeth the nettles under his feet while he gathereth good herbs. Whereby he taketh no damage, or if he be stung he maketh little of it and shortly forgetteth it. Semblably if he do read wanton matter mixed with wisdom, he putteth the worst under foot and sorteth out the best, or, if his courage be stirred or provoked, he remembreth the little pleasure and great detriment that should ensue of it, and withdrawing his mind to some other study or exercise shortly forgetteth it.[17]

4. Nicholas Udall, Prologue to *Ralph Roister Doister* (1538)

What Creature is in health, either young or old,
But some mirth with modesty will be glad to use
As we in this Interlude shall now unfold,
Wherein all scurillity we utterly refuse,
Avoiding such mirth wherein is abuse:
Knowing nothing more commendable for a man's recreation
Than Mirth which is used in an honest fashion:

For Mirth prolongeth life, and causeth health.
Mirth recreates our spirits and voideth pensivenesse,
Mirth increaseth amitie, not hindering our wealth,
Mirth is to be used both of more and less,
Being mixed with virtue in decent comliness.
As we trust no good nature can gainsay the same:
Which mirth we intend to use, avoiding all blame.

---

[17] This section on the reading of poetry has much affinity with parts of Milton's *Aeropagitica,* for example: "Good and evil we know in the field of this world grow up together almost inseparably; and the knowledge of good is so involved and interwoven with the knowledge of evil, and in so many cunning resemblances hardly to be discerned, that those confused seeds which were imposed on Psyche as an incessant labor to cull out and sort asunder were not more intermixed […] To all men such books are not temptations nor vanities, but useful drugs and materials wherewith to temper and compose effective and strong medicines which man's life cannot want."

The wise Poets long time heretofore,

Under merry Comedies secrets did declare,

Wherein was contained very virtuous lore,

With mysteries and forewarnings very rare.

Such to write neither *Plautus* nor *Terence* did spare,

Which among the learned at this day bears the bell:

These with such other therein did excell.

5. Thomas Wilson, 'Of Delighting the Hearers and Stirring Them to Laughter', from *The Arte of Rhetoric* (1560)

Of delighting the hearers and stirring them to laughter

Considering the dullness of man's nature, that neither it can be attentive to hear, nor yet stirred to like or allow any tale long told except it be refreshed or find some sweet delight, the learned have by wit and labor devised much variety. Therefore, sometimes in telling a weighty matter, they bring in some heavy tale and move them to be right sorry, whereby the hearers are more attentive. But after, when they are wearied either with tediousness of the matter or heaviness of the report, some pleasant matter is invented both to quicken them again and also to keep them from satiety. But surely few there be that have this gift: in due time to cheer men. Neither can any do it whom nature hath not framed and given an aptness thereunto. Some man's countenance will make pastime, though he speak never a word. Yea, a foolish word uttered by an apt man or a gesture strangely used by some pleasant body sets men full oft upon a laughter. And whereas some think it a trifle to have this gift, and so easy that every varlet or common jester is able to match with the best, yet it appeareth that they which wittily can be pleasant, and when time serveth can give a merry answer or use a nipping taunt, shall be able to abash a right worthy man and make him at his wit's end through the sudden quip and unlooked frump given. I have known some so hit of the thumbs that they could not tell in the world whether it were best to fight, chide, or to go their way. And no marvel, for where the jest is aptly applied, the hearers laugh immediately, and who would gladly be laughed to scorn? Some can prettily, by a word spoken, take occasion to be right merry. Others can jest at large and tell a round tale pleasantly, though they have none occasion at that time given. But assuredly that mirth is more worth which is moved by a word newly spoken than if a long tale should pleasantly be told. Forasmuch as both it cometh unlooked for and also declares a quickness of wit worthy of commendation.

There are five things which Tully noteth concerning pleasant talk:

1 What it is to delight hearers

2 Whereof it cometh

3 Whether an orator may move laughter

4 How largely he may go, and what measure he must use

5 What are the kinds of sporting or moving to laughter

Now to tell you in plain words what laughter is, how it stirreth and occupieth the whole body, how it altereth the countenance and suddenly brasteth out that we cannot keep it in, let some merry man on God's name take this matter in hand. For it passeth my cunning, and I think even they that can best move laughter would rather laugh merrily when such a question is put forth than give answer earnestly what and how laughter is in deed.

The occasion of laughter and the mean that maketh us merry (which is the second observation) is the fondness, the filthiness, the deformity, and all such evil behavior as we see to be in others. For we laugh always at those things which either only or chiefly touch handsomely and wittily some especial fault or fond behavior in some one body or some one thing. Sometimes we jest at a man's body that is not well proportioned, and laugh at his countenance if either it be not comely by nature or else he, through folly, cannot well see it. For if his talk be friendly, a merry man can want no matter to hit him home, yet may be assured. Some jest is made when it toucheth no man at all, neither the demander, neither the standers-by, nor yet any other, and yet delighteth as much the hearers as any the other can do. Now when we would abash a man for some words that he hath spoken, and can take none advantage of his person or making of his body, we either dolt him at the first and make him believe that he is no wiser than a goose, or else we confute wholly his sayings with some pleasant hest, or else we extenuate and diminish his doings by some pretty means, or else we cast the like in his dish and with some other device dash him out of countenance, or last of all we laugh him to scorn outright, and sometimes speak almost never a word but only in countenance show ourselves pleasant. But howsoever we make sport, either the delight is uttered by countenance, or by pointing to something, or else showed at large by some tale, or else occasion taken by some word spoken.

The third question is whether it standeth with an orator's profession to delight the hearers with pleasant reports and witty sayings, or no. Assuredly it behooveth a man that must talk much evermore to have regard to his audience, and not only to speak so much as is needful, but also to speak no longer than they be willing to hear. Even in this our time, some offend much in tediousness, whose part it were to comfort all men with cheerfulness. Yea, the preachers of God mind so much edifying of souls that they often forget we have any bodies. And therefore some do not so much good with telling the truth as they do harm with dulling the hearers, being so far gone in their matters that oftentimes they cannot tell when to make an end. Plato, therefore, the father of learning and the well of all wisdom, when he heard Antisthenes make such a long oration that he stark wearied all his hearers: "Fie, for shame man," quoth he, "dost thou not know that the measuring of an oration standeth not in the speaker but in the hearers." But some perhaps will say unto me, "Pascite quantum in vobis est," to whom I answer, "Estote prodentes." And now because our sense be such that in hearing a right wholesome matter we either fall asleep when we should most hearken, or else are wearied with still hearing one thing without any change, and think that the best part of his tale resteth in making an end, the witty and learned have used delightful sayings and quick sentences ever among their weighty causes, considering that not only goodwill is got thereby (for what is he that loveth not mirth?), but also men wonder at such a head as hath men's hearts at his commandment, being able to make them merry when he list, and that by one word speaking, either in answering something spoken before, or else oftentimes in giving the onset being not provoked thereunto. Again, we see that men are full oft abashed and put out of countenance by such taunting means, and those that have so done are compted to be fine men and pleasant fellows, such as few dare set foot with them.

Thus, knowing that to move sport is lawful for an orator or anyone that shall talk in any open assembly, good it were to know what compass he should keep that should thus be merry. For fear he take too much ground and go beyond his bounds. Therefore no such should be taunted or jested withal that either are notable evil livers and heinous offenders, or else are pitiful caitiffs and wretched beggers. For everyone thinketh it a better and a meeter deed to punish naughty packs than to scoff at their evil demeanor; and as for wretched souls or poor bodies, none can bear to have them mocked, but think rather that they should be pitied, except they foolishly vaunt themselves. Again, none such should be made any laughingstocks that either are honest of behavior or else are generally well beloved. As for others, we may be bold to talk with them and make such game and pastime as their good wits shall give good cause. But yet this one thing we had need ever to take with us: that in all our jesting we keep a mean, wherein not only it is meet to avoid all gross bourding and alehouse jesting, but also to eschew all foolish talk and ruffian manners, such as no honest ears can once abide, nor yet any witty man can like well or allow.

6. George Gascoigne, Prologue to *The Glasse of Governement* (1575)

What man hath mind to hear a worthy Jest,

Or seeks to feed his eye with vain delight:

That man is much unmeet to be a guest,

At such a feast as I prepare this night.

Who list lay out some pence in such a Mar,

Bellsavage fair were fittest for his purse,

I list not so to misbestow mine art,

I have best wares, what need I then show worse?

An Interlude may make you laugh your fill,

Italian toys are full of pleasant sport:

Plaine speeche to use, if wanton be your will,

You may be gone, wide open stands the port.

But if you can contented be to hear,

In true discourse how high the virtuous climb,

How low they fall which live withouten fear

Of God or man, and much mispende their time:

What right rewards a trusty servant earns,

What subtle snares these Sycophants can use,

How soon the wise such crooked guiles discerns,

Then stay a while: give ear unto my Muse.

A Comedie, I mean for to present,

No *Terence* phrase: his tyme and mine are twain:

The verse that pleased a *Romane* rash intent,

Might well offend the godly Preachers vain.

Deformed shows were then esteemed much,

Reformed speech doth now become us best,

Men's words must weigh and tried be by touch

Of God's own word, wherein the truth doth rest.

Content you then (my Lords) with good intent,

Grave Citizens, you people great and small,

To see your selves in Glasse of Government:

Behold rash youth, which dangerously doth fall

On craggy rocks of sorrows nothing soft,

When sober wits by Virtue climes aloft.

7. Stephen Gosson, *The School of Abuse: Containing a Pleasant Invective Against Poets, Pipers, Players, Jesters, etc.* (1579)

How Often hath her Majesty, with the graue aduice of her honorable Council, set down the limits of apparel to euery degree, and how soon again hath the pride of our hearts ouerflowen the chanel? How many times hath access to theaters been restrained, and how boldly again haue we re-entered.

Now if any man ask me why my self haue penned comedies in time past, and inueigh so eagerly against them here, let him know that *Semel insaniuimus omnes* [we have all been crazy once]: I have sinned, and am sorry for my fault: he runs far that neuer turns, better late than neuer. I gaue my self to that exercise in hope to thriue but I burnt one candle to seek another, and lost both my time and my trauel, when I had doone.

I take upon me to driue you from plays, when mine own works are daily to be seen upon stages, as sufficient withnesses of mine own folly, and seuere judges against my self.

8. Sir Philip Sidney, *An Apology for Poetry*, 'Comedy', 'Tragicomedy', 'The Nature of Laughter', from *The Defence of Poesie* (1595)

No, perchance it is the Comic, whom naughty play-makers and stage-keepers have justly made odious. To the argument of abuse I will answer after. Only thus much now is to be said, that the Comedy is an imitation of the common errors of our life, which he representeth in the most ridiculous and scornful sort that may be, so as it is impossible that any beholder can be content to be such a one.

Now, as in Geometry the oblique must be known as well as the right, and in Arithmatic the odd as well as the even, so in the actions of our life who seeth not the filthiness of evil wanteth a great foil to perceive the beauty and virtue. This doth the Comedy handle so in our private and domestical matters, as with hearing it we get as it were an experience, what is to be looked for of a niggardly Demea, of a crafty Davus, of a flattering Gnatho, of a vainglorious Thraso; and not only to know what effects are to be expected, but to know who be such, by the signifying badge given them by the comedian. And little reason hath any man to say than men learn evil by seeing it so set out; since, as I said before, there is no man living but, but the force truth hath in nature, no sooner seeth these men play their parts, but wisheth them *in pistrinum* ["in the pond"]; although perchance the sack of his own faults lie so behind his back that he seeth not himself dance the same measure; whereto yet nothing can more open his eyes than to find his own actions contemptibly set forth.

But besides these gross absurdities, how all their plays be neither right tragedies, nor right comedies, mingling kings and clowns, not because the matter so carrieth it, but thrust in clowns by head and shoulders, to play a part in majestical matters, with neither decency nor discretion, so as neither the admiration and commiseration, nor the right sportfulness is by their mongrel tragic-comedies, as Plautus hath *Amphitrio*. But, if we mark them well, we shall find that having indeed no right comedy, in that comical part of our tragedy we have nothing but scurrility, unworthy of any chaste ears, or some extreme show of doltishness, indeed be full of delight, as the tragedy should be still maintained in a well-raised admiration. But our comedians think there is no delight without laughter; which is very wrong, for though laughter may come with delight, yet cometh it not of delight, as though delight should be the cause of laughter; but well may one thing breed both together. Nay, rather in themselves they have, as it were, a kind of contrariety; for delight we scarcely do but in things that have a conveniency to ourselves or to the general nature; laughter almost even cometh of things most disproportioned to ourselves and nature. Delight hath a joy in it, either permanent or present. Laughter hath only a scornful tickling.

For example, we are ravished with delight to see a fair woman, and yet are far from being moved to laughter. We laugh at deformed creatures, wherein certainly we cannot delight. We delight in good chances, we laugh at mischances; we delight to hear the happiness of our friends, or country, at which he were worthy to be laughed at would laugh. We shall, contrarily, laugh sometimes to find a matter quite mistaken and go down the hill against the bias, in the mouth of some such men, as for the respect of them one shall be heartily sorry, yet he cannot choose but laugh; and so is rather pained than delighted with laughter. Yet deny I not but that they may go well together. For as in Alexander's picture well set out we delight without laughter, and in twenty mad antics we laugh without delight, so in Hercules, painted with his great beard and furious countenance, in woman's attire, spinning at Omphale's commandment. For the representing of so strange a power in love procureth delight: and the scornfulness of the action stirreth laughter. But I speak to this purpose, that all the end of the comical part be not upon such scornful matters as stirreth laughter only, but mixed with it, that delightful teaching which is the end of Poesy. And the great fault even in that point of laughter, and forbidden plainly by Aristotle, is that they stir laughter in sinful things, which are rather execrable than ridiculous; or in miserable, which are rather to be pitied than scorned. For what is it to make folks gape at the wretched beggar, or a

beggarly clown; or against the law of hospitality, to jest at strangers because they speak
not English so well as we do? What do we learn, since it is certain:

> *Nil habet infelix paupertas durius in se,*
> *Quam quod ridiculos homines facit?*
> [Poverty has nothing in it harsher
> than that it makes one funny.]

But rather a busy loving courtier, a heartless threatening Thraso, a self-wise-seeming
schoolmaster, an awry-transformed traveler – these if we saw walk in stage names,
which we play naturally, therein were delightful laughter, and teaching delightfulness;
as in the other, the tragedies of Buchanan do justly bring forth a divine admiration. But
I have lavished out too many words of this play matter.

9. Ben Jonson, *Every Man Out of his Humour* (1599)

[Prologue]

Though need make many poets, and some such
As art and nature have not better'd much;
As he dare serve the ill customs of the age,
Or purchase your delight at such a rate,
As, for it, he himself must justly hate:
To make a child now swaddled, to proceed
Man, and then shoot up, in one beard and weed,
Past threescore years; or, with three rusty swords,
And help of some few foot and half-foot words,
Fight over York and Lancaster's king jars,
And in the tyring-house bring wounds to scars.
He rather prays you will be pleas'd to see
One such to-day, as other plays should be;
Where neither chorus wafts you o'er the seas,
Nor creaking throne comes down the boys to please;
Nor nimble squib is seen to make afeard
The gentlewomen; nor roll'd bullet heard
To say, it thunders; nor tempestuous drum
Rumbles, to tell you when the storm doth come;
But deeds, and language, such as men do use,

And persons, such as comedy would choose,

When she would shew an image of the times,

And sport with human follies, not with crimes.

Except we make them such, by loving still

Our popular errors, when we know they're ill.

I mean such errors as you'll all confess,

By laughing at them, they deserve no less:

Which when you heartily do, there's hope left then,

You, that have so grac'd monsters, may like men.

[...]

Mitis. You have seen this play, Cordatus; pray you, how is it?

Cordatus. Faith, sir, I must refrain to judge; only this I can say of it, 'tis strange, and of a particular kind by itself, somewhat like *Vetus Comoedia*;[18] a work that hath bounteously pleased me; how it will answer the general expectation, I know not.

Mit. Does he observe all the laws of comedy in it?

Cor. What laws mean you?

Mit. Why, the equal division of it into acts and scenes,[19] according to the Terentian manner; his true number of actors; the furnishing of the scene with Grex or Chorus; and that the whole argument fall within compass of a day's business.[20]

Cor. O no, these are too nice observations.

Mit. They are such as must be received, by your favor, or it cannot be authentic.[21]

Cor. Troth, I can discern no such necessity.

Mit. No?

Cor. No, I assure you, signor. If those laws you speak of had been delivered us *ab initio,* and in their present virtue and perfection, there had been some reason of obeying their powers; but 'tis extant that that which we call *Comoedia* was at first nothing but a simple and continued song sung by one only person, till Susario invented a second; after him, Epicharmus a third; Phormus and

---

[18] Old Comedy. Aristophanes is its most famous representative.

[19] For the division into acts, see Horace, *Art of Poetry.*

[20] This speech gives much that the Elizabethans thought necessary for the "authentic" play. The emphasis on the chorus, something that seems strange to us, is normal. The "day's business," or so-called unity of time, found support in Aristotle's *Poetics*, v, 49b9, and was developed by Castelvetro.

[21] *Authentic:* in harmony with classical practice as interpreted by the Italian critics.

Chionides devised to have four actors, with a prologue and chorus; to which Cratinus, long after, added a fifth and sixth; Eupolis, more; Aristophanes, more than they; every man in the dignity of his spirit and judgment supplied something. And though that in him this kind of poem appeared absolute and fully perfected, yet how is the face of it changed since! In Menander, Philemon, Cecilius, Plautus, and the rest, who have utterly excluded the chorus, altered the property of the persons, their names, and natures, and augmented it with all liberty, according to the elegancy and disposition of those times wherein they wrote.[22] I see not then, but we should enjoy the same license or free power to illustrate and heighten our invention as they did; and not be tied to those strict and regular forms which the niceness of a few, who are nothing but form, would thrust upon us.[23]

10. Battista Guarini, *Compendium of Tragicomic Poetry* (1601) edited by Allan H. Gilbert

[Components common to tragedy and comedy]

Let us consider the parts of these two poems that are both opposed and in harmony with each other, in order to see that the mixed tragicomic is reasonable. Tragedy shares with comedy presentation on the stage, and all the rest of the apparatus, rhythm, harmony, limited time, dramatic plot, probability, recognition, and reversal. I mean that each makes use of the same things, though in the method of use there is some difference between them. Other qualities are then peculiar to one and to the other, and these qualities not only vary in their use, as do the other things that have been mentioned, but they diversify the species in such a way that they become differences between them. And I have no doubt that he who would think of making one of these pass entire into the confines of the other, and of using in tragedy what belongs to comedy alone, or *vice versa*, would produce an unseemly and monstrous story. But the point is that one should see whether these specific differences cause so much opposition that it is in no way possible to form a third species that can be a legitimate and reasonable poem.

---

[22] Jonson gives here the evolution of comedy, and suggests the fitness of different types to different ages.
[23] A strong declaration of independence from classical practice and precept.

[Comic characters in tragedy]

In tragedy these differences are the character of high rank, the serious action, terror and commiseration. In comedy, they are private character and affairs, laughter, and witty speeches. As to the first, I confess, and admit it is the doctrine of Aristotle, that characters of high rank are fitting to tragedy, and those of humble station are suited to comedy;[24] but I deny that it is contrary to nature and to poetic art in general that persons great and those not great should be introduced into one plot. What tragedy has there ever been that did not have many more servants and other persons of similar station than men of great consequence? Who unfastens the admirably tied knot in the *Oedipus* of Sophocles? Not the king, not the queen, not Creon, not Tiresias, but two servants, guardians of herds. Then it is not contrary to the nature of the stage that there should be united in a play persons of high rank and those of low station, not merely under the name of a mixed poem, such as is tragicomedy, but also under that of pure tragedy, and comedy as well, if Aristophanes is alluded to, who mixes men and gods, citizens and countrymen, and even brings in beasts and clouds to speak in his plays.

[Grave and light are to be reconciled]

With respect to actions that are great and not great, I cannot see for what reason it is unfitting that they should appear in one same plot, not entirely tragic, if they are inserted with judgment. Can it not be that amusing events intervene between serious action? Are they not many times the cause of bringing perils to a happy conclusion? But then, do princes always act majestically? Do they not at times deal with private affairs? Assuredly they do. Why, then, cannot a character of high importance be presented on the stage at a time when he is not dealing with important matters? Certainly Euripides did this in his *Cyclops*, where he mixed grave danger for the life of Odysseus, a tragic character, with the grave drunkenness of the Cyclops, which is a comic action. And among the Latins, Plautus did the same thing in *Amphitryo*, mingling the laughter and the jests of Mercury with persons of importance, not merely Amphitryo, but the king of the gods. It is, then, not unreasonable that in one story for the stage there can be at the same time persons of high rank and those not of high rank.

---

[24] This is rather the Renaissance Aristotle than the Greek himself; see *Poetica*, II, end, above. For example, the Latin grammarian Diomedes (fourth century CE) wrote: "Comedy differs from tragedy in that heroes, generals, and kings are introduced into tragedy, into comedy humble and private persons" (Kiel, *Grammatici Latini*, I, 488). Diomedes was known in the Middle Ages and there were several editions of his work in the sixteenth century. See the index for further quotations.

[Pity and laughter not inharmonious]

The same can be said of commiseration and laughter, qualities of which one is tragic and the other comic. And indeed to me they do not appear so completely opposite that the same story cannot include them under diverse occasions and persons. On reading in Terence the fate of Menedemus,[25] who willingly mortified himself because of the severity he adopted toward his son, what man is not moved to pity, and does not with Chremes, who does not restrain his tears, weep over it? And in the same play there is laughter at the art with which the astute Syrus mocks and deceives Chremes. I do not say that there can be happiness and sorrow in the same story, but there can be pity with laughter. Thus all the sum of this contradiction is seen to be reduced to a single difference, that is, the terrible, which can never occur except in a tragic plot, nor can any comedy be mixed with it, since terror is never introduced except by means of serious and mournful dramas; where it is found, there is never any room for laughter and sport.

[Are tragedy and comedy too diverse for union?]

All the things I have said above can be brought forward in defense of tragicomic poetry. But I do not wish to avail myself of them, and am content to hand over to tragedy kings, serious actions, the terrible, and the piteous; to comedy I assign private affairs, laughter, and jests; in these things are the specific differences between the two. I wish for the present to concede that one may not enter into the jurisdiction of the other. Will it follow from this that, since they are of diverse species, they cannot be united to make up a third poem? Certainly it cannot be said that this is an opposition to the practice of nature, and much less to that of art.

[Tragic and comic elements that cohere]

He who composes tragicomedy takes from tragedy its great persons but not its great action, its verisimilar plot but not its true one, its movement of the feelings but not its disturbance of them, its pleasure but not its sadness, its danger but not its death; from comedy it takes laughter that is not excessive, modest amusement, feigned difficulty, happy reversal, and above all the comic order, of which we shall speak in its place. These components, thus managed, can stand together in a single story, especially when they are handled in a way in accord with their nature and the kind of manners that pertains to them. We conclude, then, that the ability of the tragic poet, naturally fitted to produce tragedy, will not produce either comedy or tragicomedy when the parts

---

[25] In the *Heautontimorumenos*.

other than I have mentioned appear in their vigor and entirety, but only when they are not all present. And if instead of tragic components we speak of those of comedy, the comic power will never work toward the formation of a tragic poem; on the contrary the contest between the tragic parts and the comic will render that power very weak and destroy its capacity for being put into practice […].

[Selection by art]

Art observes that tragedy and comedy are composed of heterogeneous parts, and that therefore if an entire tragedy and an entire comedy should be mixed, they would not be able to function properly together as in a natural mixture, because they do not have a single intrinsic natural principle, and it would then follow that in a single subject two forms contrary to each other would be included. But art, a most prudent imitator of nature alters the parts after they are united, art alters them before they are joined in order that they may be able to exist together and, though mixed, produce a single form.

[Tragicomedy the highest form]

But it would be possible here to raise a new question, namely, what actually is such a mixture as tragicomedy? I answer that it is the mingling of tragic and comic pleasure, which does not allow hearers to fall into excessive tragic melancholy or comic relaxation. From this results a poem of the most excellent form and composition, not merely fully corresponding to the mixture of the human body, which consists entirely in the tempering of the four humors,[26] but much more noble than simple tragedy or simple comedy, as that which does not inflict on us atrocious events and horrible and inhumane sights, such as blood and deaths, and which, on the other hand, does not cause us to be so relaxed in laughter that we sin against the modesty and decorum of a well-bred man. And truly if today men understood well how to compose tragicomedy (for it is not an easy thing to do), no other drama should be put on the stage, for tragicomedy is able to include all the good qualities of dramatic poetry and to reject all the bad ones; it can delight all dispositions, all ages, and all tastes – something that is not true of the other two, tragedy and comedy, which are at fault because they go to excess.[27] For this reason one of them today is abhorred by many great and wise men, and the other is little regarded.

---

[26] The psychology and physiology of the time believed that in a healthy body the four humors – blood, phlegm, black bile, and yellow bile – were mixed in the right proportions.

[27] A bold declaration of the superiority of the new Renaissance drama to that of antiquity.

[The end of tragicomedy]

But I should not appear to have completed my task if, after I have made known the parts or forms, as it were, that tragicomedy ought to have as a good and legitimate poem, I should fail to prove the same thing of its end. Someone, perhaps, may wish to know what its end is, whether tragic or comic or mixed, as it seems that he might ask its function, since it is a mixed story. This cannot be explained without much difficulty, for each art has its end, toward which it is directed as it works; and if it has two of them, one of them is dependent on the other, in such a way that one thing alone is the chief end toward which the art is directed. Now if we concede that tragicomedy is a reasonable mixture, what does it attempt to do? What end has it? Does it wish laughter or tears? For the two cannot be done at once. Then what does it do first? What next? What is of less importance? What of chief importance? What is subaltern? To such questions one can hardly give answers without first determining what the end of tragedy is and what the end of comedy. To understand those matters one must realize that each art, in addition to the principal end of which we have spoken before, has another end. One of them is that by means of which the artist as he works introduces into the matter which he has in hand the form that is the end of the work. The other is that for the good and advantage of which he labors at the work he wishes to carry to its end. In that sense Aristotle says that man is the end of all things. We call one of these ends instrumental, and the other, using Aristotle's own word, architectonic. Both of these appear in both tragic and comic art.

[The ends of comedy]

Beginning with comedy, its instrumental end is to imitate those actions of private men which by their deficiency move us to laughter; this is Aristotle's notion.[28] But the architectonic end is not mentioned in his extant writings, for we lack the discussion of comedy in that treatise of his called the *Poetics*, though it may be supposed that there he gave an end for comedy as he did for tragedy. But from the instrumental end we are able to conjecture what he would assign as the architectonic end, since this is the exemplar which the artist sets before himself. Hence, if we consider that the Bacchic songs, all full of drunkenness and phallic license, gave rise to comedy, and, besides this, seeing that the same Aristotle distinguishes it from tragedy by means of its plebian persons, assigning laughter to it as its specific difference, it appears to me

---

[28] *Poetics*, v, above. Guarini gives us a very Renaissance Aristotle, when he changes Aristotle's 'men worse than the average' to private citizens as opposed to men of rank.

that it can have no end other than that of purging men's minds of those passions that are caused in us by labors both private and public. It purges melancholy, an emotion so injurious that often it leads a man to grow mad and to inflict death on himself, in the same way as, according to Aristotle's teaching, melody purges the feeling the Greeks call enthusiasm; the Sacred Scriptures teach us, is necessary to recreate us and enable us to gain that restoration of which human life has so great need, so comedy, with its gay and ridiculous presentations, refreshes our spirit. As a breeze is wont to drive away the thickened air, comedy by moving us to laughter shakes off that gloomy and foggy humor, generated in us by too much mental concentration, which often renders us slow and obtuse in our activities. For this reason comedy represents only private persons, with defects covering but a short time and ending happily. Such is the architectonic end of comedy.

[Tragicomedy does not purge pity and terror]

Though tragicomedy, like the others, has two ends, the instrumental, which is the form resulting from the imitation of tragic and comic affairs mixed together, and the architectonic, which is to purge the mind from the evil affection of melancholy, an end which is wholly comic and wholly simple, yet I say that tragicomedy can be connected in no way with tragedy. […] If a poet wishes to make use of any subject in such a way as not to purge terror, he must temper it with laughter and other comic qualities in such a manner that, though it is by nature terrible and pitiable, yet it has not the power of producing either terror or compassion, and much less of purging them, but remains with the single virtue of delighting by imitating. […].

[The decay of comedy]

On the other side comedy has come to be so tedious and is so little valued that if she is not accompanied with the marvels of the intermezzi, there is today no one who can endure her. This is because of mercenary and sordid persons who have contaminated her and reduced her to a vile state, carrying here and there for vile pay that excellent poem which was once accustomed to crown its makers with glory. In order to raise comic poetry from such a state of disgrace, that it may be able to please the unwilling ears of a modern audience, the makers of tragicomedy – following the steps of Menander and Terence, who raised it to dignity graver and more entitled to respect – have undertaken to mingle with the pleasing parts of comedy those parts of tragedy that can suitably accompany comic scenes to such an extent that they strive for the purgation of sadness. They defend themselves, and not badly, by explaining that as the ancient Romans, according to the testimony of Horace,[29] introduced satyrs, who were ridiculous persons, into the severity of the tragic poem, as will be shown below, for no other reason than the solace and recreation of their hearers, so, in order to remove the dislike and distaste which the world today has for simple and ordinary comedies, we should be permitted to temper them with such tragic gravity as is not repugnant to the architectonic end of purging sadness.

[Description of Tragicomedy]

But to conclude once for all that which it was my first intention to show, I say that to a question on the end of tragicomedy I shall answer that it is to imitate with the resources of the stage an action that is feigned and in which are mingled all the tragic and comic parts that can coexist in verisimilitude and decorum, properly arranged in a single dramatic form, with the end of purging with pleasure the sadness of the hearers. This is done in such a way that the imitation, which is the instrumental end, is that which is mixed, and represents a mingling of both tragic and comic events. But the purging, which is the architectonic end, exists only as a single principle, which unites two qualities in one purpose, that of freeing the hearers from melancholy. And as in mixed bodies found in nature, though in these all four of the elements are found in an abated state,[30] as has been said, yet each of them retains a particular quality of either one or another of the elements that is dominant and surpasses the others and toward which especially that which is most like it is directed, so in the mixed form of which I speak, though its parts are altogether tragic and comic, it is still not impossible for the plot to have more of one quality than of another, according to the wish of him who composes it, if only he will remain within the bounds that have been mentioned above. The *Amphitryo* of Plautus has more of the comic, the *Cyclops* of Euripides more of the tragic. Yet it is not true that the first or the second is not a tragicomedy, since neither of them has as its end the purging of terror and compassion, for this purgation cannot exist where there is laughter, which disposes the spirits to expand, and not to restrain themselves.

---

[29] *Art of Poetry*, 220–4, above.

[30] The reference is to the four elements, earth, air, fire, and water.

3

Restoration to Romanticism

INTRODUCTION

This chapter tells a story about comic theory that is both very large and very small. It is large in the sense that it spans more than a century, arguably more than one epoch, and encompasses diverse systems of thought. However, it is small in the sense that those systems of thought – and comic theory of the time – focused on personal autonomy, details of middle-class experience and private life. Heroic ideals fell before individual self-interest. As the German theorist G. E. Lessing wrote in his great theoretical work *Hamburg Dramaturgy* (c. 1767), 'The names of princes and heroes […] contribute nothing to our emotion. The misfortunes of those whose circumstances most resemble our own, must naturally penetrate most deeply into our hearts.' For Lessing, comedy could contribute to the health of the new bourgeois society by helping spectators to discern the ridiculous in everyday life. 'Comedy', he wrote, 'is to do us good through laughter'. The Dutch-British political writer Bernard Mandeville characterized this *modern*, increasingly capitalistic world in his 1723 satire *The Fable of the Bees* as a hive of self-interest: 'These Insects lived like Men, and all / Our Actions they perform'd in small.' The presiding genius of this society was John Locke (1632–1704), inventor of classical liberalism, a philosophy which privileged individual freedom, and empiricism, a theory that knowledge derives from sensory experience not metaphysics. The following pages will show that capitalism, liberalism and empiricism transformed and were transformed by new theories of comedy.

After the death of Shakespeare in 1616, until the 1660s, French theory dominated the European stage. One reason for the relative importance of the French was that English theatres were closed for nearly twenty years, following the commencement of the English Civil War in 1642 and before the monarchy was restored in 1660. The

French had imported neoclassical ideas from Italy in the 1500s, and these theories, with their emphasis on the distinctness of comedy and tragedy, on unities of time, space, and action, universal character-types and decorum, took hold in the 1630s under the stewardship of Cardinal Richelieu, a figure of immense cultural and political authority and First Minister to King Louis XIII. Pierre Corneille and Jean Racine were the leading tragedians of the period, and Molière, stage name of Jean Baptiste Poquelin (1622–73), raised French comedy to a level comparable to that of tragedy. A great comic actor and director as well as playwright, Molière borrowed from Roman comedy, medieval farce, *commedia dell'arte*, and Spanish stories. His eccentrics, such as the misanthrope and the miser, critiqued extremism and bad manners. Defending his satire of religious hypocrisy in *Tartuffe, ou l'Imposteur* (1664), Molière theorized: 'The business of comedy is to represent in general all the faults of men, especially those of our time. [...] The duty of comedy being to correct men while amusing them, I was of the opinion that in my position I could do no better than to attack, by means of ridiculous portrayal, the vices of my age.' *Tartuffe*, a moralistic comedy, written for and then censored by King Louis XIV, under intense political pressure from offended clergy, ridiculed the vice of religious hypocrisy. Conservative in spirit, it ended by celebrating the beneficence of the king.

Two decades of English Civil War led to extensive traffic of ideas between France and England, as the Prince of Wales (later King Charles II) and many intellectuals, including his sometime tutor, philosopher Thomas Hobbes, fled to the continent. When he returned to reclaim his crown in 1660, Charles, known as the Merry Monarch, would be a very different kind of ruler than his predecessors. He loved the theatre, even taking as his mistress the most famous actress of the period, Nell Gwyn, with whom he had two children. Thus, with the return of theatre to London in the 1660s, comedy and comic theory, under no such royal restraint as the kind that inhibited Molière, underwent a radical change whose impact would be felt throughout Europe and beyond.

In simplest terms, Restoration Comedy is the comedy of London upper-class life during the period between 1660 and 1710. In 1642, at the start of the First English Civil War (1642–6), the Puritan military leader and Lord Protector Oliver Cromwell had ordered all the theatres to be closed. Stage sets were destroyed; actors were publicly whipped, jailed, and driven out of England. Puritans, like Cromwell, rose largely from what were called the middling classes and represented a quasi-democratic social movement. In 1649 they chopped off the head of King Charles I. They regarded theatres as dens of vice, but they were also suspicious of all forms of pomp, whether in politics or religion. Puritans distrusted both artifice and art. The House of Commons appointed a Provost Marshall whose duty it was 'to seize all ballad-singers, and to suppress stage-plays'. In 1660, the year of the English Restoration, Charles II came to power and issued letters patent that allowed for the opening of two theatres that were licensed to perform spoken drama. Thomas Killegrew, a comic dramatist who had followed Charles to exile in France, became the first royal patentee, served as the King's jester, and later was appointed Master of the Revels. In 1665, the plague struck London, and a year later the Great Fire destroyed more than half the city, but the theatres survived.

The years that followed were guided by two main principles: the *carpe diem* motto of seizing life's pleasures, and, in the works of John Locke and Thomas Hobbes, the rise of modern social contract theory. The central problem of this society was how to limit some freedoms in order to protect others. The libertinism of Restoration culture is often overdrawn, for while aristocrats returning from France brought with them a hedonistic way of life, social, political, and economic changes sped by the Puritans could not be totally undone. Thomas Hobbes (1588–1679), a personal favourite of Charles II, was the central English political philosopher of the period. Hobbes believed that men were motivated principally by self-interest. His concept of the social contract, in his pivotal 1651 book *Leviathan, or the Matter, Form, and Power of a Commonwealth, Ecclesiastical and Civil,* established the foundation of Western political thought. Written during the English Civil War, *Leviathan* argued that lacking government and laws, men are in a condition of 'war, as is of every man against every man'. However, though self-interested, men are rational and more or less equal to each other; so, they will choose to avoid life in a state of nature, which would be 'solitary, poor, nasty, brutish and short', and forge a social contract, which, Hobbes believed, required accepting the authority of a strong sovereign. This choice between an unconstrained state of nature and the well-governed social order is at the core of Restoration drama and, with it, dramatic and literary criticism which flowered in England as never before. The intellectual centre of gravity swung back to England from France. John Dryden's *Essay of Dramatic Poesy* (1668) debates the merits of French versus English drama, and concludes that the new comedy would be distinguished, in Dryden's words, by 'the improvement of our [English] wit, language, and conversation'.

For John Locke (1632–1704), whose view of the state of nature was less harsh than that of Hobbes, the social contract depended on the consent of the governed and would be characterized not by absolute authority or the divine right of kings but by social conventions and laws. He argued in *Two Treatises on Government* that political

authority comes from the people, who retain the right to overthrow unjust governments. These ideas echo across the century not only in the American Revolution but in
Beaumarchais's 1781 comedy *The Marriage of Figaro* (made into an opera by Mozart).
At the end of the play, Figaro, a jack-of-all trades and a budding democrat, declares
that he won't allow the scheming Count to steal his fiancée: 'No, my dear Count, you
won't have my Suzanne. Just because you're an aristocrat, you think you're also a great
genius. Nobility, fortune, rank, position – you're so proud of these trappings. But what
the hell did you do to deserve them? You took the trouble of being born – that's it.' This
speech reflects an increasing emphasis on middle-class values throughout Western
Europe, and has been viewed as symptomatic of sentiments that led to revolutions in
America and France.

Locke also developed the idea of private property. For Locke, the basis of the
social contract and civil society was the protection of private property. It was for this
protection that individuals willingly gave up the state of nature. Modern theories of
comedy, too, increasingly reflected the hazards of the state of nature, the dangers of
egoism, private versus public life, property as an attribute of modern identity, and
a tension between freedom and social union, often signified at the end of comedies
by marriage. Hobbes's view of the human condition was quickly applied to gender
relations. Thus, the Restoration saw the boudoir as a potential place of sexual warfare.
Men gained esteem proportionate to the number of women they seduced, while
women increased their reputations according to how long they resisted. Woman's
virtue was a fortress to be conquered, and the theme of the fall of the virtuous woman
and the progress of the libertine seducer (the rake) dominated most Restoration
comedies – this theme points to an uncomfortable reality about eighteenth-century
comedy: first, sexual violence, including threat of rape, was a routine subject of comic
mirth, and, second, women authors, performers, and audiences, as well as men,
produced and consumed this cruel humour. On the other hand, Locke's theory of
consent also informs the marriage plots of late Restoration comedies such as *The Way
of the World*, in which men and women negotiate (money is also at the centre of many
of these plays). The obsession with virginity was not new to the Restoration; what
was new was the more open and honest treatment of social norms. The distinction
between private and public space also shaped and was shaped by the evolution of new
theatres and stage architecture. Theatre represents the way people in a given culture
inhabit space, and Restoration comedies show how men and women met in public
spaces such as parks, often hiding behind a fan or a mask, as well as in the privacy of
their boudoirs. This comedy was designed for an indoor stage (unlike Shakespeare's

open-air Globe Theatre), yet the actors still played close to the audience, sharing the same light, creating a sense of intimacy. In the eighteenth century, however, theatres grew, and auditoriums were darkened. A proscenium arch would cut off the area of darkness from the lit stage, and relations between performers and spectators reflected changing attitudes toward privacy.

With the Restoration and the reinstatement of theatres in London, comedies played for cliquish aristocratic audiences. However, they represented what might be termed a democratization of tastes. In 1684, a French monk, François Hédelin, Abbé d'Aubignac penned a definition of comedy, which became widely accepted by French and English critics. 'The purpose of comedy', he wrote, 'is to represent the actions of ordinary people, including the debaucheries of the young, the knaveries of servants, the guiles of prostitutes, love affairs, deceptions, jokes, marriages and other accidents of ordinary life.' In 1702, Irish playwright George Farquhar noted that British comedy followed the tastes of its public: 'The rules of English comedy don't lie in the compass of Aristotle or his followers but in the pit, box, and galleries.' Dramatists and theorists acknowledged the power of audiences who were (or thought they were) in the know. In 1664, playwright George Etherege, in his prologue *The Comical Revenge, or, Love in a Tub*, sarcastically described 'desperate critics' as 'most reverent judges', determined to decide whether the play were 'good' or 'bad'. The moralizing in dramatic meta-texts indicates what the middle class was up against in trying to assert new values. Thus, in his preface to *An Evening's Love; or, The Mock Astrologer* (performed 1668; published 1671), Dryden, a theatre critic, poet and playwright (1631–1700), defended himself against the accusation that he elevates debaucheries and his protagonists who indulge in them. William Wycherley, in his 1677 epistle dedicated to *The Plain-Dealer*, expresses ironic regrets that some ladies were offended at his play (the play attacks female hypocrisy). The first major woman playwright, Aphra Behn, in her 1687 dedication to *The Lucky Chance* – a play in which one character gains permission to take another's place in the marriage bed by winning a game of dice – rebutted the charge that her play was 'not fit for the Ladys'. The fact that Restoration playwrights felt the need to write prefaces to almost every play, explaining and justifying their dramatic choices, shows that the Puritans, among others, had raised new questions about where moral authority came from and how to determine questions of ethical judgement and aesthetic taste. Playwrights like Thomas Shadwell, self-appointed defenders of the comic tradition of Ben Jonson, attacked the newer style of comedy on moral grounds. So did critics, often clergy, who were fundamentally anti-theatrical. Prefaces served as vehicles for these ongoing debates.

Tragedy had been the privileged genre in ancient and Renaissance theatres, and it continued to hold its place as the more prestigious form. Comedy, however, was far more popular, and the Restoration elevated comedy socially, developing a genre in which, to quote Dryden, 'Gentlemen will now be entertained with the follies of each other.' Many theorists rejected the argument that the proper role of comedy was to ridicule vice and extol virtue. Aristotle was reinterpreted to mean by 'low characters' not those of humble birth, but those deficient in accomplishments of a gentleman. From these comedies of manners emerged a key character-type of Restoration comedy, the fop, later called the dandy; other character-types included the libertine rake, the prude, the coquette, the cuckolded husband, the naïve wife and the country bumpkin. Restoration playwrights were not particularly concerned with the well-structured plots or neo-classical unities. English playwright and architect John Vanbrugh wrote that 'the chief entertainment [in comedy] [...] lies much more in the Character and the Dialogue, than in the Business and the Event'. In these comedies, marriage, with its exchange of dowry and titles, was often a business deal. Consequently, Restoration comedy satirized arranged marriages and the culture of fathers selling off their daughters, unsatisfied wives, and the hypocritical society that agreed to maintain the façade of propriety. New comedies and comic theory focused on personal pleasure and social freedom. They privileged artifice. Clothes and manners made the man or the woman. Yet to be awkward or extreme in fashion made one ridiculous; the characters most dedicated to artificial, fashionable dress were the fops. Moreover, wealth is central to these plays, and young lovers are unlikely to sacrifice potential wealth for love. Instead, they scheme to have it all, and the blocking parents usually give in.

The most famous comedies of the Restoration era – George Etherege's *The Man of Mode* (1676), William Wycherley's *Country Wife* (1675), and William Congreve's *The Way of the World* (1700) – follow similar plotlines. The foolish youthful lover of the Renaissance becomes a skilful schemer, who is not ashamed to admit it. Hypocrisy governs human relations, enabling characters to satisfy, for the moment, both the demands of the flesh and those of social acceptability. But overt hypocrisy is usually exposed and punished in the end. 'Honour' is a dubious and much debated concept. Morality is ambiguous, and everything seems permitted as long as one manages to maintain the appearance of propriety. The story of the next hundred years of comedy would be of how didacticism and sentiment made their way back into the mix, as writers reassessed the moral function of comedy in an increasingly egalitarian and individualistic world. *Schadenfreude* did not disappear; but laughing at others' suffering was the flip side of a comedic coin, which also increasingly promoted ideals of politeness and sentiment. New research indicates that sentimental ideals were far from dominant in eighteenth-century Britain. Literary historian Simon Dickie suggests that there was a gulf between theory and practice. Throughout the period, women and men wrote curses, lampoons, bawdy epigrams, and verses about boxing, farting, and puking. Theorists may have privileged sympathy and rationality, but ordinary people laughed at the disabled, beggars, and rape victims. It was an impolite world that theorized about politeness.

The stipulation by royal patent that only women could play women's parts also contributed to the sensuality of the Restoration stage. Allowing women to play women's parts enabled theatre to represent and exploit different sexual tensions. Long flirtatious scenes, kissing, bawdy talk, even attempted rape made comedies more explicit in the Restoration, at least about heterosexual sex, than their predecessors. The new approach to stage sexuality also reflected changing attitudes toward women and morality. Some dramatists critiqued double standards with regard to women's sexuality and their lack of rights in marriage. When a strong female character, like 'wild' Hellena in Behn's *The Rover* (1677) or Millamant in Congreve's *The Way of the World* (1700), does eventually agree to marry, she may seek to secure some degree of independence and equality, though dominance is still gendered masculine. The first English woman to earn her living as an author, Behn did not moralize or propose to write about 'Characters genteel and fine'. In the prologue and epilogue to *The Rover*, she disparages 'gentle things', finding 'Sport' in 'Debauches'. Like Behn's male characters, the feisty Hellena acknowledges and acts on her own desires, though like other female characters she has to act fast to escape rape. Yet even in the 1670s some critics craved a more edifying comedy. In 1671, playwright Thomas Shadwell, quarrelling with Dryden about the nature of comedy, argued against the notion that plays should merely amuse. Most agreed that comedy should follow the Horatian line (to delight and to instruct), but Shadwell unpacked the implications in that relationship. In the prologue to *The Squire of Alsatia* (1688), he invokes a more conservative aim for the dramatist: 'to correct and to inform'.

The eighteenth century was a great age of satire, one goal of which was to ridicule folly, and the relationship between satire and comedy became a major theoretical topic. The point of satirical comedy was to shed light on society's shortcomings and serve as a social corrective. Dryden wrote satires, epigrams, and plays that provided poetic models for his contemporaries. He said that the goal of satire was 'the amendment of vices'. The problem was how to ridicule and correct without offending. Dryden's most elaborate discussion of comedy is in his preface to *An Evening's Love*, which defends a preference for witty repartee against the attack made on him by Shadwell. Dryden argues that wit is crucial for providing the audience with a model that will help them reject vice. Like most critics of his day, he believed that comedy had a vital social function; the controversial part is the defence of wit, as it 'causes laughter in those who can judge of men and manners, by the lively representation of their folly and corruption'. The Irish satirist Jonathan Swift, author of *Gulliver's Travels*, said that 'Satire is a sort of glass wherein beholders generally discover everybody's face but their own, which is the chief reason for that kind of reception it meets in the world, and that so very few are offended with it.' Yet, in Hobbes's view laughter was morally questionable because it tended to generate hostility between people. In *Leviathan*, he argued that laughter is an expression of one's feeling of superiority, and that therefore it should not be encouraged:

> Sudden glory is the passion which maketh those grimaces called laughter; and is caused either by some sudden act of their own that pleaseth them; or by the apprehension of some deformed thing in another, by comparison whereof they suddenly applaud themselves. And it is incident most to them that are conscious of the fewest abilities in themselves; who are forced to keep themselves in their own favour by observing the imperfections of other men. And therefore much laughter at the defects of others is a sign of pusillanimity. For of great minds one of the proper works is to help and free others from scorn, and compare themselves only with the most able.

Hobbes suggests that it is possible to laugh without being hurtful only if one is able to abstract the laughter from the actual person: 'Laughter without offence, must be at absurdities and infirmities abstracted from persons, and where all the company may laugh together.' Right-minded people who are humble and noble can laugh in a way that is not offensive. Hobbes's theory of laughter found little purchase among the satirists of the eighteenth century.

While satire had a conservative dimension as a social corrective, the moral relativism that characterized much of the sexual comedy of manners provoked intense opposition, shifting comedy and comic theory in a new direction. Jeremy Collier's *A Short View of the Immorality and Profaneness of the English Stage* (1698) argued that the post-Puritan era had produced demoralizing entertainment that promoted vice and disrespect for the church and religion. *A Short View* opens with a pronouncement on what Collier took to be the British drama's failures of the old neo-classical notion of decorum: 'The Business of Plays is to recommend Virtue, and discountenance

Vice; to show the Uncertainty of Human Greatness, the suddain Turns of Fate, and the unhappy Conclusions of Violence and Injustice: 'tis to expose the Singularities of Price and Fancy, to make Folly and Falsehood contemptible, and to bring every Thing that is ill under Infamy, and Neglect.' Collier critiqued Restoration comedy's 'liberties', calling them 'intolerable' 'with respect to morality and religion'. He condemned the glorification of libertines' 'success in their debauchery', 'their smuttiness of expression; their swearing, profaneness and lewd application of scripture; their abuse of the clergy'. Collier's essay provoked rebuttals. Two playwrights, Vanbrugh and Congreve, who were Collier's main targets, published rejoinders. In a preface to *A Short Vindication of the Relapse* (1698), Vanbrugh commented: 'The business of comedy is to show people what they should do by representing them upon the stage doing what they should not do'. Congreve explained, 'Men are to be laughed out of their vices in comedy'. Yet even Collier's adversaries seem influenced by his complaint. Whatever the degree of Collier's influence (which is much debated by historians), his work was symptomatic of the culture's growing distaste for the bawdiest of Restoration comedies. Although, like a true Platonist, Collier opposed all theatre, his attacks encouraged some of the elements that became associated with sentimental comedy.

While Restoration comedy had a loose attitude toward 'morality and religion', the sentimental comedy of the eighteenth century adopted a relatively simple moral stance. Sentimental comedy underwent two distinct stages of development. Moving away from French neo-classical values, it reflected an interest in tragicomedy. The mixing of tragic and comic elements eventually produced a sentimental tone that glorified virtue and punished vice via elaborate, tear-inducing plots. The shift in moral attitudes toward sentimentality at the turn of the century was influenced by the reigns of William III and the anti-theatrical Mary II, and then Mary's sister Queen Anne, who disapproved of raunchy comedies, as well as a growing cultural conservatism that accompanied the rise of the so-called 'middling' classes. In 1704, Queen Anne issued a proclamation declaring that 'nothing be acted in either of the Theatres contrary to morals or good manners'. Moreover, in 1691 the Society for the Reformation of Manners was formed. Collier's *Short View* had taken advantage of the momentum such organizations created. In 1708, 3,299 people were convicted in London for 'lewd and scandalous' acts, which included drunkenness and swearing. The Society sent spies into the theatres to inform on actors who violated the ordinances against profanity, and rebukes were issued to those who overstepped.

In comedy, sentimentalism aimed for an emotional response and a happy ending. Early sentimental comedy was called 'the weeping comedy', as its goal was to induce tears and laughter in order to generate pity for the characters. The moralizing tone of sentimental comedy was a return to earlier models of comedy as a normative and didactic tool, yet it reflected a bourgeois attitude, which privileged the psychological needs of ordinary citizens, the capacity of spectators to sympathize with others, and the underlying assumption that morality was grounded in the emotions. In his 1759 *Theory of Moral Sentiments*, Adam Smith wrote, 'The poets and romance writers, who best paint the refinements and delicacies of love and friendship, and of all other private and domestic affections [...] are, in such cases, much better instructors' than philosophers. Similarly, in the prologue to Richard Steele's *The Conscious Lovers* (1722), Leonard Welsted asserted that the objective of comedy is to 'please by Wit, that scorns the Aids of Vice', to 'chasten wit, and moralize the stage'. Welsted promoted the notion that comedy has, above all, a moralizing function. Steele, an Irish writer often called the father of sentimental comedy, was the first playwright to fully utilize the sentimental formula. Renowned as co-founder of the periodicals *The Spectator* and *The Guardian,* which targeted the growing urban middle class, Steele first made a name for himself by publishing a moralizing booklet, *The Christian Hero* (1701), which argued that 'no principles but those of religion are sufficient to make a great man'. The pamphlet reflected shifting attitudes toward religion and morality. In 1702, Steele published his first comedy, *The Funeral, or, Grief à la Mode,* a satire directed against lawyers and undertakers. In 1704, he wrote the equally successful *Tender Husband.* William Hazlitt (1778–1830) argued that Steele's comedies 'were the first that were written expressly with a view, not to imitate the manners, but to reform the morals of the age', though, Hazlitt adds, 'It is almost a misnomer to call them comedies; they are rather homilies in dialogue.'

Eighteenth-century authors continued to pen satires and parodies, aimed at the weepy stories extolled by some contemporaries, but these polemics also reflected the rise of the English novel and mutually reinforcing relations between novelistic and stage comedy. In his 1742 preface to his novel *Joseph Andrews,* Henry Fielding argued that burlesque is more beneficial to health than sentimental comedy, as it 'contributes more to exquisite mirth and laughter than any other; and these are probably more wholesome physic for the mind, and conduce better to purge away spleen, melancholy and ill affections, than is generally imagined'. Fielding's masterpiece, *Tom Jones,* is characterized by quick wit and robust humour. Between 1729 and 1737 Fielding wrote twenty-five plays, but his greatest success came with satirical novels and parodies of popular sentimental stories, the most famous of which was *Shamela* (1741), a parody of Samuel Richardson's melodramatic novel, *Pamela,* which transformed Richardson's virtuous servant girl into a gold-digger who aims to trap her master, Squire Booby, into marriage. *Joseph Andrews*, which Fielding called a 'comic epic poem in prose', along the lines of Cervantes's *Don Quixote*, was another parody of Richardson's sentimental fiction. Nonetheless, Fielding insisted that satire be a weapon of virtue. 'The only source of the true ridiculous', he wrote in the preface to *Joseph Andrews*, 'is affectation.' The ridiculousness of affectation comes from 'vanity, or hypocrisy: for as vanity puts us on affecting false characters, in order to purchase applause; so hypocrisy sets us on an endeavour to avoid censure by concealing our vices under an appearance of their opposite virtues.' Fielding considered the exaggerated humour of burlesque the perfect mirror of this phenomenon, for 'what *caricatura* is in painting, burlesque is in writing; and in the same manner the comic writer and painter correlate with each other'.

By the mid-eighteenth century, the pressures to write in a clear, didactic mode intensified. Playwrights suspected of flouting the rules were criticized. In his 1758 essay on French theatre, for example, Jean-Jacques Rousseau (1712–78) accused Molière's plays of being 'a school of vices and bad morals even more dangerous than the very books which profess to teach them'. '[Molière's] greatest care', writes Rousseau, 'is to ridicule goodness and simplicity and to present treachery and falsehood so that they arouse our interest and sympathy'. Rousseau said that Molière had 'not the slightest wish to correct vices', focusing on Molière's *Misanthrope,* in which, Alceste, 'a sincere, worthy, truly a good man', is made into 'a ridiculous character' and a 'highly virtuous character is presented as laughable'. As a political philosopher, Rousseau opposed Hobbes's concept of human nature, arguing in the *Discourse on the Origin and Basis of Inequality among Men* against Hobbes's idea that since man in the 'state of nature [...] has no idea of goodness, he must be naturally wicked'. On the contrary, Rousseau believed that humans (particularly in childhood) are naturally good, and that 'uncorrupted morals' prevail in the 'state of nature'. In the novel *Julie, ou la nouvelle Héloïse,* which explores the notion of authenticity, Rousseau argued that authentic morality based on emotions should supersede rational moral principles. Rousseau regarded Molière's Alceste as a man of virtue, uncorrupted by the vices of civilization. Such a man, Rousseau believed, should not be 'presented as laughable'. His conception of human nature contributed to the sentimental ideas of his age and helped to inspire the birth of Romanticism. Sentimental comedy idealized female virtue, the wisdom of the old, the innocence of children, and the idyllic simplicity of the past. Since they were thought to be closer to nature and perceived as childlike, women were idealized for their supposed purity and innocence. In Steele's *The Lying Lover* (1704), for example, the hero declares, 'A Woman methinks is a Being between us and Angels.' Late eighteenth-century British comedies such as Oliver Goldsmith's *She Stoops to Conquer* (1773) and Richard Brinsley Sheridan's *The School for Scandal* (1777) bear witness to the growing concern for authenticity. The idealization of women was partially inspired by the courtly love of the Middle Ages and, in turn, inspired the Romantic notion of conscience as an inner sentiment and the *amour fou* of nineteenth-century fiction.

Sentimentalists believed in the innate goodness of the human being, his or her purity, virtue, and courage. The tone of the sentimental comedy was also informed by the wave of egalitarianism that eventually produced the Declaration of the Rights of Man (1789) and the idea of class equality. Denis Diderot, a French philosopher often considered the father of the Enlightenment, was an enthusiastic promoter of sentimentalism in drama, adhering to the belief that human nature is intrinsically good and that the poet should bring it to the fore. In his essay on dramatic poetry, Diderot writes: 'Poet, are you a man of sensibility and of tender feelings? Then strike that note, and you will hear it resound or tremble in every heart.' Human nature is good as 'everything in nature is good [...]. It is wretched conventionalities that pervert man.' Elevating the virtue of uncultivated nature, sentimental comedy often revolved around rich, educated characters overcoming their social status, and learning the value of 'goodness and simplicity' from lower-class characters. Morally drifting men would eventually learn the value of true virtue from a virtuous woman. The pleasure of watching such plots derived less from laughter than from the tears that followed the recognition of untainted virtue.

By evoking sentimental feelings of pity toward the wretched, sentimental comedy paradoxically promoted 'Enlightenment'. Sentimentalism was a force for social reform and humanitarianism. With the rise of commerce and global trade, money became more important than birth in determining status, creating new socioeconomic relations. To enjoy money, prestige, and influence, the wealthy were encouraged to bestow pity and charity on the poor. When Jonas Hanway wrote *A Sentimental History of Chimney Sweepers* (1775), his objective was to arouse an outcry against child labour. However, the idealization of the lower classes also provoked criticism, as it presumed the purity of motivations of those whom one was to pity. Oliver Goldsmith, a dramatist and critic who often championed social causes, was keenly aware of the economic disruptions caused by capitalism. He argued, in 'A Comparison between Laughing and Sentimental Comedy' (1773), that comedy should not excuse folly. On the contrary, 'Comedy should excite our laughter by ridiculously exhibiting the follies of the lower part of mankind.' Laughter and tears should not happen at the same time. 'If we are permitted to make comedy weep', he wrote, we would have an equal right 'to make tragedy laugh'. Thus, the weeping comedy is a 'species of bastard tragedy', 'a kind of *mulish* production'. The formula of sentimental comedy provided a blueprint for what we call today the romantic comedy: lovers are separated by status, misunderstanding, or their own psychological obstacles (stubbornness, pride, shyness); they reject one another, only to forgive at the happy end.

Since it often dealt with characters from the lower classes (though they were rarely the leads), the humour of the sentimental comedy was considerably less sharp than the wit of the Restoration comedy. Entering a conversation that went back to Congreve in 1700, William Hazlitt, considered one of the greatest essayists in the English language, distinguished between 'wit' and 'humour' in an 1819 essay: 'Humour is the describing the ludicrous as it is in itself; wit is the exposing it, by comparing or contrasting it with something else.' If wit was the domain of Restoration comedy, humour was the domain of the sentimental. Hazlitt analysed the nature of laughter: what causes it and how it affects us. He would develop a version of what has come to be known as the incongruity theory, which is the notion that humour arises from a perception of the discrepancy between expectation and actuality. This theory dates to the German philosopher, Immanuel Kant, who writes, 'Laughter is an affect that arises if a tense expectation is transformed into nothing.' This quick change of perspective, which, in theory, produces a pleasure from the free play of sensations, gratifies us, Kant says, because it illuminates 'our own mistake in reaching for some object that is otherwise indifferent to us'. Incongruity is basic to the structure of modern humour, just as it is to our consumer-driven modern economy. Hazlitt would argue similarly that laughter is the result of broken expectations: 'The ludicrous is where there is the same contradiction between the object and our expectations, heightened by some deformity or inconvenience, that is, by its being contrary to what is customary or desirable.' While humour is the product of happy accidents, however, 'wit is, in fact, the eloquence of indifference.'

By the nineteenth century, sentimental comedy and its reliance on feeling as a guide to moral truth raised new questions. Charles Lamb's essay 'On the Artificial Comedy of the Last Century' (1822) calls for the return of the moral ambiguity of Restoration comedy. Sentimental comedy, Lamb writes, is not natural (as it pretended) but artificial, and therefore false, because 'the moral point is every thing'. The moral 'disorder' of Restoration drama, he believed, was truer to life: 'In our anxiety that our morality should not take cold, we wrap it up in a great blanket of precaution against the breeze and sunshine.' The characters of sentimental comedy are 'walking bundles of manners and customs', which is unrealistic. Debates about sentimental comedy, informed by massive historical changes – including revolutions in America and France, rapid urbanization, industrialism, African slavery (with sentimental comedies of plantation life) and the growth of European empires, which idealized the 'noble savage' and other comic stereotypes – continue to this day. However, Romanticism did not eschew feeling; on the contrary, the comic spirit was understood in the late-eighteenth and early nineteenth-century to be deeply human, intensely emotional, unconstrained by convention, and ultimately liberating. For Romantic theorists, history itself unfolded as a comic plot. German philosopher G. W. F. Hegel (1770–1831) imagined history as progress to a higher end of freedom and rationality. In his 1807 *Phenomenology of Spirit*, he described a new level of human development as 'a state of spiritual well-being and repose therein, such as is not to be found anywhere outside this Comedy'. In his view, history would unfold as comedy toward a happy end. Friedrich Schiller (1759–1805) also believed that comedy was liberating. In contrast to Hobbes's view that laughter was invariably hurtful, Schiller privileged comedy over tragedy in his 1784 essay 'Theatre as a Moral Institution', precisely because the stage is a mirror 'to reflect fools and their thousand forms of folly, which are there turned to ridicule. [...] If a comparison be made between tragedy and comedy [...] we should probably give the palm to the latter.' Schiller envisioned theatre as a domain counter to that of the absolutist state, and comedy illustrates a morally responsible form of freedom. Thus, comedy is one of the human spirit's freest and highest expressions.

Neither Romantic optimism nor this high estimate of comedy lasted into the Victorian period, as we will see in the next section. Charles Dickens, a lover of theatre, would write comic novels that deployed sentimental tropes and devices, but their humour was also, often, ironic and self-conscious. Contemporary with Dickens, Karl Marx would apply Hegel's dialectical theory – the notion that there is always a tension between any present state of affairs and what it was becoming – to 'real world' problems arising from capitalism. In his 'Contribution to the Critique of Hegel's Philosophy of Law', Marx would apply the Romantic thinker's insights to history: 'History is thorough and goes through many phases when carrying an old form to the grave. The last phase of a world-historical form is its *comedy*. [...] Why this course of history? So that humanity should part with its past *cheerfully*.' Marx's materialist conception of history brought Hegel's idealism down to earth, a kind of comic move in itself. History, Marx would show, was the creation of labouring men. In short, people became increasingly self-conscious about history and the cultural forms that they inherited and remade. Comic theory epitomized such self-consciousness.

Finally, the British Romantic poet and theorist Samuel Taylor Coleridge, who was also deeply influenced by German thinkers such as Kant and Hegel, articulated a crucial distinction between what he called mechanical and organic models of literary form in his famous lectures on Shakespeare. 'The form is mechanical', he wrote, 'when on any given material we impress a predetermined form, not necessarily arising out of the properties of the material, as when to a mass of wet clay we give whatever shape we wish it to retain when hardened. The organic form, on the other hand, is innate; it shapes as it develops itself from within, and the fullness of its development is one and the same with the perfection of its outward form. Such is the life, such the form.' By the end of the next century, this distinction would give rise to a new conception of the significance of comedy in a modern, mechanized world. By the early 1800s, the spirit of the times appeared to be changing, or at least moving into new forms, and so too would aesthetic taste in comedy.

Bibliography

Burns, Edward. *Restoration Comedy: Crises of Desire and Identity*. New York: St. Martin's, 1987.

Burra, Peter. *Baroque and Gothic Sentimentalism: An Essay*. Bel Air, CA: Folcroft Library Editions, 1974.

Canfield, J. Douglas. *Tricksters and Estates: On the Ideology of Restoration Comedy*. Lexington, KY: University of Kentucky, 1997.

Corman, Brian. *Genre and Generic Change in English Comedy, 1660–1710*. Toronto: University of Toronto Press, 1993.

Dickie, Simon. *Cruelty and Laughter: Forgotten Comic Literature and the Unsentimental Eighteenth Century*. Chicago: University of Chicago Press, 2011.

Dixon, Michael Bigelow and Michele Volansky, eds. 1993. *Kiss and Tell: Restoration Comedy of Manners: Monologues, Scenes and Historical Context*. Newbury, VT: Smith and Kraus.

Domingo, Darryl P. 'The Natural Propensity of Imitation or Pantomimic Poetics and the Rhetoric of Augustan Wit'. *Journal of Early Modern Cultural Studies* 9 (2) (Fall/Winter 2009): 51–95.

Dykstal, Timothy. 'Provoking the Ancients: Classical Learning and Imitation in Fielding and Collier'. *College Literature* 31 (3) (Summer 2004): 102–22.

Ellis, Frank H. *Sentimental Comedy: Theory and Practice*. Cambridge: Cambridge University Press, 1991.

Ewin, Robert E. 'Hobbes on Laughter'. *The Philosophical Quarterly* 51 (202) (January 2001): 29–40.

Felheim, Marvin. *Comedy: Plays, Theory, and Criticism*. New York: Harcourt, Brace & World, 1962.

Gill, Pat. *Interpreting Ladies: Women, Wit, and Morality in the Restoration Comedy of Manners*. Athens: University of Georgia, 1994.

Hokenson, Jan. *The Idea of Comedy: History, Theory, Critique*. Madison, NJ: Fairleigh Dickinson University Press, 2006.

Hume, Robert D. 'Jeremy Collier and the Future of the London Theatre in 1698'. *Studies in Philology* 96 (4) (Autumn 1999): 480–511.

Ingram, Allan. 'Sentimental Comedy: Theory and Practice'. *Modern Language Review* 88 (3) (July 1993): 729–30.

Owen, Susan J., ed. *A Companion to Restoration Drama*. Oxford: Blackwell, 2001.

Rousseau, Jean-Jacques (1758). 'The French Theatre: Comedy: Molière and His Successors', in *Politics and the Arts: Letter to M. d'Alembert on the Theatre*, translated with notes and introduction by Allan Bloom. Ithaca, NY: Cornell University Press, 1968. (Based on the text edited by Michel Laurnay. Garnier Flammarion, Paris, 1967.)

Styan, J. L. *Restoration Comedy in Performance*. Cambridge: Cambridge University Press, 1986.

Young, Douglas M. *The Feminist Voices in Restoration Comedy: The Virtuous Women in the Play-worlds of Etherege, Wycherley, and Congreve*. Lanham, MD: University Press of America, 1997.

TEXTS

1. Samuel Butler, *Characters and Passages from Notebooks* (c. 1650)

A humorist

Is a peculiar Fantastic, that has a wonderful natural Affection to some particular Kind of Folly, to which he applied himself, and in Time becomes eminent. 'Tis commonly some out-lying Whimsie of *Bedlam*, that being tame and unhurtful is suffered to go at Liberty. The more serious he is, the more ridiculous he becomes, and at the same Time pleases himself in Earnest, and others in Jest. He knows no mean; for that is inconsistent with all Humour, which is never found but in some Extreme or other. Whatsoever he takes to, he is very full of, and believes every Man else to be so too; as if his own Taste were the same in every Man's Palate. If he be a *Virtuoso*, he applied himself with so much Earnestness to what he undertakes that he puts his Reason out of Joint, and strains his Judgment: And there is hardly any Thing in the World so slight or serious, that some one or other had not squandered away his Brains, and Time, and Fortune upon, to no other Purpose but to be ridiculous. He is exempted from a dark Room and a Doctor, because there is no Danger in his Frenzy; otherwise he has as good a Title to fresh Straw as another. Humour is but a Crookedness of the Mind, a disproportioned Swelling of the brain, that draws the Nourishment from the other Parts, to stuff an ugly and deformed Crup-Shoulder. If it have the Luck to meet with many of its own Temper, instead of being ridiculous, it becomes a Church, and from Jest grows to Earnest.

Wit and folly

Wit is very chargeable, and not to bee maintaind in its Necessary Leasure, at an ordinary Rate: It is the worst Trade in the world to live upon, and a Commodity that no man thinks he has neede of, for those who have the least, believe they have as much as the best, and injoy greater Priviledges, for as they are their own Judges, they are subject to no Censures which they cannot easily reverse, and it is incredible how much upon that Accompt they will disise all the world, which those who have more wit dare not do, and the more wit they have, are but the more severe to themselves, and their own Performances, and have just confidence enough to keep them from utterly Renouncing of it, which they are apt to do upon the smallest Check, if something else than their own Inclination did not oppose them in it.

The Condition of those who are born to Estates, and those who are born only to wit, are very neare the same: For very few of both know how to make a Right use of either, but generally as the first live above their Estates, so do the later below their wit; And when both meete in the same Person, it is seldom seen that either of them Prospers, while Who are born to neither, if they have but Industry (which no man of Wit, or Fortune, is so capable of) do commonly thrive better in the world than either of them. For as they are both in their kindes, above the Ordinary alloy of Mankinde (and so most frequently associate together) they cannot submit to that Slavery, and Drudgery, which those who have neither must indure, either to thrive, or get into Preferment. For all that men can get in this world (setting Fortune aside) is but the Sallary, and Pay of their Paines, and Drudgery: which fine wits are no more fit for, than fine Cloaths to labour, and Sweat in. For Nature where shee has once given a Man wit, thinke's she has don enough for him; and after leave's him to himself, as she has don all Mankinde (in respect of other Creatures) in Providing them neither Food, nor Cloaths, nor Armes (as she has don Beasts at her own Charge) but such as they can invent and prepare for themselves. And hence as they can invent, and prepare for themselves. And hence it is that Fooles are Commonly so fortunate in the world, and wiser men so unhappy and miserable. To say nothing of the Craft and Subtlety which she has given all helpless Creatures (as Hares, and Foxes) with which they are able to preserve themselves, from being utterly destroy'd by their stronger and Docile Enemies, who if they were not assisted by men, would be able to do them very little Harm. Nor is it Improbably, but Fooles may be as Fit for great Imployments as wiser men, for what they want of wit, and Ingenuity, is commonly abundantly supply'd with Care and Industry. And wee see dayly such men as have nothing but Formality and Dul gravity to set them off, do rise in Church, and State, sooner to Preferment, than those of Freer and Readier Parts. For the Truth is Fooles are much fitter to have the Management of things of Formality, and show (as the greatest part of all State Affayres are) for they do them Naturally, and in earnest, which wise men do but Counterfet and dissemble And so become the more unapt for them.

There are as many Sorts of Fooles, as there are of Dogs; from the largest of Mastives and Irish Greyhounds, to the smallest of Currs, and Island Shocks, and all equally Fooles as the rest are Dogs.

Men that are mad upon many things, are never so extravagant, as those who are possest with but one. For one Humor diverts another, and never suffers the Caprich to fix. And as those who apply themselves to many Studies, never become excellent in any one: So those that are Distracted with severall Sorts of Freakes, are never so solidly, and Profoundly mad as those that are wholy taken up with some one Extravagance. For sottishness and Folly, which is nothing else but Natural Madnes, is neither so ridiculous, nor Serious in its way, as that which men fall into by Accident or their own ungovern'd Passions. And although a Mad man in his Intervals, is much wiser than a Naturall Fool: yet a Fool (if he be not very stupid) has (al things considerd) much the Advantage of him. For Nature never made anything so bad as the Deviations from her have render'd it: Nor is she more Improv'd by Art, and Ingenuity, then Impayr'd by Artificiall Folly, and Industrious Ignorance. And therefor the Author of Don Quixot, makes Sancho (though a Natural Fool) much more wise and Politique than his Master with all his Study'd, and acquir'd Abilities.

A Blinde Man knows he cannot see, and is glad to be led, though it bee but by a Dog, But hee that is Blinde in his understanding (which is the worst Blindeness of all others) believe's he see's as well as the Best, and Scorne's a Guide, and the more, the more he neede's one. For all Men are very sensible of the Defects of their Senses, but none of their Intellects. For the understanding being Judge of all their Abilities, is either so Partiall to it self, that it is Impossible it should ever discover it's own wants, or else is incapable of Doing it, by being depriv'd of right Information, the only meanes, by which it is to be don.

For mens wits and Judgements, (how excellent so ever in their kindes) will [n]ever be brought to stand in Tune together. For good wits do not always Jump. There is no Theft so easy as that of Wit; that is so cheap, it will not beare the Charges of being lock'd up, or look'd after. But though it be less Difficult then to rob an Orchard that is unfenc'd, yet he who think's he can steal Judgment is as Ridiculous as he that believe's he can run away with the Trees, or because he can steale the Oare, suppose's he can convey away the Mine. For there is no tru wit that is not produc'd by a great Deal of Judgment, For wit and Fancy are but the Cloaths, and Ornaments of Judgment, and when they are Stollen by those whom they will not fit, they serve them to no Purpose, or that which is worse then none, to make them Ridiculous, For almost all Plants, and Animals too, degenerate where they are not Naturally produc'd, and he that believe'd otherwise of wit, is as ignorant as those silly Indians, that buy Gunpowder of our Merchants, and so it in the Earth, believe it will grow there.

That Providence that Cloaths and Feede's Beasts, because they know not how to help themselves, Provides for all Sorts of Fooles, that are equally incapable of Relieving themselves without it.

Though wit be ever so Contemptible to the Ignorant: yet those who have none of their own Growth, and are forc'd to buy it, are sure to pay Deare for it; although it be the most slight, and Course of all others, as all things that are made for Sale usually are, to pass the easier of by their Cheapnes: only Bought wit is the Dearer for being vile and Paultry. For a Cheat is worse then a Thiefe, and do's not only Rob a man of his Goodes (as a thiefe do's) but his Reputation also, and makes him Combine and take Part against himself: Steale's and convey's him, out of his Reason, and Senses (as Changlings are sayd to be serv'd by witches out of the Cradle). And is not so Civil as to beg the Tuition of him, but assume's a Power, and Authority to make himself his Guardian, upon what Tearmes he pleases.

Fooles are always wrangling and Disputing, and the lesse Reason they have, the more earnest they are in controversy: As beggars are always Quarrelling about divideing an Almes; And the Paultryest Trades will higgle more for a Penny, then the Richer will do for a Pound. For those who have but a Little, ought to make as much of it as they can.

All Mad men are Humorists, and wholly possest with some Foolish extravagant Fancy, which they are never to be redeem'd from, but by the Recovery of their Wits, which are commonly so wasted with the violence of the Frenzy, that they are never good for anything after. For Mad men are more earnest, and serious, in their wildest Apprehension, then those that are in their wits and are in their greatest Probabilities of Reason, so much has error the odds of Truth wheresoever they meet; That the Kingdom of Darknes is more frequently taken by violence then that of Heaven. For Truth is so often baffled, and outwitted in the Affaires of the world, that wise men are discourag'd to ingage in her Right. For as it was crucify'd in the Person of our Saviour (who was truth itself) so it has been ever since and wilbe to the end of the world.

[...]

There is nothing that provokes and Sharpens wit like Malice, and Anger si Natura negat facit Indignatio &c. And hence perhaps came the first occasion of calling those Raptures Poeticall Fury. For Malice is a kinde of Madnes (For if Men run mad for Love, why should they not as well do so for Hate?) And as mad men are say'd to have in their fits double the Strength they had before, so have Malitious men the wit. He who first found out Iambiques; and before with all his wit and Fancy could not prevayle with the Father of his Mistress to keep but his Promise with him; has no sooner turn'd his Love into Hate, but he forc'd him with the bitternes of his New Rhimes so to hang himself. So much Power has Malice above all other Passions, to highten wit and Fancy, for Malice is Restles, and never finds ease untill it has vented itself. And therefore Satyrs that are only provok'd with the Madness and Folly of the world, are found to conteine more wit, and Ingenuity then all other writings whatsoever, and meet with a better Reception from the world, that is always more delighted to heare the Faults and vices though of itself well describd, then all the Panegyriques that ever were, which are commonly as Dull as they are False, And no man is Delighted with the Flattery of another. Among all Sports and shows that are used none are so Delightfull as the Military; that do but imitate and Counterfet Fights. And in Heroicall Poetry, that has nothing to do with Satyr; what is there that do's so much captivate the Reader, as the prodigious Feates of Armes of the Heroes, and the Horrid Distruction they make of their Enemies? There is no sort of Cuning in the world so subtle and Curious, as that which is used in doing of Mischief; Nor any true wisdom and Politie so ingenious, as the Artifices of Cheates and Impostors. Against which all the wisdom of Laws is so unable to prevail that they will turne all their best and surest Guards upon themselves, in spight of all the caution and Care which the wisest Governments can possibly contrive. How far more cunning and Crafty have the Wits of Men been in finding out that Prodigious variety of offencive weapons, in comparison of those Few who have invented only for Defence? though their own Preservation ought in Reason to be more Considerable, to them then the Distruction of others. What made the Serpent so subtle, as to out-wit Adam in Paradise, though a Copy drawn from the original of wisdom itself, but only the Malice of his Designe? So Active and Industrious is the Devill to do mischief. For Malice is the Reason of State of Hell, as Charity is of Heaven, and therefor the Proceedings of both are directly Contrary. For God who made the world, and all that is in it in six days, was forty Days and Nights too in Drowning of it, besides so many yeares in executing what he had resolv'd, whose Punishments extend but to the third or fourth Generation, but his Mercy unto thousands. Malice is so great an Odds in any Contest between Man and man; that the Law do's not condemne one man for killing another, for any Reason so much, as for having Malice Prepensd on his side; as if it were one of those Illegal weepons, which the Statute of Stabbing provide's against. What a Stupendious operation has the Malice of witches (for nothing else Qualify's them to be such,) who if the Laws of the Land are but true and just, are able to do feates, which the wisest men in the world are not able to understand? And hence it is that Envie and Emulation, which is but a kinde of Malice, has power to inable some men to do things which had otherwise been far above their Naturall Abilities. It is not only a wicked vice, but its own Punishment also: For it always afflict those more, that beare it, then those, for whose sakes they indure the slavery to maintain it. He who in a Rage threw his Pencill at his Picture, because he could not please himself in Drawing the Fome of a Mad Dog; came nearer to Nature both in his Performance, and the way of Doing it, then all his sober study and care could ever have brought him. For all the best Productions of most Judicious mens Studys proceed from nothing more, then their Restles vexation of thought which all Passions naturally produce in the minde, and put the Spirits into a quicker motion then they are capable of in a quiet Temper. But notwithstanding the many Advantages that wit receives from Passion, there is nothing in Nature so pernicious, and Distructive to all manner of Judgment: for all Passion is so Partiall and Prepossest that it is not capable of making a true Judgment of anything thoughever so Plaine, and Easy. And although there are but few Passions of the Naturall Temper of Judgment, As Feare Sorrow Shame &c., yet where they Prevayl, they are as averse to it, and sometime more, then those of a direct contrary Nature. For Judgment is like a Ballance that measure's all things by weight, and therefore the more light, and less solid anything is, the less apt it is to be examin'd that way.

2. Molière, Preface to *Tartuffe* (1667), translated by Paul Lauter

Here is a comedy about which people have raised quite a stir, which has long been persecuted, and the people it mocks have made plain that they were more powerful in France than all those I have mocked heretofore. The marquises, the precious ladies, the cuckolds, and the doctors have suffered the portrayal in peace, and have even made a show of being amused, like everyone else, by the sketches we made of them. But the hypocrites could not take mockery; they were immediately affrighted, and found it strange that I should be so bold as to make sport of their grimacing and wish to criticize an occupation meddled in by so many honest folk. It is a crime they could not forgive, and they all took up arms against my comedy with a frightful furor. They were careful not to attack it through the side that hurt them – they are too politic for that, and know too well how to get along in the world to unveil the depths of their soul. Following their praiseworthy custom, they concealed their private interests with the cause of God, and in their words *Tartuffe* is a play that offends religion. From one end to the other it is full of abominations, and there is nothing in it that does not deserve the flames. All its syllables are impious; even the gestures are criminal; and the slightest glance, the slightest shake of the head, the slightest step to left or right hide mysteries which they manage to explain to my disadvantage.

In vain I have submitted it to my friends' judgment and to everybody's censure; the corrections I have been able to make, the judgment of the king and queen, who have seen it, the approval of the great princes and ministers, who have publicly honored it with their presence, the testimony of upright people, who found it useful – all that has not helped at all. They will not let go; and every day, still, they prompt the public outcry of indiscreet zealots, who insult me piously and damn me from charity.

I should care very little about anything they can say, were it not for the artifice by which they create for me enemies whom I respect, and thrust onto their side truly worthy people, whose good faith they catch unawares, and who in their enthusiasm for Heaven's best interests are easily impressionable. That is what obliges me to defend myself. It is to the truly pious that I wish everywhere to justify myself about the conduct of my comedy; and I beseech them with all my heart not to condemn things before seeing them, to rid themselves of all prejudice, and not to serve the passion of those whose grimacing dishonors them.

If one takes the trouble to examine my comedy in good faith, one will see without a doubt that my intentions throughout are innocent and that it in nowise tends to make sport of things that we must revere; that I have treated it with all the precautions required by the delicate nature of the subject and that I have put all the art and all the care possible to distinguish clearly between the character who is the hypocrite and the one who is truly devout. To that end, I have used two whole acts to prepare the arrival of my scoundrel. He does not keep the spectator in suspense for a single moment; he is recognized immediately by the characteristics that I give him; and, from one end to the other, he does not say a word, he does not do one action, that does not depict for the spectators the character of a wicked man or enhance the character of the truly upright man whom I place next to him as a foil.

Of course I know that in reply those gentlemen try to insinuate that it is not up to the theater to speak of these subjects, but I beg leave to ask them on what basis they establish this fine maxim. This is merely a hypothetical premise, which they in nowise prove; and it would present absolutely no difficulty to point out to them that ancient drama had its origins in religion and was a part of their mysteries; that our neighbors, the Spaniards, mingle drama into the celebration of practically all their holy days, and that even with us the theater owes its birth to the cares of a confraternity that today still owns the Hotel de Bourgogne; that it is a place that was given for the presentation of the most important mysteries of our faith; that one can still see plays printed in gothic type under the name of a Sorbonne doctor, and, without going so far afield, that in our own time Monsieur de Corneille's religious plays were produced and were admired by all of France.

If the mission of comedy is to correct men's vices, I fail to see why some should be privileged. In the State, this one is of an importance much more dangerous than all the others; and we have seen that the theater is a great force for correction. The finest points of a serious morality are usually less powerful than those belonging to satire; and most men are scolded by nothing quite so well as by the portrayal of their faults.

It is a great blow to vice to expose it to everyone's laughter. We can easily stand being reprehended, but we cannot stand being mocked. We are willing to be wicked, but we will not be ridiculous.

I have been reproached for having placed terms of piety in the mouth of my impostor. Well! Could I help it in properly representing the character of a hypocrite? To me, it seems enough for me to make known the criminal motives that make him say those things, and for me to have cut out sacred terms, for it would have been repugnant to hear him make bad usage of them. – "But in the fourth act he propounds a pernicious morality." But is not this morality something we have heard about over and over again? Does it say anything new in my comedy? And can it be feared that things so widely detested should have any influence over people's minds, or that they should gain authority in the mouth of a scoundrel? There is no probability in that; and the comedy *Tartuffe* should be approved, or else all comedies condemned.

And that is precisely what has recently been raging, and never have some people been so furious against the theater. I cannot deny that there have been Fathers of the Church who condemned the drama, but no one can deny that there have also been some who treated it a little more gently. Thus, the authority on which the proposed censure is based is destroyed by this division, and the only conclusion that can be drawn from this diversity of opinions in minds enlightened by the same intelligence is that they have considered the drama differently, and that some have taken it in its pure state while the others have looked at its corruption and have confused it with those base spectacles which have been correctly called "spectacles of turpitude."

And indeed, since one should discourse on things and not words, and since most contradictions come from lack of understanding and from wrapping up contrary things in the same word, one need merely lift the veil of equivocation and look at what comedy is per se to see whether it is reprehensible. It will be agreed, no doubt, that, being nothing other than a skillful poem which, by agreeable lessons, reprimands men's defects, it could not be censured save unjustly; and, if we wish to hear the witness of antiquity on this matter, she will tell us that her most famous philosophers praised comedy, they who professed such austere restraint and who incessantly cried out against the vices of their age. She will point out to us that Aristotle consecrated his night watches to the drama and took the trouble of reducing the art of making comedies to precepts. She will teach us that her greatest and highest ranking men gloried in composing some themselves, that there were others who did not scorn to recite in public those which they had composed; that Greece manifested her esteem for this art by the glorious prizes and the splendid theaters with which she did it honor;

and that in Rome itself this same art also received extraordinary honors. I do not mean in Rome debauched under licentious emperors, but in Rome disciplined under austere consuls, in the time of vigorous Roman virtue.

I admit that there have been times when comedy was corrupt. But what is there in the world that is not corrupted every day? There is nothing so innocent that men cannot stain it with crime, no art so salutary that they cannot reverse its intentions, nothing so good in itself that they cannot turn it to bad uses. Medicine is a beneficial art and everyone respects it as one of the most excellent things we have, yet there have been times when it became odious and often it has been made into an art for poisoning men. Philosophy is a gift of Heaven; it was given to us to lead our minds to the knowledge of God through contemplating the miracles of nature; nevertheless, everyone is aware that it has often been perverted from its function and publicly used to uphold impiety. Even the holiest of things are not safe from men's corrupting, and we see scoundrels who every day abuse piety and wickedly make it serve the greatest crimes. But for all of that one does not fail to make the necessary distinctions. One does not bundle together into one false conclusion the true excellence of the things being corrupted and the malice of the corruptors. One goes on separating the bad usage from the goal of the art, and just as we do not take it into our heads to forbid medicine because it was banished from Rome or philosophy because it was publicly condemned in Athens, likewise we should not wish to interdict comedy because it has been criticized at certain times. That censure had its reasons, which do not exist today. It was restricted to what it could see, and we must not draw it out beyond its own self-appointed limits, nor stretch it further than is right, and make it embrace the innocent with the guilty. The comedy it aimed to attack is not the one that we would defend. One must be careful not to confuse the one with the other. They are two persons whose manners and morals are completely opposite. They have no connection with each other beyond the similarity of the name; and it would be a frightful injustice to want to condemn Olympe, who is an upright woman, because there is an Olympe who was depraved. Judgments like that would perforce cause a great disorder in the world. By that system everything would be condemned; and since we do not hold that severity against so many things that are abused every day, we should then grant the same grace to comedy and approve plays wherein we see instruction and propriety reign.

I know that there are some souls who are so dainty that they cannot suffer any comedy, who say that the most proper are the most dangerous, that the passions depicted are all the more touching in that they are filled with virtue, and that souls are moved to tenderness by those kinds of representations. I cannot see that it is such a great crime to be moved at the sight of a chaste passion, and it is a high plane of virtue, that complete insensitivity to which they would lift up our soul. I doubt that such a perfection lies within the strength of human nature, and I do not know whether it is not better to work at rectifying and tempering men's passions rather than trying to do away with them altogether. I admit that there are better places to frequent than the theater; and if we are going to reprove all the things that do not directly concern God and our salvation, it is certain that comedy must be among them, and I find no fault at its being condemned with the rest; but if we allow, as is true, that the exercises of piety suffer intervals and that men need diversion, I maintain that they cannot find a more innocent one than comedy. But this has been too protracted. Let us finish with a *mot* from a great prince about the comedy *Tartuffe.*

A week after it was forbidden, a play called *Hermit Scaramouche* was presented before the court; on leaving, the king said to this great prince, "I should really like to know why the people who are so scandalized about Molière's comedy don't say a word about *Scaramouche.*" To which the prince replied, "The reason is that the comedy *Scaramouche* makes sport of Heaven and religion, which those gentlemen don't care a hang about, but Molière 's comedy makes sport of *them,* which is what they cannot stand."

3. William Congreve, Dedication to *The Double-Dealer* (1693)

I grant, that for a Man to Talk to himself, appears absurd and unnatural; and indeed it is so in most Cases; but the circumstances which may attend the occasion, make great alteration. It oftentimes happens to a Man, to have designs which require him to himself [sic], and in their Nature, cannot admit of a Confident. Such, for certain, is all Villainy; and other less mischievous intentions may be very improper to be Communicated to a second Person. In such a case therefore the Audience must observe, whether the Person upon the Stage takes any notice of them at all, or no. For if he supposes any one to be by, when he talks to himself, it is monstrous and ridiculous to the last degree. Nay, not only in this case, but in any sort of a Play, if there is expressed any knowledge of an Audience, it is insufferable. But otherwise when a Man in Soliloquy reasons with himself, and *Pro's* and *Con's*, and weighs all his Designs: We ought not to imagine that this Man either talks to us, or to himself: he is only thinking, and thinking such Matter, as were inexcusable Folly in him to speak. But because we are conceal'd Spectators of the Plot in agitation, and the Plot finds it necessary to let us know the whole Mystery of his Contrivance he is willing to inform us of this Person's Thoughts; and to that end is forced to make use of the expedient of Speech, no other better way being yet invented for the Communication of Thought.

Another very wrong Objection has been made by some who have not taken leisure to distinguish the Characters. The Hero of the Play, as they are pleas'd to call him, (meaning *Mellefont*) is Gull, and made a Fool and cheated. Is every Man a Gull and a Fool that is deceiv'd? At that rate I'm afraid the two Classes of Men, whill be reduc'd to one, and the Knaves themselves be at a loss to justifie their Title: But if an Open-hearted Honest Man, who has an entire Confidence in one whom he takes to be his Friend, and whom he has obliged to be so; and who (to confirm him in his Opinion) in all appearance, and upon several trials has been so: If this Man be deceived by the Treachery of the other; must he of necessity commence Fool [*sic*] immediately, only because the other has proved a Villain? Ay, but there was Caution given to *Mellefont* in the first Act by his Friend *Careless*. Of what Nature was this Caution? Only to give the Audience some light into the Character of *Maskwell*, before his appearance; and not to convince *Mellefont* of his Treachery; for that was more than *Careless* was then able to do: He never knew *Maskwell* guilty of any Villainy; he was only a sort of Man which he did not like. As for his suspecting his Familiarity with my Lady *Touchwood*: Let 'em examine the Answer that *Mellefont* makes him, and compare it with the Conduct of *Maskwell's* Character through the Play.

I would have 'em again look into the Character of *Maskwell*, before they accuse any Body of weakness for being deceiv'd by him. For upon summing up the enquiry into his Objection, [I] find they have only mistaken Cunning in the Character, for Folly in another.

But there is one thing which I am more concerned than all the false Criticisms that are made upon me; and that is, some of the Ladies are offended: I am heartily sorry for it, for I declare I would rather disoblige all the Criticks in the World, than one of the Fair Sex. They are concerned that I have represented some Women Vicious and Affected: How can I help it? It is the Business of a Comick Poet to paint the Vices and Follies of Humane kind; and there are but two sexes I know, *viz. Men and Women*, which have a Title to Humanity: And if I leave one half of them out, the Work will be imperfect. I should be very glad of an opportunity to make my Compliment to those Ladies who are offended: But they can no more expect it in a Comedy, than to be Tickled by a Surgeon, when he's letting 'em Blood. They who are Virtuous or Discreet, I'm sure cannot be offended, for such Characters as these distinguish them, and make their Beauties more shining and observ'd: And they who are of the other kind, may nevertheless pass for such, by seeming not to be displeased, or touched with the Satyr of this *Comedy*. Thus have they also wrongfully accused me of doing them a prejudice, when I have in reality done them a service.

I have heard some whispering, as if they intended to accuse this Play of Smuttiness and Bawdy: But I declare I took a particular care to avoid it, and if they find any in it, it is of their own making, for I did not design it to be so understood. But to avoid my saying any thing upon a Subject, which has been so admirably handled before, and for their better instruction, I earnestly recommend to their perusal, the Epistle Dedicatory before the *Plain-Dealer*.

You will pardon me, Sir, for the freedom I take of making Answers to other People, in an Epistle which ought wholly to be sacred to you: But since I intend the Play to be so too, I hope I may take more liberty of Justifying it, where it is in the right. I hear a great many of the Fools are angry at me, and I am glad of it; for I Writ at them, not to 'em. This is a bold confession, and yet I don't think I shall disoblige one Person by it; for no Body can take it to himself, without owning the *Character*.

4. John Dryden, *Of Dramatick Poesie, an Essay* (1668)

Neither, indeed, do I value a reputation gained from comedy so far as to concern myself about it any more than I needs must in my own defence: for I think it, in its own nature, inferior to all sorts of dramatic writing. Low comedy especially requires, on the writer's part, much of the conversation with the vulgar: and much of ill nature in the observation of their follies. But let all men please themselves according to their several tastes: that which is not pleasant to me may be to others who judge better; and, to prevent an accusation from my enemies, I am sometimes ready to imagine that my disgust of low comedy proceeds not so much from my judgment as from my temper; which is the reason why I so seldom write it; and that when I succeed in it (I mean so far as to please the audience), yet I am nothing satisfied with what I have done; but am often vexed to hear people clap, as they perpetually do, where I intended 'em no jest; while they let pass the better things without taking notice of them. Yet even this confirms me in my opinion of slighting popular applause, and of contemning that approbation which those very people give, equally with me, to the zany of the mountebank; or to the appearance of an antic on the theatre, without wit on the poet's part, or any occasion of laughter from the actor besides the ridiculousness of his habit and grimaces.

But I have descended, before I was aware, from comedy to farce;[1] which consists

---

[1] One of the earliest recorded uses of the word as a kind of play. Howard had already used it in this sense in his preface to *The Great Favorite* (1668), quoted derisively by Dryden in his 'Defense'.

principally of grimaces. That I admire not any comedy equally with tragedy is, perhaps, from the sullenness of my humour; but that I detest those farces which are now the most frequent entertainments of the stage, I am sure I have reason on my side. Comedy consists, though of low persons, yet of natural actions and characters; I mean such humours, adventures, and designs as are to be found and met with in the world. Farce, on the other side, consists of forced humours and unnatural events. Comedy presents us with the imperfections of human nature. Farce entertains us with what is monstrous and chimerical: the one causes laughter in those who can judge of men and manners, by the lively representation of their folly or corruption; the other produces the same effect in those who can judge of neither, and that only by its extravagances. The first works on the judgment and fancy; the latter on the fancy only: there is more of satisfaction in the former kind of laughter, and in the latter more of scorn. But how it happens that an impossible adventure should cause our mirth, I cannot so easily imagine. Something there may be in the oddness of it, because on the stage it is the common effect of things unexpected to surprise us into a delight: and that is to be ascribed to the strange appetite, as I may call it, of the fancy; which, like that of a longing woman, often runs out into the most extravagant desires; and is better satisfied sometimes with loam, or with the rinds of trees, than with the wholesome nourishments of life. In short, there is the same difference betwixt farce and comedy as betwixt an empiric and a true physician:[2] both of them may attain their ends; but what the one performs by hazard, the other does by skill. And as the artist is often unsuccessful while the mountebank succeeds; so farces more commonly take the people than comedies. For to write unnatural things is the most probable way of pleasing them, who understand not nature. And a true poet often misses of applause because he cannot debase himself to write so ill as to please his audience.

After all, it is to be acknowledged that most of these comedies which have been lately written have been allied too much to farce; and this must of necessity gall out till we forbear the translation of French plays: for the poets, wanting judgment to make or to maintain true characters, strive to cover their defects with ridiculous figures and grimaces. While I say this, I accuse myself as well as others: and this very play would rise up in judgment against me, if I would defend all things I have written to be natural: but I confess I have given too much to the people in it, and am ashamed for them as well as for myself, that I have pleased them at so cheap a rate. Not that there is anything

---

[2] An "empiric" is given to prescribing according to private observation rather than scientific theory – hence, a quack.

here which I would not defend to an ill-natured judge (for I despise their censures, who I am sure would write worse on the same subject): but because I love to deal clearly and plainly, and to speak of my own faults with more criticism than I would of another poet's. Yet I think it no vanity to say that this comedy has as much of entertainment in it as many others which have been lately written: and, if I find my own errors in it, I am able at the same time to arraign all my contemporaries for greater. As I pretend not that I can write humour,[3] so none of them can reasonably pretend to have written it as they ought. Jonson was the only man of all ages and nations who has performed it well, and that but in three or four of his comedies: the rest are but a *crambe bis cocta*;[4] the same humours a little varied and written worse. Neither was it more allowable in him than it is in our present poets to represent the follies of particular persons; of which many have accused him. *Parcere personis, dicere de vitiis*[5] is the rule of plays. And Horace tells you that the Old Comedy amongst the Grecians was silenced for the too great liberties of the poets:

> in vitium libertas excidit et vim
> dignam lege regi: lex est accepta, chorusque
> turpiter obticuit, sublato jure nocendi.[6]

Of which he gives you the reason in another place: where, having given the precept.

> neve immunda crepent, ignominiosaque dicta,

he immediately subjoins,

> offendenduntur enim quibus est equus, et pater, et res.[7]

But Ben Jonson is to be admired for many excellencies; and can be taxed with fewer failings than any English poet. I know I have been accused as an enemy of his writings; but without any other reason than that I do not admire him blindly, and without looking into his imperfections. For why should he only be exempted from those frailties from which

---

[3] Evidently used in a sense more modern than Jonsonian, though its meaning in the following sentence is less clear. Dryden had defined the Elizabethan sense of the word with pedantic thoroughness in *Of Dramatic Poesy*; but, as this preface repeatedly suggests, the word had already evolved far beyond this point.

[4] Juvenal, *Satires*, VII.154 has "crambe repetita" ("the mess served up again and again").

[5] "To spare individuals and speak of vices" (Latin tag).

[6] *Ars Poetica*, II. 282–4: "Liberty turned to license, and to an excess that called for legal restraint. A law was passed and, the right of libel gone, the chorus to its shame fell silent."

[7] *Ars poetica*, II. 247–8: "nor should they give way to foul and scurrilous expressions, for persons of rank, birth, and fortune are offended by them."

Homer and Virgil are not free? Or why should there be any *ipse dixit* in our poetry, any more than there is in our philosophy? I admire and applaud him where I ought: Those who do more do but value themselves in their admiration of him and, by telling you they extol Ben Jonson's way, would insinuate to you that they can practise it. For my part, I declare that I want judgment to imitate him; and should think it a great impudence in myself to attempt it. To make men appear pleasantly ridiculous on the stage was, as I have said, his talent; and in this he needed not the acumen of wit, but that of judgment. For the characters and representations of folly are only the effects of observation; and observation is an effect of judgment. Some ingenious men, for whom I have a particular esteem, have thought I have much injured Ben Jonson when I have not allowed his wit to be extraordinary: but they confound the notion of what is witty with what is pleasant.[8] That Ben Jonson's plays were pleasant, he must want reason who denies: but that pleasantness was not properly wit, or the sharpness of conceit, but the natural imitation of folly: which I confess to be excellent in its kind, but not to be of that kind which they pretend. Yet if we will believe Quintilian in his chapter *De movendo risu*, he gives his opinion of both in these following words: *stulta reprehendere facillimum est; nam per se sunt ridicula: et a derisu nin procul abest risus: sed rem urbanum facit aliqua ex nobis adjectio.*[9]

And some perhaps would be apt to say of Jonson as it was said of Demosthenes: *non displicuisse illi jocos, sed non contigisse.*[10]

I will not deny but that I approve most the mixed way of comedy; that which is neither all wit, nor all humour, but the result of both. Neither so little of humour as Fletcher shows, nor so little of love and wit as Jonson; neither all cheat, with which the best plays of the one are filled, nor all adventure, which is common practice of the other. I would have the characters well chosen, and kept distant from interfering with each other; which is more than Fletcher or Shakespeare did: but I would have more of the *urbana, venusta, salsa, faceta,*[11] and the rest which Qunitilian reckons up as the ornaments of wit; and these are extremely wanting in Ben Jonson. As for repartee in particular; as it is the very soul of conversation, so it is the greatest grace of comedy, where it is proper to the characters. There may be much of acuteness in a thing well

---

[8] I.e. amusing.

[9] *Institutio oratoria*, VI.iii.71: "It is easy to make fun of folly, for folly is ridiculous in itself; but something of our own makes the joke graceful."

[10] Ibid., VI.iii.2: "not to have disliked jokes, but to have lacked the power to make them."

[11] Ibid., VI.iii.17–20, where Quintilian distinguishes a number of words by which wit is described, the first four being *urbanitas* (of the language of cities and learning), *venustus* (graceful, charming), *salsus* (salty, piquant), and *facetus* (polished, elegant).

said; but there is more in a quick reply: *sunt enim longe venustiora omnia in respon-dendo quam in provocando.*[12] Of one thing I am sure, that no man ever will decry wit but he who despairs of it himself; and who has no other quarrel to it but that which the fox had to the grapes. Yet, as Mr. Cowley (who had greater portion of it than any man I know) tells us in his character of wit, rather than all wit let there be none.[13] I think there's no folly so great in any poet of our age as the superfluity and waste of wit was in some of our predecessors: particularly we may say of Fletcher and of Shakespeare what was said of Ovid, *in omni ejus ingenio, facilius quod rejici, quam quod adjici potest, invenies.*[14] The contrary of which was true in Virgil, and our incomparable Jonson.

Some enemies of repartee have observed to us that there is a great latitude in their characters which are made to speak it: and that it is easier to write wit than humour, the poet is confined to make the person speak what is only proper to it. Whereas all kind of wit is proper in the character of a witty person. But, by their favour, there are as different characters in wit as in folly. Neither is all kind of wit proper in the mouth of every ingenious person. A witty coward and a witty brave must speak differently. Falstaff and the Liar speak not like Don John in the *Chances,* and Valentine in *Wit without Money.*[15] And Jonson's Truewit in the *Silent Woman* is a character different from all of them. Yet it appears that this one character of wit was more difficult to the author than all his images of humour in the play: for those he could describe and manage from his observations of men; this he has taken, at least a part of it, from books: witness the speeches in the first act, translated *verbatim* out of Ovid *De arte amandi*; to omit what afterwards he borrowed from the sixth satire of Juvenal against women.[16]

5. Aphra Behn, 'Epistle to the Reader', from *The Dutch Lover* (1673)

I will have leave to say that in my judgement the increasing number of our latter Plays have not done much more towards the amending of men's Morals, or their Wit,

---

[12] Quintilian, VI.iii.13: "for wit always looks more graceful in reply than in attack."

[13] "Ode: Of Wit" ll.35–6

    Jewels at nose, and lips but ill appear;

    Rather than all things, Wit, let none be there.

[14] Quintilian, VI.iii.5 ("posit, invenient"): "In all his wit you will find it easier to reject than to add."

[15] Two of Fletcher's comedies.

[16] E.g. *Epicoene,* I.i.105–9 and *Ars amatoria,* III.135–40; *Epicoene,* I.i.114–26 and *Ars,* 217–18, 225–34, etc. Cf. *Herford & Simpson,* X.7f. Jonson's portrait of the Collegiate Ladies owes something to Juvenal.

than hath the frequent Preaching, which this last age hath been pester'd with (indeed without all Controversie they have done less harm), nor can I once imagine what temptation anyone can have to expect it from them; for sure I am no Play was ever writ with that design. If you consider Tragedy, you'll find their best of Characters unlikely patterns for a wise man to pursue: For he that is the Knight of the Play, no sublunary feats must serve his Dulcinea; for if he can't bestrid the Moon, he'll ne'er make good his business to the end, and if he chance to be offended, he must without considering right or wrong confound all things he meets, and put you half-a-score likely tall fellows into each pocket; and truly if he come not something near this Pitch I think the Tragedy's not worth a farthing; for Playes were certainly intended for the exercising of men's passions not their understandings, and he is infinitely far from wise that will bestow one moment's meditation on such things: And as for Comedie, the finest folks you meet with there are still unfitter for your imitation, for though within a leaf or two of the Prologue, you are told that they are people of Wit, good Humour, good Manners, and all that: yet if the Authors did not kindly add their proper names, you'd never know them by their Characters; for whatsoe'er's the matter, it hath happen'd so spightfully in several Playes, which have been prettie well received of late, that even those persons that were meant to be the ingenious Censors of the Play, have either prov'd the most debauch'd, or most unwittie people in the Company: nor is this error very lamentable, since as I take it Comedie was never meant, either for a converting or a conforming Ordinance: In short, I think a Play the best divertisement that wise men have: but I do also think them nothing so who do discourse as formallie about the rules of it, as if 'twere the grand affair of humane life. This being my opinion of Plays, I studied only to make this as entertaining as I could, which whether I have been successful in, my gentle Reader, you may for your shilling judge. To tell you my thoughts of it, were to little purpose, for were they very ill, you may be sure I would not have expos'd it; nor did I so till I had first consulted most of those who have a reputation for judgement of this kind; who were at least so civil (if not kind) to it as did encourage me to venture it upon the Stage, and in the Press: Nor did I take their single word for it, but us'd their reasons as a confirmation of my own.

Indeed that day 'twas Acted first, there comes me into the Pit, a long, lither, phleg-matick, white, ill-favour'd, wretched Fop, an Officer in Masquerade newly transported with a Scarf & Feather out of France, a sorry Animal that has nought else to shield it from the uttermost contempt of all mankind, but that respect which we afford to Rats and Toads, which though we do not well allow to live, yet when considered as a part of God's Creation, we make honourable mention of them. A thing, Reader—but no more of such a Smelt: This thing, I tell ye, opening that which serves it for a mouth, out issued such a noise as this to those that sate about it, that they were to expect a woful Play, God damn him, for it was a woman's. Now how this came about I am not sure, but I suppose he brought it piping hot from some who had with him the reputation of a villanous Wit: for Creatures of his size of sense talk without all imagination, such scraps as they pick up from other folks. I would not for a world be taken arguing with such a propertie as this; but if I thought there were a man of any tolerable parts, who could upon mature deliberation distinguish well his right hand from his left, and justly state the difference between the number of sixteen and two, yet had this prejudice upon him; I would take a little pains to make him know how much he errs. For waving the examination why women having equal education with men, were not as capable of knowledge, of whatsoever sort as well as they: I'll only say as I have touch'd before, that Plays have no great room for that which is men's great advantage over women, that is Learning; We all well know that the immortal Shakespeare's Plays (who was not guilty of much more of this than often falls to women's share) have better pleas'd the World than Johnson's works, though by the way 'tis said that Benjamin was no such Rabbi neither, for I am inform'd that his Learning was but Grammar high; (sufficient indeed to rob poor Salust of his best orations) and it hath been observ'd that they are apt to admire him most confoundedly, who have just such a scantling of it as he had; and I have seen a man the most severe of Johnson's Sect, sit with his Hat remov'd less than a hair's breadth from one sullen posture for almost three hours at *The Alchymist*; who at that excellent Play of *Harry the Fourth* (which yet I hope is far enough from Farce) hath very hardly kept his Doublet whole; but affectation hath always had a greater share both in the action and discourse of men than truth and judgement have; and for our Modern ones, except our most unimitable Laureat, I dare to say I know of none that write at such a formidable rate, but that a woman may well hope to reach their greatest heights. Then for their musty rules of Unity, and God knows what besides, if they meant anything, they are enough intelligible and as practible by a woman; but really methinks they that disturb their heads with any other rule of Playes besides the making them pleasant, and avoiding of scurrility, might much better be employed in studying how to improve men's too imperfect knowledge of that ancient English Game which hight long Laurence: And if Comedy should be the picture of ridiculous mankind I wonder anyone should think it such a sturdy task, whilst we are furnish'd with such precious Originals as him I lately told you of; if at least that Character do not dwindle into Farce, and so become too mean an entertainment for those persons who are us'd to think. Reader, I have a complaint or two to make to you and I have done;

Know then that this Play was hugely injur'd in the Acting, for 'twas done so imperfectly as never any was before, which did more harm to this than it could have done to any of another sort; the Plot being busie (though I think not intricate) and so requiring a continual attention, which being interrupted by the intolerable negligence of some that acted in it, must needs much spoil the beauty on't. My Dutch Lover spoke but little of what I intended for him, but supplied it with a great deal of idle stuff, which I was wholly unacquainted with until I had heard it first from him; so that Jack-pudding ever us'd to do: which though I knew before, I gave him yet the Part, because I knew him so acceptable to most o'th' lighter Periwigs about the Town, and he indeed did vex me so, I could almost be angry: Yet, but Reader, you remember, I suppose, a fusty piece of Latine that has past from hand to hand this thousand years they say (and how much longer I can't tell) in favour of the dead. I intended him a habit much more notably ridiculous, which if ever it be important was so here, for many of the Scenes in the three last Acts depended upon the mistakes of the Colonel for Haunce, which the ill-favour'd likeness of their Habits is suppos'd to cause. Lastly my Epilogue was promis'd me by a Person who had surely made it good, if any, but he failing of his word, deput'd one, who has made it as you see, and to make out your penyworth you have it here. The Prologue is by misfortune lost. Now, Reader, I have eas'd my mind of all I had to say, and so sans farther compliment, Adieu.

6. John Dryden, 'A Discourse Concerning the Original and Progress of Satire' (1693)

There has been a long dispute among the modern critics, whether the Romans derived their satire from the Grecians, or first invented it themselves. Julius Scaliger and Heinsius are of the first opinion; Casaubon, Rigaltius, Dacier and the publisher of the Dauphin's Juvenal maintain the latter. If we take satire in the general signification of the word, as it is used in all modern languages for an invective, it is certain that it is almost as old as verse; and though hymns, which are praises of God, may be allowed to have been before it, yet the defamation of others was not long after it. After God had cursed Adam and Eve in Paradise, the husband and wife excused themselves by laying the blame on one another, and gave a beginning to those conjugal dialogues in prose, which the poets have perfected in verse. The third chapter of Job is one of the first instances of this poem in Holy Scripture, unless we will take it higher, from the latter end of the second – where his wife advises him to curse his Maker.

Scaliger the father will have it descend from Greece to Rome; and derives the word satire from Satyrus, that mixed kind of animal; or, as the ancients thought him, rural god, made up betwixt a man and a goat; with a human head, hooked nose, pouting lips, a bunch or struma under the chin, pricked ears, and upright horns; the body shagged with hair, especially from the waist, and ending in a goat, with the legs and feet of that creature. But Casaubon and his followers, with reason condemn this derivation, and prove that from Satyrus, the word *satira*, as it signifies a poem, cannot possibly descend. For *satira* is not properly a substantive but an adjective, to which the word *lanx*, in English a charger or large platter, is understood, so that the Greek poem, made according to the manner of a satyr, and expressing his qualities, must properly be called satirical, and not satyr. And thus far it is allowed that the Grecians had such poems; but that they were wholly different in species from that to which the Romans gave the name of satyr.

I will not insist on this opinion, but rather judge in general, that since all poetry had its original from religion, that of the Grecians and Romans had the same beginning: both were invented at festivals of thanksgiving: and both were prosecuted with mirth and raillery, and rudiments of verse; amongst the Greeks, by those who represented satyrs; and amongst the Romans by real clowns.

But what is yet more wonderful, that most learned critic takes notice also, in his illustrations on the first episode of the second book, that as the poetry of the Romans, and that of the Grecians, had the same beginning, at feasts of thanksgiving, as it has been observed: and the old comedy of the Greeks which was invective, and the satire of the Romans which was of the same nature, were begun on the very same occasion, so the fortune of both, in process of time, was just the same; the old comedy of the Grecians was forbidden, for its too much license in exposing of particular persons, and the rude satire of the Romans was also punished by a law of the Decemviri […].

And here it will be proper to give the definition of the Greek satiric poem, from Casaubon, before I leave this subject. The satiric, says he, is a dramatic poem, annexed to a tragedy; having a chorus, which consists of satyrs; the persons represented in it are illustrious men; the action of it is great; the style is partly serious, and partly jocular; and the event of the action most commonly is happy.

The Grecians, besides these satiric tragedies, had another kind of poem, which they called Silli; which were more of kin to the Roman satire; those Silli were indeed invective poems, but of a different species from the Roman poems of Ennius, Pacuvius, Lucilius, Horace, and the rest of their successors. They were so called, says Casaubon in one place, from Silenus, the foster-father to Bacchus; but in another place, bethinking himself better, he derives their name from their scoffing and petulancy. From some fragments of the Silli, written by Timon, we may find, that they were satiric poems, full of parodies; that is, of verses patched up from great poets, and turned into another sense than their author intended them. Such among the Romans is the famous Cento of Ausonius, where the words are Virgil's; but by applying them to another sense, they are made the relation of a wedding. Of the same manner are our songs, which are turned into burlesque, and the serious words of the author perverted into a ridiculous meaning.

[...] Diomedes, the grammarian, in effect says this: "Satire, among the Romans, but not among the Greeks, was a biting invective poem, made after the model of the ancient comedy for the reprehension of vices: such as were the poems, which were composed of several sorts of verses: such as were made by Ennius and Pacuvius: more fully expressing the etymology of the word satire, from *satura*, which we have observed."

This is what I have to say in general of satire: only, as Dacier has observed before me, we may take notice that the word satire is of a more general significance in Latin, than in French, or English. For amongst the Romans it was not only used for those discourses which decried vice, or exposed folly; but for others also, where the very name of satire is formidable to those persons, who would appear to the world, what they are not in themselves. For in English, to say satire, is to mean reflection, as we use that word in the worse sense; or as the French call it, more properly, *médisance*. In the criticism of spelling it ought to be with *i* and not with *y* to distinguish its true derivation from *satura*, not from *Satyrus*. And if this be so, then it is false spelled throughout this book; for here it is written satyr. Which having not considered at the first, I thought it not worth afterwards. But the French are more nice, and never spell it any other way than satire.

That former sort of satire, which is known in England by the name of lampoon, is a dangerous sort of weapon, and for the most part unlawful. We have no moral right on the reputation of other men. It is taking from them what we cannot restore to them. There are only two reasons for which we may be permitted to write lampoons; and I will not promise that they can always justify us: the first is revenge, when we have been affronted in the same nature, or have been any ways notoriously abused, and can make ourselves no other reparation. And yet we know, that, in Christian charity, all offenses are to be forgiven, as we expect the like pardon for those which we daily commit against Almighty God. And this consideration has often made me tremble when I was saying our Saviour's prayer; for the plain condition of forgiveness which we beg, is the pardoning of others the offenses which they have done to us: for which reason I have many times avoided the commission of that fault, even when I have been notoriously provoked. Let not this, my Lord, pass for vanity in me; for it is truth. More libels have been written against me, than almost any man now living: and I had reason on my side, to have defended my own innocence; I speak not on my poetry, which I have wholly given up to the critics; let them use it as they please; posterity, perhaps, may be more favourable to me: for interest and passion will lie buried in another age; and partiality and prejudice be forgotten. I speak of my morals, which have been sufficiently aspersed; that any sort of reputation ought to be dear to every honest man, and is to me. But let the world witness for me, that I have been often wanting to myself in that particular; I have seldom answered any scurrilous lampoon, when it was in my power to have exposed my enemies: and, being naturally vindicative, have suffered in silence, and possessed my soul in quiet.

Anything, though never so little, which a man speaks of himself, in my opinion, is still too much; and therefore I will waive this subject and proceed to give the second reason, which may justify a poet, when he writes against a particular person: and that is, when he is become a public nuisance. And those, whom Horace in his satires, and Persius and Juvenal have mentioned in theirs, with a brand of infamy, are wholly such. It is an action of virtue to make examples of vicious men. They may and ought to be upbraided with their crimes and follies: both for their own amendment, if they are not yet incorrigible, and for the terror of others, to hinder them from falling into those enormities, which they see are so severely punished in the persons of others. The first reason was only an excuse for revenge; but this second is absolutely of a poet's office to perform: but how few lampooners are there now living who are capable of this duty? When they come in my way, it is impossible sometimes to avoid reading them. But, good God! how remote they are, in common justice, from the choice of such persons as are the proper subject of satire! and how little wit they bring, for the support of their injustice! The weaker sex is their most ordinary theme; and the best and fairest are sure to be the most severely handled. Amongst men, those who are prosperously unjust, are entitled to panegyric; but afflicted virtue is insolently stabbed with all manner of reproaches; no decency is considered, no fulsomeness omitted; no venom is wanting, as far as dullness can supply it: for there is a perpetual dearth of wit; a barrenness of good sense and entertainment. The neglect of the readers will soon put an end to this sort of scribbling. There can be no pleasantry where there is no wit: no impression can be made, where there is no truth for the foundation.

Nature: how easy it is to call rogue and villain, and that wittily! But how hard to make a man appear a fool, a blockhead, or a knave, without using any of those opprobrious terms! To spare the grossness of the names, and to do the thing yet more severely, is to draw a full face, and to make the nose and cheeks stand out, and yet not to employ any depth of shadowing. This is the mystery of that noble trade, which yet no master can teach to his apprentice: he may give the rules, but the scholar is never the nearer in his practice. Neither is it true, that this fineness of raillery is offensive. A witty man is tickled while he is hurt in this manner; and a fool feels it not. The occasion of an offence may possibly be given, but he cannot take it. If it be granted, that in effect this way does more mischief; that a man is secretly wounded, and though he be not sensible himself, yet the malicious world will find it out for him: yet there is still a vast difference betwixt the slovenly butchering of a man, and the fineness of a stroke that separates the head from the body, and leaves it standing in its place.

As in a play of the English fashion, which we call a tragic-comedy, there is to be but one main design: and, though there be an under-plot, or second walk of comical characters and adventures, yet they are subservient to the chief fable, carried along under it, and helping to it; so that the drama may not seem a monster with two heads. Thus the Copernican system of the planets makes the moon to be moved by the motion of the earth, and carried about her orb, as a dependant of hers. Mascardi, in his discourse of the "Doppia favola," or double tale in plays, gives an instance of it, in the famous pastoral of Guarini, called "Il Pastor Fido"; where Corsica and the satire are the under-parts; yet we may observe that Corsica is brought into the body of the plot, and made subservient to it. It is certain that the divine wit of Horace was not ignorant of this rule, that a play, though it consists of many parts, must yet be one in action, and must drive on the accomplishment of one design; for he gives this very precept, "Sit quodvis simplex duntaxat et unum"; yet he seems not so much to mind it in his satires, many of them consisting of more arguments than one; and the second without dependence on the first. Casaubon has served without dependence on the first. Casaubon has observed this before me, in his preference of Persius to Horace: and will have his own beloved author to be the first, who found out, and introduced this method of confining himself to one subject. I know it may be urged in defence of Horace, that this unity is not necessary; because the very word *satura* signifies a dish plentifully stored with all variety of fruit and grains.

In general all virtues are everywhere to be praised and recommended to practice; and all vices to be reprehended, and made either odious or ridiculous: or else there is a fundamental error in the whole design.

I have already declared who are the only persons that are the adequate object of private satire, and who they are that may properly be exposed by name for public examples of vice and follies: and therefore I will trouble your Lordship no further with them. Of the best and finest manner of satire, I have said enough in the comparison betwixt Juvenal and Horace; it is that sharp, well-mannered way of laughing at folly out of countenance, of which your Lordship is the best master of in this age. I will proceed to the versification, which is most proper for it, and add somewhat to what I have said already on that subject. The sort of verse which is called burlesque, consisting of eight syllables, or four feet, is that which our excellent Hudibras has chosen. I ought to have mentioned him before, when I spake of Donne; but by a slip of an old man's memory, he was forgotten. The worth of his poem is too well known to need any commendation, and he is above my censure: his satire is of the Varronian kind, though unmixed with prose. The choice of his numbers is suitable enough to his design, as he has managed it: but in any other hand, the shortness of his verse, and the quick returns of rhyme, had debased the dignity of style. And besides, the double rhyme (a necessary companion of burlesque writing) is not so proper for manly satire, for it turns earnest too much to jest, and gives us a boyish kind of pleasure. It tickles awkwardly with a kind of pain, to the best sort of readers; we are pleased ungratefully, and, if I may say so, against our liking. We thank him not for giving us that unreasonable delight, when we know he could have given us better, and more solid.

7. Jeremy Collier, *A Short View of the Immorality and Profaneness of the English Stage* (1698)

[… That the contemporary stage is harmful to public good] I shall endeavour to prove by showing the misbehaviour of the stage with respect to morality and religion. Their liberties in the following particulars are intolerable, namely their smuttiness of expression; their swearing, profaneness and lewd application of scripture; their abuse of the clergy; their making their top characters libertines, and giving them success in their debauchery.

[On indecent language:] […] among the curiosities of this kind we may reckon Mrs. Pinchwife, Horner and Lady Fidget in *The Country Wife* (by William Wycherly); Widow Blackacre and Olivia in *The Plain Dealer* (also by Wycherly). These, though not all the exceptionable characters, are the most remarkable. I'm sorry the author should stoop his wit thus low, and use his understandings so unkindly. Some people appear coarse and slovenly out of poverty; they can't well go to the charge of sense. They are offensive, like beggars, for want of the necessaries. But this is none of the *Plain Dealer's* case; he can afford his muse a better dress when he pleases. (pp. 3–4)

[On "smut" as a camouflage for lack of ideas or talent:] Smuttiness is a fault in behaviour as well as religion. 'Tis a very coarse diversion, the entertainment of those who are generally the least both in sense and station; the looser part of the mob have no true relish of decency and honour, and want education and thought, to furnish out a gentle conversation! Barrenness of fancy often makes them up with those scandalous liberties. A vicious imagination may blot a great deal of paper at this rate with ease enough; and 'tis possible convenience may sometimes invite to the expedient. The modern poets seem to use smut as old ones did machines, to relieve a fainting imagination. When *Pegasus* is jaded and would stand still, he is apt, like other *Tits*, to run into every puddle.

The *Double Dealer* [by Congreve] is particularly remarkable. There are but four ladies in this play, and three of the biggest of them are whores. A great compliment to quality, to tell them there is not above a quarter of them honest!

[On sexual jokes with double meanings:] They have sometimes not so much as the poor refuge of a double meaning to fly to. So that you are under the necessity either of taking ribaldry or nonsense. And when the sentence has two handles, the worst is generally turned to the audience. The matter is so contrived that the smut and scum of the thought rises uppermost; and, like a picture drawn to sign, looks always upon the company.

[Ancient comedy was much less obscene:] Notwithstanding the latitudes of paganism, the Roman and Greek theaters were much more inoffensive than ours. To begin with Plautus: this comedian, tho' the most exceptionable, is modest on the comparison. He rarely gives any of the above mentioned liberties to women; and when there are any instances to the contrary, 'tis only in prostituted and vulgar people – and even these don't come up to the grossness of the modern stage. [...] Several of our single plays shall far outdo all this put together. [...] These Roman lasses are mere Vestal Virgins, comparatively speaking.

The Stage-poets make their principal characters vicious, and reward them at the end of the play. To put lewdness into a thriving condition, to give it an equipage of quality, and to treat it with ceremony and respect, is the way to confound the understanding, to fortify the charm, and to make the mischief invincible. [...] The stage seems eager to bring matters to this issue. [...] If this be not their aim, why is lewdness so much considered in character and success? Why are their favorites atheistical, and their fine gentlemen debauched? [...] Wildblood [in Dryden, *The Mock Astrologer*] sets up for debaucher, ridicules marriage, and swears by Mahomet. Bellamy [in *The Mock Astrologer*] makes sport with the devil, and Lorenzo [in Dryden, *Spanish Friar*] is vicious and calls his father "bawdy magistrate." Horner [in Wycherly, *The Country Wife*] is horridly smutty, and Harcourt false to his friend who used him kindly. In *The Plain Dealer* Freeman talks coarsely, cheats the widow, debauches her son, and makes him undutiful. [...] These sparks generally marry the top ladies, and those that do not are brought to no penance, but go off with the character of fine gentlemen. [...] To sum up the evidence: a fine gentleman is a fine whoring, swearing, smutty, atheistical man. These qualifications, it seems, complete the idea of honour. They are the top improvements of fortune, and the distinguishing glories of birth and breeding! [...]

8. Anthony Ashley Cooper, third Earl of Shaftesbury, 'The Freedom of Wit and Humour', from *Sensus Communis: An Essay on the Freedom of Wit and Humour* (1709)

Section 1

When in conversation the other day I spoke in defence of raillery, you were surprised; and I have been thinking about why. Is it possible that you have supposed me to be such a grave person that I would dislike all conversation of this kind? Or were you afraid that if you put me to the test by the use of raillery I would fail? I must confess that you had reason enough for your caution if you thought me to be basically such a true zealot that I couldn't bear the least raillery on my own opinions. I know there are many people like that. Anything that they think is grave or solemn must, they hold, be treated only in a grave and solemn way; though they don't mind treating differently anything that others think—they are eager to try the edge of ridicule against any opinions except their own. Is it fair for them to take this attitude? Isn't it just and reasonable to handle our own opinions as freely as we do other people's? To be sparing with our own opinions may be regarded as a piece of selfishness. We might be accused of willful ignorance and blind idolatry, for having taken opinions on trust and consecrated in ourselves certain idol-notions that we won't allow to be unveiled or seen in day light.

The items that we carefully tuck away in some dark corner of our minds may be monsters rather than divinities or sacred truths; the spectres can impose on us if we refuse to turn them every way and view their shapes and complexions in every light. Something that can be shown only in a certain light is questionable. Truth, they say, can stand any light; and one of the principal lights [...] by which things are to be viewed in order to evaluate them thoroughly is ridicule itself, i.e. the form of test through which we discover whatever is vulnerable to fair raillery in any subject. [...] So I want you to know fully what my views are regarding this, so that you can judge whether I was sincere the other day in defending raillery, and can still plead for those able friends of ours who are often criticised for their humour of this kind, and for the freedom they take in this airy way of conversing and writing.

Section 2

Seriously, thinking about how this species of wit is sometimes employed, and how excessively some of our contemporaries have been using it lately, one may be a little confused and unsure what to think of the practice or where this rallying frame of mind will eventually take us. It has passed from the men of pleasure to the men of business. Politicians have been infected with it, so that grave affairs of state have been treated with an air of irony and banter. The ablest negotiators have been known as the most notable clowns; the most celebrated authors have shown themselves as the greatest masters of burlesque.

There is indeed a kind of defensive raillery (if I may so call it) which I am willing enough to allow—in affairs of any kind—when the spirit of inquiry would force a discovery of more truth than can conveniently be told, and the raillery is a device for heading off inquiry. In some contexts the worst harm we can do to truth is to discover too much of it. It's the same with understandings as with eyes: for a given size and structure just so much light is necessary, and no more; anything beyond that brings darkness and confusion. It is real humanity and kindness to hide strong truths from tender eyes. And it is easier and more civil to do this by pleasant humour than by a harsh denial or by remarkable Reserve. But to work at confusing men by creating mysteries, and getting advantage or pleasure from the perplexity you are throwing them into by such uncertain talk, is as mean when it is done through raillery as when it is done with the greatest seriousness in a solemn attempt to deceive. It may still be necessary, as it was long ago, for wise men to speak in parables with a double meaning, so that the enemy will be confused and only those who have ears to hear will hear. (This echoes Matthew 13:9, where Jesus, after presenting a parable, says 'Who hath ears to hear, let him hear'.) But it is certainly a mean, impotent, and dull sort of 'wit' that confuses everyone and leaves even one's friends unsure what one's real opinions are on the topic in question.

This is the crude sort of raillery that is so offensive in good company. And indeed there's as much difference between the two sorts of raillery as between fair-dealing and hypocrisy, or between the most genteel wit and the most scurrilous clowning. But this illiberal kind of wit will lose its credit—i.e. will be exposed for the low device that it is—by freedom of conversation. That is because wit is its own remedy; its true value is settled by free trade in it; the only danger is setting up an embargo. The same thing happens here as in the case of trade: tariffs and restrictions reduce trade to a low ebb; nothing is as advantageous to it as a free port. We have seen in our own time the decline and ruin of a false sort of wit that delighted our ancestors so much that their poems and plays, as well as their sermons, were full of it. All humour involved some sort of play on words; the very language of the royal court was full of puns. But now such word-play is banished from the town and from all good company; there are only a few signs of it in the country; and it seems at last to have been restricted to the schools, as the chief entertainment of teachers and their pupils. Other kinds of wit will also improve in our hands, and humour will refine itself, as long as we take care not to tamper with it and hold it down by severe discipline and rigorous prohibitions. Everything that is civilised in conversation is due to liberty: we polish one another, and rub off our corners and rough sides by a sort of friendly collision. To restrain this is inevitably to cause men's understandings to rust. It is to destroy civility, good breeding, and even charity itself, under a pretence of maintaining it.

9. Richard Blackmore, *Essay upon Wit* (1716)

Since the Power of Wit is so prevalent, and has obtained such Esteem and Popularity, that a Man endow'd with this agreeable Quality, is by many look'd on as a Heavenly Being, if compar'd with others, who have nothing but Learning and a clear arguing Head; it will be worth the while to search into its Nature, and examine its Usefulness, and take a View of those fatal Effects which it produces, when it happens to be misapply'd.

Tho perhaps the Talent which we call Wit, like that of Humour, is as clearly under-stood by its simple Term, as by the most labour'd Description; an Argument or which is this, That many ingenious Persons, by their unsuccessful Essays to explain it, have rather obscur'd than illustrated its Idea; I will notwithstanding adventure to give the Definition of it, which tho it may fall short of Perfection, yet I imagine, will come nearer to it, than any that has yet appear'd. *Wit is a Qualification of the Mind, that raises and enlivens cold Sentiments and plain Propositions, by giving them an elegant and surprizing Turn.*

It is evident, that Wit cannot essentially consist in the Justness and Propriety of the Thoughts, that is, the Conformity of our Conceptions to the Objects we conceive; for this is the Definition of Truth, when taken in a Physical Sense; nor in the Purity of Words and Expression, for this may be eminent in the Cold, Didactick Stile, and in the correct Writers of History and Philosophy. But Wit is that which imparts spirits to our Conceptions and Diction, by giving them a lively and novel, and therefore an agreeable Form: And thus its Nature is limited and diversify'd from all other intellectual Endowments. Wit therefore is the Accomplishment of a warm, sprightly, and fertile Imagination, enrich'd with great Variety of proper Ideas; which active Principle is however under the Direction of a regular Judgment, that takes care of the Choice of just and suitable Materials, prescribes to the tighter Facilities the due Bounds of their Sport and Activity, and assists and guides them, while they imprint on the Conceptions of the Mind their peculiar and delightful Figures. The Addition of Wit to proper Subjects, is like the artful Improvement of the Cook, who by his exquisite Sauce gives to a plain Dish, a pleasant and unusual Relish. A Man of this Character works on simple Proportions a rich Embroidery of Flowers and Figures, and imitates the curious Artist, who studs and inlays his prepar'd Steel with Devices of Gold and Silver. But Wit is not only the Improvement of a plain Piece by intellectual Enameling; besides this, it animates and warms a cold Sentiment, and makes it flow with Life and Vigor; and this it effects, as is express'd in the last Part of the Definition, by giving it as elegant [*sic*] and surprizing Turn. It always conveys the Thought of the Speaker or Writer cloath'd in a pleasing but foreign Dress, in which it never appear'd to the Hearer before, who however had been long acquainted with it; and this Appearance in the Habit of a Stranger must be admirable, since Surprize naturally arises from Novelty, as Delight and Wonder result from Surprize; which I have more fully explained in the former Essay.

As to its efficient Cause, Wit owes its Production to an extraordinary and peculiar Temperament in the Constitution of the Possessors of it, in which is found a Concurrence of regular and exalted Ferments, and an Affluence of Animal Spirits refin'd and rectify'd to a great degree of Purity; whence being endow'd with Vivacity, Brightness and Celerity, as well in their Reflexions as direct Motions, they become proper Instruments for the sprightly Operations of the Mind; by which means the Imagination can with great Facility range, the wide Field of Nature, contemplate an infinite Variety of Objects, and by observing the Similitude and Disagreement of their several Qualities, single out and abstract, and then suit and unite those Ideas, which will best serve its purpose. Hence beautiful Allusions, surprizing Metaphors and admirable Sentiments are always ready at hand: And while the Fancy is full of Images collected from innumerable Objects and their different Qualities, Relations and

Habitudes, it can at pleasure dress a common Notion in a strange, but becoming Garb; by which, as before observ'd, the same Thought will appear a new one, to the great Delight and Wonder of the Hearer. What we call Genius results from this particular happy Complexion in the first Formation of the Person that enjoys it, and is Nature's Gift, but diversify'd by various specifick Characters and Limitations, as its active Fire is blended and allay'd by different Proportions of Phlegm, or reduc'd and regulated by the Contrast of opposite Ferments. Therefore as there happens in the Composition of a facetious Genius a greater or less, tho still an inferior degree distinguished from another. That Distinction that seems common to Persons of this Denomination, is an inferior Degree of Wisdom and Discretion; and tho these two Qualities, Wit and Discretion, are almost incapable of a friendly Agreement, and will not, but with great Difficulty, be work'd together and incorporated in the Constitution of any Individual; yet this Observation is not so conspicuous in any, as in those, whose native distemper'd Elevation of the Spirits: Nothing is more common, than to see Persons of thise Class always Think the same Time to be pity'd for their want of Prudence and common Sense; abounding with excellent Maxims and instructive Sentiments, which however are not of the least Use to themselves in the Conduct of their Lives. And hence it is certain, that tho the Gentlemen of a pleasant and witty Turn of Mind often make the industrious Merchant, and grave Persons of all Professions, the Subjects of their Raillery, and expose them as stupid Creatures, not supportable in good Company; yet these in their Turn believe they have as great a right, as indeed they have, to reproach the others for want of Industry, good Sense, and regular Oecomony, much more valuable Talens than those, which any mere Wit can boast of, and therefore wise Parents, who from a tender Concern for the Honour and Happiness of their Children, earnestly desire they may excel in intellectual Endowments, should, instead of refin'd Parts and a Genius turn'd for pleasant Conversation, wish them a solid Understanding and a Faculty of close and clear Reasoning, these Qualifications being likely to make them good Men, and the other only good Companions.

The Objects about which Wit is exercis'd, are the common and less important Actions of Life. It is the Province of the Civil Magistrate to make Laws against enormous Crimes and great Immoralities, and by punishing Offenders, to deter men from the like Trangressions; but they take no notice of lower Errors, either because they have not such noxious Influence on the State, or because it is impossible to foresee and enumerate their numberless Classes, and prevent their Growth; Where then the Legislator ends, the Comick Genius begins, and presides over the low and ordinary Affairs and Manners of Life. It extends its Power and Jurisdiction over the wide Field of inferior Faults and ridiculous Follies, over the Districts of Indiscretion, Indecency, and Impertinence, and is Visitor of the Regions void of Discipline, Politeness, and Civility.

Wit is employ'd in its own Province, when the Possessor of it exercises his Genius on the ordinary Customs and Manners of Life, either in Conversation, or Comick Writing. It has therefore no place in the Works where severe Knowledge and Judgment are chiefly exercis'd; those superior Productions of the Understanding must be express'd in a clear and strong manner, without intervening Strains of Wit or facetious Fancies, which, were they admitted, would appear incongruous and impertinent, and diminish the Merit of the Writing. Hence Wit has no place in History, Philology, Philosophy, or in the greater Lyrick or Epick Poems; the two last of which containing either the Praises of Deities or Demi-Gods, or treating of lofty and illustrious Subjects; such as the Foundation, Rise, and Revolution of Kingdoms, Commotions of State, Battles, Triumphs, solemn Embassies, and various other important Actions of Princes and Heroes, are exalted above the Sphere of Wit and Humour. The Strength and Dignity of the sublime Stile is debas'd and adulterated by the foreign and improper Mixture of light Sentiments, and pretty Fancies. These Sallies and Sports of the Imagination, will no more advance the Beauty of such superior Productions, than the Addition of glittering Tinsel and glass Beads will improve the Imperial Purple, or adorn the Crowns of great Monarchs. And therefore we see, with what judicious Care *Virgil* has avoided this Error; how clear are his celebrated Writings from the least sprinkling of Wit and pleasant Conceits, which corrupt the Purity, debase the Majesty, and sully the Lustre of the greater Species of Poetry? And as the Gravity and Chastness of the sublime Stile, in the Works last mention'd, will not endure the gay Ornaments of Fancy; so does that light Dress more misbecome the pious and wise Discourses, that come from either the Pulpit or the Press. Wit is so far from being a Grace or Improvement of Divine Eloquence, that on the contrary, it destroys its Dignity, breaks its Force, and renders it base and puerile.

But this excellent and amiable Qualification of the Mind is too apt to be abus'd and perverted to ill purposes. Instead of being ingag'd on the Side of Vertue, and us'd to promote just Notions and Regularity of Life, it is frequently employ'd to expose the most Sacred Things, to turn Gravity and reserv'd Behavior into Ridicule, to keep in Countenance Vice and Irreligion, and with a petulant and unrestrain'd Liberty, to deride the Principles and Practices of the wisest and best of Men. The Conversation of ingenious Libertines generally turns upon Revel'd Religion and the venerable Teachers of it; or on those of the Laity, who seem most sincere in the Belief of Christianity, and express the greatest Conformity in their Actions to the Precepts of it. Nothing gives so high a Seasoning to their Raillery, and more improves the Taste of their Jests, than some sharp and pointed Ingredients, that wound Religion and the Professors of it; whereof some are made the Entertainment of the Company by these facetious Scoffers, and expos'd as Persons fetter'd with Prepossessions, and biass'd by Notions of Vertue, deriv'd from Education and the early Instructions of canting Parents. Others are represented as indebted for their Piety to the Prevalency of the Spleen, and an immoderate mixture of Melancholy in their Complexion, which, say they, give to the Mind a superstitious Turn, and fill the Head with religious Chimeras, frightful Phantomes of Guilt, and idle Fears of imaginary Punishments; while others are ridicul'd as Men of a cold and phleg-matick Complexion, without Spirit and native Fire; who derive, say they, their Vertue, not from Choice or Restraint of Appetite, but from their deadness and indisposition to Pleasure; not from the Power of their Reason, but the Weakness of their Passions. It would be endless to enumerate the various Ways which the atheistical Wit and merry Libertine employ, to take off all Veneration of Religion, and expose its Adherents to publick Derision. This is certainly the greatest Abuse of Wit imaginable. In all the Errors and monstrous Productions of Nature, can any appear more deform'd than a Man of Parts, who employs his admirable Qualities in bringing Piety into Contempt, putting Vertue to the Blush, and making Sobriety of Manners the common Subject of his Mirth; while with Zeal and Industry, he propagates the malignant Contagion of Vice and Irreligion, poisons his Friends and Admirers, and promotes the Destruction of his native Country? And if these foolish Wits and ingenious Madmen could reflect, they would soon be convinc'd, that while they are engaged against Religion they hurt themselves; and that Wit and Humour thus misapply'd, will prove but a wretched Compensation for their want of Vertue.

Tho the Persons addicted to this impious Folly, expose the sacred Mysteries of Christianity, and make its Votaries the common Topick of their Raillery, it cannot thence be concluded, that they are certain that those whom they thus deride, as whimsical, stupid, and deluded Men, have not the least Reason to support their Religious Principles and Practice; for if they were sure of this, they would treat such unhappy Persons as Men rob'd of their Senses, with Tenderness and Compassion; for none will allow such distemper'd Minds to be proper Subjects of Ridicule and Derision; But those, who attentively observe the Manner and Air of these jesting Libertines, when they laugh at Vertue, will plainly see their licentious Mirth springs from other Principles; either from this, That the Example of many Persons, who in earnest embrace and profess the Articles of Religion, continually disturbs their Opinion of themselves, and creates severe Misgivings and Distrust in their Minds, lest their Notions about

Religion should not be true, when they observe, that many Persons of eminent Parts, superior Reason and Erudition, maintain with Zeal quite contrary Sentiments; or else it proceeds from their Hatred of Men of Vertue, founded in the Dissimilitude of Dispositions and Manners, and Disagreements in Interest, Employments and Designs; or from an Envy of their great Merit, innocent Life, and worthy Actions, which from the prevailing Power of their own vicious Inclinations, they are unable to imitate; for after all their Raillery and Expressions of Contempt, Vertue has that native Lustre and amiable Appearance, that will compel Men secretly to esteem it, even while they deride the Possessors of it. Such is the Pride and Vanity of degenerate Nature, that loose Men will always endeavor to level the eminent Characters of religious and sober Persons, and reduce them to the inferior Degree of their own; And for that end, they will labour to sink the Opinion and Esteem of any Excellence or Merit, to which themselves can make no Pretence. While they cannot equal the bright Example of Vertue in others, they strive to sully or efface it, and by turning it into Ridicule, make it seem rather the Dishonour and Deformity, than the Beauty and Perfection of the Mind: And if they can disgrace Religion, and subvert all moral Distinction, Men will be valu'd only for their intellectual Endowments, and then they imagine they have gain'd their Point, since the Superiority of Wit, as they suppose, is on their Side. These seem to me the genuine and natural Causes, why Men of great Parts and extraordinary Wit, but of loose Principles and immoral Lives, who above all others affect Popularity and gasp after Applause, take so much Pleasure, without the least regard to Modesty and Decency, in a Christian Country to mock Religion and jerk with spiteful Satire Men of Vertue and inoffensive Behavior.

Wit is likewise misapply'd, when exercis'd to ridicule any unavoidable Defects and Deformities of Body or Mind; for since nothing is a moral Blemish, but as it is the Effect of our own Choice, nothing can be disgraceful but what is voluntary, and brought freely upon our selves; and since nothing is the proper Object of Raillery and Ridicule, but what is shameful, it must be a Violence to Reason and Humanity, to reproach and expose another for any thing that was not in his Power to escape. And therefore to make a Man contemptible, and the Jest of the Company, by deriding him for his mishapen Body, ill figur'd Face, stammering Speech, or low Degree of Understanding, is a great abuse of ingenious Faculties.

Nor is it a less criminal Use of this Talent, when it is exercis'd in lascivious and obscene Discourses. The Venom is not less, but more infectious and destructive, when convey'd by artful Insinuation and a delicate Turn of Wit; when impure Sentiments are express'd by Men of a heavy and gross Imagination, in direct and open Terms, the Company are put out of Countenance, and nauseate the Coarseness of the Conversation: but a Man of Wit gilds the Poison, dresses his wanton Thoughts in a beautiful Habit, and by slanting and side Approaches, possesses the Imagination of the Hearers, before his Design is well discover'd; by which means he more effectually gains admission to the Mind, and fills the fancy with immodest Ideas.

Nothing can be more ill-manner'd, or disagreeable to Persons of Vertue and Sobriety of Manners, than wanton and obscene Expressions; on which Subject the excellent Archbishop *Tillotson* has the following Paragraph: 'Nothing that trespasses upon the Modesty of the Company, and the Decency of Conversation, can become the Mouth of a wise and vertuous Person. This kind of Conversation would fain pass for Wit among some sort of Persons, to whom it is acceptable; but whatever savours of Rudeness and Immodesty, and Ill-Manners, is very far from deserving that Name; and they that are sober and vertuous cannot entertain any Discourse of this kind, with Approbation and Acceptance. A well bred Person will never offend in this way. And therefore it cannot but be esteem'd as an Affront to modest Company, and a rude presuming upon their Approbation, impudently taking it for granted, that all others are as lewd and dissolute as themselves.'

No doubt a Comedy may be so contriv'd, that it may at once become delightful, and promote Prudence and Sobriety of Manners; that is, when the Characters are well chosen, justly delineated, and every where distinguish'd; when the various Manners are exactly imitated and carry'd on with Propriety and Uniformity; when the principal Action contains an instructive Moral, and all the Parts in a regular Connexion, Dependence and Proportion, illustrate and support each other, and have a manifest Influence on the main Event; When the Incidents are well imagin'd, and result from the Manners of the Dramatick Persons, when the Turns are surprizing, the Knots or Obstructions natural and unconstrain'd, and the unraveling of them, tho unforeseen, yet free and easy; and when the Diction is pure, proper and elegant, as well as chaste and inoffensive to the modest and vertuous Hearers. So regular and beautiful a Piece as this cannot but greatly please and divert, as well as instruct the Audience. Nor is it, I imagine, from want of Knowledge of the Rules of Writing, nor of sufficient Genius, in which this Nation abounds, that so few Comedies, distinguish'd by these Perfections, have been produc'd: But this Defect arises partly from this, that the Comick Poets are often Men of loose Manners, and therefore unlikely Persons to undertake the Promotions and Encouragement of Vertue, of which they have no Taste, and to discountenance Imprudence and Immorality, when by doing so, they must expose their own Character to derision; tho sometimes it may happen, that a loose Poet as well as Preacher, merely from his just Manner of Thinking, and his Sense of Decency in forming Discourses becoming his Character, may entertain the Audience with laudable Performances.

Another, and the chief Cause of the Immorality of the Theatre, is the ill Taste of the People, who, notwithstanding they have applauded several clean and regular Tragedies, such as those which have of late, appear'd that are worthy of the greatest Commendation, especially *Cato* and the Plays for the most part of Mr. *Row*, as great a Genius for Tragedy as any Nation in any Age has produc'd, yet still frequent and encourage the loosest Comedies. It happens, that the greatest part of Men of Wit and Humour, who not being easy in their Fortunes, work for the Stage, and are Day-Labourers to the Muses, lie under a Necessity of bringing those Productions to Market, which are in Fashion, and therefore vendible; while others, tho of ever so much greater Value, would be turn'd back upon their Hands; nor would the Actors, who live by their Employment, as the Comick Writers do by theirs, undertake to represent an Innocent, and much less a Comedy of yet higher Merit.

Tho several Assaults have been made upon the Comick Poets in Fashion, and many Batteries have been rais'd against the Theatre, yet hitherto they have prov'd unsuccessful; the Stage is become Impregnable, where loose Poets, supported by Numbers, Power, and Interest, in Defiance of all Rules of Decency and Vertue, still provide new Snares and Temptations to seduce the People, and corrupt their Manners. Notwithstanding the earnest Cries of this great City, that importune these Writers to reform the Theatre, and no longer to infest her Youth, and draw their Inclinations from their Professions and Employments; notwithstanding the Sighs and Tears of many once flourishing, but now disconsolate Families, ruin'd by the dissolute Lives of their chief Branches, who lost their Vertue by frequenting the fatal Entertainments of the Theatre; notwithstanding the wise and sober part of the Kingdom earnestly sollicit them to spare the People, to stop the spreading Plague and slay the destroying Pen, they persevere with intrepid Resolution and inexorable Cruelty, to poison the Minds, and ruin the Morals of the Nation.

The great Archbishop *Tillotson* has set our present Theatre in a true Light in his Discourse upon *Corrupt Communication*:

"I shall only speak a few words concerning Plays, which as they are now order'd among us, are a mighty Reproach to the Age and Nation.

"To speak against them in general, may be thought too severe, and that which the present Age cannot so well brook, and would not perhaps be so just and reasonable; because it is very possible they might be so fram'd and govern'd by such Rules, as not only to be innocently diverting, but instructing and useful, to put some Vices and Follies out of Countenance, which cannot perhaps be so decently reprov'd, nor so effectually expos'd and corrected any other way. But as the Stage now is, they are intollerable, and not fit to be permitted in a civiliz'd, much less a Christian Nation. They do most notoriously minister both to Infidelity and Vice. By the Profaneness of them, they are apt to instil bad Principles into the Minds of Men, and to lessen that awe and reverence which all Men ought to have for God and Religion: and by their Lewdness they teach Vice, and are apt to infect the Minds of Men, and dispose them to lewd and dissolute Practices.

"And therefore I do not see how any Persons pretending to Sobriety and Vertue, and especially to the pure and holy Religion of our Blessed Saviour, can, without great Guilt, and open Contradiction to his holy Profession, be present at such lewd and immodest Plays, much less frequent them, as too many do, who yet would take it very ill to be shut out of the Communion of Christians, as they would most certainly have been in the first and purest Ages of Christianity."

And not only wise and sober Men have declar'd their detestation of the Immorality of the Stage, but eminent Poets themselves, who have written the most applauded Comedies, have own'd, that the Theatre stands in great need of Restraints and Regulation, and wish'd that Plays were compil'd in such an inoffensive Manner, that not only discreet and vertuous Persons of the Laity, but a Bishop himself, without being shock'd, might be present while they were acted. Mr. *Dryden* has, up and down in his Prefatory Discourses and Dedications, freely aeknowledg'd the Looseness of our Dramatick Entertainments, which sometimes he charges upon the Countenance given to it by the dissolute Court of King *Charles* the Second, and sometimes upon the vitiated Taste of the People. In his Dedication of *Juvenal*, made *English*, to the late famous Earl of *Dorset*, he thus bespeaks him; "As a Counsellor bred up in the Knowledge of the Municipal and Statute Laws may honestly inform a just Prince how far his Prerogative extends, so I may be allow'd to tell your Lordship, who by an indisputed Title are the King of Poets, what an Extent of Power you have, and how lawfully you may exercise it over the petulant Scriblers of the Age. As Lord Chamberlain, you are absolute by your Office, in all that belongs to the Decency and good Manners of the Stage; You can banish thence Scurrility and Profaneness, and restrain the licentious Insolence of the Poets and their Actors, in all things that shock the publick Quiet or the Reputation of private Persons, under the Notion of *Humour*." Hence it evidently appears, that Mr *Dryden* look'd on the Decency of the Stage to be violated in his Time, by licentious and insolent Poets; and I wish I could say, that there is less

Reason of Complaint in ours; In a Copy of Verses, publish'd in one of the Volumes of the Miscellany Poems, the same celebrated Author inveighs against the Lewdness and Pollutions of the Stage in the strongest Expressions that can be conceiv'd; and in his latter days, when his Judgment was more Mature, he condemns all his loose and profane Writings to the Flames, which, he says, they justly deserve: Which is not only a free and ingenious Confession of his Fault, but a considerable Mark of Repentance, and worthy to be imitated by his Successors, who have broken in upon the Rules of Vertue and Modesty in the like manner.

Tho all Men of Vertue, who wish well to Mankind, and are zealous for the Happiness of their Country, cannot but observe the mischievous Effects of these licentious Dramatick Compositions, yet they will find it very difficult to suggest an effectual Remedy for the Cure of so obstinate an Evil. The ingenious *Spaniard* mention'd before, for stopping the Progress of this contagious Lewdness in his Country, propos'd to the Government, that an Officer or Inspector might be establish'd, with Authority to peruse and correct the Poet's Writings, and that no Comedies should be presented to the Publick without his Licence and Approbation.

The Clergy lie under such manifest Obligations to attack publick Immorality, wherever it is found, and by whatsoever Patrons of Power, Dignity, and Interest it is shelter'd and supported, that, as I have suggested, it is not easy to imagine whence their Lenity and Tenderness for the Theatre can proceed. But if the true Reason of it, whatever it is, and which is so hard to be accounted for, were remov'd, and our Divines would interest themselves with Zeal in the Cause of Vertue, in respect to our Dramatick Entertainments, as they espouse and defend it in all other Instances, I cannot believe that the Stage, without a Regulation, would be able to stand, when batter'd with Vigor from the Pulpit. The Poets and Players would soon find themselves oblig'd to restrain their licentious Conduct, reform the Theatre, and present to the Town, if not instructive, at least inoffensive and unshocking Diversions. And it is very desirable, that this Expedient were set on foot, that the Honour of the English Theatre may be retriev'd; that while we justly boast of our Priority in Wit and Humour to our Neighbours, we may not be oblig'd to acknowledge the great Inferiority of our Comedies, in respect of Cleanness and moral Beauty: that we may not be reproach'd, that while we profess a Reform'd and pure Religion, we encourage an immodest and unreform'd Theatre, and that we are very defective in the Practice of Vertue and Regularity of Manners, while these Abominations are indulg'd, and these unhallow'd Groves and High Places of Immorality are frequented without Disturbance.

10. Henry Fielding, selections from the Preface to *Joseph Andrews* (1742)

Now a comic romance is a comic epic-poem in prose; differing from comedy, as the serious epic from tragedy: its action being more extended and comprehensive; containing a much larger circle of incidents, and introducing a greater variety of characters. It differs from the serious romance in its fable and action, in this: that as in the one these are grave and solemn, so in the other they are light and ridiculous; it differs in its characters, by introducing persons of inferior rank, and consequently of inferior manners, whereas the grave romance, sets the highest before us; lastly in its sentiments and diction, by preserving the ludicrous instead of the sublime. In the diction I think, burlesque itself may be sometime admitted; of which many instances will occur in this work, as in the descriptions of battles, and some other places, not necessary to be pointed out to the classical reader; for whose entertainment those parodies or burlesque imitations are chiefly calculated.

But tho' we have sometimes admitted this in our diction, we have carefully excluded it from our sentiments and characters; for there it is never properly introduced, unless in writings of the burlesque kind, which this is not intended to be. Indeed, no two species of writing can differ more widely than the comic and the burlesque: for as the latter is ever the exhibition of what is monstrous and unnatural, and where our delight, if we examine it, arises from the surprising absurdity, as in appropriating the manners of the highest to the lowest, or *e converso*; so in the former, we should ever confine ourselves strictly to nature from the just imitation of which, will flow all the pleasure we can this way convey to a sensible reader. And perhaps, there is one reason, why a comic writer should of all others be the least excused for deviating from nature, since it may not be always so easy for a serious poet to meet with the great and the admirable; but life every where furnishes an accurate observer with the ridiculous.

I have hinted this little, concerning burlesque; because, I have often heard that name given to performances, which have been truly of the comic kind, from the author's having sometimes admitted it in his diction only; which as it is the dress of poetry, doth like the dress of men establish characters, (the one of the whole poem, and the other of the whole man,) in vulgar opinion, beyond any of their greater excellencies: but surely, a certain drollery in style, where the characters and sentiments are perfectly natural, no more constitutes the burlesque, than an empty pomp and dignity of words, where every thing else is mean and low, can entitle any performance to the appellation of the true sublime.

And I apprehend, my Lord Shaftesbury's opinion of mere burlesque agrees with mine, when he asserts, 'There is no such thing to be found in the writings of the antients.' But perhaps, I have less abhorrence than he professes for it: and that not because I have had some little success on the stage this way; but rather, as it contributes more to exquisite mirth and laughter than any other; and these are probably more wholesome physic for the mind, and conduce better to purge away spleen, melancholy and ill affections, than is generally imagined. Nay, I will appeal to common observation, whether the same companies are not found more full of good-humour and benevolence, after they have been sweeten'd for two or three hours with entertainments of this kind, than when soured by a tragedy or a grave lecture.

But to illustrate all this by another science, in which, perhaps, we shall see the distinction more clearly and plainly: let us examine the works of a comic history-painter, with those performances which the Italians call *caricatura*; where we shall find the true excellence of the former, to consist in the exactest copying of nature; insomuch, that a judicious eye instantly rejects any thing *outré*; any liberty which the painter hath taken with the features of that *alma mater*. – Whereas in the *caricatura* we allow all license. Its aim is to exhibit monsters, not men; and all distortions and exaggerations whatever are within its proper province.

Now what *caricatura* is in painting, burlesque is in writing; and in the same manner the comic writer and painter correlate with each other. And here I shall observe, that as in the former, the painter seems to have the advantage; so it is in the latter infinitely on the side of the writer: for the *monstrous* is much easier to paint than describe, and the *ridiculous* to describe than paint.

And tho' perhaps this latter species doth not in either science so strongly affect and agitate the muscles as the other; yet it will be owned, I believe, that a more rational and useful pleasure arises to us from it. He who should call the ingenious Hogarth a burlesque painter, would, in my opinion, do him very little honour: for sure it is much easier, much less the subject of admiration, to paint a man with a nose, or any other feature of a preposterous size, or to expose him in some absurd or monstrous attitude, than to express the affections of men on canvas. It hath been thought a vast commendation of a painter, to say his figures *seem to breathe*; but surely, it is a much greater and nobler applause, *that they appear to think*.

But to return – the ridiculous only, as I have before said, falls within my province in the present work. – Nor will some explanation of this word be thought impertinent by the reader, if he considers how wonderfully it hath been mistaken, even by writers who have profess'd it: for to what but such a mistake, can we attribute the many attempts to ridicule the blackest villanies; and what is yet worse, the most dreadful calamities? What could exceed the absurdity of an author, who should write *The Comedy of Nero, with the merry Incident of ripping up his Mother's Belly;* or what would give a greater shock to humanity, than an attempt to expose the miseries of poverty and distress to ridicule? And yet, the reader will not want much learning to suggest such instances to himself.

Besides, it may seem remarkable, that Aristotle, who is so fond and free of definitions, hath not thought proper to define the ridiculous. Indeed, where he tells us it is proper to comedy, he hath remarked that villany is not its object: but he hath not, as I remember, positively asserted what is. Nor doth the Abbe Bellegarde, who hath writ a treatise on this subject, tho' he shews us many species of it, once trace it to its fountain.

The only source of the true ridiculous (as it appears to me) is affectation. But tho' it arises from one spring only, when we consider the infinite streams into which this one branches, we shall presently cease to admire at the copious field it affords to an observer. Now affectation proceeds from one of these two causes, vanity, or hypocrisy: for as vanity puts us on affecting false characters, in order to purchase applause; so hypocrisy sets us on an endeavour to avoid censure by concealing our vices under an appearance of their opposite virtues. And tho' these two causes are often confounded, (for there is some difficulty in distinguishing them) yet, as they proceed from very different motives, so they are as clearly distinct in their operations: for indeed, the affectation which arises from vanity is nearer to truth than the other; as it hath not that violent repugnancy of nature to struggle with, which that of the hypocrite hath. It may be likewise noted, that affectation doth not imply an absolute negation of those qualities which are affected: and therefore, tho', when it proceeds from hypocrisy, it be nearly allied to deceit; yet when it comes from vanity only, it partakes of the nature of ostentation: for instance, the affectation of liberality in a vain man, differs visibly from the same affectation in the avaricious; for tho' the vain man is not what he would appear, or that not the virtue he affects, to the degree he would be thought to have it; yet it sits less awkwardly on him than on the avaricious man, who *is* the very reverse of what he would *seem* to be.

From the discovery of this affectation arises the ridiculous – which always strikes the reader with surprise and pleasure; and that in a higher and stronger degree when the affectation arises from hypocrisy, than when from vanity; for to discover anyone to be the exact reverse of what he affects, is more surprising, and consequently more ridiculous, than to find him a little deficient in the quality he desires the reputation of. I might observe that our Ben Jonson, who of all men understood the *ridiculous* the best, hath chiefly used the hypocritical affectation.

Now from affectation only, the misfortunes and calamities of life, or the imperfections of nature, may become the objects of ridicule. Surely he hath a very ill-framed mind, who can look on ugliness, infirmity, or poverty, as ridiculous in themselves: nor do I believe any man living who meets a dirty fellow riding through the streets in a cart, is struck with an idea of the ridiculous from it; but if he should see the same figure descend from his coach and six, or bolt from his chair with his hat under his arm, he would then begin to laugh, and with justice. In the same manner, were we to enter a poor house, and behold a wretched family shivering with cold and languishing with hunger, it would not incline us to laughter (at least we must have very diabolical natures, if it would): but should we discover there a grate, instead of coals, adorned with flowers, empty plate or china dishes on the side-board, or any other affectation of riches and finery either on their persons or in their furniture; we might then indeed be excused, for ridiculing so fantastical in appearance. Much less are natural imperfections the objects of derision: but when ugliness aims at the applause of beauty, or lameness endeavours to display agility; it is then that these unfortunate circumstances, which at first moved our compassion, tend only to raise our mirth.

The poet carries this very far;

None are for being what they are in fault,
But for not being what they would be thought.

Where if the metre would suffer the word *ridiculous* to close the first line, the thought would be rather more proper. Great vices are the proper objects of our detestation, smaller faults of our pity: but affectation appears to me the only true source of the ridiculous.

But perhaps it may be objected to me, that I have against my own rules introduced vices, and of a very black kind into this work. To which I shall answer: First, that it is very difficult to pursue a series of human actions and keep clear from them. Secondly, that the vices to be found here, are rather the accidental consequences of some human frailty, or foible, than causes habitually existing in the mind. Thirdly, that they are never set forth as the objects of ridicule but destination. Fourthly, that they are never the principal figure at the time on the scene; and lastly, they never produce the intended evil.

11. Samuel Johnson, 'The Difficulty of Defining Comedy', *The Rambler* (1751)

Comedy has been particularly unpropitious to definers; for though perhaps they might properly have contented themselves, with declaring it to be such a dramatick representation of human life, as may excite mirth, they have embarrassed their definition with the means by which the comick writers attain their end, without considering that the various methods of exhilarating their audience, not being limited by nature, cannot be comprised in precept. Thus, some make comedy a representation of mean and others of bad men; some think that its essence consists in the unimportance, others in the fictitiousness of the transaction. But any man's reflections will inform him, that every dramatick composition which raises mirth, is comick; and that, to raise mirth, it is by no means universally necessary, that the personages should be either mean or corrupt, nor always requisite, that the action should be trivial, nor ever, that it should be fictitious.

If the two kinds of dramatick poetry had been defined only by their effects upon the mind, some absurdities might have been prevented, with which the compositions of our greatest poets are disgraced, who, for want of some settled ideas and accurate distinctions, have unhappily confounded tragick with comick sentiments. They seem to have thought, that as the meanest of personages constituted comedy, their greatness was sufficient to form a tragedy; and that nothing was necessary but that they should crowd the scene with monarchs, and generals, and guards; and make them talk, at certain intervals, of the downfall of kingdoms, and the rout of armies. They have not considered, that thoughts or incidents, in themselves ridiculous, grow still more grotesque by the solemnity of such characters; that reason and nature are uniform and inflexible: and that what is despicable and absurd, will not, by any association with splendid titles, become rational or great; that the most important affairs, by an intermixture of an unseasonable levity, may be made contemptible; and that the robes of royalty can give no dignity to nonsense or to folly.

"Comedy," says Horace, "sometimes raises her voice"; and Tragedy may likewise on proper occasion abate her dignity; but as the comick personages can only depart from their familiarity of style, when the more violent passions are put in motion, the heroes and queens of tragedy should never descend to trifle, but in the hours of ease, and intermissions of danger.

12. Oliver Goldsmith, 'A Comparison between Laughing and Sentimental Comedy' (1773)

Essay XXVII[17]

A comparison between laughing and sentimental comedy

The theatre, like all other amusements, has its fashions and its prejudices; and when satiated with its excellence, mankind begin to mistake change for improvement. For some years tragedy was the reigning entertainment; but of late it has entirely given way to comedy, and our best efforts are now exerted in these lighter kinds of composition. The pompous train, the swelling phrase, and the unnatural rant are displaced for that natural portrait of human folly and frailty of which all are judges, because all have sat for the picture.

But as in describing nature it is presented with a double face, either of mirth or sadness, our modern writers find themselves at a loss which chiefly to copy from; and it is now debated whether the exhibition of human distress is likely to afford the mind more entertainment than that of human absurdity.

Comedy is defined by Aristotle to be a picture of the frailties of the lower part of mankind, to distinguish it from tragedy, which is an exhibition of the misfortune of the great. When comedy therefore ascends to produce the characters of princes or generals upon the stage, it is out of its walk, since low life and middle life are entirely its object. The principal question, therefore, is, whether in describing low or middle life an exhibition of its follies be not preferable to a detail of its calamities? Or, in other words, which deserves the preference – the weeping sentimental comedy, so much in fashion at present, or the laughing and even low comedy, which seems to have been last exhibited by Vanburgh and Cibber?[18]

If we apply to authorities, all the great masters in the dramatic art have but one opinion. Their rule is, that as tragedy displays the calamities of the great, so comedy should excite our laughter by ridiculously exhibiting the follies of the lower part of mankind. Boileau, one of the best modern critics, asserts that comedy will not admit of tragic distress:

> "Le comique, ennemi des soupirs et des pleurs,
> N'admet point dans ses vers de tragiques doulers."

---

[17] From the *Westminster Magazine* for 1778 (vol. i. p. 4), introduced into the volume of Essays published in 1797 by Isaac Reed, and included by Percy in the Miscellaneous Works of 1801.

[18] "The undertaking of a comedy not merely sentimental was very dangerous; and Mr. Colman, who saw the piece in its various stages, always thought it so." – Goldsmith, *Dedication to Dr. Johnson of "She Stoops to Conquer."*

Nor is this rule without the strongest foundation in nature, as the distresses of the mean by no means affect us so strongly as the calamities of the great. When tragedy exhibits to us some great man fallen from his height, and struggling with want and adversity, we feel his situation in the same manner as we suppose he himself must feel, and our pity is increased in proportion to the height from whence he fell. On the contrary, we do not so strongly sympathize with one born in humbler circumstances, and encountering accidental distress: so that while we melt for Belisarius, we scarce give halfpence to the beggar who accosts us in the street. The one has our pity, the other our contempt. Distress, therefore, is the proper object of tragedy, since the great excite our pity by their fall; but not equally so of comedy, since the actors employed in it are originally so mean that they sink but little by their fall.

Since the first origin of the stage, tragedy and comedy have run in distinct channels, and never till of late encroached upon the provinces of each other. Terence, who seems to have made the nearest approaches, yet always judiciously stops short before he comes to the downright pathetic; and yet he is even reproached by Caesar for wanting the *vis comica*. All other comic writers of antiquity aim only at rendering folly or vice ridiculous, but never exalt their characters into buskined pomp, or make what Voltaire humorously calls "a tradesman's tragedy."

Yet notwithstanding this weight of authority, and the universal practice of former ages, a new species of dramatic composition has been introduced under the name of *sentimental comedy*, in which the virtues of private life are exhibited, rather than the vices exposed; and the distresses rather than the faults of mankind make our interest in the piece. These comedies have had of late great success, perhaps from their novelty, and also from their flattering every man in his foible. In these plays almost all the characters are good, and exceedingly generous; they are lavish enough of their *tin* money on the stage; and though they want humor, have abundance of sentiment and feeling. If they happen to have faults or foibles, the spectator is taught not only to pardon, but to applaud, them, in consideration of the goodness of their hearts; so that folly, instead of being ridiculed, is commended, and the comedy aims at touching our passions, without the power of being truly pathetic. In this manner we are likely to lose one great source of entertainment on the stage; for while the comic poet is invading the province of the tragic muse, he leaves her lovely sister quite neglected. Of this, however, he is no way solicitous, as he measures his fame by his profits.

But it will be said that the theatre is formed to amuse mankind, and that it matters little, if this end be answered, by what means it is obtained. If mankind find delight in weeping at comedy, it would be cruel to abridge them in that or any other innocent pleasure. If those pieces are denied the name of comedies, yet call them by another name, and if they are delightful, they are good. Their success, it will be said, is a mark of their merit, and it is only abridging our happiness to deny us an inlet to amusement.

These objections, however, are rather specious than solid. It is true that amusement is a great object of the theatre; and it will be allowed that these sentimental pieces do often amuse us; but the question is, whether the true comedy would not amuse us more? The question is, whether a character supported throughout a piece, with its ridicule still attending, would not give us more delight than this species of bastard tragedy, which only is applauded because it is new?

A friend of mine, who was sitting unmoved at one of the sentimental pieces, was asked how he could be so indifferent? "Why, truly," says he, "as the hero is but a tradesman, it is indifferent to me whether he be turned out of his counting-house on Fish Street Hill, since he will still have enough left to open shop in St. Giles's."

The other objection is as ill-grounded; for though we should give these pieces another name, it will not mend their efficacy. It will continue a kind of mulish production, with all the defects of its opposite parents, and marked with sterility. If we are permitted to make comedy weep, we have an equal right to make tragedy laugh, and to set down in blank-verse the jests and repartees of all the attendants in a funeral procession.

But there is one argument in favor of sentimental comedy which will keep it on the stage in spite of all that can be said against it. It is of all others the most easily written. Those abilities that can hammer out a novel are fully sufficient for the production of a sentimental comedy. It is only sufficient to raise the characters a little: to deck out the hero with a ribbon or give the heroine a title; then to put an insipid dialogue, without character or humor, into their mouths; give them mighty good hearts, very fine clothes; furnish a new set of scenes; make a pathetic scene or two with a sprinkling of tender melancholy conversation through the whole; and there is no doubt but all the ladies will cry and all the gentlemen applaud.

Humor, at present, seems to be departing from the stage; and it will soon happen that our comic players will have nothing left for it but a fine coat and a song. It depends upon the audience whether they will actually drive those poor merry creatures from the stage, or sit at a play as gloomy as at the tabernacle. It is not easy to recover an art when once lost; and it would be but a just punishment that when, by our being too fastidious, we have banished humor from the stage, we should ourselves be deprived of the art of laughing.

13. Immanuel Kant, 'Comparison of the Aesthetic Value of the Various Fine Arts', from *Critique of Judgment*, translated by Werner S. Pluhar (1790)

As we have frequently shown, there is an essential difference between *what we like when we merely judge it*, and what *gratifies* us (i.e., what we like in sensation). The second is something that, unlike the first, we cannot require of everyone. Gratification (even if its cause happens to like in ideas) seems always to consist in a feeling that a person's life is being furthered generally [*gesamt*], and [this feeling] thus includes furtherance of his bodily well-being, i.e., his health. To this extent, then, when *Epicurus* claimed that all gratification is basically bodily sensation, he was perhaps not mistaken but only misunderstood himself in including intellectual and even practical liking among the gratifications. If we bear this latter distinction in mind, we can explain how a gratification can be disliked by the very person who feels it (for example the joy felt by a needy but upright person at being made the heir of his loving but stingy father), or how profound grief may yet be liked by the person suffering it (as a widow's sadness over the death of her worthy husband), or how a gratification may be liked in addition (as our gratification in the sciences we pursue), or how a pain (such as hatred, envy, or a thirst for revenge) may be disliked on addition. The liking or disliking in these cases is based on reason and is the same as *approval or disapproval*. Gratification and pain, on the other hand, can rest only on the feeling of being well or unwell (whatever the cause), or on the prospect of possibly being so.

Any changing free play of sensations (that are not based on an intention) gratifies us, because it furthers our feeling of health, and it does not matter whether in our rational judgment we like the object of this play, or like the gratification itself. [...] The play of *thought* arises merely from the change of presentation in judgment; although it produces no thought that carries any interest with it, it does quicken the mind.

How gratifying such play must be, without our having to assume an underlying interested intention, is shown by all our evening parties; for without play almost none of them could keep itself entertained. But many affects are at play there—hope, fear, joy, anger, and scorn, alternating constantly—and are so lively that they amount to an inner motion that seems to further all the vital processes in the body, as is proved by how sprightly the mind becomes as a result, even though nothing has been won or learned. But since the play of chance is not beautiful play, we shall here set it aside. But music and something to laugh about are two kinds of play with aesthetic ideas, or for that matter with presentations of the understanding, by which in the end nothing is thought; it is merely the change they involve that still enables them to gratify us in a lively way. This shows rather clearly that in both of them the quickening is merely bodily, even though it is aroused by ideas of the mind, and shows that all the gratification [we find] at a lively party, extolled as being so refined and inspired consists [merely] in the feeling of health that is produced by an intestinal agitation corresponding to such play. It is not our judging of the harmony we find in tones or in flashes of wit—this harmony, with its beauty, merely serves as a necessary vehicle—but the furtherance of the vital processes in the body, the affect that agitates the intestines and the diaphragm, in a word the feeling of health (which we cannot feel without such promptings), which constitutes the gratification we find in the fact that we can reach the body through the soul as well, and use the soul as the physician of the body.

In music this play proceeds from bodily sensation to aesthetic ideas (of the objects of affects), and from these back again [to the body], but with the force exerted on the body concentrated [*vereinigt*]. In jest (which, just as much as music, deserves to be considered more an agreeable than a fine art) the play starts from thoughts, all of which, as far as they seek sensible expression, engage the body also. In the exhibition involved in jest, the understanding, failing to find what it expected, suddenly relaxes, so that we feel the effect of this slackening in the body by the vibration of our organs, which helps restore their equilibrium and has a beneficial influence on our health.

Whatever is to arouse lively, convulsive laughter must contain something absurd (hence something that the understanding cannot like for its own sake). *Laughter is an affect that arises if a tense expectation is transformed into nothing.* This same transformation certainly does not gladden the understanding, but indirectly it still gladdens us in a very lively way for a moment. So the cause of this must consist both in the influence that the presentation has on the body and in the body's reciprocal effect on the mind—but not because the presentation is objectively an object of our gratification (for how could an expectation that turned out to be false gratify us?), but solely because it is a mere play of presentations which produces in the body an equilibrium of the vital forces.

Suppose someone tells us this story: An Indian at an Englishman's table in Surat saw a bottle of ale being opened, and all the beer, turned out to froth, rushing out. The Indian, by repeated exclamations, showed his great amazement.—Well, what's so amazing in that? asked the Englishman.—Oh, but I'm not amazed at its coming out, replied the Indian, but at how you managed to get it all in.—This makes us laugh, and it gives us a hearty pleasure. This is not because, say, we think we are smarter than this ignorant man, nor are we laughing at anything that is to our liking and that we noticed through our understanding. It is rather that we had a tense expectation that suddenly vanished, [transformed] into nothing. Or suppose that the heir of a rich relative wants to arrange for him a very solemn funeral service, but complains that things are not quite working out: For (he says), the more money I give my mourners to look grieved, the more cheerful they look.—This evokes ringing laughter in us, and the reason is that we have an expectation that is suddenly transformed into nothing, not into the positive opposite of an expected object, for that is always something and may frequently grieve us. For if someone tells us a story that arouses great expectations in us, but at the close we see immediately that it is untrue, this arouses our dislike. An example of this is the story about people whose hair is said to have turned grey overnight from great grief. Suppose, on the other hand, that in response to a story like this some rogue gives us a longwinded account of the grief of some merchant who, during his return trip from India to Europe, with all his fortune in merchandise, was forced by a heavy storm to throw everything overboard, and whose grief was such that whose grief was such that [it made his *wig* turn grey that very night.—This will make us laugh; and] it gratifies us because we treat our own mistake in reaching for some object that is otherwise indifferent to us, or rather the idea we had been pursuing, as we might a ball: we continue to knock it back and forth for a while, even though all we mean to do is seize [it] and hold on to [it]. What arouses our gratification here is not that we are dismissing someone as a liar or a fool. For even on its own account the latter story, told with an assumed seriousness, would make a party roar with laughter, whereas dismissing someone as a liar or a fool would not ordinarily merit attention.

It is noteworthy that in all such cases the joke must contain something that can deceive us for a moment. That is why, when the illusion vanishes, [transformed] into nothing, the mind looks at the illusion once more in order to give it another try, and so by a rapid succession of tension and relaxation the mind is bounced back and forth and made to sway; and such swaying, since whatever was stretching the string, as it were, snapped suddenly (rather than by a gradual slackening), must cause a mental agitation and an inner bodily agitation in harmony with it, which continues involuntarily, and which gives rise to fatigue while yet also cheering us up (these are the effects of a[n] inner motion conducive to our health).

For if we assume that all our thoughts are, in addition, in a harmonious connection with some agitation in the body's organs, then we can pretty well grasp how, as the mind suddenly shifts alternately from one position to another in order to contemplate its object, there might be a corresponding alternating tension and relaxation of the elastic parts of our intestines that is communicated to the diaphragm (such as ticklish people feel). The lungs, meanwhile, rapidly and intermittently expel air, and so give rise to an agitation that is conducive to our health. It is this agitation alone, and not what goes on in the mind, that is the actual cause of our gratification in a thought [by] which [we] basically present nothing. Voltaire said that heaven has given us two things to counterbalance the many hardships in life: *hope* and *sleep*. He might have added *laughter*, if only the means for arousing it in reasonable people were as easy to come by, and if the wit or whimsical originality needed for it were not just as rare, as the talent is common for people to write, as mystical ponderers do, things that *break your head*, or to write, as geniuses do, things that *break your neck*, or to write, as sentimental novelists do (also, I suppose, sentimental moralists), things that *break your heart*.

It seems to me, therefore, that Epicurus may certainly be granted that all gratification, even if it is prompted by concepts that arouse aesthetic ideas, is animal (i.e., bodily) sensation. For granting this does not in the least impair the intellectual feeling of respect for moral ideas, which is not gratification but self-esteem (of the humanity within us) elevating us above the need for gratification—and indeed does not impair even the less noble feeling of taste.

[...]

The *whimsical* manner may also be included with whatever is cheerful and closely akin to the gratification derived from laughter, and which belongs to originality of intellect, but which certainly does not belong to the talent for fine art. For *whimsicality*, in its favorable sense, means the talent enabling us to put ourselves at will into a certain mental disposition, in which everything is judged in a way quite differently from the usual ones (even vice versa), but yet is judged in conformity with certain principles of reason [present] in such a mental attunement. A person who is subject to such changes involuntarily is moody [*launisch*]. But someone who can adopt them at will and purposively (so as to enliven his description of something by means of a contrast arousing laughter) is called whimsical [*launig*], as is also the way he conveys [his thoughts]. However, this manner belongs more to agreeable than to fine arts, because the object of fine art must always show itself as having some dignity; and so an exhibition of it requires a certain seriousness, just as taste does when it judges the object.

14. Jean Paul Richter, 'On the Ridiculous' and 'The Comic in Drama' (1804)

'Definition of The Ridiculous'

The ridiculous has always resisted the definitions of philosophers except by accident, because the sense of the ridiculous takes on as many forms as there are deformities; it alone among feelings has a subject matter as inexhaustible as the multitude of crooked lines. Cicero and Quintilian found the ridiculous refractory to any description; this Proteus is dangerous in his metamorphoses for anyone who would bind him. Even the modern Kantian definition, according to which the ridiculous arises from a sudden resolution of expectation into nothing, has much to be said against it. First, not every resolution into nothing is ridiculous, not one which is immoral, rational, spiritual, or pathetic because of pain or pleasure. Second, people often laugh when the expectation of nothing is resolved by something. Third, every expectation is immediately left behind at the threshold of perfectly humorous moods and presentations. Finally, this formula better describes the epigram and a certain kind of wit which pairs the great with the small, but which in itself awakens no laughter, any more than does the juxtaposition of a seraph and worm. And if a laugh did result, this would hurt more than help the definition, since the effect is the same if the worm comes before the seraph.

Kant's explanation is just as indefinite and hence just as true as if I said that the ridiculous consists in the sudden resolution of the expectation of something serious into a ridiculous nothing. The old definition by Aristotle, who will never be surpassed as the Argos of perception and the Geryon of erudition, is at least on the right road to the goal, if not at the goal itself: The ridiculous stems from harmless incongruity. But such incongruity in animals or in the insane is not comic; nor is the greatest absurdity of whole peoples, like that of the Kamtschadals, who represent their god Kutka as worshipping his own frozen excrement as a goddess of beauty before it thaws. Flögel professes to find a comic effect in Linguet's notion that bread is poisonous, in Rousseau's preference for savage life, or in the opinion of the dull contemptible dreamer Postel that his Venetian whore Johanna was the redeemer of women. But how can such errors, with which every library teems without therefore becoming a *théâtre aux italiens* or *des variétés amusantes*, be given the attraction of comic beauty unless by artistic endowment? Wrong, as Flögel is to consider as comic mere spiritual absurdity without embodiment, he is equally wrong to consider as comic physical absurdity without spiritualization. Thus he finds ridiculous the juxtaposition of a relief of Christ's Passion and a juggler's dance, or a Negro on horseback and a Roman emperor with a double nose, in the collection of the Prince of Pallagonia in Palermo, known as the "Hell" Breughel of sculpture. But the spiritual meaning is lacking in these sculptural distortions of reality, as it is in that caricature of man, the animal.

The acute reviewer of the *School* in the *Jena Literary Journal* attributes the comic to a disruption of complete understanding. Since, however, there are several kinds of such interruptions, ranging from serious error to madness, one must first distinguish the comic from every other type through a definition of the comic itself (more later about the ingenious objections of this reviewer). Schiller explains comic poetry as a degradation of the object to a position below reality itself. But the distance which raises the serious ideal so inaccessibly far above reality does not apply inversely to the comic, since reality itself harbors the comic. The fool of the stage at times appears unaltered in life, while the tragic hero never does. And how should a dislocated, degraded reality please us, when the natural prosaic reality already saddens us? In any case, since degradation to a position below reality also appears in the serious poet's treatment of the sinner, it cannot provide the essential distinction of the comic.

The modern definition by A. W. Schlegel, Schelling, and Ast of the comic as "the representation of ideal infinite freedom, thus of the negative infinite life or of the infinitely determinable and of free will," I leave here to do battle with one more useful for the artist, the quite recent definition by Stephan Schütze, which explains the comic as the perception of conflict between necessity and freedom, with necessity victorious. But since sickness, impotence, unmerited poverty, and the defeat of nobility by numbers show the victory of necessity often without any comic effect, its comic force must first be assured through distinguishing marks.

But why wage this prolonged battle against the definitions of others? Set up your own and *if* it is valid, they will die before it on their own, just as eagle feathers destroy other feathers in their proximity. Besides, no author can meet all hostile definitions, even if he has the desire and ability to do so, since so many and perhaps even the majority will come forward and march out against him only after his death, so that finally after he is buried he must trust the entire victory to his own definition.

Besides our definition of the ridiculous, we must also seek something much harder to find: the reason why the ridiculous, although it is the sense of imperfection, still produces pleasure not only in poetry, which gives flowers even to mold and flowering garlands to the coffin, but in arid life itself.

A feeling is best plumbed by inquiring after its opposite. What then is the converse of the ridiculous? Neither the tragic nor the sentimental, as the very expressions "tragicomic" and "sentimental comedy" prove. Shakespeare cultivates his humorous

Northern growths to full height in the midst of the fire of pathos as well as in the frost of comedy. Indeed, a Sterne changes Shakespeare's simple succession of the pathetic and the comic into a *simultaneum* of the two.

But let anyone insert a single comic line from either writer into a heroic epic and the work is dissolved. *Derision*, or moral indignation, is consistent in Homer, Milton, and Klopstock along with the continuation of sublime feeling; but never *laughter*. In brief, the hereditary enemy of the *sublime* is the ridiculous. "Comic heroic poem" is a contradiction in terms; one should speak of a comic epic. The ridiculous consequently is the infinitely small; and what constitutes this ideal smallness?

When a writer of theoretical courses who wishes to analyze the ridiculous begins by dealing with the sublime, his theoretical course readily becomes practical.

The infinitely great which astonishes must have as its opposite something equally small which evokes the opposite feeling.

But in the moral realm nothing is small. Inward morality begets self-respect and respect for others, and inward immorality begets contempt; outward morality awakens love, and outward immorality, hate. The ridiculous is too insignificant for contempt and too good for hate. Thus its only place is in the realm of understanding and, within that, in the lack of understanding, or folly. But in order to evoke any feeling this folly must be perceived sensuously in an action or situation; and that is possible only when the action both represents and belies the rational intention of the understanding as the wrong means to an end, or when the situation both presents and contradicts a certain interpretation of the situation.

We are not yet at that goal. The simply physical cannot be ridiculous, nor the inanimate, except though personification, nor the simple mental, neither pure error nor pure folly. The question then is what physical phenomenon mirrors the mentally ridiculous and what mental phenomenon is ridiculous?

An error in itself is not ridiculous, any more than ignorance. Otherwise the various religious parties and social classes would always find each other ridiculous. The ridiculous must manifest itself in some effort or action. Thus an idolatry which seems serious in concept becomes ridiculous in practice. A healthy man who considered himself to be sick would seem comic to us only in taking significant measures against his distress. The effort and situation must be equally clear in order to raise their contradiction to a comic pitch. But we still have only a clearly expressed finite error; it is not yet infinitely absurd. For no man in any given case can act contrary to his own conception of it. When Sancho suspended himself over a shallow ditch all night because he assumed an abyss gaped beneath him, his effort on this assumption was quite understandable.

And he would have been truly mad if he had risked being dashed to pieces. Why do we nevertheless laugh? Here comes the main point: We lend *our* insight and perspective to *his* effort and produce through this contradiction the infinite absurdity. Our imagination, which here as in the sublime is the mediator between inner and outer realms, is enabled to make this transfer as in the sublime, only by sensuous clarity, in this case, that of the error. It is our self-deception in attributing to the other person a knowledge and motivation contradictory to his effort which produced that minimum of understanding, that perceived nonsense, at which we laugh. As a result, the comic like the sublime never resides in the object, but in the subject.

We can mock or approve one and the same inner and outer action, according to whether or not we project our own insight. No one laughs at the insane patient who believes himself to be a merchant and his doctor his debtor, nor do we laugh at the doctor who tries to cure him. But in Foote's *Cozeners* when this very thing happens (or seems to happen, for the patient is inwardly as rational as the doctor), we do laugh at the real merchant (the patient) who expects payments for real goods from a doctor who had been told by the woman who stole them that the demand for payment is an *idée fixe*. Through the illusion of the comic we attribute *our* knowledge of the woman's deception to the actions of both rational men.

No man's actions can appear ridiculous to himself, except an hour later, when he has already become a second self and can attribute the insights of the second to the first. A man can either respect or scorn himself in the midst of an act which is the appropriate object of either attitude, but he cannot laugh at himself, any more than he can love and hate himself at the same moment. When for the same virtue a genius and a dunce think equally well of themselves (which implies great pride) and when the two make this pride apparent with the same physical signs, although the pride and the signs are the same, we laugh only at the dunce, simply because it is only to him that we lend any extra knowledge. Complete stupidity or lack of understanding does not easily become ridiculous, because it hampers or prohibits the projection of our contrasting insight.

Hence the usual definitions of the ridiculous are false because they suppose only a simple, real contrast, instead of the second, apparent one. The ridiculous being and its deficiency must at least have the appearance of freedom. We laugh only at the more *intelligent* animals which make a personifying, anthropomorphic projection possible. The ridiculous increases with the intelligence of the ridiculous person. The man who raises himself above life and its motives prepares for himself the most sustained comedy, since he can attribute his own higher motives to the lower efforts of the mass and thereby make these absurd. But the most wretched person can reciprocate all this by attributing his own lower motives to the higher effort. A whole mass of courses, learned reporters and reports, and the heaviest bales of the German book trade, which in reality crawl along in an annoying and disgusting way, at once assume wings as works of art if anyone imagines (and thereby lends them higher motives) that they have been written for parodic amusement.

For a *situation* or an *action* to be ridiculous, we must see in the comic subject not only a true contradiction with the external but a fictive internal contrast, although it may often be as difficult to realize this arid rule in the exuberance of our vivid feeling as it is to trace the framework of animal creation, the skeleton of a fish, in every given animal.

For the sake of brevity in the rest of this inquiry let me give the following names to the three elements of the ridiculous or the sensuously perceived infinite lack of under-standing: the contradiction between the effort or existence of the ridiculous being and the sensuously perceived circumstance I call the *objective* contrast; the circumstance itself I call the *sensuous* element; and the second contradiction between the two, which we impose on them by projecting our mind and point of view, I call the *subjective* contrast.

When artificially transfigured, these three elements of the ridiculous must give rise through a shift in emphasis to the various comic modes. Plastic or ancient poetry allows the *objective* contrast between circumstance and sensuous effort to predominate in the comic; the subjective is hidden behind the mime's copy. All imitation was originally mocking; among all peoples drama began with comedy. For the playful imitation of actions inspiring love or fear, a higher stage of history was necessary. And then, the mime more easily aped the comic, with its three elements. Mime rose into poetry. But in the comic, as in the serious, the ancients were true to their plastic objectivity comedy's crown of laurels hung only at their theaters, while moderns hang it elsewhere. The distinction will become more obvious when we investigate the nature of the romantic comic and examine and distinguish satire, humor, irony, and whimsy.

'The Difference between Satire and the Comic'

The realm of satire adjoins that of the comic – the small epigram is the boundary marker – but each realm bears its own inhabitants and fruits. Juvenal, Persius, and their kind express through the lyric serious moral indignation at vice; they make us serious and elevate us. Even the accidental contrasts in their paintings, through their bitterness, shut the mouth to laughter. The comic, on the contrary, carries on its poetic game with the smallness of nonsense and makes us cheerful and free. The immorality mocked is no illusion, but the absurdity ridiculed is half one. Folly is too innocent and ignorant for the blow of satire, just as vice is too ugly for the tickle of laughter, although in folly the immoral side may be derided and in vice the foolishness laughed at. Language itself sharply opposes sarcasm, mockery, lampoons, and derision to jesting, laughter, and merry-making. The satiric as half the moral realm is the smaller, because one cannot mock arbitrarily; the realm of laughter is infinitely large, as large as that of the understanding or of the finite universe, because for every grade of being a subjective contrast can be invented which makes it smaller. In satire we are morally bound, in laughter we are freed poetically. The jest knows no goal but its own existence. The poetic blossom amid its nettles does not prick and one hardly feels the blow of its burgeoning leafy rod. It is an accident if in a genuine comic work any sharp satiric thrust is made; the comic mood is thereby disrupted. When characters in comedies direct serious satires against each other, they interrupt the play by the moral importance which they thereby lend each other.

We are tormented by the simultaneous enjoyment of discordance in works such as Young's *Satires* and Pope's *Duncaid*, which constantly mix satiric indignation with laughing jest, as philosophy frequently fuses reason and understanding. Lyrical writers easily become satiric, e.g., Tacitus, J.J. Rousseau, Schiller in *Don Carlos*, Klopstock, Herder; but epic writers are more readily comic, especially in the forms of irony and stage comedy. The mixture of the satiric and comic has a moral implication and danger. If one laughs at the profane, one makes it a matter of the *understanding*; the sacred will then also be hauled before that improper tribunal. Thus the German and French writers of comedies pervert serious vice into farce. If satire punishes folly, then it is unjust; it calls the *will* guilty, when chance and illusion are alone responsible. Here the English satirists sin.

But the transition between the two and their mixture are easy. The moral wrath of satire must be directed against the two sacraments of the devil, against the dual moral *want* of *love* and of *honor*. In its war against dishonor satire will encounter the *jest*, which wounds the *vanity* of folly in its skirmish with this lack of understanding. The persiflage of worldly fashion, a true mediator between satire and jest, is the child of our time.

Among the theories which derive comic pleasure from mental laughter, that of Hobbes, which derives this pleasure from pride, is the least well founded. First, the feeling of pride is very serious and not at all related to the comic, although it is related to the equally serious feeling of scorn. While laughing one feels less that one is exalted (often perhaps the opposite) than that the other is *lowered*. The comic pleasure of the tickle of self-comparison would have to enter into every perception of another's error and another's degradation, and it would be the more agreeable the higher one stood. But in fact one often feels just the reverse, and another's subjection gives one pain.

And what particular sense of superiority is possible when, as is often true, the object of laughter stands on such a comparatively low, completely incommensurable level, like the ass mentioned above with Philemon, or the physically ridiculous acts of stumbling, squinting, or the like? Laughers are good-humored and often set themselves among the rank and file of those laughed at. Children and women laugh the most; the proud self-comparers the least. The Harlequin who pretends to be nothing laughs at everything; the proud Moslem at nothing. No one is ashamed of having laughed; but anyone would keep more secret such a clear sense of superiority as Hobbes presupposes. Finally, no laugher takes it ill, but rather in good part, when another hundred thousand laugh with him and thus a hundred thousand self-elevations set themselves up around his own. This, however, if Hobbes were right, would be impossible. Among all conceivable societies and fraternities, one composed of none but proud people would be the least tolerable, much worse than a liberal society of misers or even cutthroats.

Pleasure in the ridiculous in *nature* must derive not from the absence, but like any other feeling from the presence of a good element. To explain this pleasure, as some have done, as a retroactive effect of pleasure in the comic in *art* is to derive the mother from her similar but more beautiful daughter. Laughers preceded the writers of comedy. Indeed, comic pleasure like any other may be analyzed by the understanding into several elements according to the context and the influencing circumstances. But in the focal point of feeling itself, all these elements melt together (like the components of glass) into a dense translucent flow. The essence of the comic elements of pleasure is the enjoyment of *three* sequences of thought presented and fixed in a single perception: (1) our own true sequence, (2) the other person's true sequence, and (3) the illusory one attributed by us to the other person. Clarity impels us to an alternating interplay of these three conflicting sequences, but this coercion is lost in gay caprice through their incompatibility. The comic is thus the enjoyment, or imagination and poetry, of the whole understanding released and at liberty, which develops playfully, dancing to and fro along the three syllogistic or flowery chains. *Three* aspects distinguish this enjoyment of the understanding from any other. *First*, no strong feeling intrudes to disturb its free course; the comic glides without friction past the reason and the heart, and the understanding ranges freely in a broad airy realm without meeting any obstacle. This pleasure is left so free that it can carry on its play even with beloved and respected persons without injuring them; for the ridiculous is indeed only a light thrown *from* and *within* us ourselves, and in this mock-light the other person can readily suffer himself to be seen.

The *second* element is the affinity of the comic with wit, but the comic has an advantage over wit and extends its refreshing rule far beyond. Since wit – as unfortunately will be demonstrated extensively in the second little volume of the *School* – is actually perceptible understanding or sensuous acumen, the confusion of it with the comic has been too seductively easy, despite many contradictory examples of a serious and sublime wit and of a comic free of wit. The most important difference between the two is that in wit the understanding explores and enjoys only simple relationships of *things*, while in the comic it enjoys the complex relationships of *persons*. Wit plays with a few intellectual elements, the comic with practical elements as well. In wit the relationships are fleeting and lack a stable basis; in the comic countless relations reside in a single man. His personality can not only give the heart room to play but can give the understanding an even more indefinite and vast arena. To all this the comic adds also the advantage of sensuous vividness. Although mere wit at times appears comic, one must consider that it can derive this power only from a comic environment or atmosphere. When, for example, in Pope's *Rape of the Lock* the heroine worries whether she will "stain her honour, or her new brocade; / Forget her prayers, or miss a masquerade; / Or lose her heart, or necklace, at a ball," the comic force springs only from the point of view of the heroine, not from the pairing of the very heterogeneous objects which are present. In Campe's *Dictionary* the staining of clothes followed by the figurative staining of honor would appear without any comic effect.

A *third* aspect of comic pleasure is the charm of indecision, the tickling effect of the alternation between apparent displeasure (caused by the minimum of another's understanding) and the pleasure in one's own projected insight, which, since it is dependent on our will, touches and teases us the more piquantly. To this extent, therefore, the comic approaches physical tickling, which vibrates like a foolish diphthong or *double entendre* between pain and pleasure. Strangely enough and almost comically, there is one circumstance which coincides allegorically with my definition ridiculous in the first edition of this work, and which I recognize in the second edition for the first time: We feel the physical tickling of our shoulder or our heel half-voluntarily when we imagine ourselves into *another's* finger. Our own finger has no such effect, and if we tickle ourselves with someone else's hand, we feel a fourth of the effect when we move it at our own will, but the whole effect as soon as it moves independently, even though we continue to hold it in our own hand. Such is man, as foolish as the body to which he cleaves.

The ridiculous is therefore the eternal consequence of spiritual finitude. When in the still unpublished twenty-ninth installment of *Walt and Vult*, the flautist *Quod dues vult* complains – although probably more in jest than in earnest – that he often has troubled hours when he imagines too vividly the prospect of being saved and living out eternities, perfect among the perfect, without any of what here below is called jest or sport, the man is surely tormenting himself in vain. The comic illusion of exchanged points of view will still remain and depend on a contemplating as well as contemplated finitude, only it will be a different illusion at a higher level. There will always be an angel to laugh at, even when one is the archangel.

15. William Hazlitt, 'On Wit and Humour' (1819)

On wit and humour

Man is the only animal that laughs and weeps; for he is the only animal that is struck with the difference between what things are, and what they ought to be. We weep at what thwarts or exceeds our desires in serious matters: we laugh at what only disappoints our expectations in trifles. We shed tears from sympathy with real and necessary distress; as we burst into laughter from want of sympathy with that which is unreasonable and unnecessary, the absurdity of which provokes our spleen or mirth, rather than any serious reflections on it.

To explain the nature of laughter and tears, is to account for the condition of human life: for it is in a manner compounded by these two! It is a tragedy or a comedy – sad or merry, as it happens.

To understand or define the ludicrous, we must first know what the serious is. Now the serious is the habitual stress which the mind lays upon the expectation of a given order of events, following one another with a certain regularity and weight of interest attached to them. When this stress is increased beyond its usual pitch of intensity, so as to overstrain the feelings by the violent opposition of good to bad, or of objects to our desires, it becomes the pathetic or tragical. The ludicrous, or comic, is the unexpected loosening or relaxing this stress below its usual pitch of intensity, by such an abrupt transposition of the order of our ideas, as taking the mind unawares, throws it off its guard, startles it into a lively sense of pleasure, and leaves no time nor inclination for painful reflections.

The essence of the laughable then is the incongruous, the disconnecting one idea from another, or the jostling of one feeling against another. The first and most obvious cause of laughter is to be found in the simple succession of events, as in the sudden shifting of a disguise, or some unlooked-for accident, without any absurdity of character or situation. The accidental contradiction between our expectations and the event can hardly be said, however, to amount to the ludicrous: it is merely laughable. The ludicrous is where there is the same contradiction between the object and our expectations, heightened by some deformity or inconvenience, that is, by its being contrary to what is customary or desirable; as the ridiculous, which is the highest degree of the laughable, is that which is contrary not only to custom but to sense and reason, or is a voluntary departure from what we have a right to expect from those who are conscious of absurdity and propriety in words, looks, and actions.

Misunderstandings, *(mal-entendus)* where one person means one thing, and another is aiming at something else, are another great source of comic humour, on the same principle of ambiguity and contrast. There is a high-wrought instance of this in the dialogue between Aimwell and Gibbet, in the "Beaux' Strategem", where Aimwell mistakes his companion for an officer in a marching regiment, and Gibbet takes it for granted that the gentleman is a highwayman. The alarm and consternation occasioned by some one saying to him, in the course of common conversation, "I apprehend you," is the most ludicrous thing in that admirably natural and powerful performance, Mr. Emery's Robert Tyke. Again, unconsciousness in the person himself of what he is about, or of what others think of him, is also a great heightener of the sense of absurdity. It makes it come the fuller home upon us from his insensibility to it. His simplicity sets off the satire, and gives it a finer edge. It is a more extreme case still where the person is aware of being the object of ridicule, and yet seems perfectly reconciled to it as a matter of course. So wit is often the more forcible and pointed for being dry and serious, for it then seems as if the speaker himself had no intention in it, and we were the first to find it out. Irony, as a species of wit, owes its force to the same principle. In such cases it is the contrast between the appearance and the reality, the suspense of belief, and the seeming incongruity, that gives point to the ridicule, and makes it enter the deeper when the first impression is overcome. Excessive impudence, as in the Liar; or excessive modesty as in the hero of "She Stoops to Conquer"; or a mixture of the two, as in the Busy Body, are equally amusing. Lying is a species of wit and humour. To lay any thing to a person's charge from which he is perfectly free, shews spirit and invention; and the more incredible the effrontery, the greater the joke.

There is nothing more powerfully humorous than what is called *keeping* in comic character, as we see it very finely exemplified in Sancho Panza and Don Quixote. The proverbial phlegm and the romantic gravity of these two celebrated persons may be regarded as the height of this kind of excellence. The deep feeling of character strengthens the sense of the ludicrous. Keeping in comic character is consistency in absurdity; a determined and laudable attachment to the incongruous and singular. The regularity completes the contradiction; for the number of instances of deviation from the right line, branching out in all directions, shews the inveteracy of the original bias to any extravagance or folly, the natural improbability, as it were, increasing every time with the multiplication of chances for a return to common sense, and in the end mounting up to an incredible and unaccountably ridiculous height, when we find our expectations as invariably baffled. The most curious problem of all, is this truth of absurdity to itself. That reason and good sense should be consistent, is not wonderful: but that caprice, and whim, and fantastical prejudice, should be uniform and infallible in their results, is the surprising thing. But while this characteristic clue to absurdity helps on the ridicule, it also softens and harmonises its excesses; and the ludicrous is here blended with a certain beauty and decorum, from this very truth of habit and sentiment, or from the principle of similitude and dissimilitude. The devotion to non-sense, and enthusiasm about trifles, is highly affecting as a moral lesson: it is one of the striking weaknesses and greatest happinesses of our nature. […]

There is another source of comic humour which has been but little touched on or attended to by the critics – not the infliction of casual pain, but the pursuit of uncertain pleasure and idle gallantry. Half the business and gaiety of comedy turns upon this. Most of the adventures, difficulties, demurs, hair-breadth 'scapes, disguises, deceptions, blunders, disappointments, successes, excuses, all the dextrous manoeuvres, artful innuendos, assignations, billets-doux, *double entendres*, sly allusions, and elegant flattery, have an eye to this – to obtaining of those "favours secret, sweet and precious," in which love and pleasure consist, and which when attained, and the *equivoque* is at an end, the curtain drops, and the play is over. All the attractions of a subject that can only be glanced at indirectly, that is a sort of forbidden ground to the imagination, except under severe restrictions, which are constantly broken through; all the resources it supplies for intrigue and invention; the bashfulness of the clownish lover, his looks of alarm and petrified astonishment; the foppish affectation and easy confidence of the happy man; the dress, the airs, the languor, the scorn, and indifference of the fine lady; the bustle, pertness, loquaciousness, and tricks of the chambermaid; the impudence, lies, and roguery of the valet; the match-making and unmaking; the wisdom of the wise; the sayings of the witty, the folly of the fool; "the soldier's, scholar's, courtier's eye, tongue, sword, the glass of fashion and the mould of form," have all a view to this. […]

Humour is the describing the ludicrous as it is in itself; wit is the exposing it, by comparing or contrasting it with something else. Humour is, as it were, the growth of nature and accident; wit is the product of art and fancy. Humour, as it is shewn in books, is an imitation of the natural or acquired absurdities of mankind, or of the ludicrous in accident, situation, and character: wit is the illustrating and heightening the sense of that absurdity by some sudden and unexpected likeness or opposition of one thing to another, which sets off the quality we laugh at or despise in a still more contemptible or striking point of view. Wit, as distinguished from poetry, is the imagination or fancy inverted, and so applied to given objects, as to make the little look less, the mean more light and worthless; or to divert our admiration or wean our affections from that which is lofty and impressive, instead of producing a more intense admiration and exalted passion, as poetry does. Wit may sometimes, indeed, be shewn in compliments as well as satire; as in the common epigram –

"Accept a miracle, instead of wit:
See two dull lines with Stanhope's pencil writ."

But then the mode of paying it is playful and ironical, and contradicts itself in the very act of making its own performance a humble foil to another's. Wit hovers round the borders of the light and trifling, whether in matters of pleasure or pain; for as soon as it describes the serious seriously, it ceases to be wit, and passes into a different form. Wit is, in fact, the eloquence of indifference, or an ingenious and striking exposition of those evanescent and glancing impressions of objects which affect us more from surprise or contrast to the train of our ordinary and literal preconceptions, than from any thing in the objects themselves exciting our necessary sympathy or lasting hatred. [...] Mere wit, as opposed to reason or argument, consists in striking out some casual and partial coincidence which has nothing to do, or at least implies no necessary connection with the nature of the things, which are forced into a seeming analogy by a play upon words, or some irrelevant conceit, as in puns, riddles, alliteration, &c. The jest, in all such cases, lies in the sort of mock-identity, or nominal resemblance, established by the intervention of the same words expressing different ideas, and countenancing as it were, by a fatality of language, the mischievous insinuation which the person who has the wit to take advantage of it wishes to convey. [...] Wit and humour (comparatively speaking, or taking the extremes to judge of the gradations by) appeal to our indolence, our vanity, our weakness, and insensibility; serious and impassioned poetry appeals to our strength, our magnanimity, our virtue, and humanity. Any thing is sufficient to heap contempt upon an object; even the bare suggestion of a mischievous allusion to what is improper, dissolves the whole charm, and puts an end to our admiration of the sublime or beautiful. Reading the finest passage in Milton's "Paradise Lost" in a false tone, will make it seem insipid and absurd. The caviling at, or invidiously pointing out, a few slips of the pen, will embitter the pleasure, or alter our opinion of a whole work, and make us throw it down in disgust. […]

Lear and the Fool are the sublimest instance I know of passion and wit united, or of imagination unfolding the most tremendous sufferings, and of burlesque on passion playing with it, aiding and relieving its intensity by the most pointed, but familiar and indifferent illustrations of the same thing in different objects, and on a meaner scale. The Fool's reproaching Lear with "making his daughters his mothers," his snatches of proverbs and old ballads, "The hedge-sparrow fed the cuckoo so long, that it had its head bit off by its young," and "Whoop jug, I know when the horse follows the cart," are a running commentary of trite truisms, pointing out the extreme folly of the infatuated old monarch, and in a manner of reconciling us to its inevitable consequences. […]

The four chief names for comic humour out of our own language are Aristophanes and Lucian among the ancients, Molière and Rabelais among the moderns. Of the two first shall I say, for I know, but little. I should have liked Aristophanes better, if he had treated Socrates less scurvily, for he has treated him most scurvily both as to wit and argument. His Plutus and his Birds are striking instances, the one of dry humour, the other of airy fancy. – Lucian is a writer who appears to deserve his full fame: he has the licentious and extravagant wit of Rabelais, but directed more uniformly to a purpose; and his comic productions are interspersed with beautiful and eloquent descriptions, full of sentiment, such as the exquisite account of the fable of the halcyon put into the mouth of Socrates, and the heroic eulogy on Bacchus, which is conceived in the highest strain of glowing panegyric.

The two other authors I proposed to mention are modern, and French. Molière, however, in the spirit of his writings, is almost as much an English as a French author – quite a *barbare* in all in which he really excelled. He was unquestionably one of the greatest comic geniuses that ever lived; a man of infinite wit, gaiety, and invention – full of life, laughter, and whim. […] What can exceed, for example, the absurdity of the Misanthrope, who leaves his mistress, after every proof of her attachment and constancy, for no other reason than that she will not submit to the *technical formality* of going to live with him in a wilderness? The characters, again, which Celimene gives of her female friends, near the opening of the play, are admirable satires, (as good as Pope's characters of women,) but not exactly in the spirit of comic dialogue. The strictures of Rousseau on this play, in his Letter to D'Alembert, are a fine specimen of the best philosophical criticism. – The same remarks apply in a greater degree to the

"Tartuffe." The long speeches and reasonings in this play tire one almost to death: they may be very good logic, or rhetoric, or philosophy, or any thing but comedy. If each of the parties had retained a special pleader to speak his sentiments, they could not have appeared more verbose or intricate. The improbability of the character of Orgon is wonderful. This play is in one point of view invaluable, as a lasting monument of the credulity of the French to all verbal professions of wisdom or virtue; and its existence can only be accounted for from that astonishing and tyrannical predominance which words exercise over things in the mind of every Frenchman. The *Ecole des Femmes,* from which Wycherly has borrowed his Country Wife, with the true spirit of original genius, is, in my judgment, the masterpiece of Molière. The set speeches in the original play, it is true, would not be borne on the English stage, nor indeed on the French, but that they are carried off by the verse. The *Critique de l'Ecole des Femmes,* the dialogue of which is prose, is written in a very different style. Among other things, this little piece contains an exquisite, and almost unanswerable defence of the superiority of comedy over tragedy. Molière was to be excused for taking this side of the question.

16. Charles Lamb, 'On the Artificial Comedy of the Last Century' (1822)

The artificial Comedy, or Comedy of manners, is quite extinct on our stage. Congreve and Farquhar show their heads once in seven years only, to be exploded and put down instantly. The times cannot bear them. Is it for a few wild speeches, an occasional license of dialogue? I think not altogether. The business of their dramatic characters will not stand the moral test. We screw every thing up to that. Idle gallantry in a fiction, a dream, the passing pageant of an evening, startles us in the same way as the alarming indications of profligacy in a son or ward in real life should startle a parent or guardian. We have no such middle emotions as dramatic interests left. We see a stage libertine playing his loose pranks of two hours' duration, and of no after consequence, with the severe eyes which inspect real vices with their bearings upon two worlds. We are spectators to a plot or intrigue (not reducible in life to the point of strict morality) and take it all for truth. We substitute a real for a dramatic person, and judge him accordingly. We try him in our courts, from which there is no appeal to the dramatis personae!, his peers. We have been spoiled with – not sentimental comedy but a tyrant far more pernicious to our pleasures which has succeeded to it, the exclusive and all devouring drama of common life; where the moral point is every thing; where, instead of the fictitious half-believed personages of the stage (the phantoms of old comedy) we recognise ourselves, our brothers, aunts, kinsfolk, allies, patrons, enemies, – the same as in life, – with an interest in what is going on so hearty and substantial, that we cannot afford our moral judgment, in its deepest and most vital results, to compromise or slumber for a moment. What is there transacting, by no modification is made to affect us in any other manner than the same events or characters would do in our relationships of life. We carry our fire-side concerns to the theatre with us. We do not go thither, like our ancestors, to escape from the pressure of reality, so much as to confirm our experience of it; to make assurance double, and take a bond of fate. We must live our toilsome lives twice over, as it was the mournful privilege of Ulysses to descend twice to the shades. All that neutral ground of character, which stood between vice and virtue; or which in fact was indifferent to neither, where neither properly was called in question; that happy breathing-place from the burthen of a perpetual moral questioning – the sanctuary and quiet Alsatia of hunted casuistry – is broken up and disfranchised, as injurious to the interests of society. The privileges of the place are taken away by law. We dare not dally with images, or names, of wrong. We bark like foolish dogs at shadows. We dread infection from the scenic representation of disorder; and fear a painted pustule. In our anxiety that our morality should not take cold, we wrap it up in a great blanket surtout of precaution against the breeze and sunshine.

I confess for myself that (with no great delinquencies to answer for) I am glad for a season to take an airing beyond the diocese of the strict conscience, – not to live always in the precincts of the law-courts, – but now and then, for a dream-whim or so, to imagine a world with no meddling restriction – to get into recesses, whither the hunter cannot follow me -

> – Secret shades
> Of woody Ida's inmost grove,
> While yet there was no fear of Jove –

I come back to my cage and my restraint the fresher and more healthy for it. I wear my shackles more contentedly for having respired the breath of an imaginary freedom. I do not know how it is with others, but I feel the better always for the perusal of one of Congreve's – nay, why should I not add even of Wycherley's – comedies. I am the gayer at least for it; and I could never connect those sports of a witty fancy in any shape with any result to be drawn from them to imitation in real life. They are a world of themselves almost as much as fairy-land. Take one of their characters, male or female (with few exceptions they are alike), and place it in a modern play, and my virtuous indignation shall rise against the profligate wretch as warmly as the Catos of the pit could desire; because in a modern play I am to judge of the right and the wrong. The standard of police is the measure of political justice. The atmosphere will blight it, it cannot live here. It has got into a moral world, where it has no business, from which it must needs fall headlong; as dizzy, and incapable of making a stand, as a Swedenborgian bad spirit that has wandered unawares into the sphere of one of his Good Men, or Angels. But in its own world do we feel the creature is so very bad? – The Fainalls and the Mirabels, the Dorimants and the Lady Touchwoods, in their own sphere, do not offend my moral sense; in fact they do not appeal to it at all. They seem engaged in, their proper element. They break through no laws, or conscientious restraints. They know of none. They have got out of Christendom into the land – what shall I call it ? – of cuckoldry – the Utopia of gallantry, where pleasure is duty, and the manners perfect freedom. It is altogether a speculative scene of things, which has no reference whatever to the world that is. No good person can be justly offended as a spectator, because no good person suffers on the stage. Judged morally, every character in these plays – the few exceptions only are mistakes – is alike essentially vain and worthless. The great art of Congreve is especially shown in this, that he has entirely excluded from his scenes, – some little generosities in the part of Angelica perhaps excepted, – not only any thing like a faultless character, but any pretensions to goodness or good feelings whatsoever. Whether he did this designedly, or instinctively, the effect is as happy, as the design (if design) was bold. I used to wonder at the strange power which his Way of the World in particular possesses of interesting you all along in the pursuits of characters, for whom you absolutely care nothing – for you neither hate nor love his personages – and I think it is owing to this very indifference for any, that you endure the whole. He has spread a privation of moral light, I will call it, rather than by the ugly name of palpable darkness, over his creations; and his shadows flit before you without distinction or preference. Had he introduced a good character, a single gush of moral feeling, a revulsion of the judgment to actual life and actual duties, the impertinent Goshen would have only lighted to the discovery of deformities, which now are none, because we think them none.

Translated into real life, the characters of his, and his friend Wycherley's dramas, are profligates and strumpets, – the business of their brief existence, the undivided pursuit of lawless gallantry. No other spring of action, or possible motive of conduct, is recognised; principles which, universally acted upon, must reduce this frame of things to a chaos. But we do them wrong in so translating them. No such effects are produced in their world. When we are among them, we are amongst a chaotic people. We are not to judge them by our usages. No reverend institutions are insulted by their proceedings,

– for they have none among them. No peace of families is violated – for no family ties exist among them. No purity of the marriage bed is stained, – for none is supposed to have a being. No deep affections are disquieted, – no holy wedlock bands are snapped asunder, – for affection's depth and wedded faith are not of the growth of that soil. There is neither right nor wrong, – gratitude or its opposite, – claim or duty, – paternity or sonship. Of what consequence is it to virtue, or how is she at all concerned about it, whether Sir Simon, or Dapperwit, steal away Miss Martha; or who is the father of Lord Froth's, or Sir Paul Pliant's children.

The whole is a passing pageant, where we should sit as unconcerned at the issues, for life or death, as at a battle of the frogs and mice. But, like Don Quixote, we take part against the puppets, and quite as impertinently. We dare not contemplate an Atlantis, a scheme, out of which our coxcombical moral sense is for a little transitory ease excluded. We have not the courage to imagine a state of things for which there is neither reward nor punishment. We cling to the painful necessities of shame and blame. We would indict our very dreams.

Amidst the mortifying circumstances attendant upon growing old, it is something to have seen the School for Scandal in its glory. This comedy grew out of Congreve and Wycherley, but gathered some allays of the sentimental comedy which followed theirs. It is impossible that it should be now acted, though it continues, at long intervals, to be announced in the bills. Its hero, when Palmer played it at least, was Joseph Surface. When I remember the gay boldness, the graceful solemn plausibility, the measured step, the insinuating voice – to express it in a word – the downright acted villainy of the part, so different from the pressure of conscious actual wickedness, – the hypocritical assumption of hypocrisy, – which made Jack so deservedly a favourite in that character, I must needs conclude the present generation of play-goers more virtuous than myself, or more dense. I freely confess that he divided the palm with me with his better brother; that, in fact, I liked him quite as well. Not but there are passages, like that, for instance, where Joseph is made to refuse a pittance to a poor relation, incongruities which Sheridan was forced upon by the attempt to join the artificial with the sentimental comedy, either of which must destroy the other – but over these obstructions Jack's manner floated him, so lightly, that a refusal from him no more shocked you, than the easy compliance of Charles gave you in reality any pleasure; you got over the paltry question as quickly as you could, to get back into the regions of pure comedy, where no cold moral reigns. The highly artificial manner of Palmer in this character counteracted every disagreeable impression which you might have received from the contrast, supposing them real, between the two brothers. You did not believe in Joseph with the same faith with which you believed in Charles. The latter was a pleasant reality, the former a no less pleasant poetical foil to it. The comedy, I have said, is incongruous; a mixture of Congreve with sentimental incompatibilities: the gaiety upon the whole is buoyant; but it required the consummate art of Palmer to reconcile the discordant elements.

A player with Jack's talents, if we had one now, would not dare to do the part in the same manner. He would instinctively avoid every turn which might tend to unrealise, and so to make the character fascinating. He must take his cue from his spectators, who would expect a bad man and a good man as rigidly opposed to each other as the death-beds of those geniuses are contrasted in the prints, which I am sorry to say have disappeared from the windows of my old friend Carrington Bowles, of St. Paul's Church-yard memory – (an exhibition as venerable as the adjacent cathedral, and almost coeval) of the bad and good man at the hour of death; where the ghastly apprehensions of the former, – and truly the grim phantom with his reality of a toasting fork is not to be despised, – so finely contrast with the meek complacent kissing of the rod, – taking it in like honey and butter, – with which the latter submits to the scythe of the gentle bleeder, Time, who wields his lancet with the apprehensive finger of a popular young ladies' surgeon. What flesh, like loving grass, would not covet to meet half-way the stroke of such a delicate mower? – John Palmer was twice an actor in this exquisite part. He was playing to you all the while that he was playing upon Sir Peter and his lady. You had the first intimation of a sentiment before it was on his lips. His altered voice was meant to you, and you were to suppose that his fictitious co-flutterers on the stage perceived nothing at all of it. What was it to you if that half-reality, the husband, was over-reached by the puppetry – or the thin thing (Lady Teazle's reputation) was persuaded it was dying of a plethory? The fortunes of Othello and Desdemona were not concerned in it. Poor Jack has past from the stage in good time, that he did not live to this our age of seriousness. The pleasant old Teazle King, too, is gone in good time. His manner would scarce have past current in our day. We must love or hate – acquit or condemn – ensure or pity – exert our detestable coxcombry of moral judgment upon every thing. Joseph Surface, to go down now, must be a downright revolting villain – no compromise – his first appearance must shock and give horror – his specious plausibilities, which the pleasurable faculties of our fathers welcomed with such hearty greetings, knowing that no harm (dramatic harm even) could come, or was meant to come of them, must inspire a cold and killing aversion. Charles (the real canting person of the scene – for the hypocrisy of Joseph has its ulterior legitimate ends, but his brother's professions of a good heart centre in down-right self-satisfaction) must be loved, and Joseph hated. To balance one disagreeable reality with another, Sir Peter Teazle must be no longer the comic idea of a fretful old bachelor bride-groom, whose teasings (while King acted it) were evidently as much played off at you, as they were meant to concern any body on the stage, – he must be a real person, capable in law of sustaining an injury – a person towards whom duties are to be acknowledged – the genuine crim-con antagonist of the villanous seducer Joseph. To realise him more, his sufferings under his unfortunate match must have the downright pungency of life – must (or should) make you not mirthful but uncomfortable, just as the same predicament would move you in a neighbour or old friend. The delicious scenes which give the play its name and zest, must affect you in the same serious manner as if you heard the reputation of a dear female friend attacked in your real presence. Crabtree, and Sir Benjamin – those poor snakes that live but in the sunshine of your mirth – must be ripened by this hot-bed process of realization into asps or amphisbaenas; and Mrs. Candour – O! frightful! become a hooded serpent. Oh who that remembers Parsons and Dodd – the wasp and butterfly of the School for Scandal – in those two characters; and charming natural Miss Pope, the perfect gentlewoman as distinguished from the fine lady of comedy, in this latter part – would forego the true scenic delight – the escape from life – the oblivion of consequences – the holiday barring out of the pedant Reflection – those Saturnalia of two or three brief hours, well won from the world – to sit instead at one of our modern plays – to have his coward conscience (that forsooth must not be left for a moment) stimulated with perpetual appeals – dulled rather, and blunted, as a faculty without repose must be – and his moral vanity pampered with images of notional justice, notional beneficence, lives saved without the spectators' risk, and fortunes given away that cost the author nothing?

No piece was, perhaps, ever so completely cast in all its parts as this manager's comedy. Miss Farren had succeeded to Mrs. Abingdon in Lady Teazle; and Smith, the original Charles, had retired, when I first saw it. The rest of the characters, with very slight exceptions, remained. I remember it was then the fashion to cry down John Kemble, who took the part of Charles after Smith; but, I thought, very unjustly. Smith, I fancy, was more airy, and took the eye with a certain gaiety of person. He brought with him no sombre recollections of tragedy. He had not to expiate the fault of having pleased beforehand in lofty declamation. He had no sins of Hamlet or of Richard to atone for. His failure in these parts was a passport to success in one of so opposite a tendency. But, as far as I could judge, the weighty sense of Kemble made up for more personal incapacity than he had to answer for. His harshest tones in this part came steeped and dulcified in good humour. He made his defects a grace. His exact declamatory manner, as he managed it, only served to convey the points of his dialogue with more precision. It seemed to head the shafts to carry them deeper. Not one of his sparkling sentences was lost. I remember minutely how he delivered each in succession, and cannot by any effort imagine how any of them could be altered for the better. No man could deliver brilliant dialogue – the dialogue of Congreve or of Wycherley – because none understood it – half so well as John Kemble. His Valentine, in Love for Love, was, to my recollection, faultless. He flagged sometimes in the intervals of tragic passion. He would slumber over the level parts of an heroic character. His Macbeth has been known to nod. But he always seemed to me to be particularly alive to pointed and witty dialogue. The relaxing levities of tragedy have not been touched by any since him – the playful court-bred spirit in which he conde-scended to the players in Hamlet – the sportive relief which he threw into the darker shades of Richard – disappeared with him. He had his sluggish moods, his torpors – but they were the halting-stones and resting-places of his tragedy – politic savings, and fetches of the breath – husbandry of the lungs, where nature pointed him to be an economist – rather, I think, than errors of the judgment. They were, at worst, less painful than the eternal tormenting unappeasable vigilance, the "lidless dragon eyes," of present fashionable tragedy.

4

The Industrial Age

INTRODUCTION

The Victorian era, which takes its name from the sixty-three year reign of England's sober, matriarchal Queen Victoria, is not generally considered to be remarkable for comedy, at least not until the last decades of the century when the ethos of bourgeois respectability became the target not only of Oscar Wilde, in brilliant comedies of manners, but also of avant-garde artists on the Continent, who developed radical new kinds of comedy. The nineteenth century in Western Europe and North America was a time of industrial revolution, rapid urbanization, economic development, the growth of the middle class, and the cult of domesticity. Philosophers and psychologists authored functional analyses of laughter, humour, and jokes. Industrial capitalism had produced new forms of work, but it also generated a new understanding of leisure as a distinct non-work time. Workers began to pay for leisure activities in this modern, commercial culture. The duality of work and play would become essential to what Ralph Waldo Emerson labelled in his essay, 'The Comic' (1843), a 'taste for fun'.

The Victorian period emphasized, as Wilde brilliantly satirized it in 1895, the importance of being *earnest* – along with related virtues of seriousness, sincerity, and industriousness. The longstanding opposition between 'jest' and 'earnest' took on new meaning. Earnestness implied deep and genuine feeling, not irony, levity, or absurdity. To be earnest was to be serious, not comical. In German, the word for serious is *ernst*. Aestheticism, the movement with which Wilde is often associated, took an anti-utilitarian view of art – advocating 'art for art's sake' – in reaction against the materialism, the dull mechanical labour, and capitalism of the age. 'In matters of grave importance, style, not sincerity, is the vital thing', Wilde wrote paradoxically in *The Importance of Being Earnest: A Trivial Comedy for Serious People*, comically inverting the assumption that people should be in earnest (not jest) about 'important' subjects. However, as Wilde knew, style depends on social status and economic privilege, and comic theory of this period reflected growing class divisions and cultural hierarchies ('high' versus 'low' culture), drawing sharp distinctions between kinds of laughter and ways of producing it. Different forms of comedy might be more or less appropriate to different audiences.

Comic theory of the nineteenth century both demonstrated and reacted against the continuing influence of Romanticism and its deep earnestness. Eighteenth-century German theorists such as G. E. Lessing and Friedrich Schiller had embraced the view that drama was a genre for moral reflection, critical inquiry, and instruction, and their work profoundly shaped subsequent cultural attitudes. Yet their thinking about comedy was equivocal. Schiller believed that the goal of comedy was a state of perfect freedom and equilibrium, 'the highest thing man has to strive for', yet it remained an unrealized ideal. In theory, comedy might represent the highest human ends – earthly and spiritual freedom – but the real world and real comedy were more problematic. In his *Philosophy of Fine Art* (first published in 1835 from lectures on aesthetics), G. W. F. Hegel complained that modern comedy gives play on stage to private interests, the laughable features of social life, its peculiar habits and follies. Modern comedy offered only partial perspectives; whereas, he believed, true comedy possessed 'an infinite geniality and confidence capable of rising superior to its own contradictions'. Hegel idealized ancient Greek 'joviality' or the way Aristophanes' exuberant comedies resolved conflicts and represented human wholeness. Emerson suggests a similar, Platonic understanding of comedy, in his essay 'The Comic', when he writes, 'The essence of all jokes, of all comedy, seems to be an honest or well-intended halfness.'

The German aesthetic tradition tended to privilege tragedy, often frowning on laughter. In *The World as Will and Representation* (first published in 1818, expanded in 1844), Arthur Schopenhauer (1788–1860) describes tragedy as the highest of the poetic arts. Life, he believed, is a constant struggle or assertion of 'will'. Tragedy enables us to achieve a momentary experience of 'will-less knowing', or relief from everyday struggle. Comedy, on the other hand, asserts the will and is therefore caught in a constant state of disappointed longing. This idea of comedy and frustrated striving led Schopenhauer to develop a version of the incongruity theory of laughter. We laugh when we realize 'the terrible truth by which firmly cherished expectations are shown to be delusive', and this 'bitter' laughter expresses our sense 'of the incongruity between the thoughts entertained by us in our foolish confidence in men or in fate, and the reality unveiled'. Humour consists in a discrepancy between concepts and reality, seriousness in the 'exact suitability of the two'. Schopenhauer says that when others laugh at what we do seriously we discover a 'great incongruity between our concepts and objective reality'. Comedy cannot be serious. 'The opposite of laughter and joking', he claims, 'is *seriousness [ernst]*'. Wilde later deconstructed this notion in his 'trivial comedy for serious people'. The historical experience of rapid change, social mobility, heterogeneity and incongruity is a crucial context for Schopenhauer's discussion of humour, which 'arises from the miserable mania for giving things a more distin-guished name than belongs to them, and hence the name of a class standing above them'. Humour reveals humans' dark desires. At the end of the century, the father of psychoanalysis, Sigmund Freud, would develop Schopenhauer's incongruity theory in his own empirical work on jokes, humour, and the unconscious.

The incongruity theory took a different turn with Danish philosopher and theologian Søren Kierkegaard (1813–55), who refers to it and the influence of Hegelian philosophy in his *Concluding Unscientific Postscript* (1846). 'Wherever there is contra-diction', he writes, 'the comical is present'. After his dissertation *On the Concept of Irony with Continual Reference to Socrates* (1841), Kierkegaard's first major work *Either/Or* (1843) rejected both Hegel's tragic resolution and Schopenhauer's tragic resignation. Kierkegaard adopted a Socratic method, using different voices or personae, different prose styles, and ironic juxtapositions to express different life views; in a sense, he employs a comic form to make a comic argument. No single view can claim access to ultimate truth. Irony, he explains, 'arises from the constant placing of the particu-larities of the finite together with the infinite ethical requirement, thus permitting the contradiction to come into being'. In short, Kierkegaard shows that comedy and irony are the dominant modes of a modern age characterized by individualism, fragmen-tation, and isolation. Harmony would become possible only at a higher, religious stage of existence. Kierkegaard sounds somewhat like Schiller when he proposes that at the highest stage of being the 'power in the comic is a vitally necessary legitimation for anyone who is to be regarded as authorized in the world of spirit'. Nineteenth-century thinkers returned frequently to the relationship between two moral ideas: the signifi-cance of ordinary life and the ideal of universal benevolence, individualism and a larger sense of moral order.

Tensions between the individual and the mass, the inner and the outer, the private and the public informed both the social history and the comic theory of this era. Often these categories had gender connotations (a key feature of nineteenth-century incon-gruity theory), and feminist historians have described an ideology of separate spheres of women and men that emerged during the Industrial Revolution. In Kierkegaard, irony and humour are gendered. Women, he believed, are more childish and more sympathetic than men, who are more self-assured. 'In irony there is no sympathy, there is self-assurance', he theorized. 'Hence in woman one often finds humour but never irony.' The relative social positions of men and women, including their emotional and intellectual capacities, would become a major subject of late nineteenth-century comic theory, specifically in George Meredith and Bernard Shaw and the concept of the 'New Woman'. As the woman's suffrage movement gained momentum, late-Victorian comedy increasingly questioned traditional gender roles. Male and female comic writers took diverse positions on the ideal of the strong, well-educated New Woman, often traced to Henrik Ibsen's play *A Doll's House* (1879). On the one hand, Emma Schiff's 1882 comedy *The Rights of Women* rejected women's liberation in favour of traditional marriage. On the other, Constance Campbell's 1914 *One of the Old Guard*, mocked gender stereotypes and promoted women's rights.

Romanticism had emphasized intense emotion, non-conformity, and self-consciousness. In doing so it also represented a new spirit of democracy, which included the notion that truth, as Jean-Jacques Rousseau wrote in *The Social Contract* (1762), 'is not graven on tablets of marble or brass, but on the hearts of the citizens'. Comedy also reflected aspects of this democratic spirit, both in putting new emphasis on the redemptive capacity of romance and in responding to the financial requirement to appeal to popular tastes. After patronage came to an end in France, dramatists had to look to the public to make a living. During the French Revolution theatres had been filled with soldiers and workmen partial to strong effects. Melodrama, a new kind of theatre characterized by moralism and high emotion, emerged on the boulevards of Paris. With its romance and happy endings, melodrama, as Northrop Frye suggests, is 'comedy without the humor.' It features the triumph of moral virtue over villainy, grand gestures rather than verbal wit. It also became the target of middle-class theorists who preferred more refined forms of comedy later in the century.

Eighteenth-century thinkers had been concerned with 'moral sentiments', such as sympathy, and how comedy might encourage social virtues. Comedy of the Victorian drawing room also tended toward the sentimental, usually without the intense feeling of melodrama. It offered a light look at human folly, and concluded with a lesson in conventional morality. In 1821, an American critic described the history of comedy in metaphorical terms as an evolution from 'a robust buxom dame, whose fat sides ever shook with laughter' to one that 'has since lost much of her portliness, is greatly addicted to punning, fond of caricatures and ever apes the newest fashion'. Restoration dramatists remained a touchstone, compared to which Victorian comedy often seemed tame both in the performance – as actors retreated behind the proscenium arch into a pictorial set – and in comic writing. In his 1851 lectures on English humorists of the eighteenth century, for instance, satirical novelist William Makepeace Thackeray (1811–63) singled out William Congreve. 'The Congreve Muse is dead', he opined, 'and her song choked in Time's ashes'. In marking a contrast with the past, he remarks that 'Congreve's comic feast flares with lights … the wildest jests and ribaldry'. By Thackeray's day, far less wild comedies of manners reflected the social mobility and commercial culture of the time, as in Edward Bullwer-Lytton's 1840 moralistic satire *Money*. Victorian stage comedy and comic theory evolved with the marketplace it represented. Money mediates every relationship in Bullwer-Lytton's play, driving people apart but also drawing them together. It reduces greedy people to automatons, anticipating Henri Bergson's theory of comedy as the 'mechanical encrusted upon the living', and enables the generous to prove their value.

Money is also the central metaphor of playwright Anna Cora Mowatt's *Fashion* (1845), which she described as 'a good-natured satire upon some of the follies incident to a new country, where foreign dross sometimes passes for gold, while native gold is cast aside as dross'. *Fashion*, arguably the most important comedy by an American of the nineteenth century, drew on Congreve's comedies of manners, American stock characters, such as the rough American farmer Adam Trueman, and the racist theatrical practice of blackface minstrelsy, in which white men caricatured African Americans. Edgar Allan Poe critiqued its artificiality, but most contemporaries viewed *Fashion* as a triumph of stage realism and lively action (the subtitle is *Life in New York*). The play reflects concerns about the financial instability of capitalism and American national culture. Mowatt transplants the British comedy of manners to raise questions about cultural identity and the challenge of forging a shared public discourse in a pluralistic, urban, liberal society. Her New World comedy concludes by moralizing on the difference between Nature and Fashion: 'Here let [the world] see portrayed its ruling passion, / And learn to prize at its just value – Fashion'. Comedy puts city dwellers in touch with Nature and represents the dream of regaining an ideal state of harmony. In nineteenth-century comedies and comic theory, the opposition between the natural and the artificial, the organic and the mechanical, became both increasingly important and increasingly problematic.

Reflecting broad currents in Victorian culture, Mowatt represents a blend of Christian and Enlightenment ideas. She channels the traditional Sacred into secular terms, both personal and nationalistic; for instance, Trueman urges 'economy, true independence, and home virtues'. In some ways, the Victorian era was more pious than the eighteenth century. But it was a worldly piety, which contributed to the rise of social reform movements from abolitionism to women's rights and reflected a belief in progress, which combined rationally planned improvements and Christian faith. The English felt that they possessed the true comic spirit, which could not have developed without a history of tolerance and political freedom. But few compelling stage comedies remain from this period in any language. For the utilitarian Victorian middle class, comedy needed a purpose greater than the entertainment offered by circuses and burlesques. Comedy was not to be overindulged or to be enjoyed for its own sake. Victorian comic theory, drawing much on the French, emphasized the necessity of strict formal constraints, balancing humour with realism. Mowatt's *Fashion* subordinates Romanticism's dream of freedom to social responsibility. It represents a central paradox in Victorian comic theory: punishing difference (those who fail to be good citizens) to assert the value of freedom.

The tension between instruction and entertainment in comedy was decided in favour of the latter by the prolific and hugely successful French playwright Eugene Scribe, who churned out hundreds of fluffy yet profitable 'well-made plays' (*pièces bien faites*) between 1820 and 1850. The well-made play was an influential formula, which involved a five-act structure that pivoted on a misunderstanding and led to a speedy resolution that sent the audience home happy. Scribe's system assumed a theory of comedy that coupled reason with sentiment: his 'good' characters won happiness, but they had to outsmart their opponents. The son of a silk merchant, Scribe epitomized the new professionalism in playwriting. He had begun as a writer of *comédies en vaudeville*, farcical sketches that interpolated songs and dances, and by 1836 was so successful that he was elected to the Académie Française. In his inaugural speech, he argued that the purpose of his comedy (and of all drama) was to entertain, not to instruct: 'You go the theatre not for instruction or correction, but for relaxation and amusement.' We are amused by fantasy not everyday life, he added: 'To represent what is before your eyes every day is not the way to please you; but what does not come to you in your usual life, the extraordinary, the romantic, that is what charms you, that is what one is eager to offer you.' Playwrights of the next generation adopted Scribe's methods of plot-construction but applied a more earnest worldview. From 1845 to 1875 Alexandre Dumas *fils* and Émile Augier brought Scribe's system into relation with their social environment. They emphasized the utilitarian aspect of drama, advocated by eighteenth-century French philosopher Denis Diderot, who had conceived of a kind of drama between comedy and tragedy, which he called the *genre sérieux*. It would feature neither ridiculous nor vicious characters, but following the Roman playwright

Terence, virtue and duty. The principal development of this theory appears in the emphasis on marriage on the nineteenth-century French stage in the 'thesis plays' (*pièces à these*) of Dumas and Augier. They did not move beyond the well-made play in form, but they tried to bring it into relation with their social environment and to generate debates on moral questions. Love was the highest value, and these plays are characterized by sermonizing, which, though not comical in itself, had an important impact on comic theory at the end of the century, particularly in the 'discussion plays' of Bernard Shaw. These works were by and for the middle class.

The first half of the century in England saw the democratization of Shakespeare not only in theatres and music halls but also in newspapers and magazines. In England and America, Shakespeare was treated as a popular author whose work could be improved. So, the tragedy *King Lear* was performed with a moralistic, happy ending in which Cordelia survives to marry Edgar, who insists in the final line 'That Truth and Virtue shall at last succeed.' Shakespeare was also routinely burlesqued on the popular stage; *Richard III*, for instance, became *Bad Dicky*. The most innovative comic writing appeared in the pre-eminent literary form of the period, the novel. In their fiction, Charles Dickens and Mark Twain showed the influence of Ben Jonson's satires more than Shakespeare's romances. Both, however, made hilarious use of Shakespeare to satirize the social conditions of their day. In Dickens's *Great Expectations* (1861), Pip, the protagonist, goes to the theatre to see a terrible production of *Hamlet* in which the prince is played by a clerk who moved to London to pursue a theatrical career, and an actor who plays the Ghost has a terrible cough and can't remember his lines. In *The Adventures of Huckleberry Finn* (1886), two rogues perform Shakespearean scenes to raise money in poor towns along the banks of the Mississippi in a mish-mash of burlesque speeches and tomfoolery. As they recognize, 'these Arkansaw lunk-heads couldn't come up to Shakespeare; what they wanted was low comedy – and maybe something rather worse than low comedy'. Twain's story takes place in the 1840s, but he published it in the 1880s, at which point low comedy was splitting from the high culture that Shakespeare came to epitomize.

As numerous theorists of the nineteenth and twentieth centuries would argue, comedy focuses on social life. British author George Meredith (1828–1909) said that comedy presents 'a version of the ordinary worldly understanding of our social life,' and the French philosopher Henri Bergson (1859–1941) would add, 'We laugh not at immorality but at unsociability.' Comedy is thus a social corrective, and Victorian comic theory returns to the question of whether the function of comedy is to allow for a release of social pressure or to ridicule vice and punish difference. Romantic thought and the revolutions of the previous century had celebrated freedom, and popular entertainment flourished throughout the century. But the flip side of individualism and populism was mass culture, which seemed intellectually barren and hostile to individuality. In this context, a cultural hierarchy evolved in the nineteenth century, which distinguished between mass or popular culture and the more refined, intellectual and spiritual preferences of the educated elite. Shakespeare became required reading in the state school curriculum in England with the Education Act of 1870. His plays were transformed into quasi-sacred texts and no longer performed as part of an evening that included farces, magicians, singers, acrobats, minstrels, and comics. In his 1869 book *Culture and Anarchy*, Matthew Arnold defined culture as 'a study of perfection' to be discovered in 'an inward condition of the mind and spirit, not in an outward set of circumstances'. This concept was hostile not only to belly laughs and slapstick comedy but also to the material concerns – money, domestic squabbles, buffoonery, sexual intrigue – that comedy takes as its subject and to mass culture as a whole.

Culture cannot be a 'frivolous and useless thing', says Arnold. Instead, it 'has a very important function to fulfil for mankind'. Furthermore, he adds, 'this function is particularly important in our modern world, of which the whole civilization is ... mechanical and external, and tends constantly to become more so'. In the opposition between culture and anarchy, the organic and the mechanical, Arnold indicates a paradox that appeared in comic theory too. Can comedy *force* us to be free? If so, which is more important, force or freedom? Is comedy anarchic, or does it serve as a social corrective? Arnold reacted to the same industrial reality as Karl Marx, yet he turned to the idealism of Plato and away from the material requirements of life. 'If it were not for this purging effect wrought upon our minds by culture', Arnold worried, the whole world 'would inevitably belong to the Philistines'. In 1877, George Meredith tried to justify comedy in similar terms in 'An Essay on Comedy'. He argued that what the world needed was a 'society of cultivated men and women ... wherein ideas are current, and the perceptions quick'.

Meredith reflects the late Victorian middle-class anxiety that the 'semi-barbarism' of popular culture could lead to an imbalance between sobriety and mirthfulness. The laughter of comedy, he asserts in terms that would have amazed Aristophanes, 'is of unrivalled politeness ... It laughs through the mind, for the mind directs it.' His essay set the terms for late Victorian theory by drawing a contrast between the 'hyperglasts' or 'excessive laughers ... who are so loosely put together that a wink will shake them' and the 'agelasts' or non-laughers, who 'are in that respect as dead bodies'. In his view, the 'comic spirit' occupied a middle ground between 'puritanism and Bachannalism'.

Meredith reflected a broader cultural discourse about the propriety of laughter and the function of comedy in the terms of human evolution derived from Charles Darwin. Over the next few decades, theorists drawing on social Darwinism even suggested that working-class humour was lower on the evolutionary ladder than the more refined laughter of the cultured elite. Meredith suggests that laughter is like wine, evoking comedy's Dionysian origins, but this Victorian wine is curiously conducive to 'sobriety'. It is rational and civilizing. An early advocate of women's rights, Meredith went so far as to suggest that countries in which women are severely oppressed cannot produce comedy: 'There has been fun in Bagdad. But there never will be civilization where Comedy is not possible; and that comes of some degree of social equality of sexes.' Meredith believed that comedy 'lifts women to a station offering them free play for their wit, as they usually show it, when they have it, on the side of sound sense'. The relation of 'free play' to 'sound sense' indicates a crucial conflict in modern comic theory: the function of comedy may be to release people from boring routines and work, but rather than freeing us from 'common sense', it restores us to sanity. Comedy, according to this theory, is not anarchic or revolutionary, but therapeutic. In the late Victorian period, theories of release and those of domination turn into one another. This form of freedom sounds limited indeed. Henri Bergson would define comedy as 'something mechanical encrusted on the living'. We become free through laughter (an automatic response) only when we are compelled to recognize that we have been behaving mechanically.

Elsewhere, a new form of comedy was evolving that represented the opposite of Meredith's appreciation of comic refinement. On the Continent, the Hydropaths, a group of writers and performers that met in a café in Paris, artists such as Émile Cohl, a caricaturist, often regarded as the father of the animated cartoon, the French poet and inventor Charles Cros, and many others created provocative nonsense that was a precursor of surrealism and Dadaism. Their work often seemed truly anarchic, illogical (not 'well-made'), juvenile, and lacking recognizable aesthetic rules. They aimed not only to satirize but also to explode conventional forms of culture. Like aesthetes urging art for art's sake, they rejected the notion that comedy ought to have a moral purpose. The French symbolist Alfred Jarry's radical comedy *Ubu Roi* – first performed in Paris in 1896 – demolished traditional comic playwriting and actually caused riots. Unlike the well-made plays of Scribe, *Ubu Roi* got rid of coherent dramatic form. It parodied Shakespeare's *Macbeth*, recalled the crazy violence of Punch and Judy puppet shows, and spewed obscenity. It became a precursor of modernism and what would later be called Theatre of the Absurd. Jarry attacked the greed and complacency of the bourgeoisie in the fat, ugly Père Ubu, whose first word is 'Merdre!' (French for 'shit', intentionally misspelt). Yet avant-garde comedy was also an outgrowth of bourgeois society, dependent on what it parodied. It evokes Sigmund Freud's explanation of the pleasure of humour in *Jokes and Their Relation to the Unconscious* (1905) as a 'release of affect'.

Freud (1856–1939) entered medical school at the University of Vienna in 1873 and pursued thereafter the career not of a conventional physician but of a philo-sophical-scientific researcher into human psychology that led him to coin the term 'psychoanalysis' in 1896. His psychoanalytic description of 'the economics of laughter' treats the nervous system like both a financial statement that needs to be balanced and a power grid that periodically needs to discharge buildups of excess energy. It is quantitative and physiological. His analysis of three laughter situations – *der Witz*, often translated as 'jokes', 'the comic', and 'humour' – draws upon his 'science of the mind'. Freud associates joking with play and with freedom, but his view of comedy as an economy, or energy system, returns us to the central conflict of Victorian comic theory. Does comedy liberate from dull routine, offering anarchy over sound sense, or does it cure or correct, even punish those who challenge dominant social norms, as suggested by Ben Jonson and Thomas Hobbes? In spite of the avant-garde, Freud's work shows, humour is hardly revolutionary; nor is the release it allows truly radical. As his economic vocabulary suggests, the comic release of pent-up nervous energy allows the system to work better: 'the pleasure is derived from an economy'. Laughter balances the books. We feel relief because, after a comic expenditure, we no longer need to work at suppressing forbidden emotions.

Like Freud, Henri Bergson was a European Jew who applied a scientific education to philosophical subjects. His essay *Laughter* (*Le Rire*, 1900) presents the period's most influential version of the incongruity theory of laughter. Its compelling central metaphor (Comedy is 'something mechanical encrusted on the living') encapsulated a key feature of the modern experience: the pervasive mechanization of both work and leisure, and the incongruity between the rigid and the flexible, repetition and sponta-neity. Bergson picks up on the Romantic distinction between the organic and the mechanical and the notion that all that is 'serious' in our life comes from our freedom, at a time when urban, industrial society had grown exponentially more mechanized. People laugh, he says, at mechanical uniformity, as Charlie Chaplin would later show in his comic performance of assembly-line work, which continues out of the workplace, in the silent film *Modern Times*. Modern individuals start to behave like automatons and act without thought or spontaneity. Even at home they behave merely by habit.

Human events take on a clockwork arrangement; so, we become inflexible and, thus, comical. In brief, the comic side of a person reveals his or her likeness to a thing or a machine. Laughter, then, is a social gesture that restores our humanity. Comedies present types on stage, but in everyday life people also conform to stereotypes, as when they transpose ideas into technical jargon. In being mechanical rather than 'natural', they become laughable. Laughter reminds us that we are human, restoring to us the gracefulness and vitality crucial to an intellectual and moral life.

For Bergson, when we are diverted from the spiritual to the physical or material realm, we generate laughter. A man running along the street stumbles and falls, or a clown slips on a banana peel. Everyone laughs because he has been clumsy, carried involuntarily by momentum not his own volition. The laughable element 'consists of a certain *mechanical inelasticity*', whereas the comic spirit is a living thing (*chose de vivant*). But in performing everyday routines, even just walking absentmindedly, the living body inevitably becomes rigid like a machine. Laughter forces us to be free, punishes absentmindedness and restores our subjectivity. The vice capable of making us comic, Bergson says, comes from without, like a ready-made frame into which we step. Although he privileges the organic and free over the mechanical and absent-minded, Bergson's notion of laughter is also cruel. It requires a 'momentary anaesthesia of the heart'. We don't feel the pain of the clown who falls. The comic appeals to the intelligence not the emotions. Laughter itself can seem like a mechanical reaction, a physiological response any good comedian knows how to produce with a 'routine'. Nonetheless, when it occurs, Bergson says, laughter reveals absentmindedness for what it is and corrects manners. He may echo Hobbes's superiority theory in suggesting the corrective role of laughter, but his theory is more complex, combining a theory of release with one of punishment.

The most important dramatist to venture into the conversation about the function of comedy as a social corrective in the increasingly bureaucratic, modern world was George Bernard Shaw (1856–1950) whose famous discussion plays also represented his theories in dramatic form. Shaw aimed to demonstrate what was at stake ideologically for playwrights who employed humour to reveal hypocritical aspects of social dynamics, and his political targets included severe inequalities in class and in gender. Like Wilde, Shaw was an Irishman who moved to London, and his outsider position rendered him an effective ironist of the dominant culture as well. In his *Fabian Essays in Socialism* Shaw argued that socialism is the only system that addresses the bitterness of inequality, and he saw comedy as a tool of social change that could expose paradoxes within capitalism while advocating 'common sense'. In the preface to his comedy *Major*

Barbara (1907), Shaw argues against the sentimental impulses of the era, arguing that comedy arises from 'the tragi-comic irony of the conflict between real life and the romantic imagination'. Thus, comedy can illuminate reality as it is, not as we wish it to be.

In a famous response to George Meredith, 'Meredith on Comedy' (1897), Shaw accused the latter of both condoning the moral complacency of the English bourgeois audience and knowing little about the actual theatre: 'Mr. Meredith knows more about plays than about playgoers.' He felt that it was vital to provoke the audience to question their assumptions and prejudices. Englishmen's supposed 'common sense', which meant valuing success 'more than anything else … makes comedy impossible, because it would not seem like common sense at all if it were not self-satisfied unconscious of its moral and intellectual bluntness, whereas the function of comedy is to dispel such unconsciousness by turning the searchlight of the keenest moral and intellectual analysis right on to it'. According to Shaw, comedy ought to promote social justice by exposing hypocrisy and combating evil. So he combined elements of the well-made play with self-reflexive dialogue to challenge both the audience's acceptance of conventional plots and complacent Victorian attitudes more broadly. In his preface to *Major Barbara*, Shaw mocks the melodramatic conventions that romanticize poverty without an awareness of the social and psychological toll it takes on the individual: "'Poor but honest', and 'respectable poor', and such phrases are as intolerable and as immoral as 'drunken but amiable', 'fraudulent but a good after-dinner speaker.'" Poverty is evil, Shaw writes, because it pits one man against another, and 'if a man cannot look evil in the face without illusion, he will never know what it really is, or combat it effectually'.

Comedy, Shaw believed, has a social function, namely to draw fresh attention to serious problems of the day, whether in education, sexual double-standards, class privilege, or other areas. In *Pygmalion* (1913), he focused on the education of a poor flower girl by a wealthy linguistics professor. The play is part parody of romance, part comedy of manners, and part parable of socialism. It updates the Greek myth of a sculptor whose work comes to life and draws upon the classical types of Greek comedy – the *eirôn* (the self-deprecator) and the a*lazôn* (the braggart) – to subvert the prevalent belief that every human possesses an unchanging soul and to raise questions about who we are and what social and economic conditions make us that way. Shaw's Pygmalion-figure, Professor Higgins, turns a human being into a mechanical doll, but the flower-girl turned duchess, Eliza, manages to assert her humanity in the end. In this and other overtly political comedies, Shaw both draws upon the thesis-play model of Dumas and Augier and reflects a move in British comedy to a sharper more politically engaged theory and practice.

In sum, comic theory from the early-Victorian period to the early twentieth century represents a peculiar collision of idealism and realism. The major thinkers of the era, Charles Darwin in evolutionary biology and Karl Marx in political history and economics, demolished old systems of belief. They substituted materialist for theological explanations of experience. The nineteenth century became increasingly anti-idealist under their influence. Critiquing the idealism of his Romantic predecessor Hegel, Marx advanced a theory of history as an unfolding joke in an essay on the French coup of 1851 by Louis-Napoléon Bonaparte. 'Hegel remarks somewhere that all great world-historic facts and personages appear, so to speak, twice', writes Marx. 'He forgot to add: the first time as tragedy, the second time as farce.' History has a dramatic form, and the form matters because, as Marx says, while men make their own history, they do not make it just as they please but under circumstances given and transmitted from the past. Yet in his own way Marx was also an heir to Romanticism, which suggested an alternative to the increasingly bureaucratic, industrial society, and his materialist conception of history is sustained by a belief in social progress. This dialectic of freedom and constraint, which is related to that of the particular and the universal, the subjective and the objective, is at the core of nineteenth-century thought. In bringing key features of Hegel's idealism into the real world, Marx was both making a comic move and indicating the historicist turn that comic theory would take over the next hundred years. For Marx, the key ingredient in an understanding of human history is a comprehension of productive activity – the way people obtained their means of subsistence by labour. This conception of history, which connects our here-and-now with self-awareness of our role as shapers of our 'world', points to crucial developments in comic theory, away from the universal and toward the tensions and contradictions of particular socio-cultural experience.

Bibliography

Bartlett, Jami. 'Meredith and Ends'. *ELH* 76 (3) (Fall 2009): 547–76.

Bennett, Benjamin. *Modern Drama and German Classicism: Renaissance from Lessing to Brecht.* Ithaca, NY: Cornell University Press, 1979.

Boyd, Brian. 'Laughter and Literature: A Play Theory of Humor'. *Philosophy and Literature* 28 (1) (April 2004): 1–22.

Brooks, Peter. *The Melodramatic Imagination: Balzac, Henry James, and the Mode of Excess.* New Haven, CT: Yale University Press, 1976.

Carlson, Susan. 'Conflicted Politics and Circumspect Comedy: Women's Comic Playwriting in the 1890s'. In *Women and Playwriting in Nineteenth-Century Britain,* ed. Tracy C. Davis and Ellen Donkin, 257–76. Cambridge, New York: Cambridge University Press, 1999.

Grimsted, David. *Melodrama Unveiled: American Theater & Culture: 1800–1850*, repr. 1968. Berkeley: University of California Press, 1987.

Henkle, Roger B. *Comedy and Culture: England 1820–1900*. Princeton, NJ: Princeton University Press, 1980.

Jenkins, Henry. *What Made Pistachios Nuts? Early Sound Comedy and the Vaudeville Aesthetic*. New York: Columbia University Press, 1992.

Kierkegaard, Søren. *The Humor of Kierkegaard: An Anthology*, ed. and intro. Thomas C. Oden. Princeton, NJ: Princeton University Press, 2004.

Levine, Lawrence W. *Highbrow / Lowbrow: The Emergence of Cultural Hierarchy in America*. Cambridge, MA: Harvard University Press, 1988.

Martin, Robert Bernard. *The Triumph of Wit: A Study of Victorian Comic Theory*. Oxford: Clarendon, 1974.

North, Michael. *Machine-Age Comedy*. New York: Oxford University Press, 2009.

Sanders, Valerie. *The Tragi-comedy of Victorian Fatherhood*. Cambridge, NY: Cambridge University Press, 2009.

Schoch, Richard W. *Not Shakespeare: Bardolatry and Burlesque in the Nineteenth Century*. Cambridge, NY: Cambridge University Press, 2002.

Wagner-Lawlor, Jennifer A., ed. *The Victorian Comic Spirit: New Perspectives*. Aldershot and Brookfield, VT: Ashgate, 2000.

Weeks, Mark. 'Milan Kundera: A Modern History of Humor Amid the Comedy of History'. *Journal of Modern Literature* 28 (3) (Spring 2005): 130–48.

TEXTS

1. Søren Kierkegaard, 'The Reality of Suffering (Humor);' 'Humor as an Incognito for Religiosity;' 'Humor – The Religiosity of Hidden Inwardness', from *Concluding Unscientific Postscript* (1846), translated by David F. Swenson

The comical is brought out when the hidden inwardness comes into relationship with an environment, in that the religious individual comes to hear and see that which when brought into conjunction with his inward passion, produces a comic effect. Hence even when two religious individuals converse with one another, the one will produce a comic impression on the other, for each of them will constantly have his own inwardness in mind, and will not hear what the other says in the light of this, and hear it as comical, because neither dares directly express the secret inwardness; at most they will entertain a suspicion of one another because of the humoristic undertone.

A principle propounded by Lord Shaftesbury, which makes laughter a test of truth, was the occasion during the last century for the appearance of one or another little inquiry as to whether this is so or not. In our time the Hegelian philosophy has desire to give preponderance to the comical, which might seem a particularly strange thing for the Hegelian philosophy to do, since this philosophy is surely least of all equipped to withstand an attack from that side. In ordinary life we laugh when something is made to seem ridiculous, and after having laughter we sometimes say: but one is really not justified in making such a thing ridiculous. But if the comic interpretation is well done, one cannot restrain oneself from laughing and spreading the story further, – naturally accompanied by the edifying afterthought: but it is not right to make such a thing ridiculous. It goes unnoticed how ridiculous this is, that there is a contradiction in the fictitious attempt to act ethically by means of an edifying afterthought, instead of renouncing the illegitimate antecedent. Now when this is so, when the advance and wider dissemination of culture and polished manners, when the refinement of life continues to develop a sense for the comic, so that an overwhelming partiality for the comical is characteristic of our time, which both in the correct and the incorrect sense seems to rejoice in the Aristotelian view that lays stress on a sense for the comic as a distinguishing mark of man's nature – in such circumstances the religious address much long since have taken note of how the comical stands related to the religious. For what occupied the minds of men so much, what constantly recurs in conversation, in intercourse, in books, in the modifications of the entire view of life, that is something that the religious dare not ignore; unless indeed the Sunday performances in church are meant to constitute a kind of indulgence, where at the price of a grumpy devotionalism for an hour's time, one buys immunity to laugh unchecked the whole week through. The question of the legitimacy of the comic, of its relationship to the religious, of whether it does not have a place in the religious address itself – this question is of essential significance for a religious existence in our times, where the comical everywhere runs away with the victory. To cry alas and alack over this tendency only proves how little the champions of religious respect what they fight for. It is surely an indication of far greater respect for the religion to demand that it be given its proper place in daily life, than to keep it at a Sunday-distance away from life, in high-flown eccentricity.

The matter is quite simple. The comical is present at every stage of life (only that the relative positions are different), for wherever there is life, there is contradiction, and wherever there is contradiction, the comical is present. The tragic and the comic are the same, in so far as both are based on contradiction; but *the tragic is the suffering contradiction, the comical, the painless contradiction*. That something which the comic apprehension envisages as comical may entail imaginary suffering for the comical individual, is quite irrelevant. In that case, for example, it would be incorrect to apprehend the hero of Holberg's *The Busy Man* as comical. Satire also entails pain, but this pain has a dialectic which gives it a teleology in the direction of a cure. The difference between the tragic and the comic lies in the relationship between the contradiction and the controlling idea. The comic apprehension evokes the contradiction or makes it manifest by having in mind the way out. The tragic apprehension sees the contradiction and despairs of a way out. It is a matter of course that this much be understood so that the various nuances of the comic are again kept subject to the qualitative dialectic of the different spheres, which passes judgment upon all subjective arbitrariness. Thus if one proposed to make everything comical by means of nothing, it is clear at once that his comedy is nowhere at home, since it lacks a foothold in any sphere. The discoverer of this type of comedy would himself be open to comic apprehensions from the standpoint of the ethical sphere, because as an existing individual he must himself in one way or another have a foothold in existence.

If one were to say: repentance is a contradiction, *ergo* it is comical, it would at once be apparent that this is nonsense. Repentance belongs in the ethico-religious sphere, and is hence so placed as to have only one higher sphere above it, namely, the religious in the strictest sense. But it was not the religious it was proposed to make use of in order to make repentance ridiculous; *ergo* it must have been something lower, in which case the comic is illegitimate, or something only chimerically higher, as for example the sphere of abstraction; and then our friend of laughter is himself comical, as I have frequently in the preceding sought to show over against speculative philosophers, namely, that in consequence of having made themselves fantastic, and in that manner having attained to the highest standpoint, they have made themselves comical. The lower can never make the higher comical, i.e. it cannot legitimately apprehend the higher as comical, and has not the power to make it comical. It is another thing that the lower, by being brought into conjunction with the higher, may make the relationship ridiculous. Thus it is possible for a horse to be the occasion for a man showing himself in a ridiculous light, but the horse has no power to make him ridiculous.

The different existential stages take rank in accordance with their relationship to the comical, depending on whether they have the comical within themselves or outside themselves; yet not in the sense that the comical is the highest stage. The immediate consciousness has the comical outside itself, for wherever there is life there is contradiction, but the contradiction is not represented in the immediate consciousness, which therefore has the contradiction coming from the outside. A finite, worldly wisdom presumes to apprehend immediacy as comical, but thereby itself becomes comical; for the supposed justification of its comic apprehension is that it definitely knows the way out, but the way out which it knows is still more comical. This, then, is an illegitimate comic apprehension. Wherever there exists a contradiction and the way out is not known, where the contradiction is not cancelled and corrected in something higher, there the contradiction is not painless; and where the correction is based on something only chimerically higher (from the frying-pan into the fire), it is itself still more comical, because the contradiction is greater. Thus in the relationship between immediacy and finite worldly wisdom. A comic apprehension on the basis of despair is also illegitimate, for despair is despair because it does not know the way out, does not know the contradiction cancelled, and ought therefore to apprehend the contradiction tragically, which is precisely, the way to its healing.

Humor has its justification precisely in its tragic side, in the fact that it reconciles itself to the pain, which despair seeks to abstract from, although it knows no way out. Irony is justified as over against immediacy, because its state of equilibrium, not as mere abstraction but as an existential art, is higher than the immediate consciousness. Only an existential ironist is therefore justified over against immediacy; total irony once for all, like a bargain-priced notion set down on paper, is, like all abstractions, illegitimate over against every sphere of existence. Irony is indeed an abstraction, and an abstract pitting together of things, but the justification of the existential ironist that he expresses this himself existentially, that he preserves his life in it, and does not toy with the grandeurs of irony while himself having his life in Philistinism; for then his comic apprehension is illegitimate.

The immediate consciousness has the comical outside itself; irony has it *within* itself. The ethicist who has irony as his incognito can again see the comic side of irony, but assures himself of justification only through constantly holding himself to the ethical, and therefore sees the comical only as constantly vanishing.

Humor has the comical *within* itself, and is justified in the existential humorist; for humor once for all *in abstracto* is as illegitimate as everything else that is in this manner abstract; the humorist earns his justification by having his life in his humor. Against religiosity only it is not justified, but it is justified against everything that courts recognition as religiosity. The religiosity which has humor as its incognito can also see the humoristic as comical, but preserves its justification only by constantly keeping itself in religious passion with respect to the God-relationship, and hence it sees the comic aspect of humor only vanishingly.

Now we have reached the limit. The religiosity of hidden inwardness is *eo ipso* inaccessible to comic apprehension. The comical cannot be outside it, precisely, because it is hidden inwardness, and therefore cannot come into contradiction with anything. The sphere of contradiction which humor dominates, including as it does the higher range of the comical, is something that such religiosity has itself brought to consciousness, and it has it within itself as something lower. Thus it is absolutely secured against the comical, or is by means of the comical secured against the comical.

When the religious in church and state has sometimes sought the assistance of legislation and the police against the comical, this may be very well intentioned, but the question is whether the motivation is in the last analysis religious in character; and it is certainly unjust to the comical to regard it as an enemy of the religious. The comical is not more than the dialectical an enemy of the religious. Which everything on the contrary serves and obeys. But the religiosity which essentially pretends to externality, essentially makes the external commensurable, needs to look to itself, and the fear itself more than the comical (lest it become aesthetics); the comical might indeed legitimately help it get its eyes open. Much in Catholicism may serve as an example of this. And as far as the individual is concerned, the principle holds that a religious individual who wants everything to be serious, perhaps even serious in the same manner that he is, because he is stupidly serious, is involved in a contradiction, and the religious individual who cannot endure, if it comes to that, that all others laugh at what interests him absolutely, is lacking in inwardness, and hence desires the consolation of an illusion, the knowledge that many are of the same opinion as he, aye, of the same type of countenance; and he will be edified by adding the weight of the world-historical to his own bite of reality, "since now everywhere a new life is beginning to stir, the heralded new era, with eye and heart for the cause."

The hidden inwardness is inaccessible to the comical, as can also be seen from the fact that if such a religious individual could be incited suddenly to externalize his religiosity, if for example he so far forgot himself as to come into conflict with a comparative religious individual, and again so forgot himself and the absolute requirement of inwardness as to wish comparatively to be regarded as more religious than the other, then he is comical, and the contradiction consists in his wishing at one and the same time to be visible and invisible. Humor makes use of the comical over against presumptuous forms of the religious, precisely because a religious individual must know the way out if he merely wills to know it. If this cannot be presumed, such a comic apprehension of him becomes dubious in the same sense as a comic apprehension of Holberg's hero in *The Busy Man*, if it were assumed that he really was weak-minded.

The law for the comical is quite simple: it exists wherever there is contradiction, and where the contradiction is painless because it is viewed as cancelled; for the comical does not indeed cancel the contradiction, but a legitimate comic apprehension can do so, otherwise it is not legitimate. Talent in this field consists in the ability to represent the comical *in concreto*. The test of the comical is to be found in the relationship between the spheres which the comical presupposes; if this relationship is not correct, the comic apprehension is illegitimate; and a comic apprehension which has no foothold anywhere is *eo ipso* illegitimate. The sophistical in relation to the comic therefore has its foothold in nothing, in the realm of pure abstraction, and this is expressed by Gorgias in the abstract proposal to annihilate seriousness by means of the comical, and the comical again by means of seriousness (cf. Aristotles's *Rhetoric* 3:18). The balance of the account here ends in both, and the dubiousness of the procedure is easily perceived, in the fact that an existing individual has transformed himself into a fantastic letter "X"; for it must surely be an existing individual who proposes to use this procedure, which can only serve to make him ridiculous when one uses against him the formula of exorcism against speculative philosophers proposed in an earlier passage: "May I have the honor to ask with whom I have the honor to converse; is it a human being, etc.?" For Gorgias with his invention lands in the fantastic exaggeration of pure being; for when he annihilates the one by the other there is nothing left. However, Gorgias has perhaps in the first stance wished merely to characterize the trickiness of a pettifogger, who seeks a victory by changing his weapons in relation to the weapons of his opponent. But a pettifogger has no standing in relation to the comical, he will have to whistle for his justification – and be content with the profit, which, as is well known, has always been the favorite result with all sophists: money, money, money, or whatever is on the same level with this.

Humor as the border line for the religiousness of hidden inwardness comprehends guilt-consciousness as a totality. The humorist therefore talks rather rarely of this or that guilt because he comprehends guilt totally, or if occasionally he accentuates this or that particular, it is because the totality is thereby expressed. The humorous effect is produced by letting the childlike trait reflect itself in the consciousness of totality. Intellectual culture on an absolute scale put together with childishness produces humor. One often enough encounters men who are full grown, confirmed, and "men of heart", who in spite of being older in years do everything or leave undone like a child, and who even in their fortieth year would undeniably be regarded as promising children if it were the custom for every man to become two hundred and fifty years old. But childishness and loutish pranks are very different from humor. The humorist possesses the childlike quality but is not possessed by it, constantly prevents it from expressing itself directly, but lets it only shimmer through an absolute culture. Hence when one puts together an absolute culture and a child, they always in combination bring the humorous to evidence: the child utters it and does not recognize it, the humorist recognized that it was uttered. On the other hand, relative culture put together with a child discovers nothing, for it looks down upon the child and its foolishness.

Precisely because the pleasantry of humor consists in revocation (a start being made with profundity, which is revoked) it naturally is often a regression to childhood. If a man like Kant who stands at the pinnacle of scientific culture were to say regarding the proofs for God's existence, "Well, I know nothing more about it except that my father told me it was so," this would be humorous, and he would be saying more than a whole book on the proofs, in case such a book forgets this item. But because humor is always a concealed pain, it is also an instance of sympathy. In irony there is no sympathy, there is self-assurance, and therefore its sympathy is sympathetic in an entirely indirect way, not with any man in particular, but with the idea of self-assurance as the possibility of every man. Hence in woman one often finds humor but never irony. If an essay is made at it, it ill becomes her, and a purely womanly nature will regard irony as a kind of cruelty.

Humor reflects upon the consciousness of guilt as a totality, as is therefore truer than all comparative measuring and gauging. But the profound thought is revoked in jest, just as we saw earlier in the case of suffering. Humor comprehends guilt as a totality, but just as it comes to the point of giving an explanation, it becomes impatient and revokes it all, saying, "However, that would be too long drawn out and too profound, I therefore revoke it all and give back the money." "We are all of us debtors," the humorist would say, "many a time we fall and in various ways, all of us who belong to the animal species which Buffon thus describes …" Here might follow a definition expressed purely in terms of natural history. The contrast has here attained its highest expression: between an individual who in the eternal recollection has the totality of guilt, and a specimen of an animal species. There is therefore no analogy here to the developmental metamorphosis of a man, in so far as he has the highest experience, that of being subsumed under the absolute definition of spirit. […] The humorous swing away from the individual to the species is also a return to aesthetic concepts, and it is by no means in this that the profundity of humor consists. The totality of guilt-consciousness in the particular individual before God in relation to an eternal happiness is religiousness. Upon this humor reflects, but revokes it again. […] Humor puts the eternal recollection of guilt together with everything, but does not by this recollection relate itself to an eternal happiness. Now we come to the hidden inwardness. The eternal recollection of guilt cannot be expressed outwardly, it is incommensurable with such expression, since every outward expression finitizes guilt. But the eternal recollection of guilt which characterizes the hidden inwardness is anything but despair; for despair is always the infinite, the eternal, the total, at the instant of impatience; and all despair is a kind of bad temper. No, the eternal recollection is the mark indicative of the relationship to an eternal happiness, a mark which is as far as possible from being a plain indication, but which is always sufficient to prevent the leaping aside of despair.

Humor discovers the comic by putting the total guilt together with the relativity as between man and man. The comic lies in the fact that the total guilt is the foundation which supports the whole comedy. In case essential innocence or goodness were at the basis of the relative, the situation is not comic, for it is not comic that the more of the less is defined within the positive definition. But when relativity rests upon the total guilt, the more or the less rests upon that which is less than nothing, and this is the contradiction which the comic detects. In so far as money is a something, the relativity as between richer and poorer is not comic, but when counters are used instead of money it is comic that there should be a relativity. When men's busy activity in running around had as its reason a possibility of escaping danger, this activity is not comic; but in case, for example, it is on a ship which is sinking, there is something comic in all this running around, for the contradiction is that in spite of all this movement they do not move away from the place where destruction is.

The hidden inwardness must also discover the comic, not for the fact that the religious man is different from others, but for the fact that he, though most heavily burdened by bearing the eternal recollection of guilt, is like all others. He discovers the comic, but inasmuch as in the eternal recollection he is constantly related to an eternal happiness, the comic is constantly evanescent.

2. William Makepeace Thackeray, *The English Humourists of the Eighteenth Century* (1853)

I fancy poor Congreve's theatre is a temple of Pagan delights, and mysteries not permitted except among heathens. I fear the theatre carries down that ancient tradition and worship, as masons have carried their secret signs and rites from temple to temple. When the libertine hero carries off the beauty in the play, and the dotard is laughed to scorn for having the young wife: in the ballad, when the poet bids his mistress to gather roses while she may, and warns her that old Time is still a-flying: in the ballet, when honest Corydon courts Phillis under the treillage of the pasteboard cottage, and leers at her over the head of grandpapa in red stockings, who is opportunely asleep; and when seduced by the invitations of the rosy youth she comes forward to the footlights, and they perform on each other's tiptoes that *pas* which you all know, and which is only interrupted by old grandpapa awaking from his doze at the paste-board chalet (whither he returns to take another nap in case the young people get an encore): when Harlequin, splendid in youth, strength, and agility, arrayed in gold and a thousand colors, springs over the heads of countless perils, leaps down the throat of bewildered giants, and, dauntless and splendid, dances danger down: when Mr. Punch, that godless old rebel, breaks every law and laughs at it with odious triumph, outwits his lawyer, bullies the beadle, knocks his wife about the head, and hangs the hangman – don't you see in the comedy, in the song, in the dance, in the ragged little Punch's puppet-show – the Pagan protest? Doesn't it seem as if Life puts in its plea and sings its comment? Look how the lovers walk and hold each other's hands and whisper! Sings the chorus – "There is nothing like love, there is nothing like youth, there is nothing like beauty of your springtime. Look! how old age tries to meddle with merry sport! Beat him with his own crutch, the wrinkled old dotard! There is nothing like youth, there is nothing like beauty, there is nothing like strength. Strength and valour win beauty and youth. Be brave and conquer. Enjoy, enjoy, enjoy! Would you know the *Segreto per esser felice*? Here it is, in a smiling mistress and a cup of Falerian." As the boy tosses the cup and sings his song – hark! what is that chaunt coming nearer and nearer? What is that dirge which *will* disturb us? The lights of the festival burn dim – the cheeks turn pale – the voice quavers – and the cup drops on the floor. Who's there? Death and Fate are at the gate, and they *will* come in.

Congreve's comic feast flares with lights, and round the table, emptying their flaming bowls of drink, and exchanging the wildest jests and ribaldry, sit men and women, waited on by rascally valets and attendants as dissolute as their mistresses – perhaps the very worst company in the world. At the head of the table sits Mirabel or Belmour (dressed in the French fashion and waited on by English imitators of Scapin and Frontin). Their calling is to be irresistible, and to conquer everywhere. Like the heroes of the chivalry story, whose long-winded loves and combats they were sending out of fashion, they are always splendid and triumphant – overcome all dangers, vanquish all enemies, and win the beauty at the end. Fathers, husbands, usurers, are the foes these champions contend with. They are merciless in old age, invariably, and an old man plays the part in the dramas which the wicked enchanter or the great blundering giant performs in the chivalry tales, who threatens and grumbles and resists – a huge stupid obstacle always overcome by the knight. It is an old man with a money-box; Sir Belmour his son or nephew spends his money and laughs at him. It is an old man with a young wife whom he locks up: Sir Mirabel robs him of his wife, trips up his gouty old heels and leaves the old hunks. The old fool, what business has he to hoard his money, or lock up blushing eighteen? Money is for youth, love is for youth, away with the old people. When Millamant is sixty, having of course divorced the first Lady Millamant, and married his friend Doricourt's granddaughter out of the nursery – it will be his turn; and young Belmour will make a fool of him. All this pretty morality you have in the comedies of William Congreve, Esquire. They are full of wit. Such manners as he observes, he observes with great humour; but ah! it's a weary feast, that banquet of wit where no love is. It palls very soon; sad indigestions follow it and lonely blank headaches in the morning.

3. Charles Baudelaire, 'On the Essence of Laughter' (1855), translated by P. E. Charvet

The wise man laughs only with fear and trembling

Let us indeed analyse this strange proposition: the wise man, that is to say he who is filled with the spirit of the Lord, he who has a divine formulary at his finger-tips, does not laugh, does not let himself go to laughter without trepidation. The wise man trembles when he has laughed; the wise man is afraid to laugh, just as he is afraid of profane entertainments or concupiscence. He holds back on the brink of laughter, as though on the brink of temptation. Thus, according to the sage, there is some secret contradiction between his character as sage and the primeval character of laughter.

If we are willing to adopt the orthodox standpoint, it is certain that human laughter is intimately connected with the accident of an ancient fall, of a physical and moral degradation. Laughter and grief express themselves through the organs that have the control and the knowledge of good and evil, the eyes and the mouth. In the earthly paradise (whether we place it in the past or in the future, in memory of prophecy, according to the theologians or the socialists), in the earthly paradise, that is to say in the surroundings, where it seemed to man that all created things were good, joy did not reside in laughter. As no sorrow afflicted him, man's countenance was simple and composed, and the laughter that nowadays shakes nations did not distort the features of his face. Neither laughter nor tears can show themselves in the paradise of bliss. They are equally the children of sorrow, and they came because enervated man lacked the bodily strength to control them. From the standpoint of my Christian philosopher, the laughter of his lips is a sign of as great a state of corruption as the tears in his eyes. God, who desired to multiply his own image, did not place lion's teeth in man's mouth – but man bites with his laughter; nor did He place, in man's eyes, all the fascinating duplicity of the serpent – but man seduces with his tears. And pray observe that it is also with his tears that man washes away man's sorrows, that it is with laughter that he sometimes softens man's heart, and draws it closer; for the phenomena produced by the Fall will become the means of redemption. [...]

The fact that would suffice by itself to show that the comic is one of the clearest marks of Satan in man, and one of the numerous pips in the symbolic apple, is the unanimous agreement of the physiologists of laughter on the primary reason for this monstrous phenomenon. Anyhow, their discovery is not all that profound and does not take us very far. Laughter, so they say, comes from superiority. I should not be surprised if, in the face of this discovery, the physiologist himself were to burst out laughing at the thought of his own superiority. And so the way it should have been put is: Laughter comes from a man's idea of his own superiority. A satanic idea if ever there was one! What pride and aberration! For it is a matter of common knowledge that all the inmates of our asylums harbour the idea of their own superiority developed to an inordinate degree. I have never heard of anyone mentally ill of humility. Note, moreover, that laughter is one of the most frequent and numerous symptoms of lunacy, and see how everything fits in; when Virginie, having stepped aside from the strict path of virtue, has come down a degree in purity, she will begin having the idea of her own superiority, she will be more sophisticated from a worldly point of view, and she will laugh.

I said earlier that there was a symptom of weakness in laughter; and indeed, what clearer sign of debility could there be than a nervous convulsion, an involuntary spasm, comparable to a sneeze, caused by the sign of another's misfortune? That misfortune is almost always a weakness in mind. Is there a more deplorable phenomenon than weakness delighting at weakness? But there is worse to come. The misfortune is sometimes of a very inferior kind, a weakness on the physical level. To take one of the most commonplace examples in life, what is there so particularly diverting in the sight of a man falling on the ice or on the road, or tripping on the edge of a pavement, that his brother in Christ should promptly double up uncontrollably, that the muscles of his face should suddenly begin to function like a clock at midday or a mechanical toy? The poor devil may at the very least have damaged his face, or perhaps have broken a vital limb. But the irresistible and sudden roar of laughter was unleashed. It is certain that if we want to explore this situation, we shall find at the very heart of the laugher's thought a certain unconscious pride. That is the start of the thing: 'I don't fall, I don't. I walk straight, I do; my footstep is steady and assured, mine is. You won't catch me being stupid enough not to see where the pavement ends, or that there is a pavingstone in my way.'

The romantic school, or more accurately, one of the subdivisions of the romantic school, the satanic school, thoroughly grasped this primeval law of laughter; or, at least, if they did not all grasp it, all of them, even in their most outrageous extravagances and exaggerations, felt its force and applied it correctly. All melodrama's miscreants, cursed, damned, inevitably marked with a rictus running from ear to ear, are in line with the purest orthodoxy of laughter. Anyhow almost all of them are legitimate or illegitimate grandchildren of the celebrated traveller, Melmoth, the great satanic creations of Charles Robert Maturin. What could be greater, what more powerful, in relation to poor humanity than this pale, bored Melmoth? And yet he has a weak, an abject, anti-divine and anti-luminous side to him. And so, how he laughs and laughs, as he constantly compares himself with human caterpillars, he so strong, so intelligent, he for whom a certain number of the physical and intellectual laws that condition humanity no longer exist! And this laughter is the perpetual explosion of his wrath and his suffering. It is, be sure and understand me, the necessary product of his dual and contradictory nature, which is infinitely great in relation to man, infinitely vile and base in relation to absolute truth and righteousness. Melmoth is a living contradiction.

He has left behind the fundamental conditions of life; his bodily organs can no longer support his thought. That is why this laughter of his freezes and wrings the guts. It is a laughter that never sleeps, like a disease for ever on its stealthy way, in execution of a providential command. And so, Melmoth's laughter, which is the highest expression of pride, is always fulfilling its function, as it tears and scorches the lips of the laugher beyond hope of pardon. [...]

Humanity works its way up, and acquires a potential for evil and an understanding of evil, proportionate to the potential it acquires for good. That is why I do not find it surprising that we, children of a better covenant than the ancient religious laws, we, the cherished disciples of Jesus, should possess more comic resources than pagan antiquity. That fact may even rank as one condition of our general intellectual power. By all means let the sworn gainsayers quote the classic anecdote of the philosopher who died of laughing at the sight of a donkey eating figs, or even the comedies of Aristophanes and those of Plautus. My answer is that, apart from these epochs being essentially civilized and beliefs having already retreated considerably, the sense of the comic in question is not entirely like our own. It even has something barbaric about it, and we can scarcely grasp it fully except by a backward effort of mind which produces what is called 'pastiche'. As for the grotesque figures that antiquity has handed down to us, the masks, the bronze statuettes, the muscular representations of Hercules, the little Priapuses with bronze tongues curling upwards and pointed ears, with prodigious brain boxes and phalli – as for the latter, on which the fair daughters of Romulus innocently ride astride, these monstrous mechanisms of generation, decked out with bells and wings, I believe all these things to have a deeply serious intention. Venus, Pan, Hercules were not figures of fun. They were laughed at only after the coming of Jesus, with the help of Plato and Seneca. I believe that antiquity was full of respect for the drum majors and for all the circus acrobats with their various turns, and that all the extravagant fetishes I have just referred to are nothing but objects of adoration, or at most symbols of strength, and not at all intentionally comic figments of mind. Indian and Chinese idols are unaware of being laughable; the comic dwells in us Christians.

[...] Joy exists of itself, but it has different manifestations. Sometimes it can hardly be detected; at others it expresses itself in tears. Laughter is merely a form of expression, a symptom, an outward sign. Symptom of what? That is the whole question. Joy is a unit. Laughter is the expression of a double or contradictory feelings: and it is for this reason that a convulsion occurs. Thus the laughter of children, which some people might vainly try to use as a counter-argument, is of a quite different nature, even in its physical expression, in its form, from the laughter of an adult attending the performance of a comedy, or looking at a caricature, or from the terrible laughter of Melmoth, or Melmoth, the social outcast, the outsider standing at the extreme limits of the human world and on the frontiers of the higher life, of Melmoth, always believing himself to be on the point of escape from his compact with the devil, for ever hoping to exchange his superhuman power, cause of his misfortune, for the pure and undefiled conscience of a simple soul, which he envies. The laughter of children is like the blossoming of a flower. It is the joy of receiving, the joy of breathing, the joy of confiding, the joy of contemplating, of living, of growing up. It is like the joy of a plant. And so, generally speaking, its manifestation is rather the smile, something analogous to the wagging tail in a dog or the purring of cats. And yet, do not forget that if the laughter of children may, after all is said and done, be distinguished from the outward signs of animal contentment, the reason is that this laughter is not entirely devoid of ambition, and that is as it should be, in mini-men or in other words Satans of early growth.

There is a case where the question is more complex. I refer to the laughter of men, and I mean genuine laughter, guffaws of laughter, at the sight of things that are not marks of weakness or misfortune of fellow-humans. I refer of course to the kind of laughter provoked by what is grotesque. Fabulous creations, beings for whose existence no explanation drawn from ordinary common sense is possible, often excite in us a wild hilarity, excessive fits and swooning of laughter. Evidently a distinction is called for here, as we are confronted with a higher form. From the artistic point of view, the comic is an imitation; the grotesque, a creation. The comic is an imitation mixed with a certain degree of creative capacity, or, in other words, of artistic ideality. Now, human pride, which always gets the upper hand, and which is the natural cause of laughter in the case of the comic, also becomes the natural cause of laughter in the case of the grotesque. which is a creation, mixed with a certain faculty of imitating elements pre-existing in nature. I mean to say that, in this case, laughter is the expression of the idea of superiority, no longer of man over man, but of man over nature. [...] Find another plausible explanation if you can. If this one appears far-fetched and hard to accept, the reason is that laughter excited by the grotesque has in itself something profound, axiomatic and primitive, which comes much closer to the life of innocence and to absolute joy than the laughter aroused by the comic derived from social manners. Setting aside all considerations of usefulness, the same difference obtains between these two types of laughter as between the literature of involvement and the school of art for art's sake. Thus the grotesque looks down on the comic from a height of like proportions.

From now on I shall refer to the grotesque as the absolute comic, in contrast to the ordinary comic, which I shall call the significative comic. The significative comic speaks a language that is clearer, easier for the common man to understand, and especially easier to analyse, its element being obviously double: art and the moral idea; but the absolute comic, coming as it does much closer to nature, appears as a unity that must be grasped intuitively. There is only one proof of the grotesque, which is laughter, a burst of instantaneous laughter; confronted with the significative comic, we may be forgiven if ours is a delayed laughter; this does not detract from its value; it is simply a matter of quick analysis.

I have used the expression 'absolute comic', but we must be on our guard. From the point of view of the definitive absolute there is only joy. The comic can be absolute only relatively to fallen humanity, and it is in that sense that I am using the term.

The exalted nature of the absolute comic makes of it the special preserve of superior artists who have in them the necessary receptivity for absolute ideas. Thus the man who until now has apprehended these ideas better than anyone else, and who has exploited some of them in his purely aesthetic as well as his creative work is Theodor Hoffmann. He was always careful to distinguish between ordinary comic and the comic he called 'innocent comic'.

[...] In the absolute comic and the significative comic we find groups and sub-groups and families. The division between them may be drawn on different principles. It may in the first place be built on the law of pure philosophy, as I began by doing, or again on the artistic law of creation. The first division is produced by the primary separation between the absolute comic and the significative comic; the second is established on the type of special qualities each artist possesses. [...]

It must be added that one of the most distinctive signs of the absolute comic is to be unconscious of itself. That is to be seen, not only in certain animals like monkeys, in whom gravity is an essential element of the funniness, and in certain sculptural carica-tures of the ancients I have already referred to, but also in those Chinese grotesque figures which we find so highly diverting, and which have much less of a comic intention than is generally believed. A Chinese idol, though an object of veneration, scarcely differs from a tumble-over, or a pot-bellied chimney-piece ornament.

And so, to make an end with all these subtleties, all these definitions, and to conclude, let me say once and for all that the dominant idea of superiority is to be found both in the absolute comic and in the significative comic, as I have – too lengthily perhaps – explained; that, in order for the comic, in other words an emanation, an explosion, an emergence of the comic, to exist, there must be two beings in the presence of each other; that it is particularly in the laugher, in the spectator, that the sense of the comic resides; but that, on the other hand, in regard to this law of unselfconsciousness, an exception must be made of those men who have made it their profession to foster in themselves the sense of the comic, and to draw it out of themselves for the enjoyment of their fellow-men, a phenomenon that belongs to the class of all artistic phenomena that show the existence in the human being of a permanent dualism, the capacity of being both himself and someone else at one and the same time.

4. George Meredith, *An Essay on Comedy and the Uses of the Comic Spirit* (1897)

There are plain reasons why the Comic poetry is not a frequent apparition; and why the great Comic poet remains without a fellow. A society of cultivated men and women is required, wherein ideas are current and the perceptions quick, that he may be supplied with matter and an audience. The semi-barbarism of merely giddy communities, and feverish emotional periods, repel him; and also a state of marked social inequality of the sexes; nor can he whose business is to address the mind be understood where there is not a moderate degree of intellectual activity.

Moreover, to touch and kindle the mind through laughter, demands more than sprightliness, a most subtle delicacy. That must be a natal gift in the Comic poet. The substance he deals with will show him a startling exhibition of the dyer's hand, if he is without it. People are ready to except the head: and it is there that he aims. He must be subtle to penetrate. A corresponding acuteness must exist to welcome him. The necessity for the two conditions will explain how it is that we count him during centuries in the singular number.

Shakespeare is a well-spring of characters which are saturated with the comic spirit; with more of what we will call blood-life than is to be found anywhere out of Shakespeare; and they are of this world, but they are of the world enlarged to our embrace by imagination, and by great poetic imagination. They are, as it were – I put it to suit my present comparison – creatures of the woods and wilds, not in walled towns, not society. Jaques, Falstaff and his regiment, the varied troop of Clowns, Malvolio, Sir Hugh Evans and Fluellen – marvellous Welshman! – Benedict and Beatrice, Dogberry, and the rest, are subjects of a special study in the poetically comic.

His Comedy of incredible imbroglio belongs to the literary section. One may conceive that there was a natural resemblance between him and Menander, both in the scheme and style of his lighter plays. Had Shakespeare lived in a later and less emotional, less heroical period of our history, he might have turned to the painting of manners as well as humanity. Euripides would probably, in the time of Menander, when Athens was enslaved but prosperous, have lent his hand to the composition of romantic comedy. He certainly inspired that fine genius.

Molière followed the Horatian precept, to observe the manners of his age and give his characters the colour befitting them at the time. He did not paint in raw realism. He seized his characters firmly for the central purpose of the play, stamped then in the idea, and by slightly raising and softening the object of study (as in the case of the ex-Huguenot, Duke de Montausier, for the study of the Misanthrope, and, according to St. Simon, the Abbe Roquette for Tartuffe), generalized upon it so as to make it permanently human. Concede that it is natural for human creatures to live in society, and Alceste is an imperishable mark of one, though he is drawn in light outline, without any forcible human colouring.

The Misanthrope was yet more frigidly received. Molière thought it dead. 'I cannot improve on it, and assuredly never shall,' he said. It is one of the French titles to honour that this quintessential comedy of the opposition of Alceste and Celimene was ultimately understood and applauded. In all countries the middle class presents a public which, fighting the world, and with a good footing in the fight, knows the world best. It may be the most selfish, but that is a question leading us into sophistries. Cultivated men and women, who do not skim the cream of life, and are attached to the duties, yet escape the harsher blows, make acute and balanced observers. Molière is their poet.

Of this class in England, a large body, neither Puritan nor Bacchanalian, have [sic] a sentimental objection to face the study of the actual world. They take up disdain of it, when its truths appear humiliating: when the facts are not immediately forced on them, they take up the pride of incredulity. They live in a hazy atmosphere that they suppose an ideal one. Humorous writing they will endure, perhaps approve, if it mingles with pathos to shake and elevate the feelings. They approve of Satire, because, like the beak of the vulture, it seems of carrion, which they are not. But of Comedy they have a shivering dread, for Comedy enfolds with the wretched host of the world, huddles them with us all in an ignoble assimilation, and cannot be used by any exalted variety as a scourge and a broom. Nay, to be an exalted variety is to come under the calm curious eye of the Comic spirit, and be probed for what you are. Men are seen among them, and very many cultivated women. You may distinguish them by a favorite phrase: 'Surely we are not so bad!' and the remark: 'If that is human nature, save us from it!' as if it could be done: but in the peculiar Paradise of the willful people who will not see, the exclamation assumes the saving grace.

Thus, for want of instruction in the Comic idea, we lose a large audience among our cultivated middle class that we should expect to support Comedy. The sentimentalist is as averse as the Puritan and as the Bacchanalian.

These bad traditions of Comedy affect us not only on the stage, but in our literature, and may be tracked into our social life. They are the ground of the heavy moralizings by which we are outwearied, about Life as a Comedy, and Comedy as a jade, when popular writers, conscious of fatigue in creativeness, desire to be cogent in a modish cynicism: perversions of the idea of idea, and of the proper esteem for the society we have wrested from brutishness, and would carry higher. Stock images of this description are accepted by the timid and the sensitive, as well as by the saturnine, quite seriously; for not many look abroad with their own eyes, fewer still have the habit of thinking for themselves. Life, we know too well, is not a Comedy, but something strangely mixed; nor is Comedy a vile mask. The corrupted importation from France was noxious; a noble entertainment spoilt to suit the wretched taste of a villainous age; and the later imitations of it, partly drained of its poison and made decorous, became tiresome, notwithstanding their fun, in the perpetual recurring of the same situations, owing to the absence of original study and vigour of conception. Scene v. Act 2 of the Misanthrope, owing, no doubt, to the fact of our not producing matter for original study, is repeated in succession by Wycherley, Congreve, and Sheridan, and as it is at second hand, we have it done cynically – or such is the tone; in the manner of 'below stairs'. Comedy thus treated may be accepted as a version of the ordinary worldly understanding of our social life; at least, in accord with the current dicta concerning it. The epigrams can be made; but it is uninstructive, rather tending to do disservice. Comedy justly treated, as you find it in Molière, whom we so clownishly mishandled, the Comedy of Molière throws no infamous reflection upon life. It is deeply conceived, in the first place, and therefore it cannot be impure. Meditate on that statement. Never did man wield so shrieking a scourge upon vice, but his consummate self-mastery is not shaken while administering it. Tartuffe and Harpagon, in fact, are made each to whip himself and his class, the false pietists, and the insanely covetous.

The source of his wit is clear reason: it is a fountain of that soil; and it springs to vindicate reason, common-sense, pervading spirit that it inspires a pun with meaning and interest. His moral does not hang like a tail, or preach from one character incessantly cocking an eye at the audience, as in recent realistic French Plays: but is in the heart of his work, throbbing with every pulsation of an organic structure. If Life is likened to the comedy of Molière, there is no scandal in the comparison.

Congreve's Way of the World is an exception to our other comedies, his own among them, by virtue of the remarkable brilliancy of the writing, and the figures of Millamant. The comedy has no idea in it, beyond the stale one, that so the world goes; and it concludes with jaded discovery of a document at a convenient season for the descent of the curtain. A plot was an afterthought with Congreve. By the help of a woodened villain (Maskwell marked Gallows to the flattest eye, he gets a sort of plot in The Double Dealer. His Way of the World might be called The Conquest of a Town Coquette, and Millamant is a perfect portrait of a coquette, both in her resistance to Mirabel and the manner of her surrender, and also in her tongue. The wit here is not so salient as in certain passages of Love for Love, where Valentine feigns madness or retorts on his father, or Mrs. Frail rejoices in the harmlessness of wounds to a woman's virtue, if she 'keeps them from air.' In The Way of the World, it appears less prepared in the smartness, and is more diffused in the more characteristic style of the speakers. Here, however, as elsewhere, his famous wit is like a bully-fencer, not ashamed to lay traps for its exhibition, transparently petulant for the train between certain ordinary words and the powder-magazine of the improprieties to be fired. Contrast the wit of Congreve with Molière's. That of the first is a Toledo blade, sharp, and wonderfully supple for steel; cast for dueling, restless in the scabbard, being so pretty when out of it. To shine, it must have an adversary. Molière's wit is like a running brook, with innumerable fresh lights on it at every turn of the wood through which its business is to find a way. It does not run in search of obstructions, to be noisy over them; but when dead leaves and viler substances are heaped along the course, its natural song is heightened. Without effort, and with no dazzling flashes of achievement, it is full of healing, the wit of good breeding, the wit of wisdom. [...]

Rousseau, in his letter to D'Alembert on the subject of the Misanthrope, discusses the character of Alceste, as though Molière had put him forth for an absolute example of misanthropy; whereas Alceste is the only a misanthrope of the circle he finds himself placed in: he has a touching faith in the virtue residing in the country, and a critical love of sweet simpleness. Nor is he the principal person of the comedy to which he gives a name. He is only passively comic. Celimene is the active spirit. While he is denouncing and railing, the trial is imposed upon her to make the best of him, and control herself, as much as a witty woman, eagerly courted, can do. By appreciating him she practically confesses her faultiness, and she is better disposed to meet him half-way than he is to bend an inch: only she is *une ame de vingt ans*, the world is pleasant, and if the gilded flies of the Court are silly, uncompromising fanatics have their ridiculous features as well. Can she abandon the life they make agreeable to her, for a man who will not be guided by the common sense of his class; and who insists on plunging into one extreme – equal to suicide in her eyes – to avoid another? That is the comic question of the Misanthrope. Why will he not continue to mix with the world smoothly, appeased by the flattery of her secret and really sincere preference of him, and taking his revenge in satire of it, as she does from her own not very lofty standard, and will by and by do from his more exalted one? [...]

Without undervaluing other writers of Comedy, I think it may be said that Menander and Molière stand alone specially as comic poets of the feelings and the idea. In each of them there is conception of the Comic that refines even to pain, as in the Menedemus of the Heautontimorumenus, and in the Misanthrope. Menander and Molière have given the principal types to Comedy hitherto. The Micio and Demea of the Adelphi, with their opposing views of the proper management of youth, are still alive; the Sganarelles and Arnolphes of the Ecole des Maris and the Ecole des Femmes, are not all buried. Tartuffe is the father of the hypocrites; Orgon of the dupes; Thraso, of the braggadocios; Alceste of the 'Manlys'; Davus and Syrus of the intriguing valets, the Scapins and Figaros. Ladies that soar in the realms of Rose-Pink, whose language wears the nodding plumes of intellectual conceit, are traceable to Philaminte and Belise of the Femmes Savantes: and the mordant witty women have the tongue of Celimene. The reason is, that these two poets idealized upon life: the foundation of their types is real and in the quick, but they painted with spiritual strength, which is the solid in Art.

The idealistic conception of Comedy gives breadth and opportunities of daring to Comic genius, and helps to solve the difficulties it creates. How, for example, shall an audience be assured that an evident and monstrous dupe is actually deceived without being an absolute fool? In Le Tartuffe the note of high Comedy strikes when Orgon on his return home hears of his idol's excellent appetite. 'Le pauvre homme!' he exclaims. He is told that the wife of his bosom has become unwell. 'Et Tartuffe?' he asks, impatient to hear him spoken of, his mind suffused with the thought of Tartuffe, crazy with tenderness, and again he croons, 'Le pauvre homme!' It is the mother's cry of pitying delight at a nurse's recital of the feats in young animal gluttony of her cherished infant. After this masterstroke of the Comic, you not only put faith in Orgon's roseate prepossession, you share it with him by comic sympathy, and can listen with no more than a tremble of the laughing muscles to the instance he gives of the sublime humanity of Tartuffe:

'Un rien Presque suffit pour le scandaliser,
Jusque-la, qu'il se vint l'autre jour accuser

D'avoir pris une puce en faisant sa prière,
Et de l'avoir tuée avec trop de colère.'

And to have killed it too wrathfully! Translating Molière is like humming an air one has heard performed by an accomplished violinist of the pure tones without flourish. [...]

There has been fun in Bagdad. But there never will be civilization where Comedy is not possible; and that comes of some degree of social equality of the sexes. I am not quoting the Arab to exhort and disturb the somnolent East; rather for cultivated women to recognize that the Comic Muse is one of their best friends. They are blind to their interests in swelling the ranks of the sentimentalists. Let them look with their clearest vision abroad and at home. They will see that where they have no social freedom, Comedy is absent: where they are household drudges, the form of Comedy is primitive: where they are tolerably independent, but uncultivated, exciting melodrama takes its place and a sentimental version of them. Yet the Comic will out, as they would know if they listened to some of the private conversations of men whose minds are undirected by the Comic Muse: as the sentimental man, to his astonishment, would know likewise, if he in similar fashion could receive a lesson. But where women are on the road to an equal footing with men, in attainments and in liberty – in what they have won for themselves, and what has been granted them by a fair civilization – there, and only waiting to be transplanted from life to the stage, or the novel, or the poem, pure Comedy flourishes, and is, as it would help them to be, the sweetest of diversions, the wisest of delightful companions.

Now, to look about us in the present time, I think it will be acknowledged that in neglecting the civilization of the Comic idea, we are losing the aid of a powerful auxiliar. You see Folly perpetually sliding into new shapes in a society possessed of wealth and leisure, with many whims, many strange ailments and strange doctors. Plenty of common-sense is in the world to thrust her back when she pretends to empire. But the first-born of common-sense, the vigilant Comic, which is the genius of thoughtful laughter, which would readily extinguish her at the outset, is not serving as a public advocate.

You will have noticed the disposition of common-sense, under pressure of some pertinacious piece of light-headedness, to grow impatient and angry. That is a sign of the absence, or at least of the dormancy, of the Comic idea. For Folly is the natural prey of the Comic, known to it in all her transformations, in every disguise; and it is with the springing delight of hawk over heron, hound after fox, that it gives her chase, never fretting, never tiring, sure of having her, allowing her not rest.

Contempt is a sentiment that cannot be entertained by comic intelligence. What is it but an excuse to be idly minded, or personally lofty, or comfortably narrow, not perfectly humane? If we do not feign when we say that we despise Folly, we shut the brain. There is a disdainful attitude in the presence of Folly, partaking of the foolishness to Comic perception: and anger is not much less foolish than disdain. The struggle we have to conduct is essence against essence. Let no one doubt of the sequel when this emanation of what is firmest in us is launched to stroke down the daughter of Unreason and Sentimentalism: such being Folly's parentage, when it is respectable.

Our modern system of combating her is too long defensive, and carried on too ploddingly with concrete engine of war in the attack. She has time to get behind entrenchments. She is ready to stand a siege, before the heavily armed man of science and the writer of the leading article or elaborate essay have primed their big guns. It should be remembered that she has charms for the multitude; and an English multitude seeing her make a gallant fight of it will be half in love with her, certainly willing to lend her a cheer. Benevolent subscriptions assist her to hire her own man of science, her own organ in the Press. If ultimately she is cast out and overthrown, she can stretch a finger at gaps in our ranks. She can say that she commanded an army and seduced men, whom we thought sober men and safe, to act as her lieutenants. We learn rather gloomily, after she had flashed her lantern, that we have in our midst able men and men with minds for whom there is no pole-star in intellectual navigation. Comedy, or the Comic element, is the specific for the poison of delusion, while Folly is passing from the state of vapour to substantial form. […]

The Satirist is a moral agent, often a social scavenger, working on a storage of bile.

The Ironeist is one thing or another, according to his caprice. Irony is the humor of satire; it may be savage as in Swift, with a moral object, or sedate, as in Gibbon, with a malicious. The foppish irony fretting to be seen, and the irony which leers, that you shall not mistake its intention, are failures in satiric effort pretending to the treasures of ambiguity.

The Humourist of mean order is a refreshing laugher, giving tone to the feelings and sometimes allowing the feelings to be too much for him. But the humourist of high has an embrace of contrasts beyond the scope of the Comic poet.

Heart and mind laugh out at Don Quixote, and still you brood on him. The juxta-position of the knight and squire is a Comic conception, the opposition of their natures most humourous. They are as different as the two hemispheres in the time of Columbus, yet they touch and are bound in one by laughter. The knight's great aims and constant mishaps, his chivalrous valiancy exercised on absurd objects, his good sense along the derision, and the admirable figure he preserves while stalking through the frantically grotesque and burlesque assailing him, are in the loftiest moods of humour, fusing the Tragic sentiment with the Comic narrative.

The stroke of the great humourist is world-wide, with lights of Tragedy in his laughter.

Taking a living great, though not creative, humourist to guide our description: the skull of Yorick is in his hands in our seasons of festival; he sees visions of primitive man capering preposterously under the gorgeous robes of ceremonial. Our souls must be on fire when we wear solemnity, if we would not press upon his shrewdest nerve. Finite and infinite flash from one to the other with him, lending him a two-edged thought that peeps out of his peacefullest lines by fits, like the lantern of the fire-watcher at windows, going the rounds at night. The comportment and performances of men in society are to him, by the vivid comparison with their mortality, more grotesque than respectable. But ask yourself, Is he always to be relied on for justness? He will fly straight as the emissary eagle back to Jove at the true Hero. He will also make as determined a swift descent upon the man of his willful choice, whom we cannot distinguish as a true one. This vast power of his, built up of the feelings and the intellect in union, is often wanting in proportion and in discretion. Humourists touching upon History and Society are given to be capricious. They are, as in the case of Sterne, given to be sentimental; for with them the feelings are primary, as with singers. Comedy, on the other hand, is an interpretation of the general mind, and is for that reason of necessity kept in restraint. The French lay marked stress on 'mesure et goût', and they own how much they owe to Molière for leading them in simple justness and taste. We can teach them many things; they can teach us in this. [...]

You must, as I have said, believe that our state of society is founded in common-sense, otherwise you will not be struck by the contrasts the Comic Spirit perceives, or have it to look to for your consolation. You will, in fact, be standing in that peculiar oblique beam of light, yourself illuminated to the general eye as the very object of chase and doomed quarry of the thing obscure to you. But to feel its presence and to see it is your assurance that many sane and solid minds are with you in what you are experiencing: and this of itself spared you the pain of satirical heat, and the bitter craving to stroke heavy blows. You share the sublime of wrath, that would not have hurt the foolish, but merely demonstrates their foolishness. Molière was contented to revenge himself on the critics of the Ecole des Femmes, by writing the Critique de Ecole des Femmes, one of the wisest as well as the playfullest of studies in criticism. A perception of the comic spirit gives high fellowship. You become a citizen of the selector world, the highest we know of in connection with our old world, which is not supermundane. Look there for your unchallengeable upper class! You feel that you are one of this our civilized community, that you cannot escape from it, and would not if you could. Good hope sustains you; weariness does not overwhelm you; in isolation you see no charms for vanity; personal pride is greatly moderated. Nor shall your title of citizenship exclude you from worlds of imagination or of devotion. The Comic spirit is not hostile to the sweetest songfully poetic.

The laughter heard in circles not pervaded by the Comic idea, will sound harsh and soulless, like versified prose, if you step into them with a sense of the distinction. You will fancy you have changed your habitation to a planet remoter from the sun. You may be among powerful brains too. You will not find poets – or but a stray one, over-worshipped. You will find learned men undoubtedly, professors, reputed philosophers, and illustrious dilettanti. They have in them, perhaps, every element composing light, except the Comic. They read verse, they discourse of art; but their eminent faculties are not under that vigilant sense of a collective supervision, spiritual and present, which we have taken note of. They build a temple of arrogance; they speak much in the voice of oracle; their hilarity, if it does not dip in grossness, is usually a form of pugnacity.

The practice of a polite society will help in training them, and the professor on a sofa with beauties on each side of him, may become their pupil and a scholar in manners without knowing it: he is at least a fair and pleasing spectacle to the Comic Muse. But the society named polite is volatile in its adorations, and to-morrow will be petting a bronzed soldier, or a black African, or a prince, or a spiritualist: ideas cannot take root in its ever-shifting soul. It is besides addicted in self-defence to gabble exclusively of the affairs of its rapidly revolving world, as children on a whirligoround bestow their attention on the wooden horse or cradle ahead of them, to escape from giddiness and preserve a notion of identity. The professor is better out of a circle that often confounds by lionizing, sometimes annoys by abandoning, and always confuses. The school that teaches gently what peril there is lest a cultivated head should still be coxcomb's, and the collisions which may befall high-soaring minds, empty or full, is more to be recom-mended than the sphere of incessant motion supplying it with material. [...]

Modern French comedy is commendable for the directness of the study of actual life, as far as that, which is but the early step in such a scholarship, can be of service in composing and colouring the picture. A consequence of this crude, though well-meant, realism is the collision of the writers in their scenes and incidents, and in their characters. The Muse of most of them is an 'Aventuriere'. She is clever, and a certain diversion exists in the united scheme for confounding her. The object of this persona is to reinstate herself in the decorous world; and either, having accomplished this purpose through deceit, she has a 'nostalgie de la boue', that eventually casts her back into it, or she is exposed in her course of deception when she is about to gain her end. A very good, innocent young man is her victim, or a very astute, goodish young man obstructs her path. This latter is enabled to be the champion of the decorous world by knowing the indecorous well. He has assisted in the progress of Aventurieres downward; he will not help them to ascend. The world is with him; and certainly it is not much of an ascension they aspire to; but what sort of figure is he? The triumph of a candid realism is to show him no hero. You are to admire him (for it must be supposed that realism pretends to waken some admiration) as a credibly living young man; no better, only a little firmer and shrewder, than the rest. If, however, you think at all, after the curtain has fallen, you are likely to think that the Aventurieres have a case to plead against him. True, and the author has not said anything to the contrary; he has but painted from the life; he leaves his audience to the reflections of unphilosophic minds upon life, from the specimen he has presented in the bright and narrow circle of a spy-glass.

5. George Bernard Shaw, 'Meredith on Comedy' (1897)

[…] Mr. Meredith knows more about plays than playgoers. […] "The English public," he says, "have the basis of the comic in them: an esteem for common sense." The Englishman is the most successful man in the world simply because he values success – meaning money and social precedence more than anything else, especially more than fine art, his attitude towards which, culture-affectation apart, is one of half diffident, half contemptuous curiosity, and of course more than clear-headedness, spiritual insight, truth, justice, and so forth. It is precisely this unscrupulousness and singleness of purpose that constitutes the Englishman's preeminent "common sense"; and this sort of common sense, I submit to Mr. Meredith, is not only not "the basis of the comic," but actually makes comedy impossible, because it would not seem like common sense at all if it were not self-satisfiedly unconscious of its moral and intellectual bluntness, whereas the function of comedy is to dispel such unconsciousness by turning the searchlight of the keenest moral and intellectual analysis right on to it. […]

The Englishman prides himself on this anti-comedic common sense of his as at least eminently practical. As a matter of fact, it is just as often as not most pigheadedly unpractical. For example, electric telegraphy, telephony and traction are invented, and establish themselves as necessities of civilized life. The unpractical foreigner recognizes the fact, and takes the obvious step of putting up poles in his streets to carry wires. This expedient never occurs to the Briton. He wastes leagues of wire and does unheard-of damage to property by tying his wires and posts to such chimney stacks as he beguiles householders into letting him have access to. Finally, when it comes to electric traction, and the housetops are out of the question, he suddenly comes out in the novel character of an amateur in urban picturesqueness, and declares that the necessary cable apparatus would spoil the appearance of our streets. The streets of Nuremberg, the heights of Fiesole, may not be perceptibly the worse for these contrivances; but the beauty of Tottenham Court Road is too sacred to be so profaned: to its loveliness the strained bus-horse and his offal are the only accessories endurable by the beauty-loving Cockney eye. This is your common-sense Englishman. His helplessness in the face of electricity is typical of his helplessness in the face of everything else that lies outside the set of habits he calls his opinions and capacities. In the theatre he is the same. It is not common sense to laugh at your own prejudices: it is common sense to feel insulted when any one else laughs at them. Besides, the Englishman is a serious person: that is, he is firmly persuaded that his prejudices and stupidities are the vital material of civilization, and that it is only by holding on to their moral prestige with the stiffest resolution that the world is saved from flying back into savagery and gorilladom, which he always conceives, in spite of natural history, as a condition of lawlessness and promiscuity, instead of, as it actually is, the extremity, long since grown unbearable, of his own notions of law and order, morality, and conventional respectability. Thus he is a moralist, an ascetic, a Christian, a truth-teller and a plain dealer by profession and by conviction; and it is wholly against this conviction that, judged by his own canons, he finds himself in practice a great rogue, a liar, an unconscionable prate, a grinder of the face of the poor, and a libertine. Mr. Meredith points out daintily that the cure for this self-treasonable confusion and darkness is Comedy, whose spirit overheard will "look humanely malign and cast an oblique light on them, followed by volleys of silvery laughter." Yes, Mr. Meredith; but suppose the patients have "common sense" enough not to want to be cured! Suppose they realize the immense commercial advantage of keeping their ideal life and their practical business life in two separate conscience-tight compartments, which nothing but "the Comic Spirit" can knock into one! Suppose, therefore, they dread the Comic Spirit more than anything else in the world, shrinking from its "illumination," and considering its "silvery laughter" in execrable taste!

No doubt it is patriotically indulgent of Mr. Meredith to say that "Our English school has not clearly imagined society," and that "of the mind hovering above congregated men and women it has imagined nothing." But is he quite sure that the audiences of our English school do not know too much about society and "congregated men and women" to encourage any exposures from "the vigilant Comic", with its "thoughtful laughter," its "oblique illumination," and the rest of it? May it not occur to the purchasers of half-guinea stalls that it is bad enough to have to put up with the prying of Factory Inspectors, Public Analysts, County Council Inspectors, Chartered Accountants and the like, without admitting this Comic Spirit to look into still more delicate matters? It is clear that the Comic Spirit would break into silvery laughter if it saw all that the nineteenth century has to show it beneath the veneer? There is Ibsen, for instance: he is not lacking, one judges, in the Comic Spirit; yet his laughter does not sound very silvery, does it? No: if this were an age for comedies, Mr. Meredith would have been asked for one before this. How would a comedy from him be relished, I wonder, by the people who wanted to have the revisers of the Authorized Version of the Bible prosecuted for blasphemy because they corrected as many of its mistranslations as they dared, and who reviled Froude for not suppressing Carlyle's diary and writing a fictitious biography of him, instead of letting out the truth? Comedy, indeed! I drop the subject with a hollow laugh.

6. Mark Twain, 'How to Tell a Story' (1897)

The Humorous Story an American Development.—Its Difference from Comic and Witty Stories

I do not claim that I can tell a story as it ought to be told. I only claim to know how a story ought to be told, for I have been almost daily in the company of the most expert story-tellers for many years.

There are several kinds of stories, but only one difficult kind—the humorous. I will talk mainly about that one. The humorous story is American, the comic story is English, the witty story is French. The humorous story depends for its effect upon the MANNER of the telling; the comic story and the witty story upon the MATTER.

The humorous story may be spun out to great length, and may wander around as much as it pleases, and arrive nowhere in particular; but the comic and witty stories must be brief and end with a point. The humorous story bubbles gently along, the others burst.

The humorous story is strictly a work of art—high and delicate art—and only an artist can tell it; but no art is necessary in telling the comic and the witty story; anybody can do it. The art of telling a humorous story—understand, I mean by word of mouth, not print—was created in America, and has remained at home.

The humorous story is told gravely; the teller does his best to conceal the fact that he even dimly suspects that there is anything funny about it; but the teller of the comic story tells you beforehand that it is one of the funniest things he has ever heard, then tells it with eager delight, and is the first person to laugh when he gets through. And sometimes, if he has had good success, he is so glad and happy that he will repeat the "nub" of it and glance around from face to face, collecting applause, and then repeat it again. It is a pathetic thing to see.

Very often, of course, the rambling and disjointed humorous story finishes with a nub, point, snapper, or whatever you like to call it. Then the listener must be alert, for in many cases the teller will divert attention from that nub by dropping it in a carefully casual and indifferent way, with the pretense that he does not know it is a nub.

Artemus Ward used that trick a good deal; then when the belated audience presently caught the joke he would look up with innocent surprise, as if wondering what they had found to laugh at. Dan Setchell used it before him, Nye and Riley and others use it today.

But the teller of the comic story does not slur the nub; he shouts it at you—every time. And when he prints it, in England, France, Germany, and Italy, he italicizes it, puts some whopping exclamation-points after it, and sometimes explains it in a parenthesis. All of which is very depressing, and makes one want to renounce joking and lead a better life. Let me set down an instance of the comic method, using an anecdote which has been popular all over the world for twelve or fifteen hundred years. The teller tells it in this way:

The wounded soldier

In the course of a certain battle a soldier whose leg had been shot off appealed to another soldier who was hurrying by to carry him to the rear, informing him at the same time of the loss which he had sustained; whereupon the generous son of Mars, shouldering the unfortunate, proceeded to carry out his desire. The bullets and cannon-balls were flying in all directions, and presently one of the latter took the wounded man's head off—without, however, his deliverer being aware of it. In no long time he was hailed by an officer, who said:

"Where are you going with that carcass?"

"To the rear, sir—he's lost his leg!"

"His leg, forsooth?" responded the astonished officer; "you mean his head, you booby."

Whereupon the soldier dispossessed himself of his burden, and stood looking down upon it in great perplexity. At length he said:

> "It is true, sir, just as you have said." Then after a pause he added, "BUT HE TOLD ME IT WAS HIS LEG!!!!!"

Here the narrator bursts into explosion after explosion of thunderous horse-laughter, repeating that nub from time to time through his gasping and shriekings and suffocatings.

It takes only a minute and a half to tell that in its comic-story form; and isn't worth the telling, after all. Put into the humorous-story form it takes ten minutes, and is about the funniest thing I have ever listened to—as James Whitcomb Riley tells it.

He tells it in the character of a dull-witted old farmer who has just heard it for the first time, thinks it is unspeakably funny, and is trying to repeat it to a neighbor. But he can't remember it; so he gets all mixed up and wanders helplessly round and round, putting in tedious details that don't belong in the tale and only retard it; taking them out conscientiously and putting in others that are just as useless; making minor mistakes now and then and stopping to correct them and explain how he came to make them; remembering things which he forgot to put in their proper place and going back to put them in there; stopping his narrative a good while in order to try to recall the name of the soldier that was hurt, and finally remembering that the soldier's name was not mentioned, and remarking placidly that the name is of no real importance, anyway—better, of course, if one knew it, but not essential, after all—and so on, and so on, and so on.

The teller is innocent and happy and pleased with himself, and has to stop every little while to hold himself in and keep from laughing outright; and does hold in, but his body quakes in a jelly-like way with interior chuckles; and at the end of the ten minutes the audience have laughed until they are exhausted, and the tears are running down their faces.

The simplicity and innocence and sincerity and unconsciousness of the old farmer are perfectly simulated, and the result is a performance which is thoroughly charming and delicious. This is art—and fine and beautiful, and only a master can compass it; but a machine could tell the other story. To string incongruities and absurdities together in a wandering and sometimes purposeless way, and seem innocently unaware that they are absurdities, is the basis of the American art, if my position is correct. Another feature is the slurring of the point. A third is the dropping of a studied remark apparently without knowing it, as if one were thinking aloud. The fourth and last is the pause.

Artemus Ward dealt in numbers three and four a good deal. He would begin to tell with great animation something which he seemed to think was wonderful; then lose confidence, and after an apparently absent-minded pause add an incongruous remark in a soliloquizing way; and that was the remark intended to explode the mine—and it did.

For instance, he would say eagerly, excitedly, "I once knew a man in New Zealand who hadn't a tooth in his head"—here his animation would die out; a silent, reflective pause would follow, then he would say dreamily, and as if to himself, "and yet that man could beat a drum better than any man I ever saw."

The pause is an exceedingly important feature in any kind of story, and a frequently recurring feature, too. It is a dainty thing, and delicate, and also uncertain and treacherous; for it must be exactly the right length—no more and no less—or it fails of its purpose and makes trouble. If the pause is too short the impressive point is passed, and the audience have had time to divine that a surprise is intended—and then you can't surprise them, of course.

7. Henri Bergson, 'Laughter' (1901), edited and translated by Wylie Sypher

What does laughter mean? What is the basal element in the laughable? What common ground can we find between the grimace of a merry-andrew, a play upon words, an equivocal situation in a burlesque and a scene of high comedy? What method of distillation will yield us invariably the same essence from which so many different products borrow either their obtrusive odour or their delicate perfume? The greatest of thinkers, from Aristotle downwards, have tackled this little problem which has a knack of baffling every effort, of slipping away and escaping only to bob up again, a pert challenge flung at philosophic speculation.

The first point to which attention should be called is that the comic does not exist outside the pale of what is strictly human. A landscape may be beautiful, charming and sublime, or insignificant and ugly; it will never be laughable. You may laugh at an animal, but only because you have detected in it some human attitude or expression. You may laugh at a hat, but what you are making fun of, in this case, is not the piece of felt or straw, but the shape that men have given it, – the human caprice whose mould it has assumed. It is strange that so important a fact, and such a simple one too, has not attracted to a greater degree the attention of philosophers. Several have defined man as "an animal which laughs." They might equally well have defined him as an animal which is laughed at; for if any other animal, or some lifeless object, produced the same effect, it is always because of some resemblance to man, of the stamp he gives it or the use he puts it to. Here I would point out, as a symptom equally worthy of notice, the *absence of feeling* which usually accompanies laughter. It seems as though the comic could not produce its disturbing effect unless it fell, so to say, on the surface of a soul that is thoroughly calm and unruffled. Indifference is its natural environment, for laughter has no greater foe than emotion. I do not mean that we could not laugh at a person who inspires us with pity, for instance, or ever with affection, but in such a case we must, for the moment, put our affection out of court and impose silence upon our pity. In a society composed of pure intelligences there would probably be no more tears, though perhaps there would still be laughter; whereas highly emotional souls, in tune and unison with life, in whom every event would be sentimentally prolonged and re-echoed, would neither know nor understand laughter. Try, for a moment, to become interested in everything that is being said and done; act, in imagination, with those who act, and feel with those who feel; in a word, give your sympathy its widest expansion: as though at the touch of a fairy wand you will see the flimsiest of objects assume importance, and a gloomy hue spread over everything. Now step aside, look upon life as a disinterested spectator: many a drama will turn into a comedy. It is enough for us to stop our ears to the sound of music in a room, where dancing is going on, for the dancers at once to appear ridiculous. How many human actions would stand a similar test? Should we not see many of them suddenly pass from grave to gay, on isolating them from the accompanying music of sentiment? To produce the whole of its effect, then, the comic demands something like a momentary anesthesia of the heart. Its appeal is to intelligence, pure and simple.

This intelligence, however, must always remain in touch with other intelligences. And here is the third fact to which attention should be drawn. You would hardly appreciate the comic if you felt yourself isolated from others. Laughter appears to stand in need of an echo. Listen to it carefully: it is not an articulate, clear, well-defined sound; it is something which would fain be prolonged by reverberating from one to another, something beginning with a crash, to continue in successive rumblings, like thunder in a mountain. Still, this reverberation cannot go on for ever. It can travel within as wide a circle as you please: the circle remains, none the less, a closed one. Our laughter is always the laughter of a group. It may, perchance, have happened to you, when seated in a railway carriage or at *table d'hôte*, to hear travelers relating to one another stories which must have been comic to them, for they laughed heartily. Had you been one of their company, you would have laughed like them but, as you were not, you had no desire whatever to do so. A man who was once asked why he did not weep at a sermon when everybody else was shedding tears replied: "I don't belong to the parish!" What that man thought of tears would be still more true of laughter. However spontaneous it seems, laughter always implies a kind of secret freemasonry, or even complicity, with other laughers, real or imaginary. How often has it been said that the fuller the theatre, the more uncontrolled the laughter of the audience! On the other hand, how often has the remark been made that many comic effects are incapable of translation from one language to another, because they refer to the customs and ideas of a particular social group! It is through not understanding the importance of this double fact that the comic has been looked upon as a mere curiosity in which the mind finds amusement, and laughter itself as a strange, isolated phenomenon, without any bearing on the rest of human activity. Hence those definitions which tend to make the comic into an abstract relation between ideas: "an intellectual contrast," "a patent absurdity," etc., definitions which, even were they really suitable to every form of the comic, would not in the least explain why the comic makes us laugh. How, indeed, should it come about that this particular logical relation, as soon as it is perceived, contracts, expands and shakes our limbs, whilst all other relations leave the body unaffected? It is not from this point of view that we shall approach the problem. To understand laughter, we must put it back into its natural environment, which is society, and above all must we determine the utility of its function, which is a social one. Such, let us say at once, will be the leading idea of all our investigations. Laughter must answer to certain requirements of life in common. It must have a *social* signification.

Let us clearly mark the point towards which our three preliminary observations are converging. The comic will come into being, it appears, whenever a group of men concentrate their attention on one of their number, imposing silence on their emotions and calling into play nothing but their intelligence. What, now, is the particular point on which their attention will have to be concentrated, and what will here be the function of intelligence? To reply to these questions will be at once to come to closer grips with the problem. But here a few examples have become indispensable.

A man, running along the street, stumbles and falls; the passers-by burst out laughing. They would not laugh at him, I imagine, could they suppose that the whim had suddenly seized him to sit down on the ground. They laugh because his sitting down is involuntary. Consequently, it is not his sudden change of attitude that raises a laugh, but rather the involuntary element in this change, – his clumsiness, in fact. Perhaps there was a stone on the road. He should have altered his pace or avoided the obstacle. Instead of that, through lack of elasticity, though absentmindedness and a kind of physical obstinacy, *as a result, in fact, of rigidity or of momentum*, the muscles continued to perform the same movement when the circumstances of the case called for something else. That is the reason of the man's fall, and also of the people's laughter.

Now, take the case of a person who attends to the petty occupations of his everyday life with mathematical precision. The objects around him, however, have all been tampered with by a mischievous wag, the result being that when he dips his pen into the inkstand he draws it out all covered with mud, when he fancies he is sitting down on a solid chair he finds himself sprawling on the floor, in a word his actions are all topsy-turvy or mere beating the air, while in every case the effect is invariably one of momentum. Habit has given the impulse: what was wanted was to check the movement or deflect it. He did nothing of the sort, but continued like a machine in the same straight line. The victim, then, of a practical joke is in a position similar to that of a runner who falls, – he is comic for the same reason. The laughable element in both cases consists of a certain *mechanical inelasticity* just where one would expect to find the wideawake adaptability and the living pliableness of a human being. The only difference in the two cases is that the former happened of itself, whilst the latter was obtained artificially. In the first instance, the passerby does nothing but look on, but in the second the mischievous wag intervenes.

All the same, in both cases the result has been brought about by an external circumstance. The comic is therefore accidental: it remains, so to speak, in superficial contact with the person. How is it to penetrate within? The necessary conditions will be fulfilled when mechanical rigidity no longer requires for its manifestation a stumbling-block which either the hazard of circumstance or human knavery has set in its own way, but extracts by natural processes, from its own store, an inexhaustible series of opportunities for externally revealing its presence. Suppose, then, we imagine a mind always thinking of what it has just done and never of what it is doing, like a song which lags behind its accompaniment. Let us try to picture to ourselves a certain inborn lack of elasticity of both senses and intelligence, which brings it to pass that we continue to see what is no longer visible, to hear what is no longer available, to say what is no longer to the point: in short, to adapt ourselves to a past and therefore imaginary situation, when we ought to be shaping our conduct in accordance with the reality which is present. This time the comic will take up its abode in the person himself; it is the person who will supply it with everything – matter and form, cause and opportunity. Is it then surprising that the absent-minded individual – for this is the character we have just been describing – has usually fired the imagination of comic authors? When La Bruyère came across this particular type, he realised, on analysing it, that he had got hold of a recipe for the wholesale manufacture of comic effects. As a matter of fact he overdid it, and gave us far too lengthy and detailed a description of *Ménalque*, coming back to his subject, dwelling and expatiating on it beyond all bounds. The very facility of the subject fascinated him. Absentmindedness, indeed, is not perhaps the actual fountain-head of the comic, but surely it is contiguous to a certain stream of facts and fancies which flows straight from the fountain-head. It is situated, so to say, on one of the great natural watersheds of laughter. [...]

What life and society require of each of us is a constantly alert attention that discerns the outlines of the present situation, together with a certain elasticity of mind and body to enable us to adapt ourselves in consequence. *Tension* and *elasticity* are two forces, mutually complementary, which life brings into play. If these two forces are lacking in the body to any considerable extent, we have sickness and infirmity and accidents of every kind. If they are lacking in the mind, we find every degree of mental deficiency, every variety of insanity. Finally, if they are lacking in the character, we have cases of the gravest inadaptability to social life, which are the sources of misery and at times the causes of crime. Once these elements of inferiority that affect the serious side of existence are removed – and they tend to eliminate themselves in what has been called the struggle for life – the person can live, and that in common with other persons. But society asks for something more; it is not satisfied with simply living, it insists on living well. What it now has to dread is that each one of us, content with paying attention to what affects the essentials of life, will, so far as the rest is concerned, give way to the easy automatism of acquired habits. Another thing it must fear is that the members of whom it is made up, instead of aiming after an increasingly delicate adjustment of wills which will fit more and more perfectly into one another, will confine themselves to respecting simply the fundamental conditions of this adjustment; a cut-and-dried agreement among the persons will not satisfy it, it insists on a constant striving after reciprocal adaptation. Society will therefore be suspicious of all *inelasticity* of character, of mind and even of body, because it is the possible sign of a slumbering activity as well as of an activity with separatist tendencies, that inclines to swerve from the common centre round which society gravitates; in short, because it is the sign of an eccentricity. And yet, society cannot intervene at this stage by material repression, since it is not affected in a material fashion. It is confronted with something that makes it uneasy, but only as a symptom – scarcely a threat, at the very most a gesture. A gesture, therefore, will be its reply. Laughter must be something of this kind, a sort of *social gesture*. By the fear which it inspires, it restrains eccentricity, keeps constantly awake and in mutual contact certain activities of a secondary order which might retire into their shell and go to sleep, and in short, softens down whatever the surface of the social body may retain of mechanical inelasticity. Laughter, then, does not belong to the province of esthetics alone, since unconsciously (and even immorally in many particular instances) it pursues a utilitarian aim of general improvement. And yet there is something esthetic about it, since the comic comes into being just when society and the individual, freed from the worry of self-preservation, begin to regard themselves as works of art. In a word, if a circle be drawn round those actions and dispositions – implied in individual or social life – to which their natural consequences bring their own penalties, there remains outside this sphere of emotion and struggle – and within a neutral zone in which man simply exposes himself to man's curiosity – a certain rigidity of body, mind and character that society would still like to get rid of in order to obtain from its members the greatest possible degree of elasticity and sociability. This rigidity is the comic, and laughter is its corrective.

Still, we must not accept this formula as a definition of the comic. It is suitable only for cases that are elementary, theoretical and perfect, in which the comic is free from all adulteration. Nor do we offer it, either, as an explanation. We prefer to make it, if you will, the *leitmotiv* which is to accompany all our explanations. We must ever keep it in mind, though without dwelling on it too much, somewhat as a skilled fencer must think of the discontinuous movements of the lesson whilst his body is given up to the continuity of the fencing-match. We will now endeavor to reconstruct the sequence of the comic forms, taking up again the thread that leads from the horseplay of a clown up to the most refined efforts of comedy, following this thread in its often unforeseen windings, halting at intervals to look around, and finally getting back, if possible, to the point at which the thread is dangling and where we shall perhaps find – since the comic oscillates between life and art – the general relation that art bears to life. […]

Now, let us go back to the point we wished to clear up. By toning down a deformity that is laughable, we ought to obtain an ugliness that is comic. A laughable expression of the face, then, is one that will make us think of something rigid and, so to speak, coagulated, in the wonted nobility of the face. What we shall see will be an ingrained twitching or a fixed grimace. It may be objected that every habitual expression of the face, even when graceful and beautiful, gives us this same impression of something stereotyped? Here an important distinction must be drawn. When we speak of expressive beauty or even expressive ugliness, when we say that a face possesses expression, we mean expression that may be stable, but which we conjecture to be mobile. It maintains, in the midst of its fixity, a certain indecision in which are obscurely portrayed all possible shades of the state of mind it expresses, just as the sunny promise of a warm day manifests itself in the haze of a spring morning. But a comic expression of the face is one that promises nothing more than it gives. It is a unique and permanent grimace. One would say that the person's whole moral life has crystallised into this particular cast of features. This is the reason why a face is all the more comic, the more nearly it suggests to us the idea of some simple mechanical action in which its personality would for ever be absorbed. Some faces seem to be always engaged in weeping, others in laughing or whistling, others, again, in eternally blowing an imaginary trumpet, and these are the most comic faces of all. Here again is exemplified the law according to which the more natural the explanation of the cause, the more comic is the effect. Automatism, *inelasticity*, habit that has been contracted and maintained, are clearly the causes why a face makes us laugh. But this effect gains in intensity when we are able to connect these characters with some deep-seated cause, a certain *fundamental absentmindedness*, as though the soul had allowed itself to be fascinated and hypnotised by the materiality of a simple action.

[…]

The attitudes, gestures and movements of the human body are laughable in exact proportion as that body reminds us of a mere machine.

There is no need to follow this law through the details of its immediate applications, which are innumerable. To verify it directly, it would be sufficient to study closely the work of comic artists, eliminating entirely the element of caricature, and omitting that portion of the comic which is not inherent in the drawing itself. For, obviously, the comic element in a drawing is often a borrowed one, for which the text supplies all the stock-in-trade. I mean that the artist may be his own understudy in the shape of a satirist, or even a playwright, and that then we laugh far less at the drawings themselves than at the satire or comic incident they represent. But if we devote our whole attention to the drawing with the firm resolve to think of nothing else, we shall probably find that it is generally comic in proportion to the clearness, as well as the subtleness, with which it enables us to see a man as a jointed puppet. The suggestion must be a clear one, for inside the person we must distinctly perceive, as though through a glass, a set-up mechanism. But the suggestion must also be a subtle one, for the general appearance of the person, whose every limb has been made rigid as a machine, must continue to give us the impression of a living being. The more exactly these two images, that of a person and that of a machine, fit into each other, the more striking is the comic effect, and the more consummate the art of the draughtsman. The originality of a comic artist is thus expressed in the special kind of life he imparts to a mere puppet.

8. Sigmund Freud, 'The Tendencies of Wit' and 'Wit and the Various Forms of the Comic,' from *Wit and Its Relation to the Unconscious* (1905), translated by A. A. Brill

The pleasurable effect of harmless wit is usually of a moderate nature; all that it can be expected to produce in the hearer is a distinct feeling of satisfaction and a light ripple of laughter. […]

We all know what is meant by a "smutty" joke. It is the intentional bringing into prominence of sexual facts or relations through speech. However, this definition is no sounder than other definitions. A lecture on the anatomy of the sexual organs or on the physiology of reproduction need not, in spite of this definition, have anything in common with an obscenity. It must be added that the smutty joke is directed towards a certain person who excites one sexually, and who becomes cognizant of the speaker's excitement by listening to the smutty joke, and thereby in turn becomes sexually excited. Instead of becoming sexually excited the listener may react with shame and embarrassment, which merely signifies a reaction against the excitement and indirectly an admission of the same. The smutty joke was originally directed against the woman and is comparable to an attempt at seduction. If a man tells or listens to obscene jokes in male society, the original situation, which cannot be realized on account of social inhibitions, is thereby also represented. Whoever laughs at a smutty joke does the same as the spectator who laughs at a sexual aggression.

The sexual element which is at the basis of the obscene joke comprises more than that which is peculiar to both sexes, it is connected with all these things that cause shame, and includes the whole domain of the excrementitious. However, this was the sexual domain of childhood, where the imagination fancied a cloaca, so to speak, within which the sexual elements were either badly or not at all differentiated from the excrementitious. In the whole mental domain of the psychology of the neuroses, the sexual still includes the excrementitious, and it is understood in the old, infantile sense.

The smutty joke is like the denudation of a person of the opposite sex toward whom the joke is directed. Through the utterance of obscene words the person attacked is forced to picture the parts of the body in question, or the sexual act, and is shown that the aggressor himself pictures the same thing. There is no doubt that the original motive of the smutty joke was the pleasure of seeing the sexual displayed.

It will only help to clarify the subject if here we go back to the fundamentals. One of the primitive components of our libido is the desire to see the sexual exposed. Perhaps this itself is a development – a substitution for the desire to touch which is assumed to be the primary pleasure. As it often happens, the desire to see has here also replaced the desire to touch. The libido for looking and touching is found in every person in two forms, active or passive, or masculine and feminine; and in accordance with the preponderance of sex characteristics it develops preponderately in one or the other direction. In young children one can readily observe the desire to exhibit themselves nude. If the germ of this desire does not experience the usual fate of being covered up and repressed, it develops into a mania for exhibitionism, a familiar perversion among grown-up men. In women the passive desire to exhibit is almost regularly covered by the masked reaction of sexual modesty; despite this, however, remnants of this desire may always be seen in women's dress. I need only mention how flexible and variable convention and circumstances make that remaining portion of exhibitionism still allowed to women.

The Transformation of the Obscenity into Obscene Wit

In the case of men a great part of this striving to exhibit remains as a party of the libido and serves to initiate the sexual act. If this striving asserts itself on first meeting the woman it must make use of speech for two motives. First, in order to make itself known to the woman; and secondly, because the awakening of the imagination through speech puts the woman herself in a corresponding excitement and awakens in her the desire to passive exhibitionism. This speech of courtship is not yet smutty, but may pass over into the same. Wherever the yieldingness of the woman manifests itself quickly, smutty speech is short-lived, for it gives way to the sexual act. It is different if the rapid yielding of the woman cannot be counted upon, but instead there appears the defense reaction. In that case the sexually exciting speech changes into obscene wit as its own end; as the sexual aggression is inhibited in its progress towards the act, it lingers at the evocation of the excitement and derives pleasure from the indications of the same in the woman. In this process the aggression changes its character in the same way as any libidinous impulse confronted by a hindrance; it becomes distinctly hostile and cruel, and utilizes the sadistical components of the sexual impulse against the hindrance.

Thus the unyieldingness of the woman is therefore the next condition for the development of smutty wit; to be sure, this resistance must be of the kind to indicate merely a deferment and make it appear that further efforts will not be in vain. The ideal case of such resistance on the part of the woman usually results from the simultaneous presence of another man, a third person, whose presence almost excludes the immediate yielding of the woman. This third person soon becomes of the greatest importance for the development of the smutty wit, but next to him the presence of the woman must be taken account of. Among rural people or in the ordinary hostelry one can observe that not till the waitress of the hostess approaches the guests does the obscene wit come out; in a higher order of society just the opposite happens, here the presence of a woman puts an end to smutty talk. The men reserve this kind of conversation, which originally presupposed the presence of bashful women, until they are alone, "by themselves." Thus gradually the spectator, now turned the listener, takes the place of the woman as the object of the smutty joke, and through such a change the smutty joke already approaches the character of wit.

Henceforth our attention may be centered upon two factors, first upon the role that the third person – the listener – plays, and secondly, upon the intrinsic conditions of the smutty joke itself.

Tendency-wit usually requires three persons. Besides the one who makes the wit there is a second person who is taken as the object of the hostile or sexual aggression, and a third person in whom the purpose of the wit to produce pleasure is fulfilled. We shall later on inquire into the deeper motive of this relationship, for the present we shall adhere to the fact which states that it is not the maker of the wit who laughs about it and enjoys its pleasurable effect, but it is the idle listener who does. The same relationship exists among the three persons connected with the smutty joke. The process may be described as follows: As soon as the libidinous impulse of the first person, to satisfy himself through the woman, is blocked, he immediately develops a hostile attitude towards this second person and takes the originally intruding third person as his confederate. Through the obscene speech of the first person, the woman is exposed before the third person, who as a listener is fascinated by the easy gratification of his own libido.

It is curious that common people so thoroughly enjoy such smutty talk, and that it is a never-lacking activity of cheerful humor. It is also worthy of notice that in this complicated process which shows so many characteristics of tendency-wit, no formal demands, such as characterize wit, are made upon "smutty wit." The unveiled nudity affords pleasure to the first and makes the third person laugh.

Not until we come to the refined and cultured does the formal determination of wit arise. The obscenity becomes witty and is tolerated only if it is witty. The technical means of which it mostly makes use is allusion, i.e., substitution through a trifle, something remotely related, which the listener reconstructs in his imagination as a full-fledged and direct obscenity. The greater the disproportion between what is directly offered in the obscenity and what is necessarily aroused by it in the mind of the listener, the finer is the witticism and the higher it may venture in good society. Besides the coarse and delicate allusions, the witty obscenity also utilizes all other means of word- and thought-wit, as can be easily demonstrated by examples. [...]

What we had presumed in the beginning seems to have been confirmed, namely, that tendency-wit has access to other sources of harmless wit, in which all the pleasure is somehow dependent upon the technique. We can also reiterate that owing to our feelings we are in no position to distinguish in tendency-wit what part of the pleasure originates from the technique and what part from the tendency. *Strictly speaking, we do not know what we are laughing about.* In all obscene jokes we succumb to striking mistakes in judgment about the "goodness" of the joke as far as it depends upon formal conditions; the technique of these jokes is often very poor while their laughing effect is enormous.

Wit and the Various Forms of the Comic

We have approached the problems of the comic in an unusual manner. It appeared to us that wit, which is usually regarded as a subspecies of the comic, offered enough peculiarities to warrant our taking it directly under consideration, and thus it came about that we avoided discussing its relation to the more comprehensive category of the comic as long as it was possible to do so, yet we did not proceed without picking up on the way some hints that might be valuable for studying the comic. We found it easy to ascertain that the comic differs from wit in its social behavior. The comic can be content with only two persons, one who finds the comical, and one in whom it is found. The third person to whom the comical may be imparted reinforced the comic process, but adds nothing new to it. In wit, however, this third person is indispensible for the completion of the pleasure-bearing process, while the second person may be omitted, especially when it is not a question of aggressive wit with a tendency. Wit is made, while the comical is found; it is found first of all in persons, and only later by transference may be seen also in objects, situations, and the like. We know, too, in the case of wit that it is not strange persons, but one's own mental processes that contain the sources for the production of pleasure. In addition we have heard that wit occasionally reopens inaccessible sources of the comic, and that the comic often serves wit as a façade to replace the fore-pleasure usually produced by this well-known technique. All of this does not really point to a very simple relationship between wit and the comic. On the other hand, the problems of the comic have shown themselves to be so complicated, and have until now so successfully defied all attempts made by the philosophers to solve them, that we have not been able to justify the expectation of mastering it by a sudden stroke, so to speak, even if we approach it along the paths of wit. Incidentally we came provided with an instrument for investigating wit that had not yet been made use of by others; namely, the knowledge of dream-work. [...]

The Naïve

The species of the comic that is most closely allied to wit is the *naïve*. Like the comic the naïve is found universally and is not made like in the case of wit. The naïve cannot be made at all, while in the case of the pure comic the question of making or evoking the comical may be taken into account. The naïve must result without our intervention from the speech and actions of other persons who take the place of the *second* person in the comic or in wit. The naïve originates when one puts himself completely outside of inhibition, because it does not exist for him; that is, if he seems to overcome it without any effort. What conditions the function of the naïve is the fact that we are aware that the person does not possess this inhibition, otherwise we should not call it naïve but impudent, and instead of laughing we should be indignant. The effect of the naïve, which is irresistible, seems easy to understand. An expenditure of that inhibition energy which is commonly already formed in us suddenly becomes inapplicable when we hear the naïve and is discharged through laughter; as the removal of the inhibition is direct, and not the result of an incited operation, there is no need for a suspension of attention. We behave like the hearer in wit, to whom the economy of inhibition is given without any effort on his part. [...]

Occurrence and Origin of the Comic

The comical appears primarily as an unintentional discovery in the social relations of human beings. It is found in persons, that is, in their movements, shapes, actions, and characteristic traits. In the beginning it is found probably only in their psychical peculiarities and later on in their mental qualities, especially in the expression of these latter. Even animals and inanimate objects become comical as the result of a widely used method of personification. However, the comical can be considered apart from the person in whom it is found, if the conditions under which a person becomes comical can be discerned. Thus arises the comical situation, and this knowledge enables us to make a person comical at will by putting him into situations in which the conditions necessary for the comic are bound up with his actions. The discovery that it is in our power to make another person comical opens the way to unsuspected gains in comic pleasure, and forms the foundation of a highly developed technique. It is also possible to make one's self just as comical as others. The means which serve to make a person comical are transference into comic situations, imitations, disguise, unmasking, caricature, parody travesty, and the like. It is quite evident that these techniques may enter into the service of hostile or aggressive tendencies. A person may be made comical in order to render him contemptible or in order to deprive him of his claims to dignity and authority. But even if such a purpose were regularly at the bottom of all attempts to make a person comical this need not necessarily be the meaning of the spontaneous comic. […]

Comic of Situation

The origin of the comic pleasure discussed here, that is, the origin of such pleasure in a comparison of the other person with one's own self in respect to the difference between the identification expenditure (*Einfuhlungsaufwand*) and normal expenditure – is genetically probably the most important. It is certain, however, that it is not the only one. We have learned before to disregard any such comparison between the other person and one's self, and to obtain the pleasure-bringing difference from one side only, either from identification, or from the processes in one's own ego, proving thereby that the feeling of superiority bears no essential relations to comic pleasure. A comparison is indispensible, however, for the origin of this pleasure, and we find this comparison between two energy expenditures which rapidly follow each other and refer to the same function. It is produced either in ourselves by way of identification with the other, or we find it without any identification in our own psychic processes. The first case, in which the other person still plays a part, though he is not compared with ourselves, results when the pleasure-producing difference of energy expenditures comes into existence through outer influences which we can comprehend as a "situation", for which reason furnishes the comic do not here come into essential consideration; we laugh when we admit to ourselves that had we been placed in the same situation we should have done the same thing. Here we draw the comic from the relation of the individual to the often all-too-powerful outer world, which is represented in the psychic processes of the individual by the conventions and necessities of society, and even by his bodily needs. […]

Comic of Expectation

The other source of the comic, which we find in our own changes of investing energy, lies in our relations to the future, which we are accustomed to anticipate through our ideas of expectation. I assume that a quantitatively determined expenditure underlies our every idea of expectation, which in case of disappointment becomes diminished by a certain difference, and I again refer to the observations made before concerning "ideational mimicry." But it seems to me easier to demonstrate the real mobilized psychic expenditure for the cases of expectation. It is well known concerning a whole series of cases that the manifestation of expectation is formed by motor preliminaries;

this is first of all true of cases in which the expected events make demands on my motility, and these preparations are quantitatively determinable without anything further. [...]

Caricature

Human beings are not satisfied with enjoying the comic as they encounter it in life, but they aim to produce it purposely, thus we discover more of the nature of the comic by studying the methods employed in producing the comic. Above all one can produce comical elements in one's personality for the amusement of others, by making one's self appear awkward or stupid. One then produces the comic exactly as if one were really so, by complying with the condition of comparison which leads to the difference of expenditure; but one does not make himself laughable or contemptible through this; indeed, under certain circumstances one can even secure admiration. The feeling of superiority does not come into existence in the other when he knows that the actor is only shamming, and this furnishes us a good new proof that the comic is independent in principle of the feeling of superiority. [...]

Unmasking

Parody and *travesty* accomplish the degradation of the exalted by other means; they destroy the uniformity between the attributes of persons familiar to us and their speech and actions: by replacing either the illustrious persons or their utterances by lowly ones. Therein they differ from caricature, but not through the mechanism of the production of the comic pleasure. The same mechanism also holds true in *unmasking*, which comes into consideration only where some one has attached to himself dignity and authority which in reality should be taken from him. [...]

The Meeting of Wit and the Comic

In this case, something else comes to the aid of wit. The faulty thinking which as a form of thinking of the unconscious, wit utilizes for its technique, appears comical to the critic, although this is not necessarily the case. The conscious giving of free play to the unconscious and to those forms of thinking which are rejected as faulty, furnishes a means for the production of comic pleasure. This can be easily understood, as a greater expenditure is surely needed for the production of the foreconscious investing energy than for the giving of free play to the unconscious. When we hear the thought which is formed like one from the unconscious we compare it to its correct form, and this results in a difference of expenditure which gives origin to comic pleasure. A witticism which makes use of such faulty thinking as its technique and therefore appears absurd can produce a comic impression at the same time. If we do not strike the trail of the wit, there remains to us only the comic or funny story.

[...] All theories of the comic were objected to by the critics on the ground that in defining the comic these theories overlooked the essential element of it. This can be seen from the following theories, with their objections. The comic depends on a contrasting idea; yes, in so far as this contrast effects one comically and in no other way. The feeling of the comic results from the dwindling away of an expectation; yes, if the disappointment does not prove to be painful. There is no doubt that these objections are justified, but they are overestimated if one concludes from them that the essential characteristic mark of the comic has hitherto escaped our conception. What depreciates the general validity of these definitions are conditions which are indispensable for the origin of the comic pleasure, but which will be searched in vain for the nature of comic pleasure. The rejection of the objections and the explanations of the contradictions to the definitions of the comic will become easy for us, only after we trace back comic pleasure to the difference resulting from a comparison of two expenditures. Comic pleasure and the effect by which it is recognized – laughter, can originate only when this difference is no longer utilizable and when it is capable of discharge. We gain no pleasurable effect, or at most a flighty feeling of pleasure in which the comic does not appear, if the difference is put to other use as soon as it is recognized. Just as special precautions must be taken in wit, in order to guard against making new use of expenditure recognized as superfluous, so also can comic pleasure originate only under relations which fulfil this later condition. The cases in which such differences of expenditure originate in our ideational life are therefore uncommonly numerous, while the cases in which the comic originates from them is comparatively very rare. [...]

Humor

An examination of the comic, however superficial it may be, would be most incomplete if it did not devote at least a few remarks to the consideration of *humor*. There is so little doubt as to the essential relationship between the two that a tentative explanation of the comic must furnish at least one component for the understanding of humor. It does not matter how much appropriate and important material was presented as an appreciation of humor, which, as one of the highest psychic functions, enjoys the special favor of thinkers, we still cannot elude the temptation to express its essence through an approach to the formulae given for wit and the comic.

It has seemed to us that the pleasure of wit originates from an *economy of expenditure in inhibition*, of the comic from an *economy of expenditure in thought*, and of humor from an *economy of expenditure in feeling*. All three activities of our psychic apparatus derive pleasure from economy. They all strive to bring back from the psychic activity a pleasure which has really been lost in the development of this activity. For the euphoria which we are thus striving to obtain is nothing but the state of a bygone time in which we were wont to defray our psychic work with slight expenditure. It is the state of our childhood in which we did not know the comic, were incapable of wit, and did not need humor to make us happy.

We have heard that the release of painful emotions is the strongest hindrance to the comic effect. Just as aimless motion causes harm, stupidity mischief, and disappointment pain;—the possibility of a comic effect eventually ends, at least for him who cannot defend himself against such pain, who is himself affected by it or must participate in it, whereas the disinterested party shows by his behavior that the situation of the case in question contains everything necessary to produce a comic effect. Humor is thus a means to gain pleasure despite the painful affects which disturb it; it acts as a substitute for this affective development, and takes its place. If we are in a situation which tempts us to liberate painful affects according to our habits, and motives then urge us to suppress these affects *statu nascendi*, we have the conditions for humor. In the cases just cited the person affected by misfortune, pain, etc., could obtain humoristic pleasure while the disinterested party laughs over the comic pleasure. We can only say that the pleasure of humor results at the cost of this discontinued liberation of affect; it originates through the *economized expenditure of affect*. [...]

Formulæ for Wit, Comic, and Humor

Now, that we have reduced the mechanism of humoristic pleasure to a formula analogous to the formula of comic pleasure and of wit, we are at the end of our task. It has seemed to us that the pleasure of wit originates from an *economy of expenditure in inhibition*, of the comic from an *economy of expenditure in thought*, and of humor from an *economy of expenditure in feeling*. All three activities of our psychic apparatus derive pleasure from economy. They all strive to bring back from the psychic activity a pleasure which has really been lost in the development of this activity. For the euphoria which we are thus striving to obtain is nothing but the state of a bygone time in which we were wont to defray our psychic work with slight expenditure. It is the state of our childhood in which we did not know the comic, were incapable of wit, and did not need humor to make us happy.

5

The Twentieth and Early Twenty-First Century

INTRODUCTION

On 14 April 1912, RMS *Titanic*, the largest passenger steamship in the world, epitome of modern engineering and bourgeois affluence, struck an iceberg. It sank in three hours, drowning 1,517 passengers. More than any other event, the sinking of the *Titanic* symbolized the end of the Victorian era and what the French called *La Belle Époque*, a period of prosperity, optimism, and supposedly of progress. Two years later, a Serbian nationalist assassinated Austrian Archduke Franz Ferdinand in Sarajevo, initiating the First World War, a global conflict that led to the collapse of empires, the rise of technologies of mass destruction – tanks, aeroplanes, and poison gas – and millions of casualties. The new epoch began with the ethnic cleansing of more than a million Armenians by the Ottomans and, in Russia, the Bolshevik Revolution. The mid-twentieth century saw the rise of fascism in Germany and Italy, the Jewish Holocaust, the detonation of the first nuclear weapons in Hiroshima and Nagasaki, China's Communist Revolution in 1949, and the Cold War. Mass migration made the new century a time of social mobility, urbanization, and, following the invention of automobiles and Henry Ford's assembly-line technique of mass production, suburban development. Irish poet William Butler Yeats captured the unprecedented pace of technological, demographic, and political change, when he wrote in 1919, 'Things fall apart; the centre cannot hold; / Mere anarchy is loosed upon the world.' It seemed, in the words of the Algerian-French novelist Albert Camus, an age of 'absurdity', in which each person was an exile in an illogical universe.

The events of the twentieth century might not seem propitious for comedy, but brilliant, innovative comedy tends to emerge in disorienting times. Aristophanes'

Old Comedy was a response to the Peloponnesian War and the collapse of Athenian democracy. Boccaccio's rollicking *Decameron* represented the bubonic plague that killed more than 100 million people, including 60 per cent of the population of Florence, where it is set. Ben Jonson satirized the greed and immorality of early capitalism. Whether comedy serves as a release from oppressive conditions or as a social corrective, it often reflects tensions between order and disorder. The modern age is not unlike other periods in being scarred by warfare, pandemics, suffering, and death, but it is extraordinary in a number of ways. In sheer scale, the human experience changed. Global population, which reached one billion for the first time in 1804, exceeded seven billion in 2012, and people around the world are interconnected in ways that were unimaginable 100 years ago. The population of London today is forty times what it was in Shakespeare's day, when it was also almost entirely white and Christian. The relentlessly inventive culture of capitalism, with new attitudes about technology, speculative investment, and commerce, has changed how people regard the future and the past, work and play, the individual and the community, the planet and the very concept of human nature. Traditional social structures have been demolished. The authority of custom has given way to the excitement of novelty, and modern comedy reflects this manic energy.

The connection between comedy and history has also become a major focus of critical theory. In the nineteenth century, theorists complained that modern comedy represented a falling off from Greek, neoclassical, or Shakespearean models. Some recent critics have gone further. In *The Death of Comedy* (2003), Erich Segal (1937–2010) argued that comedy actually died in 1896 with the production of Alfred Jarry's absurdist *Ubu Roi*, which in his view was a 'deranged travesty'. Segal claims that none of the sources of laughter have changed in 2,500 years, but he laments that the traditional happy ending or *kōmos*, which defines Greek comedy's structure and social function, is no longer possible. Rather than the revel, renewal, and rejuvenation of Aristophanes, Samuel Beckett's bleak, postwar tragicomedy *Waiting for Godot* (1953) offers only futility; 'nothing to be done', as one character says. Segal is not the only recent critic to find modern comedies inadequate compared to Greek models. In their search for a modern Aristophanes or Menander, most of these critics ignore or disparage popular comedy of the commercial stage, cinema, and television. Segal says that comedy 'always thrives upon outrage', yet he angrily dismisses 'cinematic outrages', such as Stanley Kubrick's dark satire of the nuclear age, *Dr. Strangelove: or How I Learned to Stop Worrying and Love the Bomb* (1963). He asserts the value of comic outrage but does not consider the sources or limitations of his own.

The problem may not be the comedy but the theory. Critics like Segal imagine comedy in terms of an ancient ideal, unchanging, outside of history; so they are bound to be disappointed by modern comic artists and audiences who differ from their predecessors. Yet, as Michael North (1951–) comments in *Machine-Age Comedy* (2009), the fact that comic theory founded on classical precedents cannot cope at all with any comedy after 1896 suggests another possibility: that its 'premise is wrong and that the sources of laughter change over time just as they vary from place to place'. Early in the twentieth century, authors such as British novelist Virginia Woolf (1882–1941) and American critic Constance Rourke (1885–1941) questioned whether there was a single, universal form of humour or of comedy. They believed that it was better to situate humour in local contexts than to imagine the 'true comic spirit' (in the words of Victorian author George Meredith) that transcended time and place and would ultimately help to perfect 'a society of cultivated men and women'. In 'Pure English', Woolf finds the early-modern dramatic comedy *Gammer Gurton's Needle* 'typically English'. In her brief essay, she suggests a model of humour that is connected to the modern nation-state, implying that unique forms of humour arise from and contribute to the shared customs and characteristics of a particular people. 'A Frenchman could only enjoy such a play by an effort', she remarks. 'To us it comes straightforwardly'. This view of comedy captures the feeling, common in our interconnected, modern world, that we are often unable to explain what we find funny to people from other cultures or nations. According to this way of thinking, humour is not universal but local. Comedy is an aspect of sociality; it helps to define us versus them.

Rourke, who wrote criticism for magazines such as *The Nation* and *The New Republic*, focused on American popular culture, and in doing so she made a signal contribution to American Studies and to comic theory. In *American Humor: A Study of the National Character* (1931), she discovers a distinctive form of humour in the radical democracy of Jacksonian politics and the conditions of frontier-society. Rourke studied tall tales, improvisatory entertainments in opera houses and taverns, minstrel performances, and the 'foreign influences' that contributed to Americans' efforts to define themselves against Europeans. She critiques Meredith's theory that 'esteem for common sense' is always the 'basis of the Comic'. Rourke writes, 'So far as their humour was a sign the Americans had singularly little regard for common sense. American comedy might be aggressive or competitive ... but these elements were transformed by extravagant purposes.' She also implicitly rejects the elitism of critics who disparage modern comedy for failing to be as great as the classics, but she doesn't discount the importance of class tension. Although Rourke suggests that the 'comic spirit in America was a levelling agent', she also comments that laughter 'produced the illusion of levelling obstacles', implying that the democratic (levelling) comic spirit went only so far, and might sometimes serve a conservative function.

Modernism, a theoretical and artistic movement that arose with industrial capitalism and cosmopolitanism, reflected the excitement, the challenge, and often the impossibility of coping with novelty and change. Critic Martin Esslin captured this ethos in his 1961 book, *The Theatre of the Absurd*, which analysed the bewilderingly irrational, yet often wildly comic 'anti-plays' of Beckett, Ionesco, and others. For many artists, the failure of old models was not a source of despair but of creativity. In 1909 the Italian poet Filippo Marinetti issued the Futurist manifesto, which critiqued the ideals of the past and celebrated speed, the mob, the factory, and the machine. New forms of comedy emerged with new theories of the work of art in the age of mechanical reproduction and mass culture. The development of radio, film, television, and the internet have prompted questions about the medium as well as the message of comedy. Writing about the silent film star Charlie Chaplin in 1935, literary theorist Walter Benjamin reflects, 'Whether it is his walk, the way he handles his cane, or the way he raises his hat – always the same jerky sequence of tiny movements applies the law of the cinematic image sequence to human motorial functions. Now, what is it about this behavior that is distinctly comic?' For Benjamin, the medium of film seems essentially funny. Chaplin is ideally matched to the cinema because he's always already cinematic.

Comedy has traditionally been associated with the spontaneous, the organic, and the primitive, but a new motive for modern laughter appears in mechanical reproduction itself. Inorganic objects came to life. Nothing remained fixed in place. New developments in trick photography and animation seemed inherently funny. In *Machine-Age Comedy*, North asserts that modernists found technological modernity intrinsically comic. Mass production created new aesthetic objects and new comic forms in the silent films of Chaplin and Keaton, Marcel Duchamp's 'readymades' (manufactured objects repositioned as art), and the crazy machines of cartoonist-inventor Rube Goldberg. Countering Henri Bergson's theory of comedy as a corrective to mechanization of modern life (cf. Chapter 4), North argues that artists celebrated the relationship between the mechanical and the human. Modernity itself, he suggests, is governed by a frenetic comic rhythm. Avant-garde aesthetics and popular culture find comedy in incessant novelty and dislocation, as 'new humourists favor gags and stunts, nonsensical routines that amuse because of their inconsequence, and repetitive, stereotyped bits of shtick that spark a laugh of recognition'. Modernists also found that the self was not whole or monolithic but multiple, decentred or fragmented; so their art turned from the notion of self-expression to the materials and media of art itself, whether language, the canvas, the stage, the camera, or the celluloid of film.

Italian playwright Luigi Pirandello's (1867–1936) essay 'On Humor' (*L'umorismo*, 1908) reflects modernist preoccupations with literary form and the decentred self. 'Every feeling, every thought, or every impulse that arises in the humorist', Pirandello writes, 'immediately splits into its contrary'. He defines the comic as the 'perception of the opposite' (*l'avvertimento del contrario*). Yet the essay itself is contradictory. On the one hand, it is a work of criticism that situates humour in literary history. On the other, it is an expression of Pirandello's own strategies for representing the fragmented self in fiction and drama. For Pirandello, the humourist does not try to make people laugh, or necessarily write comedies, but prompts them to perceive the conflicts in every situation. Pirandello was interested in the role-playing of everyday life, the uncertain line between sanity and madness, and the split between conscious and unconscious minds. Modern life lacks the order and coherence found in traditional works of art; so, Pirandello asks what if we have within us not one, but four or five souls, each at odds with the others? That is the divided reality the humourist perceives. In the plays he wrote later, characters fail to create coherent selves; they feel self-estranged, alienated, and homeless. Pirandello's *Six Characters in Search of an Author* (1921), began as a tragedy and turned into a comedy because after he conceived of the characters, he found that he could not impose a tragic form on them. The result is a play that takes place on multiple levels. In theory and practice, Pirandello questioned conventions of comedy in richly philosophical works that make the familiar seem strange.

For some Marxist authors, comedy suggested a form of self-conscious political action, as opposed to tragedy which represented the helplessness of the individual before nature or the gods. Bertolt Brecht (1898–1956), the German playwright, theorist and director, charges notions of self-estrangement and meta-theatricality with the idea that society can only be understood as a product of labour and its material conditions. 'Thinking above the flow of the play', he says, 'is more important than thinking from within the flow of the play'. In his theoretical and dramatic texts, Brecht focuses on the paradoxes at the core of consciousness, participating in a self-critical or dialectical tradition he traces to Marx and Hegel. In his dialogue 'On Hegelian Dialectics', Brecht calls Hegel himself 'one of the greatest humourists among the philosophers', because he couldn't think 'of order without disorder'. Like Marx, Brecht applies Hegel's dialectical method to historical problems, when he says that something comes into being where the 'sharpest antitheses between the classes appear'. His famous 'alienation effect' (*Verfremdungseffekt*) evokes the formalist notion of *estrangement* as well as techniques of the *eirôn*, or self-deprecator, of classical comedy. Above all, Brecht's comic theory is political. For Brecht, tragedy presumes inevitability in both form and content, whereas comedy is capable of leaps, dilation, and deformation. The estrangement technique divests actions of their matter-of-course quality and reveals them as decisions which could have turned out differently. The aim of such theatre is to connect our situation as audience with our experience as actors in a world of our own making. Brecht's influence is evident in the work of Swiss dramatist Friedrich Dürrenmatt (1921–90). Tragedy, according to Dürrenmatt, presupposes a formed world, whereas comedy 'supposes an unformed world, a world being made and turned upside down, a world about to fold like ours'. Rather than immersing the audience in myths from times immemorial, like tragedy, comedy creates critical distance.

Interdisciplinary approaches to comedy in the twentieth century showed that dramatic comedy was only one among many forms of culture, or social phenomena, which employed humour and dramatic structures. Sociologists, anthropologists, philosophers and literary scholars drew from structural linguistics and rhetoric to investigate how humans make meaning through myths, symbols, and narrative structures. Humour itself can seem like a mode of anthropology, as it reflects self-consciously on the strangeness of everyday actions. The first major work on dramatic comedy in this period was Francis MacDonald Cornford's *The Origin of Attic Comedy* (1914), an anthropological study of Greek drama that rooted classical comedy in the cult of Dionysus. Cultural anthropologist Mahadev Apte (1931–) argues in *Humor and Laughter: An Anthropological Approach* (1985) not only that culture is the key to under-standing humour, but also that humour helps us to understand culture. Apte offers the first comprehensive, cross-cultural work on this topic. He finds differences between men's and women's humour in diverse local settings. Although women's humour commonly reflects inequalities between the sexes, 'social factors such as marriage, advanced age, and the greater freedom enjoyed by women in groups remove some of the constraints ordinarily imposed on them and reduce the differences between men and women's humour'. From his ethnographic research, Apte concludes that restric-tions on the kinds of humour in which women can engage shed new light on social culture. With critical theory questioning the notion of gender and race, the theorists began to look at laughter as a double-edged sword: on the one hand, laughter can be a weapon against oppression; on the other hand, it can be a weapon of oppression. Thus analysis began to focus on the distribution of power within the structure of comic representation. Who laughs, and at whom? What do the jokes do? How is power estab-lished and distributed via humour? Many feminist critics began to wonder about the relation between gender and comedy. Among many voices, Jill Dolan summarizes the issue in 1984: 'Comedy usually deals with topics that are psychologically threatening in the "real world" by culling a stereotype from their complexity and holding it up for group ridicule. Comedy is essentially meant to be reassuring. Who it reassures, however, is another matter.'

Comedy functions within networks of behaviour patterns, customs, and traditions; so as a subject of study, it has crossed disciplinary boundaries. Theorists from diverse fields have explored ways in which humans use laughter to define the difference between the knowable and the unknowable. For instance, French theorist Georges Bataille (1897–1962) combined interests in literature, anthropology, philosophy, economy, and sociology. Writing under the influence of Marx and Freud, he argued that laughter is a nervous response to the unknown. For Bataille, philosophy emerges from laughter because 'the unknown makes us laugh'. Like Bataille, French-born theorist René Girard (1923–2015) is interested in philosophical anthropology. Analysing Aristotelian catharsis and the similarities of tragedy and comedy, he theorizes the function of laughter in post-war culture. The 'possibilities for comedy have never been greater', he wrote in 1973. 'Never before has the precarious, unstable, and "nervous" nature of laughter been so much in evidence.' Bataille, Girard, and others do not simply theorize comedy; they treat theory (or philosophy) *as* a form of comedy.

Jacques Derrida (1930–2004), a Jewish, French-Algerian philosopher, influenced by Bataille and Swiss linguist Ferdinand de Saussure, is a key figure in post-structuralism, a mid-twentieth-century intellectual movement across the humanities and social sciences, which started with the notion that meaning in language is a matter of difference (*up* is *not down*; *black* is *not white*). The meaning of the signifier (a word, sound, or image) derives from what it is not. As in Woolf's definition of English comedy as *not French*, identity is a matter of difference. However, though meaning is generated via binary oppositions, the two terms are not of equal value. Western culture tends to privilege one term over the other, an ordering that Derrida (who regarded himself as a historian) deconstructs. 'Male' is 'not female', but male-dominated societies assume that 'man' comes first (as Adam comes before Eve in the Bible), making 'woman' merely non-man, or less than man. Men define themselves against women, and this opposition is central to diverse comedies from Aristophanes to Mary Tyler Moore. In comedy, gender and sexuality are major subjects, most obviously in the marriage plot. But if we deconstruct the male-female opposition, we see how these terms depend on each other. Transvestite plots, in which men play women (or, in Shakespeare, boys play women playing boys) continue to be popular in film comedies such as *Tootsie, Mrs.*

Doubtfire, and *Kinky Boots*, raising questions about repression, freedom, and the theatrical construction of gender identity. Feminist theorists show that 'man' is what he is only by defining himself against what he is not. Deconstruction, thus, also informed a major ideological turn in twentieth-century theory, with implications for comedy: how do we distinguish between self and other, sense and nonsense, high and low? Comic theorists have dismantled and analysed these oppositions.

Derrida denies the possibility of an objective viewpoint. There is no solid ground upon which to construct a hierarchy of meanings. In *Writing and Difference* (1967), he calls laughter a philosophical gesture that enables us to subvert idealist or metaphysical models of truth and to question traditional modes of philosophical discourse: 'To laugh at philosophy (at Hegelianism) calls for an entire "discipline," an entire "method of meditation" that acknowledges the philosopher's byways, understands his techniques, makes use of his ruses, manipulates his cards, lets him deploy his strategy, appropriates his texts.' This mode of cultural analysis denies stable meaning or unmediated access to "reality". Laughter implicates the critic, who cannot step outside of the structures she analyses. According to Derrida, the deconstructive method itself is a form of laughter, and only such laughter can produce self-knowledge. It is a philosophical instance of comic inversion: 'Laughter alone exceeds dialectic and the dialectician: it bursts out only on the basis of an absolute renunciation of meaning, an absolute rising of death, what Hegel calls abstract negativity.' The ironic self-consciousness of postmodern theory assumes a comic stance, or an academic playfulness. Canadian literary theorist Linda Hutcheon (1947–) implicitly extends Derrida's critical position in her book, *A Theory of Parody* (1985). As a form of criticism itself, she writes, 'parody has the advantage of being both a re-creation and a creation'. It raises questions about the origins and authenticity of a work of art. Parody is a subgenre of the comic which ridicules its object, yet parody is not simply comic. It might better be called 'ironic', Hutcheon suggests, because it is a way of 'marking of difference'. Like other post-structuralist critics, she is interested in semantic inversion, the instability of meaning, breaking down the distinction between text and context. Irony and parody both raise questions about difference and identity, or in Hutcheon's terms, 'otherness and incorporation'.

Parody, an ancient form of comic imitation, assumes heightened importance in the sceptical, playful, and self-critical culture of postmodernism. Susan Sontag (1933–2004), for instance, challenged normative categories of art and identity in her iconoclastic essay 'Notes on "Camp"' (1964). This ground-breaking piece made Sontag famous as a cultural critic in the 1960s and captured the anti-authoritarian spirit of that decade. Camp is a comic vision of the world, a form of ebullient self-parody that epitomizes comic detachment. It is a sensibility that proposes itself seriously, but cannot be taken seriously because it is 'too much'. Camp art is bad to the point of being enjoyable. The antithesis of tragedy, Sontag explains, 'Camp involves a new, more complex relation to "the serious"'. One can be serious about the frivolous, frivolous about the serious. Drawing on Oscar Wilde, Sontag subverts serious/frivolous, male/female, highbrow/lowbrow oppositions. Camp takes a 'queer' approach to sexuality, for instance, finding that what is most beautiful in virile men is something feminine; what is most beautiful in feminine women is something masculine. Camp sees everything in quotation marks. One is not a woman, but a 'woman', always playing-a-role. Sontag regards homosexuals as the vanguard of Camp because the 'metaphor of life as theatre is peculiarly suited as a justification' of their situation in the 1960s. Camp taste is a mode of enjoyment, of appreciation, not of judgement. Building on the work of Sontag and Hutcheon, in *The New Republic* and *The New York Times*, a 1999 argument, between philosopher Martha Nussbaum and gender theorist Judith Butler questioned the political effectiveness of parodic language and evoked earlier debates about the didactic, corrective role of comedy. Nussbaum accused Butler of staging 'parodic performances' in her theoretical writings that were ineffective because not grounded in real political action. In response, Butler asserted the role of parodic language and Camp in creating a more just world.

Modern comic theory centres on questions of 'significance' or where meaning comes from. Language is the most basic form of social practice, and therefore it is loaded with moral values and ideological assumptions. Russian theorist Mikhail Bakhtin (1895–1975) wrote on Marxism and the philosophy of language, and on popular culture in late-medieval and early-modern Europe. His influence has extended from literary criticism, semiotics, and philosophy to sociology and anthropology. Bakhtin began his career shortly after the Russian Revolution, but his works were only translated and published in the West decades later. In his book *Rabelais and His World*, he coined the term 'carnivalesque' to define a literary mode that subverts the assumptions of the dominant style through humour. In the medieval period, carnival (the popular culture of the marketplace) offered a release from the official culture of Church and State. People led two lives: official life, which was 'serious and gloomy', and 'the *life of the carnival square*, free and unrestricted, full of ambivalent laughter, blasphemy, the profanation of everything sacred, full of debasing and obscenities, familiar contact with everyone and everything'. Bakhtin explains that both lives 'were legitimate, but separated by strict temporal boundaries'. A time of 'misrule', carnival was liberating.

Later it became ideologically significant when the radical laughter of the marketplace, the *carnivalesque*, entered the language of 'great literature'. Comic authors, according to Bakhtin, are the heirs of a popular culture that destabilizes the official worldview. Laughter is a 'social gesture', and carnival was a safety valve for the oppressed and an outlet for a proletarian voice against the ruling class.

Bakhtin's work, along with that of Derrida, historian of ideas Michel Foucault, and cultural anthropologists Clifford Geertz and Victor Turner, contributed to vital new forms of literary-historical research; though recent theorists have challenged Bakhtin's notion that the critic could detach himself from his object of study. This trend is nowhere more evident than in the 'New Historicism', a term coined by Renaissance scholar Stephen Greenblatt in 1980. The New Historicism continued the practice of crossing boundaries between history, anthropology, art, and politics, while challenging the norm of disembodied objectivity. These critics argue comedy is inseparable from the contexts in which it is produced and that Shakespeare's comedies are not ends in themselves but a source of cultural production, or 'cultural poetics'. *Twelfth Night, A Midsummer Night's Dream*, and *The Merchant of Venice*, for example, shape and are shaped by representations of gender and power in the stratified society of early-modern England, where authority is invested in men, with the significant exception of Queen Elizabeth. Comedy and jokes are symbolic acts, establishing a shared world of cultural practices and ethics. One crucial corollary of this idea is that culture is not only, in the words of Matthew Arnold, 'the best which has been thought and said', but all the material practices, customs, beliefs of a given society. Neither the comedies nor the critics are outside of history; so the criticism itself must take into account its own biases and contexts. Interpretation is informed by the historical situation of the inter-preter. Influenced by Marxism, structuralism, and cultural studies, such ideological criticism investigates how people make sense of their world and how particular worldviews reflect particular sets of interests, assumptions, and power structures and exclude others.

Related to the theory that history informs our knowledge of comedy is the idea that comedy, like other symbolic practices, shapes our understanding of history. Karl Marx had suggested such a way of viewing historical processes. History has form, and the form matters, Marx believed, because, while humans make their own history, they do not make it just as they please but under circumstances given and transmitted from the past. American theorist Kenneth Burke (1897–1993) used the term 'frames of acceptance' to describe the system of meanings by which people gauge a historical situation and adopt a role in relation to it. Burke was a theorist of rhetoric and literature who suggested in his book *Attitudes toward History* (1937) that we confront the conditions and persons of our times through diverse 'attitudes'. According to Burke, the 'comic frame' is the 'attitude of attitudes' because it is a way of viewing 'human antics as a comedy, albeit as a comedy ever on the verge of the most disastrous tragedy'. Burke renews an ancient debate about the rhetorical function of comedy, but he also extends the term 'rhetoric' to include unconscious factors and everyday life. For Burke, comedy represents the highest degree of self-consciousness or 'forensic complexity'. It exposes error to correction. 'The class that can produce good comedy', Burke writes, 'is about as happy as can be'.

Burke's 'comic attitude' is a position from which to reflect on the limitations of other attitudes and the misunderstandings that arise between them, a view reflected in the work of Milan Kundera (1929–), a Czech-born author best known for his philosophical novels. Kundera moved to France in 1975, and his work illustrates the fact that different notions of humour evolved in the liberal democracies of the West and the totalitarian regimes of the East. In his novel *The Book of Laughter and Forgetting* (1978), he suggests that humour is bound to historical and political contexts: 'We are all prisoners of a rigid conception of what is important and what is not.' However, there are several kinds of laughter. There is laughter that reinforces the status quo, laughter that is the tool of oppression, which humiliates its victims, and there is a third kind of humour, black humour, which can function as a tool against oppression. It is the humour of people 'who are far from power, make no claim to power, and see history as a blind old witch whose moral verdicts make them laugh'. Each kind of humour reflects a different political position, and each has different aims and objectives. The postmodern condition, Kundera argues, is comparable to a totalitarian regime insofar as it collapses subversive laughter into the empty laughter of mass consumption.

In Communist countries, the relationship between comedy and politics was very complicated. Communist regimes felt threatened by any uncontrolled speech. Comedy thus became a subversive affair; the audience and the actors, united in their common understanding of their political predicament, exercised the only possible form of resistance: intellectual distance from an oppressive ideology. Actors and playwrights learnt to speak between the lines, using metaphors, symbols, or sometimes just a wink to communicate their anti-establishment sentiments to their audiences. The comic strategy of that time was what Peter Sloterdijk (in 1983) called 'kynicism', that is, subversion of the official structures through irony and sarcasm, a way of 'pissing against the idealist wind'. 'Cheekiness has, in principle, two positions', writes Sloterdijk, 'namely, above and below, hegemonic power and oppositional power'. He insists that the kynic must 'challenge the public sphere because it is the only space in which the overcoming of idealist arrogance can be meaningfully demonstrated'.

Though contemporary with Kundera and Sloterdijk, American philosopher Stanley Cavell (1926–) offers a liberal, democratic theory of comedy in his analysis of popular American film comedies of the 1930s and 1940s, showing that Hollywood cinema can be both philosophically and culturally significant. The opening years of the Depression were a key moment in the history of cinema because of the advent of sound, as well as the successes of first-wave feminism, and changing attitudes about public and private life. In these American films, characters question how to live and express the utopian longings and commitments of the culture. These fast-paced 'screwball comedies' are a major achievement in the history of comedy. As comedies of manners, they inherit the preoccupations of Shakespearean romance and Greek 'Old Comedy', yet offer modern visions of community. They disquiet the foundations of their characters' lives. Cavell's *Pursuits of Happiness: The Hollywood Comedy of Remarriage* (1981) defines a new genre, emerging from this era in cinema, 'the comedy of remarriage', in which marriage is subjected to the fact or threat of divorce. The marriage and divorce of the central couple provokes questions about what a good marriage is, what makes it important and legitimate. The goal of these plots is not to get the central pair together, but to get them *back* together. Marriage, founded on mutual consent and cooperation, is a microcosm of the larger social-political union. Cavell is interested in a particular, historically contingent form of comedy, but he puts this work into conversation with a much broader philosophical tradition. He shows how the pursuit of happiness requires not the satisfaction of needs but the examination and transformation of those needs.

Although major currents of comic theory and criticism in the twentieth century took a historical, localizing turn, some theorists constructed broad, systematic approaches to human expression, and offered rigorous analyses of formal patterns in comedy across periods and cultures. American philosopher Susanne Langer (1895–1985), who defines humans as makers of symbols, aimed to construct an intellectual framework for a philosophy of art in *Feeling and Form: A Theory of Art* (1953). Art expresses emotional states, she asserts, by representing aspects of 'life'. Every work must have an 'organic character'. Her chapter on 'The Comic Rhythm' argues that comedy represents the organic processes behind a fundamental 'life rhythm'. When this rhythm is disturbed, the organism is out of balance; so it struggles to retrieve its original dynamic form by overcoming and removing the obstacle. According to this biological, quasi-Darwinian theory, comedy represents the 'pure sense of life' as it confronts a dangerous 'non-living universe'. Langer's work indicates a post-war interest in pastoralism, the idealization of a 'natural' environment, as a response to her own complex, urban, industrial society. This interest in an organic life, 'closer to nature', is neither nostalgic, nor reactionary. In the most sophisticated critics, it may be progressive, a way of interrogating tensions between self and environment, the real and the ideal, present and future. In recent years, comic theory has provided a vocabulary for eco-critics, such as Joseph Meeker, whose book *The Comedy of Survival: Literary Ecology and a Play Ethic* treats the 'comic mode' as a ritual renewal of biological welfare in spite of modern reasons for feeling metaphysical despair.

Canadian literary theorist Northrop Frye (1912–91) has provided the most important and comprehensive treatment of the structures, character-types, and themes of comedy as a broadly human poetic practice. Frye's magisterial *Anatomy of Criticism* (1957) is one of the most influential critical works of the twentieth century. It defines comedy as one of four interrelated narrative categories – comedy, romance, tragedy, and satire – that represent what Frye calls, 'the four main types of mythical movement'. These categories are archetypes behind the structures of thought that govern human responses to basic needs and drives. The 'upward movement', from threatening complications to a happy ending, is comic. The structure of comedy relies on conflict between emerging and established social orders, and results in reconciliation. Comedy, Frye argues in a liberal vein, promotes a 'pragmatically free society'. Frye shows that dramatic comedy has been remarkably tenacious in its structural principles and character types across history, and his method combines the discipline of modern science with a Romantic investment in the imagination to forge a synoptic theory of literary criticism. Criticism, he writes, is a science as well as an art. Like Langer, he situates his theory of forms and fictional modes within the rhythms of the natural world. Frye coined the term 'green world', when he called Shakespeare's type of comedy and the tradition from which it derives, 'the drama of the green world … its plot being assimilated to the ritual theme of the triumph of life and love over the waste land'. In its use of stock characters, its openness to the stuff of fantasy, comedy is formulaic. The comic plot overcomes what is fixed; its logic is evolutionary, and creation nearly always is a central theme. Through the dialectic of freedom and constraint, comedy represents the movement of one kind of society to another. 'Something gets born at the end of comedy', Frye writes, 'and the watcher of birth is a member of a busy society'.

The question as to what degree comedy serves as an integrative or disintegrating force in modern society depends on the perspective of the theorist. Groucho, Chico, and Harpo Marx performed comedies of social disruption that many called 'anarchic'. In 1932, the French theorist Antonin Artaud admired the Marx Brothers' revolt not only against social convention but also against the cultivated definition of humour that had 'lost its meaning of total liberation, of the destruction of all reality in the mind'. Most theorists today believe that modern comedy cannot be understood apart from class and cultural change, which includes new media such as film and television. As film historian Gerald Mast (1940–88) writes in *The Comic Mind* (1973), the problem with discussions of comedy is that no single definition adequately includes every work traditionally recognized as comic; on the other hand, 'it is impossible to talk about film comedy without some definitions'. Forms and themes of modern comedy may hark back to ancient models, but they are inextricable from their processes of production, distribution, and consumption.

In his book on early film comedy, *What Made Pistachio Nuts?* (1992), American media scholar, Henry Jenkins (1958–) describes entertaining and unresolvable tensions in certain movies that represent an irreducibly pluralistic culture and a new sense of humour. He also critiques Meredith's celebration of a middlebrow 'comic spirit', which is restrained and purposeful, by showing that it reflects a larger cultural discourse about the nature of laughter in the Victorian era. 'Refinement' was possible when 'cultivated' people detached themselves from popular culture, and this notion of the comic spirit betrays an elitist anxiety about mass culture. The Victorians were concerned about the propriety of laughter. They expected comedy to serve a 'serious', ethical or didactic function. Comedy would contribute to human social evolution. But working-class humour was of a lower evolutionary order than that of the cultivated middle or upper class. In the nineteenth century, many believed that human progress changed the nature of laughter. Jokes, they felt, ought to be incorporated into a narrative in respectable comedy. But at the same time new mass market publications and modes of performance emerged that produced a different discourse, challenging assumptions about purposeful laughter and suggesting that comic entertainment could be pleasurable in its own right. This idea, often called 'New Humor' clashed with the Victorian model. It advocated a loss of bodily and social control, not refinement, and it was levelling or democratic. 'New Humor' celebrated gags with a big 'pay off', slapstick routines, songs, and comic 'bits' that weren't subordinated or integrated into a narrative. Popular amusement became a social issue, as it seemed a symptom of overstimulation and a society out of control. The humour of working-class immigrants was commercialized; it rewarded mass taste not 'good taste'. Building on the idea that 'New Humor' was a unique product of twentieth-century American life, with more intense, more remunerative forms of comedy, Jenkins argues that early Hollywood cinema combined the energy of slapstick vaudeville performance with more traditional theatrical comedy, merging the affective immediacy of New Humor with the thematic complexity of 'true comedy'. Professor Andrea Most argues, similarly, that the challenge of Jewish immigrants assimilating into American culture is reflected formally in the tension between book and musical numbers in Broadway musical comedy and in their eventual integration in the work of Rodgers and Hammerstein. As Frye implied, comic plots can forge new citizens.

Comedy employs stock characters and stereotypes today that are updated versions of ancient roles, from the trickster (*eirôn*) to the boaster (*alazôn*), from young lovers to old misers, but the way people think about identity and specific comic types has changed. A modern, pluralistic society may take stereotypes as a source of humour, just as Italian *commedia dell'arte* did, but the types have evolved with attitudes toward social difference. Comic theory of the past fifty years has often centred on identity politics, or the perspectives of various, disempowered groups within a broader cosmopolitan society, and on the politics of whether particular groups produce specific kinds of humour. Who gets to make fun of whom, and how does humour negotiate relations between the physical and the metaphysical? Historians have argued that oppressed minorities have developed their own humour, appropriating stereotypes used against them as a defence mechanism or, to cite a standard theory of humour, as a release. Thus, in *Laughing Fit to Kill: Black Humor in Fictions of Slavery* (2008), Glenda Carpio shows that African American humour, which arises from oppression, 'has provided a balm, a release from anger and aggression, a way of coping with the painful consequences of racism'. In *No Joke: Making Jewish Humor* (2013), professor of Yiddish and comparative literature, Ruth Wisse (1936–) presses the question of comedy as a coping mechanism, asking whether the extreme self-ridicule of Jewish humour may go too far and backfire in the process. Her work also draws on the history, anthropology, socio-political utility, and moral value of the role humour plays in an ethnic group that historically has dwelt in the margins of the nations and cultures of others. Ethnic humour did not originate in the twentieth century, but globalism has prompted vexing questions about the relation between the universal and the particular, bringing diverse cultures into often jarring contact. Comic theorists have turned new attention to this subject.

Comedy is an insider's sport; it revels in interests and exclusions, feelings of superiority and of commonality. Aristotle said that comedy imitates the ugly or deformed, but in the new field of disability studies, theorists have asked how humour may enable the disabled. English philosopher Simon Critchley (1960–) suggests in his book *On Humor* (2002) that 'the body that is the object and subject of humour is an *abject* body – estranged, alien, weakening, failing', which suggests a 'metaphysical unease at the heart of humour'. Humour, like anxiety, makes the world seem strange, turns the familiar unfamiliar, distances us from our own bodies, but it also assumes common ground. Even in mass society there are 'in-jokes' that assume cultural distinction. Humour at the expense of the disabled is often cruel, yet for people with disabilities certain kinds of humour can be emancipating. Laughter can foster sympathetic identification and reframe otherwise painful experience. Disability humour both points at boundaries between groups and holds them together. But if comedy can serve as a social corrective, are more humane forms of humour possible? Henri Bergson had written in 1900 that comedy demands a momentary anaesthesia of the heart and that it appeals to the intelligence, not the emotions. However, in his view, the point of laughter was to restore our humanity, to prompt us to recognize that we have assumed stereotyped attitudes or assigned them, without thinking, to others. Moral questions about what kind of comedy may be appropriate or harmful date back to ancient debates about decorum, but they have different significance in a democratic culture where all people are supposed to be created equal. Altered conceptions of identity, attention to the rights of women – who achieved the right to vote in Britain in 1918 and in the United States in 1920 – changing notions of gender and sexuality, and encounters with ethnic and racial minorities have not only renovated old comic tropes but also produced new comic forms. Nineteen-thirties comedies of remarriage are intricately bound up with this phase in the history of the consciousness of women. In diverse, cosmopolitan societies, comedy did not mean the same thing to everyone. Immigration, civil rights and nationalism shaped the perception that different groups responded to different kinds of comedy, that there was such a thing as ethnic humour, but also American humour versus English or French humour or, in Carpio's terms, 'black humour', a phrase that plays on surrealist André Breton's coinage in his 1935 *Anthology of Black Humor* (*Anthologie de l'humour noir*) for humour arising from fear or disgust.

Contrary to eulogies on its alleged death, comedy today seems to be everywhere, from movies to television to the internet to comedy clubs. Comic theory has also proliferated in the academy like never before. In the 1960s academics embraced comedy as a way of challenging hierarchies of high versus low culture. Popular politics helped to give comedy legitimacy in academic discourse, as comic theory as well as comic performances helped to make the case against strict regimes. The first international conference on humour was held in Wales in 1976, generating new interest in the subject. This Reader joins several new introductions to comic theory, including

Eric Stott's *Comedy* (2005) and Matthew Bevis's *Comedy: A Very Short Introduction* (2012). Courses on comedy are taught in literature and theatre departments at nearly all universities and colleges across North America and Western Europe. A remarkable outpouring of new studies of comedy and humour, ranging from structural analyses of film comedy to works on ethnic and racial humour to analyses of comedy and disability, suggests that comic theory has at last overcome an ancient bias.

Bibliography

Ackerman, Alan. 'Comedy, Capitalism, and a Loss of Gravity'. *Discourse: Journal for Theoretical Studies in Media and Culture* 36 (2) (Spring 2014): 139–75.

Albrecht, Gary L. 'Disability Humor: What's in a Joke?' *Body Society* 5 (4) (December 1999): 67–74.

Apte, Mahadev L. 'Ethnic Humor versus "Sense of Humor": An American Sociocultural Dilemma'. *American Behavioral Scientist* 30 (3) (January/February, 1987): 27–41.

Artaud, Antonin, 'The Marx Brothers', in *Selected Writings*, ed. Susan Sontag, trans. Helen Weaver, 240–2. Berkeley: University of California Press, 1976.

Bevis, Matthew. *Comedy: A Very Short Introduction*. New York: Oxford University Press, 2012.

Brecht, Bertolt (1940–1). 'On Hegelian Dialectics'. in *Flüchtlingsgespräche* [*Refugee Conversations*] Berlin: Suhrkamp, 2000 (first published 1956).

Corley, Cheryl. 'A Raisin in the Sun'. *NPR.org*, 11 March 2002. Web. 12 May 2015. Available online: http://sandbox.npr.org/programs/morning/features/patc/raisin/index.html

Dolan, Jill. '"What, No Beans?": Images of Women and Sexuality in Burlesque Comedy'. *Journal of Popular Culture* 18 (3) (1984) 37–47.

Druker, Jonathan. 'Self-Estrangement and the Poetics of Self-Representation in Pirandello's "L'umorismo"'. *South Atlantic Review*, 63 (1) (Winter, 1998), 56–71.

Dürrenmatt, Friedrich. *Problems of the Theatre*, trans. Gerhard Nellhaus. New York: Grove Press, 1955.

Eagleton, Terry. *Literary Theory: An Introduction*. Minneapolis: University of Minnesota Press, 1983.

Esslin, Martin. *The Theatre of the Absurd*. New York: Anchor Books, 1961.

Garber, Marjorie. *Vested Interests: Cross-Dressing and Cultural Anxiety*. New York: Routledge, 1992.

Holquist, Michael. 'Bakhtin and Rabelais: Theory as Praxis'. *boundary 2*, 11 (1/2) (Autumn/Winter 1982–3): 5–19.

Kundera, Milan. *The Book of Laughter and Forgetting*, trans. Michael Henry Heim. Alfred. A. Knopf. New York. 1980.

Meeker, Joseph. *The Comedy of Survival: Studies in Literary Ecology*.New York: Scribner, 1974.

Miller, Arthur. 'Tragedy and the Common Man'. *New York Times*, 27 February 1949. Web. 12 May 2015. Available at: https://www.nytimes.com/books/00/11/12/specials/miller-common.html

Montrose, Louis Adrian, '"Shaping Fantasies": Figurations of Gender and Power in Elizabethan Culture'. *Representations* 2 (1983): 61–94.

Most, Andrea. *Making Americans: Jews and the Broadway Musical*. Cambridge, MA: Harvard University Press, 2004.

Otto, Beatrice K. *Fools Are Everywhere: The Court Jester Around the World*. Chicago: University of Chicago Press, 2001.

Sloterdijk, Peter. *Critique of Cynical Reason*, trans. Michael Eldred. Minneapolis: University of Minnesota Press, 1987.

Sontag, Susan. 'Notes on "Camp".' *Against Interpretation and Other Essays*, 275–92. New York: Farrar Straus and Giroux, 1964.

Stott, Eric. *Comedy*. London: Routledge, 2005.

Watkins, Mel. *On the Real Side: Laughing, Lying, and Signifying—: The Underground Tradition of African-American Humor That Transformed American Culture, from Slavery to Richard Pryor*. New York: Simon & Schuster, 1995.

Wendell, Susan. 'Toward a Feminist Theory of Disability', in *The Disability Studies Reader*, ed. Lennard J. Davis, 260–78. New York: Routledge, 1997. Print.

Wisse, Ruth. *No Joke: Making Jewish Humor*. Princeton, NJ, Princeton University Press, 2013.

TEXTS

1. Luigi Pirandello, *On Humor* (1908, 1920), translated by Antonio Illiano and Daniel P. Testa (1974)

Before we begin to talk about the essence, characteristics, and substance of humor, we need to clear the ground of three preliminary questions: 1) Is humor, as a literary phenomenon, exclusively modern? 2) Is it foreign to the Italians? 3) Is it peculiarly Nordic? On one hand, these questions are closely related to the broader and more complex question of the difference between modern art and ancient art – a question argued at length during the controversy over classicism and romanticism; on the other hand, they are connected with romanticism, which was considered by the Anglo-Germanic peoples as their victorious reprisal over the classicism of the Latins. In fact, we shall see that the various controversies on humor make use of the same arguments of romantic criticism, beginning with those used by Schiller, who, according to Goethe, founded all of modern aesthetics with his famous *Uber naïve und sentimentalische Dichtung.*

   Those arguments are well known: the subjectivism in the speculative-sentimental poet, representative of modern art, as opposed to the objectivism in the instinctive or ingenuous poet, representative of ancient art; the contrast between the ideal and the real; the imperturbable composure, the poised dignity, the outer beauty of ancient art as opposed to the exaltation of the emotions, the vagueness, the infinity, the indeterminateness of aspirations, the melancholic longings, the nostalgia, the inner beauty of modern art: the veristic earthiness of ingenuous poetry versus the hazy abstractions and intellectual dizziness of sentimental poetry; the impact of Christianity; the philosophical element; the incoherence of modern art as opposed to the harmony of Greek poetry; the individualized particularities set against classical typification; reason that concerns itself more with the philosophical value of content than with the beauty of external form; the deep-felt sense of an inner disunity and double nature typical of modern man, etc.

[...]

Now, one should first of all realize that, in dealing critically with an expression of art so peculiarly and uniquely original as humor [...] hasty synopses and ideal historical reconstructions cannot be accepted as valid. When a legend is created, the collective imagination rejects all the elements, features and characteristics which are at variance with the ideal nature of a given action or personality, and, instead, evokes and combines all the suitable images: the same thing happens when we draw a summary sketch of a given period and are inevitably led to overlook the many discordant details and specific manifestations. We are unable to hear the voices of protest in the midst of an overpowering chorus. We know that there are certain vivid colors that, if scattered here and there and looked at from a distance, will thin out, fade and blend with the prevailing shades of blue or gray of the landscape. In order for these colors to stand out and fully re-acquire their individual brightness, we need to draw close to them. We will then realize how and to what degree we were deceived by distance.

If we accepted Taine's theory that moral phenomena are as subject to deterministic laws as physical phenomena, that human history is a part of natural history, and that the works of art are products of specific factors and specific laws (i.e., the law of dependency with the ensuing rule of the essential traits and dominant faculties, and the law of conditions and circumstances which entails the observance of such factors as the primeval forces, race, milieu, and historical moment); if we considered the works of art only as inevitable effects of natural and social forces, we would never penetrate the inner core of art. We would be compelled to see all the artistic manifestations of a given period as concordant and concomitant, each depending on the others and all of them reflecting that characteristic which, according to our superficial conception or notion, has brought them together and produced them. We would not see reality, which is infinitely varied and constantly changing, and the individual feelings and perceptions of reality, which also are infinitely varied and constantly changing. After considering the sky, the climate, the sun, the society, customs and prejudices, we have to look at each individual in order to find out what these elements have become according to the particular psychic structure, the unique original combination of elements which makes up each individual. Where one person gives up, another rebels; where one weeps, another laughs; and there may always be someone who laughs and weeps at the same time. In the world around him, man, in this or any other period, sees only those things that interest him: from early infancy, without being aware of it in the slightest, man selects, accepts, and absorbs certain elements; later, these elements, stirred by feelings and emotions, will mix and mingle in the most varied combinations.

"Antiquity unperturbably compressed abstract forms into the harmony of the finite." Here is a generalization. All of antiquity? Is there no exception? "Either the Cyclops or the Gnome, the Graces or Parcae." And why not also the Sirens, half woman, half fish? "Life had either free men or slaves." And couldn't a free man have felt enslaved and a slave have felt inwardly free? Doesn't Arcoleo himself quote Diogenes who "enclosed the world in a barrel and would not accept the greatness of Alexander if it obstructed his view of the sun"? And what does it mean that the Greek intellect perceived the contrast and Art was incapabe of expressing it because life was different? What was life like? All tears or all laughter? How could the intellect then grasp the contrast? All abstractions are necessarily rooted in a concrete fact. What existed, therefore, was tears *and* laughter, not tears *or* laughter; and if the intellect was able to grasp the contrast, why should art have been incapable of expressing it? "At best," says Arcoleo, "the sense of contrast made its way from the sphere of the intellect to that of imagination where it became a phantasy, and this is when Aristophanes wrote his satires of the sophists and Lucian satirized the Gods." What does "at best" mean? If the sense of contrast made its way from the sphere of intellect to that [of the imagination where it turned into a phantasy, this means that it] became art. What then? Let's leave Aristophanes out of it, for, as we shall see, he had nothing to do with humor; but Lucian was not only the author of the dialogue of the Gods. And let us proceed.

"The ancients reduced the supernatural forces to plastic forms." Here is another generalization. All of the ancient world and all of the supernatural forces? Including fate? And during the Renaissance did all Italy remain "pagan and serene in their pleasures, and had no curiosity, no intimacy"? We shall see. We are now discussing humor and its artistic manifestations which, I repeat, are extraordinary and uniquely original: only one humorist would suffice; we shall find a good many in every place and period; and we shall explain why it happens that Italian humorists particularly do not seem to us to be humorists.

[...]

Furthermore, no one today would dream of denying that the ancients were quite aware of man's profound misery. It was clearly expressed, moreover, by philosophers and poets. But, as usual, some have resolved also to see an almost total difference in substance between ancient and modern suffering, and the claim has been made that there is a gloomy progression in human suffering, which evolves with the history of civilization itself and is based on the fact that human consciousness is increasingly more sensitive and delicate, irritable and dissatisfied. But if I am not mistaken, this was already said by Solomon in times of old: an increase in knowledge brings an increase in suffering.[1] And was Solomon, in times of old, really right? It remains to be seen. If human passions develop a mutual attraction and influence as they grow

---

[1] Ecclesiastes. I, 18. [tr.]

increasingly more keen and intense; if man, as it is said, is led, partly by his imagination and sensitivity, into the "process of universalization" which expands ever more rapidly and forcibly so that in one moment of affliction we seem to experience many or all afflictions, do we really suffer more because of this? No, because this increase in suffering entails a lessening in intensity. And this is precisely what motivated Leopardi's sharp observation that ancient suffering was utterly hopeless, as it usually is in nature and still is among primitive and country people, namely, a suffering that lacks the consolation of sensibility and the sweet resignation to misfortunes.[2]

Today, if we think we are unhappy, the world, in our eyes, becomes a theatre of universal misery. This is because, instead of plunging headlong into our own sorrow, we spread and extend it to the universe. We pluck out the thorn and wrap ourselves in a black cloud. Boredom grows, but the pain dulls and lessens. But what about the *tedium vitae* of the contemporaries of Lucretius? And what about Timon's feeling of misanthropic dejection?

Well, let's not indulge in a useless display of examples and quotations. These questions and disquisitions are purely academic. We needn't look too far back to find the humanity for our past for it is within us, the same as always. At most, we can admit that, due to the alleged development of sensibility and progress of civilization, those dispositions of the mind and those conditions of life which are particularly conducive to humor – to be more precise, to a *certain type* of humor – are more common; but it would be completely arbitrary to deny that the ancients had or could have had those same dispositions toward humor. Indeed Diogenes, with his cask and lantern, did not live yesterday, and in no one else are the serious and the ridiculous more closely intertwined. Are Aristophanes and Lucian exceptions as Nencioni says and Arcoleo repeats? But then swift and Sterne are also exceptions. *All* humoristic art, we say again, is and has always been an art of exception.

As the ancients wept differently from us, say these critics, so naturally they laughed differently. Jean Paul Richter's distinction between the classical comic sense and the romantic comic sense is well known; he identifies the first with gross jestings and vulgar satire derisive of vices and defects without any commiseration or pity, and the second with humor proper, a philosophical laughter mixed with pain because it stems from the comparison between the small finite world and the infinite idea, a laughter full of tolerance and sympathy.

---

[2] Giacomo Leopardio, *Zibaldone di pensieri*, no. 77.

[…]

[Leopardi speaks] of the French *esprit* as opposed to the classical sense of the ridiculous, without realizing that, as Taine said, "the spirit of conversation, the talent for *faire des mots*, the taste for lively and witty phrases, unexpected, ingenious and spiced with gaiety and malice," is also classical and quite old in France: "Duas res industriosissime persequitur gens Gallorum, rem militarem et argute loqui" ("Two things the Gauls pursue most industriously, military activity and wit").[3] This *esprit* – French in origin, and which has gradually become refined and conventional, aristocratic and elegant in certain literary periods – is certainly not modern humor and much less English humor with which Taine contrasts it on the basis that English humor is made not of "words" but of "things" or, in some respect, of common sense (if – as Joubert thought – common sense consists of useful notions while *esprit* consists of many useless ones).[4] Let's not confuse the two, then.

In 1899, Alberto Cantoni, a most acute Italian humorist who was deeply affected by the conflict between reason and feeling and who suffered for not being able to be as genuine and spontaneous as his nature prompted him to be, resumed the subject in an allegorized story called "Humour classic e moderno."[5] In this story he imagines that an attractive, ruddy and jovial old man, who represents classical humor, and a wary little man with a mawkish humor, meet in front of the statue of Gaetano Donizetti in Bergamo and immediately begin to quarrel. Then they propose in the way of a challenge that, each on his own, as though they were total strangers, they should go to Clusone, a town in the nearby countryside where a fair is being held; then in the evening, back again at the statue of Donizetti, they will recount and compare their fleeting and particular impressions of the trip. Instead of discussing and analyzing the nature, purpose, and flavor of ancient and modern humor, Cantoni relates, in a lively dialogue, the impressions gathered by the jovial old man and the circumspect little man at the Clusone fair. The old man's impressions could have been the subject by a story of Boccaccio, Firenzuola, or Bandello; the comments and sentimental variations of the little man sound like Sterne's *Sentimental Journey* or Heine's *Reisebilder*. Given his predilection for natural spontaneity, Cantoni would side with the ruddy old man if

---

[3] Hippolyte Taine, "*De l'esprit anglais*," Chap. VIII of *Notes sur l'Angleterre* (Paris, 1903), p. 399. ["Faire des mots" is the art of making witticisms. The Latin quote is from Cato, *Hist. frg.*—tr.]

[4] J. Joubert, *Pensées* (Paris, 1901), p. 50. [tr.]

[5] Cantoni calls this work "grottesco," perhaps because it mixes imagination and criticism. For a study of Cantoni's work, see L. Pirandello, "Un critic fantastic," in *Arte e scienza* (Rome: W. Modes, 1908). [now also in *Saggi poesie, scritti varii*—tr.]

he were not forced to recognize that the old man has wanted to remain as he was, much beyond what his age would tolerate, and that he is somewhat coarse and often shame-fully sensual. But Cantoni also feels and understands the conflict that constantly splits and tears the soul of the small and thin man, so he has the old man address him with harsh and biting remarks: "Because you have repeated so many times that you seem to be all smiles on the outside but that you are actually all sorrow [...] one cannot tell anymore what you seem to be or what you actually are. [...] If you could see yourself, you would not understand, as I don't, whether you feel more like crying or laughing."

> "This is true today," Modern Humour answers, "because I now think that you stopped half way. In your time the joys and the torments of life had two different forms or at least they appeared to be simpler and quite dissimilar to each other. Nothing was easier than to set them apart and then to elevate one to the detriment of the other. Then in my time came criticism, and that was the end of that. For a long time we groped in the dark wondering which was the best or the worst until the *tormenting* aspects of happiness and the *amusing* aspects of sorrow begin to emerge from their long hiding. The ancients also believed that pleasure was only the cessation of pain and that pain itself, if carefully considered, was not at all to be identified with evil. But they held these nice ideas in earnest, which is like saying that they were not in the least convinced. Now, alas, my time has come and we keep saying almost laughingly – that is, with the most profound conviction – that the two elements recently associated with joy and sorrow, have faded and have become so indefinite that it is impossible even to tell them apart, not to speak of separating them. The result is that my contemporaries no longer know how to be either very happy or very unhappy, and that you alone are no longer capable of stimulating the tempered pleasure of the first or diverting the sophistic quivering fears of the second. Since I know how to mix everything, I am now needed to disperse as many deceiving mirages as possible, on one hand, and to smoothen as many superfluous rough edges as I find, on the other, I live by makeshift and by providing protective padding ..."[6]

[...]

Like in the romantic drama that the two nice bourgeois Dupuis and Cotonet saw "dressed in black and white, laughing with one eye and crying with the other." But here we have confusion again. Cantoni, in a different way, is saying essentially what Richter and Leopardi had said. The difference is that he calls humor what the other two

---

[6] A. Cantoni, *Romanzi e racconti* (Milan 1903), pp. 593–5. [tr.]

had called the classical sense of the comic and of the ridiculous. Richter, a German, praises the romantic sense of the comic or a modern humor and severely censures the classical sense of the comic as coarse and vulgar, whereas Cantoni, like Leopardi, as a good Italian is wont to do, defends the latter type, even though he recognizes that the charge of shameful sensuality is not at all undeserved. But Cantoni also believed that modern humor is nothing but an adulterated form of the ancient. In fact, he has Classical Humour say to Modern Humour: "Well, my idea is that it has always been possible to do without you, or that you are only the worst part of me, which is now raising its cocky head as is the custom these days. It is a true saying that one is bound never to know himself well by himself! You certainly slipped away from me and I didn't even notice it."

Now is this true? Is Cantoni's Classical Humour really humor? Or doesn't Cantoni make, from one point of view, the same mistake that Leopardi made, from another, when he confused the French *esprit* with the whole of modern humor? More precisely: what Cantoni calls Classical Humour, would it not be humor in a much wider sense, one that would include jerk, mock, and wit, in short, the comic in all its varied expressions?

This is the very crux of the questions. It is not a matter of the difference between ancient and modern art nor is it a matter of ethnic prerogatives. It is rather a question of whether humor should be considered in the wide sense in which it is usually mistakenly considered, or rather in a narrower but more appropriate sense. If we take it in the wide sense, we will find a wealth of examples in both the ancient and modern literatures of all nations; if we take it in its more restricted sense, we will also find it in the ancient and modern literatures of all countries, but we will find much less of it, in fact, only very few exceptional manifestations.

2. Virginia Woolf, 'Pure English' (1920)

Gammer Gurton's Needle [sic] had for us little preliminary value. [...] Then again, one is probably justified in assuming that what is 'held to be the first comedy in our language' owed its perpetuation to curiosity rather than to sensibility. It is a mummy and not a living being, a footprint which has somehow escaped the natural obliteration of time. For such reasons, prejudices, our greeting to Gammer Gurton may have been respectful, but was certainly lacking in warmth.

But who shall trace how it is that coldness yields to curiosity, and curiosity to warmth, or satisfactorily define what constitutes that relationship between book and reader? For the essence of it is instinctive rather than rational. [...] One particular reader then, upon a particular occasion, read *Gammer Gurton's Needle* with pleasure. Perhaps one had better say no more about it. After, however, receiving that impression, which momentarily overlays all others, the unplaiting process automatically begins. One wishes to explain to oneself this warm, jovial, contented emotion; to justify it by proving it well founded. 'Warm, jovial, contented'—these three adjectives after a moment's reflection prompt the idea that we enjoy *Gammer Gurton's Needle* because it is typically English. A Frenchman could only enjoy such a play by an effort. To us it comes straightforwardly. [...] The scene is rude enough; the humour of the characters is simple, but what an energy there is in it! With what a swing and directness it goes!

[...]

But, to return to our analysis of pleasure, his straightforward method serves to release a deep current, first of joy in the English qualities, and then of relish for the plain language, the free manners, to which we have grown so little used. His characters can scarcely open their mouths without saying something which, upon reflection, we must call coarse. But this is an afterthought imposing itself upon a direct judgement that not only is indecency of this kind enjoyable, but it is also wholesome and natural. [...] Hard upon that, however, comes the reflection that though plain speaking and free acting have an irresistible charm, *Gammer Gurton* palls before the end through excess of horseplay. The characters are by no means without such rude shaping as befits their parts, but William Stevenson, if we credit him with the work, was no poet. He sang his song in praise of ale with splendid vigour, but for the majority of human pleasures, for the look of things, for love and for death he had no sense at all. At any rate, he makes no explicit mention of them. But when the story is told with such spirit, when so clear before us comes the cottage, with the end of the candle hid in the shoe behind the old brass pan, the cat's gleaming eyes, the game of cards, poor Hodge's drudgery in the fields and his desire to appear decently before his mistress on Sunday, the voice of poetry, though still dumb, seems about to burst into song. Here and there one pauses as if to listen for it. No, it is too early; the petals are furled in the buds; the birds hopping among leafless twigs. Of all these things, and of many besides, is our pleasure composed.

3. Constance Rourke, *American Humor: A Study of the National Character* (1931)

"The comic," says Bergson, "comes into being when society and the individual, freed from the worry of self-preservation, begin to regard themselves as works of art." With his triumphs fresh and his mind noticeably free, by 1815 the American seemed to regard himself as a work of art, and began that embellished self-portraiture which nations as well as individuals may undertake. No one can say when or how these efforts might have ended if the American had been left to himself. He was not. Foreign artists insisted upon producing their portraits. After a few tours of observation the French, carrying the amiable light luggage of preconceptions derived from Rousseau, declared him to be a child of nature. The phrase gained a considerable popularity and had a long life, but it was difficult to graft the florid idea upon a Yankee base. The British schooling was more constant, and went deeper.

[...]

The Negro minstrel joined with the Yankee and the backwoodsman to make a comic trio, appearing in the same era, with the same timely intensity. The era of course was the turbulent era of the Jacksonian democracy, that story time when the whole mixed population of the United States seemed to pour into the streets of Washington, and when many basic elements in the national character seemed to come to the surface. [...] The three figures loomed large, not because they represented any considerable numbers in the population, but because something in the nature of each induced an irresistible response. [...] Comic triumph appeared in them all; the sense of triumph seemed a necessary mood in the new country. Laughter produced the illusion of leveling obstacles. Laughter created ease, and even more, a sense of unity, among a people who were not yet a nation and who were seldom joined in stable communities. These mythical figures partook of the primitive; and for a people whose life was still unformed, a searching out of primitive concepts was an inevitable and stirring pursuit, uncovering common purposes and directions. [...] As the three figures were projected in stories or on the stage the effect of consciousness was greatly heightened. With all their rude poetry it was about a mind that these centred, a conscious, indeed an acutely self-conscious, mind. Masquerade was salient in them all.

[...]

American audiences enjoyed their own deflation; they liked the boldness of attack, the undisguised ridicule. Once again, as in the portraiture of the comic trio, the subject was essentially themselves. [...] [T]he comic spirit in America had maintained the purpose—or so it seemed—to fulfill the biblical cry running through so much of the revivalism of the time: to "make all things new." It was a levelling agent. The distant must go, the past be forgotten, lofty notions deflated. Comedy was conspiring toward the removal of all alien traditions, out of delight in pure destruction or as preparation for new growth.

Yet the burlesque of this long period could only have been created by a temper steeped in romanticism. If it punctured romantic feeling, it kept a breathless comic emotion of its own. Invading current fantasies, it employed fantastical forms. Indian myths might traipse across the stage in grotesque and balloonlike guises, but they only became mythical again with a broader and livelier look. It was not a realistic spirit that was abroad. The world of burlesque was still the familiar native world of phantasmagoria.

[...]

Meredith declared that to produce a comic poet, "a society of cultivated men and women is required, wherein ideas are current and the perception quick, that he may be supplied with matter and an audience. The semi-barbarism of merely giddy communities, and feverish emotional periods, repel him." The long period out of which American comedy sprang might easily be called feverish and emotional; and surely the communities within which it was produced were often giddy and semi-barbaric. No society of cultivated men and women had supplied a subject matter, though it might perhaps be granted that such a society had sometimes formed an audience.

"They have the basis of the Comic in them: an esteem for common sense," Meredith said of the English. So far as their humor was a sign the Americans had singularly little regard for common sense. American comedy might be aggressive or competitive; it often tied hard knots: but these elements were transformed by extravagant purposes.

"To know comedy you must know the real world," said Meredith: but American comedy had stepped outside the real world into that of fantasy.

For purposes of candor American comedy of the long period which stretched from the Revolution to the year 1860 may be described in a series of negations. Little of the purely human was contained within it, no deepening of the portrayal of character, nothing of a wide and interwoven web of thought and feeling where wit might freely play and the whole be gently lighted. Lincoln had revealed a human touch, but not too frequently; and this was shown for the most part toward the end of his life. Little or nothing of the philosophical element had developed even in Lincoln's stories. Satire had persistently appeared, sometimes directed toward highly focused ends, often showing only the flare of quick attack. This humor was highly competitive even in its quiet Yankee turns. To look upon the comedy of this time was to conclude that the Americans were a nation of wild and careless myth-makers, aloof from the burdens of pioneer life, bent upon proving a triumphant spirit. Yet comic these fantasies were in spite of the strictures of Meredith. If they failed to exhibit subtlety, fineness, balance, they had created laughter and had served the ends of communication among a people unacquainted with themselves, strange to the land, unshaped as a nation; they had produced a shadowy social coherence.

4. Kenneth Burke, 'Comic Correctives', from *Attitudes Toward History* (1937)

[P]oetic image and rhetorical idea can become subtly fused—a fusion to which the very nature of poetry and rhetoric makes us prone. For the practiced rhetorician relies greatly upon images to affect men's ideation (as with current terms like "power vacuum" and "iron curtain"). [...] That is, though every historical period is unique as regards its particular set of circumstances and persons, the tenor of men's policies for confronting such manifold conditions has a synthesizing function. For instance, if we feel happy on three different occasions, these three occasions are in a sense attitudinally united. [...] One now sees the importance of our stress upon the term attitudes in our title. For all the terms which we consider alphabetically in our fourth section are of a strong attitudinal sort. Even when they name a process or a condition, they name it from a meditative, or moralizing, or even hortatory point of view. And saturating the lot is the attitude of attitudes which we call the "comic frame," the methodic view of human antics as a comedy, albeit as a comedy ever on the verge of the most disastrous tragedy.

[...]

Comedy, Meredith has said, is the most civilized form of art. What reason is there to question him? The class that can produce good comedy is about as happy as can be. True, the adjustment, though admirable in itself, is often shown by subsequent events to have been a very dangerous one, as though a contented village were to have evolved its culture at the edge of a sleeping volcano that is already, in its "subconscious" depths, preparing to break forth and scatter destruction.

We should account for this dramatic irony, that subsequent history adds to our interpretation of the happy time, by suggesting that the materials incorporated within the frame are never broad enough to encompass all the necessary attitudes. Not all the significant cultural factors are given the importance that a total vision of reality would require. Class interests provide the cues that distort the interpretative frame, making its *apparent* totality function as an *actual* partiality. [...]

Like tragedy, comedy warns against the dangers of pride, but its emphasis shifts from crime to stupidity. Shakespeare, whose tragedies gravitate towards melodrama (notably in a work like *Othello*) required *villains* to make his plot work. Henry James made an essentially comic observation when saying that his plots required the intervention of *fools*. [...]

The progress of humane enlightenment can go no further than in picturing people not as *vicious*, but as *mistaken*. When you add that people are *necessarily* mistaken, that *all* people are exposed to situations in which they must act as fools, that *every* insight contains its own special kind of blindness, you complete the comic circle, returning again to the lesson of humility that underlies great tragedy. The audience, from its vantage point, sees the operation of errors that the characters of the play cannot see; thus seeing from two angles at once, it is chastened by dramatic irony; it is admonished to remember that when intelligence means *wisdom* [...], it requires fear, resignation, the sense of limits, as an important ingredient.

Comedy requires the maximum of forensic complexity. In the tragic plot the *deus ex machina* is always lurking, to give events a fatalistic turn in accordance with the old "participation" pattern whereby men anthropomorphize nature, feeling its force as the taking of sides with them or against them. Comedy must develop logical forensic causality to its highest point, calling not upon astronomical marvels to help shape the plot, but completing the process of internal organization whereby each event is deduced "syllogistically" from the premises of the informing situation. Comedy deals with *man in society*, tragedy with the *cosmic man*. [...] Comedy is essentially *humane*, leading in periods of comparative stability to the comedy of manners, the dramatization of quirks and foibles. But it is not necessarily confined to drama. The best of Bentham, Marx, and Veblen is high comedy.

[...]

We might, however, note an important distinction between comedy and humor, that is disclosed when we approach art forms as "frames of acceptance," as "strategies" for living. Humor is the opposite of the heroic. The heroic promotes acceptance by magnification, making the hero's character as great as the situation he confronts, and fortifying the non-heroic individual vicariously, by identification with the hero; but humor reverses the process: it takes up the slack between the momentousness of the situation and the feebleness of those in the situation by *dwarfing the situation*. It converts downwards, as the heroic converts upwards. Hence it does not make for so completely well-rounded a frame of acceptance as comedy, since it tends to gauge the situation falsely. In this respect it is close to sentimentality, a kinship that may explain why so many of our outstanding comedians (who are really humorists) have a fondness for antithetical lapses into orgies of the tearful. Their customary method of self-protection is the attitude of "happy stupidity" whereby the gravity of life simply fails to register; its importance is lost to them. The mimetics of this role is often complicated by some *childish* quality of voice, as with [...] the stutterers and the silent.

[...]

This notion of *ambivalence* gets us to our main thesis with regard to propagandistic (didactic) strategy. We hold that it must be employed as an essentially *comic* notion, containing two-way attributes lacking in polemical, one-way approaches to social necessity. It is neither wholly euphemistic, nor wholly debunking – hence it provides the *charitable* attitude towards people that is required for purposes of persuasion and co-operation, but at the same time maintains our shrewdness concerning the simplicities of "cashing in." [...]

A comic frame of motives avoids these difficulties, showing us how an act can "dialectically" contain both transcendental and material ingredients, both imagination and bureaucratic embodiment, both "service" and "spoils". Or, viewing the matter in terms of ecological balance [...], one might say of the comic frame: It also makes us sensitive to the point at which one of these ingredients becomes hypertrophied, with the corresponding atrophy of the other. A well-balanced ecology requires the symbiosis of the two. [...]

The comic frame of reference also opens up a whole new field for social criticism, since the overly *materialistic* coordinates of the polemical-debunking frame have unintentionally blinded us to the full operation of "alienating" processes. Historians become indignant, for instance, when reviewing the ways in which private individuals were able, in nineteenth-century America, to appropriate "legally" large areas of the public domain.

[...]

The Church thought of man as a prospective citizen of heaven. In time, the critical inaccuracy that such transcendental emphasis brought to the gauging of material relationships became bureaucratically exploited to its limits. Out of this over-emphasis, a purely antithetical over-emphasis developed. Against man as a citizen of heaven, thinkers opposed man in nature; and with the progress of efficiency in reasoning, we got simply to *man in the jungle.* A comic synthesis of these antithetical emphases would "transcend" them by stressing *man in society.* As such, it would come close to restoring the emphasis of Aristotle, with his view of man as a "political animal."

In the motives we assign to the actions of ourselves and our neighbors, there is implicit a program of socialization. In deciding *why* people do as they do, we get the cues that place us with relation to them. Hence, a vocabulary of motives is important for the forming of both private and public relationships. A comic frame of motives, as here conceived, would not only avoid the sentimental denial of materialistic factors in human acts. It would also avoid the cynical brutality that comes when such sensitivity is outraged, as it must be outraged by the acts of others or by the needs that practical exigencies place upon us.

And one is exposed indeed to the possibilities of being cheated shamelessly in this world, if he does not accumulate at least a minimum of spiritual resources that no man can take from him. The comic frame, as a *method of study* (man as eternal journeyman) is a better personal possession, in this respect, than the somewhat empty accumulation of facts such as people greedily cultivate when attempting to qualify in "Ask Me Another" questionnaires, where they are invited to admire themselves for knowing the middle name of Robert Louis Stevenson's favorite nephew (if he had one). Mastery of this sort (where, if "Knowledge is power," people "get power" vicariously by gaining possession of its "insignia," accumulated facts) may somewhat patch up a wounded psyche; but a more adventurous equipment is required, if one is to have a private possession marked by mature social efficacy.

The comic frame, in making a man the student of himself, makes it possible for him to "transcend" occasions when he had been tricked or cheated, since he can readily put such discouragements in his "assets" column, under the head of "experience." Thus we "win" by subtly changing the rules of the game – and by a mere trick of bookkeeping, like the accountants for big utility corporations, we make "assets" out of "liabilities." And can we, in our humbleness, do better than apply in our own way the wise devices of these leviathans, thereby "democratizing" a salvation device as we encourage it to filter down from the top down?

In sum, the comic frame should enable people *to be observers of themselves, while acting*. Its ultimate would not be *passiveness*, but *maximum consciousness*. One would "transcend" himself by noting his own foibles. He would provide a rationale for locating the irrational and the non-rational.

The materials for such a frame by no means require a new start. They are all about us. (We should question the proposal drastically, were it otherwise, for a man is necessarily talking error unless his words can claim membership in a collective body of thought.) The comic frame is present in the best of psychoanalytical criticism. It is highly present in anthropological catalogues like that of Frazer's *Golden Bough* which, by showing us the rites of magical purification in primitive peoples, gives us the necessary cues for the detection of similar processes in even the most practical and non-priestly of contemporary acts. It is to be found, amply, in the great formulators of "economic psychoanalysis," writers like Machiavelli, Hobbes, Voltaire, Bentham, Marx, Veblen. Yet, while never permitting itself to overlook the admonitions of even the most caustic social criticism, it does not waste the world's rich store of error, as those parochial-minded persons waste it who dismiss all thought before a certain date as "ignorance" and "superstition." Instead, it cherishes the lore of so-called "error" as a *genuine aspect of the truth*, with emphases valuable for the correcting of present emphases.

Often, we can reapply, for incorporation in the "comic" frame, a formula originally made in the euphemistic or debunking modes of emphasis, by merely changing our *attitude* towards the formula. We "discount" it for comic purposes, subtly translating it, as Marx translated Hegel, "taking over" a mystificatory methodology for clarificatory ends. This strategy even opens us to the resources of "popular" philosophy, as embodied not only in proverbs and old saws, but also in the working vocabulary of every-day relationships. Thus we can incorporate the remarkable terms of politics and business, two terminologies which quickly chart and simplify constantly recurring relationships of our society. The vocabulary of crime is equally valuable, in such ingenious shortcuts as "ganging up on" and "putting on the spot."

[...]

The comic frame of acceptance but carries to completion the translative act. It considers human life as a project in "composition," where the poet works with the materials of social relationships. Compositions, translation, also "revision," hence offering maximum opportunity for the resources of *criticism*.

The comic frame might give a man an attitude that increased his spiritual wealth, by making even bad books and trivial remarks legitimate objects of study. It might mitigate somewhat the difficulties in engineering a shift to new symbols of authority, as required by the new social relationships that the revolutions of historic environment have made necessary. It might provide important cues for the composition of one's life, which demands accommodation to the structure of others' lives.

It could not, however, remove the ravages of boredom and inanition that go with the "alienation" of contemporary society. The necessities of earning a living may induce men actually to compete "of their own free will" to get the most incredible kinds of jobs, jobs that make them rot in the dark while the sun is shining, or warp their bodies and their minds by overlong sedentary regimentation and grotesque devotion to all the unadventurous tasks of filing and recording that our enormous superstructure, for manipulating the mere abstract symbols of exchange, has built up. The need of wages may induce men "voluntarily" to scramble for such "opportunities," even plotting to elbow themselves into offices which, in earlier economies, would not have been performed at all except by slaves and criminals under compulsion. For alienations of this sort (the stifling of adventure that, as a by-product, had come with the accumulations of the venturesome) the comic frame could not, and should not, offer recompense. Its value should only reside in helping to produce a state of affairs whereby these rigors may abate.

5. Susanne Langer, 'The Comic Rhythm', from *Feeling and Form* (1953)

The pure sense of life is the underlying feeling of comedy, developed in countless different ways. To give a general phenomenon one name is not to make all its manifestations one thing, but only to bring them conceptually under one head. Art does not generalize and classify; art sets forth the individuality of forms which discourse, being essentially general, has to suppress. The sense, or "enjoyment," as Alexander would call it,[7] is the realization in direct feeling of what sets organic nature apart from inorganic; self-preservation, self-restoration, functional tendency, purpose. Life is teleological, the rest of nature is, apparently, mechanical; to maintain the pattern of vitality in a non-living universe is the most elementary instinctual purpose. An organism tends to keep its equilibrium amid the bombardment of aimless forces that beset it, to regain equilibrium when it has been disturbed, and to pursue a sequence of actions dictated by the need of keeping all its interdependent parts constantly renewed, their structure

---

[7] S. Alexander, *Space, Time and Deity*. See Vol. I, p. 12.

intact. Only organisms have needs; lifeless objects whirl or slide or tumble about, are shattered and scattered, struck together, piled up, without showing any impulse to return to some pre-eminent condition and function. But living things strive to persist in a particular chemical balance, to maintain a particular temperature, to repeat particular functions, and to develop along particular lines, achieving a growth that seems to be performed in their earliest, rudimentary, protoplasmic structure.

That is the basic biological pattern which all living things share: the round of conditioned and conditioning organic processes that produces the life rhythm. When this rhythm is disturbed, all activities in the total complex are modified by the break; the organism as a whole is out of balance. But, within a wide range of conditions, it struggles to retrieve its original dynamic form by overcoming and removing the obstacle, or if this proves impossible, it develops a slight variation of its typical form and activity and carries on life with a new balance of functions—in other words, it adapts itself to the situation. A tree, for instance, that is bereft of the sunshine it needs by the encroachment of other trees, tends to grow tall and thin until it can spread its own branches in the light. […] But the impulse to survive is not spent only in defense and accommodation; it appears also in the varying power of organisms to seize on opportunities. […] All creatures live by opportunities, in a world fraught with disasters. That is the biological pattern in most general terms.

This pattern, moreover, does not develop sporadically in midst of mechanical systems; when or where it began on the earth we do not know, but in the present phase of this planet's constitution there appears to be no "spontaneous generation." It takes life to produce further life.

[…]

The human life-feeling is the essence of comedy. It is at once religious and ribald, knowing and defiant, social and freakishly individual. The illusion of life which the comic poet creates is the oncoming future fraught with dangers and opportunities, that is, with physical or social events occurring by chance and building up the coincidences with which individuals cope according to their lights. This ineluctable future—ineluctable because its countless factors are beyond human knowledge and control—is Fortune. Destiny in the guise of Fortune is the fabric of comedy; it is developed by comic action, which is the upset and recovery of the protagonist's equilibrium, his context with the world and his triumph by wit, luck, personal power, or even humours, or ironical, or philosophical acceptance of mischance. Whatever the theme—serious and lyrical as in *The Tempest*, coarse slapstick as in the Schwänke of Hans Sachs, or clever and polite social satire—the immediate sense of life is the underlying feeling of comedy, and dictates its rhythmically structured unity, that is to say its organic form.

Comedy is an art form that arises naturally wherever people are gathered to celebrate life, in spring festivals, triumphs, birthdays, weddings, or initiations. For it expresses the elementary strains and resolutions of animate nature, the animal drives that persist even in human nature, the delight man takes in his special mental gifts that make him the lord of creation; it is an image of human vitality holding its own in the world amid the surprises of unplanned coincidence. The most obvious occasions for the performance of comedies are thanks or challenges to fortune. What justifies the term "Comedy" is not that the ancient ritual procession, the Comus, honoring the god of that name, was the source of this great art form—for comedy has arisen in many parts of the world, where the Greek god with his particular worship was unknown— but that the Comus was a fertility rite, and the god it celebrates a fertility god, a symbol of perpetual rebirth, eternal life.

Tragedy has a different basic feeling, and therefore a different form; that is why it has also quite different thematic material, and why character development, great moral conflicts, and sacrifice are its usual actions. *It is also what makes tragedy sad,* as the rhythm of sheer vitality makes comedy happy. To understand this fundamental difference, we must turn once more to the biological reflections above, and carry them a little further.

[…]

There is a close relation between humor and the "sense of life," and several people tried to analyze it in order to find the basis of that characteristically human function, laughter; the chief weakness in their attempts has been, I think, that they have all started with the questions: What sort of thing makes us laugh? Certainly laughter is often evoked by ideas, cognitions, fancies; it accompanies specific emotions such as disdain, and sometimes the feeling of pleasure; but we also laugh when we are tickled (which may not be pleasurable at all), and in hysterics. Those predominantly physiological causes bear no direct relation to humor; neither, for that matter, do some kinds of pleasure. Humor is one of the causes of laughter.

[…]

Laughter is, indeed, a more elementary thing than humor. We often laugh without finding any person, object, or situation funny. People laugh for joy in active sport, in dancing, in greeting friends; in returning a smile, one acknowledges another person's worth instead of flaunting one's own superiority and finding him funny.

But all these causes of laughter or its reduced form, smiling, which operate directly on us, belong to actual life. In comedy's the spectator's laugh has only one legitimate source: his appreciation of humor in the piece. He does not laugh with the characters, not even at them, but at their situations, their doings, their expressions, often at their dismay. M. Pagnol holds that we laugh at the characters directly, and regards that as a corroboration of his theory: our pleasure in the comic theater lies in watching people to whom we feel superior.[8]

There is, however, one serious defect in that view, namely that it supposes the spectator to be aware of himself as a being in the same "world" as the characters. To compare them, even subconsciously, to himself he must give up his psychical Distance and feel himself co-present with them, as one reads an anecdotal news item as something apart from one's own life but still in the actual world, and is moved to say: "How could she do such a thing! Imagine being so foolish!" If he experiences such a reaction in the theater, it is something quite aside from his perception of the play as a poetic fabrication; he has lost, for the moment, his distance, and feels himself inside the picture.

Humor, then, would be a by-product of comedy, not a structural element in it. And if laughter were elicited thus by the way, it should not make any difference to the value of the work where it occurred; a stage accident, a bad actor who made every amateur actor in the audience feel superior, should serve as well as any clever line or funny situation in the play to amuse the audience. We do, in fact, laugh at such failures; but we do not praise the comedy for that entertainment. In a good play the "laughs" are peptic elements. Its humor as well as its pathos belongs to the virtual life, and the delight we take in it is delight in something created for our perception, not a direct stimulus to our own feelings. It is true that the comic figures are often buffoons, simpletons, clowns; but such characters are almost always sympathetic, and although they are knocked around and abused, they are indestructible, and eternally self-confident and good-humored.

[...]

Because comedy abstracts, and reinforces for our perception, the motion and rhythm of living, it enhances our vital feeling, much as the presentation of space in painting

---

[8] *Notes sur le rire*, p. 92. There is a further discussion of this problem at the end of the present chapter.

enhances our awareness of visual space. The virtual life on the stage is not diffuse and only half felt, as actual life usually is: virtual life, always moving visibly into the future, is intensified, speeded up, exaggerated; the exhibition of vitality rises to a breaking point, to mirth and laughter. We laugh in the theater at small incidents and drolleries which would hardly rate a chuckle off-stage. It is not for such psychological reasons that we go there to be amused, nor are we bound by rules of politeness to hide our hilarity, but these trifles at which we laugh are really funnier *where they occur* than they would be elsewhere; they are employed in the play, not merely brought in casually. They occur where the tension of dialogue or other action reaches a high point. As thought breaks into speech—as the wave breaks into form—vitality breaks into humor.

Humor is the brilliance of drama, a sudden heightening of the vital rhythm. A good comedy, therefore builds up to every laugh; a performance that has been filled up with jokes at the indiscretion of the comedian or of his writer may draw a long series of laughs, yet leave the spectator without any clear impression of a very funny play. The laughs, moreover, are likely to be of a peculiar sameness, almost perfunctory, the formal recognition of a timely "gag."

[…]

There it is, in a nutshell: the contest of men and women—the most universal contest, humanized, in fact civilized, yet still the primitive joyful challenge, the self-preservation and self-assertion whose progress is the comic rhythm.

This rhythm is capable of the most diverse presentations. That is why the art of comedy grows, in every culture, from casual beginnings—miming, clowning, sometimes erotic dancing—to some special and distinctive dramatic art, and sometimes to many forms of it within one culture, yet never seems to repeat its works. It may produce a tradition of dignified drama, spring from solemn ritual, even funereal, its emotional movement too slow to culminate in humor at any point; then other means have to be found to lend it glamor and intensity. The purest heroic comedy is likely to have no humorous passages at all, but to employ the jester only in an ornamental way reminiscent of tragedy, and in fact to use many techniques of tragedy. It may even seem to transcend the amoral comic pattern by presenting virtuous heroes and heroines. But their virtue is a formal affair, a social asset. […] Humor, then, is not the essence of comedy, but only one of its most useful and natural elements It is also its most problematical element, because it elicits from the spectators what appears to be a direct emotional response to persons on the stage, in no wise different from their response to actual people: amusement, laughter.

But the fact that the rhythm of comedy is the basic rhythm of life does not mean that biological existence is the "deeper meaning" of all its themes, and that to understand the play is to interpret all the characters and symbols and the story as a parable, a disguised rite of spring or fertility magic, performed four hundred and fifty times on Broadway. The stock characters are probably symbolic both in origin and in appeal […] but their value for art lies in the degree to which their significance can be "swallowed" by the single symbol, the art work. Not the derivation of personages and situations, but of the rhythm of "felt life" that the poet puts upon them, seems to me to be of artistic importance: the essential comic feeling, which is the sentient aspect of organic unity, growth, and self-preservation.

6. Georges Bataille, 'Un-Knowing: Laughter and Tears' (1953), translated by Annette Michelson

Knowledge requires a certain stability of things known. The realm of the known is, in at least one sense, a stable one, in which we recognize ourselves, whereas although the unknown may not be in motion—it may even be quite immobile—there is no certainty of its stability. Stability may exist, but even the limits of possible movement are uncertain. The unknown is obviously and always unforeseeable.

One of the most remarkable aspects of this realm of the unforeseeable unknown is the risible, in those objects which produce in us that effect of inner upheaval, of overwhelming surprise which we call laughter. There is something extremely curious about the risible. Nothing is more easily studied, and "finally" known, than laughter. We can, with fair precision, observe and define the various themes of the laughable; it in no way eludes the clarity of knowledge or of methodical investigation. Moreover, once we have seen the cause of laughter in its various aspects, we can reproduce its effects at will. We possess veritable recipes, we can in various ways provoke laughter, in exactly the same way as all the other effects known to us. We can, in short, produce objects of laughter. Or one might say, and indeed it has been said, that knowing means knowing how. But can we say that because we know how to provoke laughter we really know what causes laughter? It would seem, from the history of the philosophical study of laughter, that such is not the case, for it is, on the whole, the history of an insoluble problem. That which first seems so accessible has constantly eluded investigation. It may even be that the domain of laughter is finally – or so it seems to me – a closed domain, so unknown and unknowable is the cause of laughter.

It is not my intention to review, on this occasion, all those existing explanations of laughter, which have never managed fully to resolve the mystery. The best-known is surely that of Bergson – the application of the mechanical to the living. This theory of Bergson's, although very well known, is, I believe, somewhat unjustifiably disparaged.

[…]

It is nonetheless true, however, that Bergson's hypothesis is so far from providing a solution to the mystery that the author himself offers it as explanation, not of laughter in general, but of one particular aspect of the risible which he terms the comic.

Thus, apart from the value of Bergson's effort, we observe that the laughter which does, nevertheless, make sense, such as that of the (chance) encounter, that of tickling, that of the child's immediate laughter, is excluded.

Actually, studies have accumulated without enabling us really to account for laughter. Apart from the authors' individual convictions or particular theories, we don't truly know the meaning of laughter. Its cause remains unknown, so that we are suddenly invaded when our habitual foundation is upset, producing in us that "sudden widening of the face," those "explosive sounds in the larynx," and those "rhythmic spasms of thorax and of abdomen" described by medical men.

There remains, perhaps, just one last theory, which has at least, to its credit, its dependence on the most outstanding and essential quality of preceding ones: *their failure*. Let us suppose that that which induces laughter is not only unknown, but unknowable. There is still one possibility to be considered. That which is laughable may simply be *the unknowable*. In other words, the unknown nature of the laughable would be not accidental, but essential. We would laugh, not for some reason which, due to lack of information, or of sufficient penetration, we shall never manage to know, but because *the unknown makes us laugh*.

We laugh, in short, in passing very abruptly, all of a sudden, from a world in which everything is firmly qualified, in which everything is given as stable within a generally stable order, into a world in which our assurance is overwhelmed, in which we perceive for, suddenly the unexpected arises, something unforeseeable and overwhelming, revelatory of an ultimate truth: the surface of appearances conceals a perfect absence of response to our expectations.

We perceive that finally, for all the exercise of knowledge, the world still lies wholly outside its reach, and that not only the world, but the being that one is lies out of reach. Within us and in the world, something is revealed that was not given in knowledge, and whose site is definable only as unattainable by knowledge. It is, I believe, at this that we laugh. And, it must at once be said, in theorizing laughter, that this is what ultimately illuminates us; this is what fills us with joy.

This theory obviously presents from the outset many difficulties, perhaps more than most.

I do not think it does not, to begin with, give us the specificity of laughter. That is obviously its main defect. I might, if necessary, be able to show that in every case of laughter we pass from the domain of the known, from that of the foreseeable, to that of the unknown and the unforeseeable. Such is the case, for example, with the unexpected meeting in the street, which may not provoke a burst of laughter, but which does usually make us laugh. And so it is with the laughter of tickling, which affects us unexpectedly. Such, I believe, is the case of the very young child, overwhelmed, as he emerges from that sort of torpor which we imagine as his embryonic existence, when, upon discovering his mother's affection, he suddenly discovers something disturbing, exciting, and wholly unlike his previous experience.

This, however, does not mean that we laugh whenever a sight which is calm and in keeping with our expectations is succeeded by a disturbance, or even by a reversal, of that sight. And the proof of this lies all too readily at hand.

Let us suppose, in effect, that suddenly – as has happened in certain cities – the earth begins to quake and the floor begins to buckle beneath our feet. None of us would, I think, dream of laughing.

Of course we can say, in spite of this, that there is in the relationship between laughter and the unknown an element that is, relatively speaking, measurable. The cause of such laughter can be said to be proportionate, in its effect, to the diminution of nature as known, or to the suppression of the known character of nature which makes us laugh. Certainly, the less we know of that which arises, the less we expect it, the harder we laugh.

And the suddenness with which the unknown element appears also plays a role. Now, this suddenness has the precise sense of intensity. The swifter the change, the more intense our feeling and perceptive experience of it. But finally, that does not make a sudden catastrophe laughable. We must, I think, in those conditions, consider the matter differently.

I believe, really, that the principal error of most attempts to discuss laughter philo-sophically lie in isolating the object of laughter. Laughter is, I think, part of a range of possible reactions to one situation. This situation, of which I have spoken, this suppression of the character of the known, can result in different reactions.

Laughter, in this respect, can seem to guide us to the path; the consideration of the cause of laughter can set us on the path leading to the understanding of this fundamental situation. But once we have settled upon this situation, we must quickly add that the sudden invasion of the unknown can, depending upon the case, produce the effect of laughter or of tears, as well as other reactions.

Laughter and tears – and this must be mentioned because it goes somewhat contrary to my claim – have not, incidentally, always been studied in isolation. The recent, interesting study of Alfred Stern, a philosopher who has lived in America, considers laughter in connection with tears. This work is entitled *The Philosophy of Laughter and Tears*.

However, as I have observed, other reactions may also be linked to the same state. For example, the sudden invasion of the unknown can result in poetic feeling, or in that of the sacred. It can also produce the effect of anguish or of ecstasy, and not only anguish but also, of course, the effect of terror. I do not, by the way, consider this to be the complete picture. Other aspects do indeed exist. It may, however, be complete insofar as certain other forms are not precisely reducible to one of those just enumerated. Such, for example, is the case of the tragic.

In any case, I think we might recognize the impossibility of discussing laughter outside the framework of a philosophy which goes beyond laughter itself, as, for example, that which I might term a philosophy of un-knowing, which I am attempting to outline before you over a series of lectures which are ordered, up to a certain point.

A certain reciprocity, in this respect, should be noted. I believe it is impossible to speak of un-knowing in any way other than in our experience of it. This experience always has an effect, as laughter or tears, the poetic feeling, anguish or ecstasy. And I do not think it possible to talk seriously of unknowing apart from these effects.

I now wish to stress, incidentally, another aspect of the difficulty involved in the interpretation of laughter. I think it pointless to try to approach laughter as a mystery to be solved by a personal philosophy formulated quite independently of any thought of laughing.

There is always something extremely interesting in the attempt, in afterthought, to test a philosophy on the problem of laughter. Its extreme interest lies in its recognition that philosophy should be able to supply the key to the problem of laughter. But this key will, I believe, provide no opening at all, if it is not made expressly for the lock in question.

I think that in straining to solve the problem of laughter, we have to begin by thinking about laughing, insofar as one does philosophical work. Philosophical reflection must, I think, bear first on laughter.

Given my immediately preceding statement, that may come as a surprise. But the contradiction is obviously a superficial one. I have said that the problem of laughter should not be isolated, that it must, on the contrary, be linked to the problem of tears, to the problem of sacrifice, and so forth. I mean by that, essentially, that we must begin with an experience of laughter as related to the experience of sacrifice, the experience of the poetic, and so forth. Let us be clear. I do not mean that these are necessarily simultaneous, but I do believe in the possibility of beginning with the experience of laughter and not relinquishing it when one passes from this particular experience to its neighbor, the sacred or the poetic. This means, if you like, finding in the given which is laughter the central given of philosophy, its very first and perhaps its ultimate given.

I now wish to explain myself on this point. I should like to make as clear and precise as possible this determinate orientation of philosophy, or at least of the reflective experience as based on the experience of laughter. And I shall therefore take my own personal experience as point of departure.

I may say indeed that insofar as I am a philosopher, mine is a philosophy of laughter. It is a philosophy founded on the experience of laughter, and which does not even make any further claim. It is a philosophy which casts off problems other than those provided by that precise experience.

I stress the fact that I prefer to speak of reflective experience. For me this has a great advantage, insofar as the word *experience* carries, despite its association with the word *reflective*, the meaning of a constantly sustained and precise effect, such as laughter, or ecstasy, or anguish.

My philosophical reflection is never pursued independently of this experience. And I must say that this is true in a double sense; for my philosophical reflection has value insofar as it modifies the effects in question, insofar as it makes of these effects conscious effects. And I think it useful to describe the way in which I should have undertaken my reflection on this point.

I should begin by stating that I am not in any way a professional philosopher. I can't say I have not studied philosophy, but I did not study in the usual way; I was not a student of philosophy. I wanted, rather systematically, by the way, to study things other than philosophy. And these studies, as things turned out – I apologize for the anecdotal character of this explanation – took me to London, and in London I was received in a house also frequented by Bergson.

Despite all this I had, as I have said, like everyone else, studied some philosophy, in that completely elementary way one does in order to pass an exam. I had indeed read a few pages of Bergson, but with the very simple reaction of one who is about to meet an important philosopher. I was embarrassed by the idea of knowing nothing, or almost nothing, of his work. So, as I have already recounted in one of my books – but I want now to relate it with more precision – I went to the British Museum and read Bergson's *On Laughter*.

It was not very satisfying reading, but I found it very interesting, nevertheless. And I have continued, in my various considerations of laughter, to refer to this theory which still seems to me one of the deepest to have been developed.

I therefore read this little book, which I found enormously gripping for reasons other than the content developed within it. What gripped me at that time was the possibility of thinking about laughter, the possibility of making laughter the object of reflection. I increasingly wanted to deepen this reflection, to distance myself from all I had remembered of Bergson's book, but from the start my thinking was directed, as I have tried to present it to you, toward both experience and reflection.

I should say, incidentally, that according to my fairly precise remembrance of the first stages of my thought as it there developed, my sole, my true interest lay in its character of experience. I went astray in difficulties of a quite secondary sort; I lacked – I was about to say – experience, but I can't use that word, since in speaking now I use it in another sense. I lacked the knowledge needed to accomplish this reflection. Still, I managed, in that reflection, a kind of plunge, from my overhanging position, toward dizziness, into the possibility of laughter.

Still, there is something in my thinking at that time that I can retain; its principle. This consisted in considering that the major problem was that of laughter. And putting this quite crudely, quite differently from the way in which I would now do so, I thought that if I could manage to learn what laughter was, I would know everything. I would have solved the problem of all philosophy. It seemed evident to me that solving the problem of laughter and solving the philosophical problem were the same thing. The object that I grasped in laughter seemed, if you like, of interest comparable to that of the object as usually posed in philosophy.

I do not seek to defend this point of view, at least in the form in which I now present it. I do need to express myself thus in order to be able to describe this experience.

I should explain that when this experience began, I was, in short, quickened by a very definite religious faith, in conformity with a dogma, and that this was very important to me, to the point where, as far as possible, I suited my action to my thoughts. Certainly, when I began to envisage the possibility of furthest descent within the sphere of laughter, the first effect was the feeling that everything offered by dogma was decomposed and swept away in a sort of deliquescent tide. I felt then that it was, after all, wholly possible to maintain faith and its related behavior, but that the tide of laughter which swept over me, made of my faith a game – a game in which I might continue to believe, but which was transcended, nonetheless, by the dynamics of the game which was given me in laughter. From that moment on, I could adhere to it only as something transcended by laughter.

It almost goes without saying that in conditions such as those, faith in dogma cannot persist, and that gradually, and as a matter of not the slightest consequence, I grew detached from all faith.

I thus emphasize that the fundamental idea I want to stress is the complete absence of presuppositions. The philosophy that I propose is, at the very least, absolutely presuppositionless.

When I now speak of un-knowing, I mean essentially this: I know nothing, and if I continue to speak, it is only insofar as I have knowledge which leads me to *nothing*. This is particularly true of that sort of knowledge which I am now considering before you, since it is in order to set myself before this *nothing* that I do talk of it, to set both myself and my listeners in confrontation with this *nothing*.

I must also say that there was, from the beginning, another aspect of this mixture of belief and laughter. It very quickly became clear to me that there was nothing in my experience of laughter which was not to be found in my former religious experience. I mean that in claiming to maintain faith within the sphere of laughter I was not expressing myself precisely enough. I did maintain them, but in such deep diffusion that I felt they could be indefinitely transposed in an impulse of laughter. I could recapture all the impulses of religious experience, mingling them with the experience of laughter without feeling that religious experience to be in any way impoverished.

I may say, too, that the impulse of what I prefer to call my life rather than my work has essentially worked toward the maintenance (in ways both unexpected and, probably, most unsatisfactory from the point of view of adherence to the limits of dogma) of the whole religious experience acquired within the limits of dogma.

Similarly, I believe that when I pass, as I am now doing, from the pure and simple consideration of laughter to the more general one of un-knowing – since by un-knowing I mean mainly an experience – I remain, despite the break with all possible knowledge, within the richness of the experience I had formerly known. Un-knowing, as I understand it, does not eliminate the possibility of an experience which I consider to be equally as rich as the religious experience present in the maximum knowledge which is revelation.

It is, in short, in considering being as problematic, as wholly unknown, and in plunging into this nonknowledge, that I find an experience not only as rich, but, to me, richer still, deeper if possible, because in this experience I further part with common experience. I part with that experience of the profane in which, after all, we adhere to objects whose hold upon us is extremely doubtful, due merely to hunger, suffering, and made possible only because our actions are often commanded by fear. Within the experience of un-knowing of which I speak, there remains a religious experience; it is wholly detached from concern with the future, it is wholly detached from the hold exerted by the possible threat of suffering, it is now only play.

I am naturally led to lay stress upon the fact that this experience of laughter is rather remote from the common experience of it. I should say first, because this may seem rather strange, that this experience may be quite as detached from those movements described by medical men as cited heretofore. It is always possible not to widen one's face without fundamentally changing anything. In that respect I can only say that, of course, the widening, the brightening of the face and even the burst of laughter are part of that experience, that we cannot suppose this experience to exclude moments of real, pealing laughter, as physiologically defined. What seems to me much more important, however, is to explain that I part with the experience and with laughter on one very important point, insofar as I understand not only theoretically what we mean in using this word, but something more.

Of course, laughter remains joyous. Notwithstanding that joy which is present in laughter and which is so paradoxically associated with objects of laughter which are not generally joyous, that joy cannot, in my view, be separated from the feeling of the tragic.

I believe, moreover, that this is not wholly exterior to the joy commonly present in laughter, insofar as for each of us, for all of us, it is always possible from the impulse of common joy to pass into the feeling of the tragic, and without any diminution of that joy. It remains true, however, that in most cases, we take care not to do so.

I would, at this point, stress something frequently stressed in my writing: the fact that this is an experience I believe to be deeply consonant with that of Nietzsche. I have frequently, I think, put things somewhat strangely, in saying that I felt at one with Nietzsche's thought, with Nietzsche himself, as well, and in some fundamental relation with Nietzsche's experience. And one may wonder if that means very much; we are all isolated; communication between one being and another is minimal; my interpretation of Nietzsche may, on the other hand, be debatable. I do nevertheless, and for a reason which is not merely an intellectual one, stress this relation between what Nietzsche was and what I am. The reason lies in a very particular kind of experience apparently proper to both Nietzsche and myself – similar, for example, to the way in which the experience of Saint Theresa was as much that of Saint John of the Cross as it was hers. They were, if you like, related on the level of communication present in dogma and in their subscribing to the same religion. This community may be present between two individuals, outside of a religious community. That is why I speak of community in speaking of Nietzsche. I mean by that precisely the following: I believe there to be a relation between the thought and experience of Nietzsche and my own, analogous to that which exists within a community.

I do want, moreover, to be clear about this. I think that Nietzsche's thought makes this experience quite clear. It is present, naturally, and in particular, in the importance which Nietzsche ascribed to laughter, and this in a great number of passages, but mainly in a rather late, posthumously published work: "To see the failure of tragic natures and to laugh, that is divine." I do not think that what I represent is general when I talk of un-knowing and of the experience of its effects can be disassociated from an expression like that.

What matters to me insofar as I speak of laughter is situating it at that point of slippage which leads to that particular experience, the laughter which becomes divine insofar as it can be one's laughter at witnessing the failure of a tragic nature. I am not sure but what there is something troubling to me in Nietzsche's expression. It is perhaps, a shade too – I would not say grandiloquent – but a shade too tragic. Indeed, once one clarifies the experience of the really tragic to the point of the ability to laugh at it, all is lightened, all is simple, and everything can be said with no pain, with no appeal to emotion other than those surmounted.

Indeed, I believe that the nature of laughter as one of that group of effects which I relate to un-knowing lay in its link to a position of dominance. In tears, for example, our experience of un-knowing, of what is present in our crying, is not one in which we have a position of dominance. One is clearly overwhelmed.

Now, it must be stated that the transcendence present in laughter is not of great interest if it is not the transcendence indicated in Nietzsche's phrase. In general we laugh on condition that our position of dominance not be at the mercy of laughter, the object of laughter. To laugh, it is necessary that one not risk losing one's position of dominance.

To return to the terms I have already employed – laughter is, let us say, the effect of un-knowing, though laughter has not, theoretically, as its object, the state of un-knowing; one does not, by laughing, accept the idea that one knows nothing. Something unexpected occurs, which is in contradiction to the knowledge we do have.

Here I would cite a phrase from an article by Charles Eubé ("The Tragic Foundation of Laughter," *Critique*, no. 68, January 1953), which I find of particular interest. I say this with slight embarrassment, since I published it in the last issue of *Critique*, but one phrase in particular I found very meaningful. Here is the way in which at one point he defines laughter. It is not, properly speaking, a definition of laughter, but of the position of him who laughs. This position implies, according to Charles Eubé, "the refusal to *accept* that which deep within ourselves, we *know*. ..."

Indeed, he who laughs does not, theoretically, abandon his knowledge, but he refuses, for a time – a limited time – to accept it, he allows himself to be overcome by the impulse to laughter, so that what he knows is destroyed, but he retains, deep within, the conviction that it is not, after all, destroyed. When we laugh we retain deep within us that which is suppressed by laughter, but it has been only artificially suppressed, just as laughter, let us say, has the power to suspend strict logic. Indeed, when we operate within this sphere we can also retain faith, and, conversely, we can know that which we simultaneously destroy as known.

I have returned to the theme which I had developed last time in talking of the lesser play as opposed to greater play. There is lesser laughter as well as greater laughter. I don't wish to limit myself today to discussion of the greater laughter, but it is never-theless to it that I essentially refer.

The most curious mystery within laughter comes from one's rejoicing in something which places a vital equilibrium in danger. We even rejoice most strongly thus. This, as I see it, is the case in which we must, once and for all, declare that a question such as this cannot be isolated within the sphere of laughter. The same indeed applies to tears.

Tears are deeply ambiguous. We all know that there is pleasure in crying, that we find in tears a kind of solace we may often not care to accept, but which overcomes us. There is something intoxicating in tears, as in laughter. One would, I think, have no difficulty, in showing that tears can be considered as related to laughter, to the invasion of the unknown, to the elimination of a part of this world which we consider as the world known in all the parts generally seen as a whole. If someone dies, for example, it is true that a familiar order is deeply altered, and that we must face the substitution, before us and in spite of us, of something that we know by something unknown to us, for example, the presence of the dead, or more precisely, the absence of the living. Tears, more than anything else, mark the disappearance, the sudden destruction of the known universe in which we belong.

But tears, like laughter, are strange in nature. And this stranger nature I shall have some difficulty in describing, for it is not a classic object of study. There exist, first of all, beyond the tears of pain, the tears of sadness, the tears of death, the tears of joy. Now of tears of joy we do frequently need to speak. But beyond tears of joy, there may be tears more curious still, which are not [usually the object of understanding. I tend to think that eyes fill with tears for] all sorts of complex reasons. I can, I believe, do no more now than provide some indications of my meaning.

There are, I think, tears of success, which are very frequent. They are obviously not so frequent that I am, for example, curious to know whether or not some of you have concrete experience, knowledge of the tears of success. Actually, I know nothing of what I call tears of success; they have not been subject to study, like laughter, not so far as I know.

For example, and unhoped-for success can bring tears to one's eyes, and so can a wholly extraordinary stroke of chance. I will cite one instance, surprising even to me, which I have never been able to mention or hear mentioned without tears filling my eyes. I know someone who, during the war, was an officer on board the *Hood*, until almost the day of the catastrophe. On that day, or perhaps the day before – it was a matter of a few hours – he left on a mission in a motor launch, so his mother naturally believed him dead. His death was moreover announced, and it was not until days and days later that his mother learned that he was alive. Now, I do not think that this unhoped-for element is something which must necessarily bring tears to one's eyes, but it can do so. And this, in my view, places it at something of a distance from what is the general, classical view of tears.

I should say that I was, in this respect, struck by something; this is not the only example familiar to me, but I generally cannot manage to recall the examples that should be present in my memory; I almost always forget. I have frequently had this experience, but have not, so to speak, ever noticed it; I am not very methodical and I generally forget it. You see, moreover, that I speak now of a domain which is still wholly open to investigation, which is wholly unknown.

I do not want to cause confusion. Certainly when I talk of the unknown, it is not of that sort that I speak. There is, however, something wholly particular which seems, nevertheless, quite clear to me: essential to this cause of tears is the element of the unhoped-for, the unanticipated, which returns us to the theme which I have generally introduced.

I shan't continue this exposition by talking more generally of the different effects heretofore enumerated. I have already, in this series of lectures, discussed the relations between eroticism and un-knowing, but I shall, this evening, limit myself to that which I have already presented.

In pronouncing the word *ecstasy*, I shall limit myself to saying merely the following: laughter, when considered as I have done, initiates a sort of general experience which is, in my view, comparable to what the theologians call "mystical theology" or "negative theology." But I must add that there is, in this respect, an essential difference to be noted: this experience, so far as I am concerned, is not negative merely within certain limits; it is totally negative. To this experience and to its accompanying reflection, I would want to give the name of "atheology," composed of the privative prefix *a* and of the word *theology*. It is an atheology whose fundamental consideration, let us say, is present in the following proposition: God is an effect of un-knowing. He can nevertheless be known as an effect of un-knowing – like laughter, like the sacred.

I can then say the following: that this experience is, on the whole, part of the general line of religions. In speaking as I do, I am aware not only of adopting a basically religious attitude, but further, of representing a kind of constituted religion. There is no question of foundation of religion. No, there is no foundation, since there is no possible presupposition; there is only a possibility of experience. But not all religions have been founded, after all; religions were able to be simply experiences constituting a more or less coherent dogma, and often less rather than more.

I will, moreover, say in conclusion that I would not in any case want to underestimate the philosophical character of this entire way of seeing. First of all, I declare with insistence that this way of seeing, despite its negative character, is necessarily linked to a positive philosophy. All that it can add to this principle – that of negation – is the recognition that positive philosophy itself is not, for him who is positioned in experience as I have described it, a sort of ineluctable necessity; it is, rather, suspended, as I have suggested that dogma might be, within laughter.

7. Northrop Frye 'Comic Fictional Modes', from *Anatomy of Criticism: Four Essays* (1965)

The theme of the comic is the integration of society, which usually takes the form of incorporating a central character into it. The mythical comedy corresponding to the death of the Dionysiac god is Apollonian, the story of how a hero is accepted by a society of gods. In Classical literature it is the theme of salvation; or, in a more concentrated form, of assumption: the comedy that stands just at the end of Dante's *Commedia*. The mode of romantic comedy corresponding to the elegiac is best described as idyllic, and its chief vehicle is the pastoral. Because of the social interest of comedy, the idyllic cannot equal the introversion of the elegiac, but it preserves the theme of escape from society to the extent of idealizing a simplified life in the country or on the frontier (the pastoral of popular modern literature is the Western story). The close association with animal and vegetable nature that we noted in the elegiac recurs in the sheep and pleasant pastures (or the cattle and ranches) of the idyllic, and the same easy connection with myth recurs in the fact that such imagery is often used, as it is in the Bible, for the theme of salvation.

The clearest example of high mimetic comedy is the Old Comedy of Aristophanes. The New Comedy of Menander is closer to the low mimetic, and through Plautus and Terence its formulas were handed down to the Renaissance, so that there has always been a strongly low mimetic bias to social comedy. In Aristophanes there is usually a central figure who constructs his (or her) own society in the teeth of strong opposition, driving off one after another all the people who come to prevent or exploit him, and eventually achieving a heroic triumph, complete with mistresses, in which he is sometimes assigned the honours of a reborn god. We notice that just as there is a catharsis of pity and fear in tragedy, so there is a catharsis of the corresponding comic emotions, which are sympathy and ridicule, in Old Comedy. The comic hero will get his triumph whether what he has done is sensible or silly, honest or rascally. Thus Old Comedy, like the tragedy contemporary with it, is a blend of the heroic and the ironic. In some plays this fact is partly concealed by Aristophanes' strong desire to get his own opinion of what the hero is doing into the record, but his greatest comedy, *The Birds*, preserves an exquisite balance between comic heroism and comic irony.

New Comedy normally presents an erotic intrigue between a young man and a young woman which is blocked by some sort of opposition, usually paternal, and resolved by a twist in the plot which is the comic form of Aristotle's "discovery," and is more manipulated than its tragic counterpart. At the beginning of the play the forces thwarting the hero are in control of the play's society, but after a discovery in which the hero becomes wealthy or the heroine respectable, a new society crystallizes on the stage around the hero and his bride. The action of the comedy thus moves toward the incorporation of the hero into society that he naturally fits. The hero himself is seldom a very interesting person: in conformity with low mimetic decorum, he is ordinary in his virtues, but socially attractive. In Shakespeare and in the kind of romantic comedy that most closely resembles his there is a development of these formulas in a more distinctively high mimetic direction. In the figure of Prospero we have one of the few approaches to the Aristophanic technique of having the whole comic action projected by a central character. Usually Shakespeare achieves his high mimetic pattern by making the struggle of the repressive and the desirable societies a struggle between two levels of existence, the former like our own world or worse, the latter enchanted and idyllic. This point will be dealt with more fully later.

For the reasons given above the domestic comedy of later fiction carries on with much the same conventions as were used in the Renaissance. Domestic comedy is usually based on the Cinderella archetype, the kind of thing that happens when Pamela's virtue is rewarded, the incorporation of an individual very like the reader into the society aspired to by both, a society ushered in with a happy rustle of bridal gowns and banknotes. Here again, Shakespearean comedy may marry off eight or ten people of approximately equal dramatic interest, just as a high mimetic tragedy may kill off the same number, but in domestic comedy such diffusion of sexual energy is more rare. The chief difference between high and low mimetic comedy, however, is that the resolution of the latter more frequently involves a social promotion. More sophisticated writers of low mimetic comedy often present the same success-story formula with the moral ambiguities that we have found in Aristophanes. In Balzac or Stendhal a clever and ruthless scoundrel may achieve the same kind of success as the virtuous heroes of Samuel Smiles and Horatio Alger. Thus the comic counterpart of the *alazon* seems to be the clever, likeable, unprincipled *picaro* of the picaresque novel.

In studying ironic comedy we must start with the theme of driving out the *pharmakos* from the point of view of society. This appeals to the kind of relief we are expected to feel when we see Jonson's Volpone condemned to the galleys, Shylock stripped of his wealth, or Tartuffe taken off to prison. Such a theme, unless touched very lightly, is difficult to make convincing, for the reasons suggested in connection with ironic tragedy. Insisting on the theme of social revenge on an individual, however great a rascal he may be, tends to make him look less involved in guilt and the society more so. This is particularly true of characters who have been trying to amuse either the actual or the internal audience, and who are the comic counterparts of the tragic hero as artist. The rejection of the entertainer, whether fool, clown, buffoon, or simpleton, can be one of the most terrible ironies known to art, as the rejection of Falstaff does, and certain scenes in Chaplin.

In some religious poetry, for example at the end of the *Paradiso*, we can see that literature has an upper limit, a point at which an imaginative vision of an eternal world becomes an experience of it. In ironic comedy we begin to see that art also had a lower limit in actual life. This is the condition of savagery, the world in which comedy consists of inflicting pain on a helpless victim, and tragedy in enduring it. Ironic comedy brings us to the figure of the scapegoat ritual and the nightmare dream, the human symbol that concentrates our fears and hates. We pass the boundary of art when this symbol becomes existential, as it does in the black man of a lynching, the Jew of a pogrom, the old woman of a witch hunt, or anyone picked up at random by a mob, like Cinna the poet in *Julius Caesar*. In Aristophanes the word *pharmakos* means simply scoundrel, with no nonsense about it. At the conclusion of *The Clouds*, where the poet seems almost to be summoning a lynching party to go and burn down Socrates' house, we reach the comic counterpart of one of the greatest masterpieces of tragic irony in literature, Plato's *Apology*.

But the element of *play* is the barrier that separates art from savagery, and playing at human sacrifices seems to be an important theme of ironic comedy. Even in laughter itself some kind of deliverance from the unpleasant, even the horrible, seems to be very important. We notice this particularly in all forms of art in which a large number of auditors are simultaneously present, as in drama, and, still more obviously, in games. We notice too that playing at sacrifice has nothing to do with any historical descent from sacrificial ritual, such as has been suggested for Old Comedy. All the features of such ritual, the king's son, the mimic death, the executioner, the substituted victim, are far more explicit in Gilbert and Sullivan's *Mikado* than they are in Aristophanes. There is certainly no evidence that baseball has descended from a ritual of human sacrifice, but the umpire is quite as much of a *pharmakos* as if it had: he is an abandoned scoundrel, a greater robber than Barabbas; he has the evil eye; the supporters of the losing team scream for his death. At play, mob emotions are boiled in an open pot, so to speak; in the lynching mob they are in a sealed furnace of what Blake would call moral virtue. The gladiatorial combat, in which the audience has the actual power of life and death over the people who are entertaining them, is perhaps the most concentrated of all the savage of demonic parodies of drama.

The fact that we are now in an ironic phase of literature largely accounts for the popularity of the detective story, the formula of how a man-hunter locates a *pharmakos* and gets rid of him. The detective story begins in the Sherlock Holmes period as an intensification of low mimetic, in the sharpening of attention to details that makes the fullest and most neglected trivia of daily living leap into mysterious and fateful significance. But as we move further away from this we move toward a ritual drama around a corpse in which a wavering finger of social condemnation passes over a group of "suspects" and finally settles on one. The sense of a victim chosen by lot is very strong, for the case against him is only plausibly manipulated. If it were really inevitable, we should have tragic irony, as in *Crime and Punishment*, where Raskolnikoff's crime is so interwoven with his character that there can be no question of any "whodunit" mystery. In the growing brutality of the crime story (a brutality protected by the convention of the form, as it is conventionally impossible that the man-hunter can be mistaken in believing that one of his suspects is a murderer), detection begins to merge with the thriller as one of the forms of melodrama. In melodrama two themes are important: the triumph of moral virtue assumed to be held by the audience. In the melodrama of the brutal thriller we come as close as it is normally possible for art to come to the pure self-righteousness of the lynching mob.

We should have to say, then, that all forms of melodrama, the detective story in particular, were advance propaganda for the police state, in so far as that represents the regularizing of mob violence, if it were possible to take them seriously. But it seems not to be possible. The protecting wall of play is still there. Serious melodrama soon gets entangled with its own pity and fear; the more serious it is, the more likely it is to be looked at ironically by the reader, its pity and fear seen as sentimental drivel and owlish solemnity, respectively. One pole of ironic comedy is the recognition of the absurdity of naïve melodrama, or, at least, of the absurdity of its attempt to define the enemy of society as a person outside that society. From there it develops toward the opposite pole, which is true comic irony or satire, and which defines the enemy of society as a spirit within that society. Let us arrange the forms of ironic comedy from this point of view.

Cultivated people go to a melodrama to hiss the villain with an air of condescension: they are making a point of the fact that they cannot take his villainy seriously. We have here a type of irony which exactly corresponds to that of two other major arts of the ironic age, advertising and propaganda. These arts pretend to address themselves seriously to a subliminal audience of cretins, an audience that may not even exist, but which is assumed to be simple-minded enough to accept at their face value the statements made about the purity of a soap or a government's motives. The rest of us, realizing that irony never says precisely what it means, take these ironically, or, at least, regard them as a kind of unreality of the villainy involved. Murder is doubtless a serious crime, but if private murder really were a major threat to our civilization it would not be relaxing to read about it. We may compare the abuse showered on the pimp in Roman comedy, which was similarly based on the indisputable ground that brothels are immoral.

The next step is an ironic comedy addressed to the people who can realize that murderous violence is less an attack on a virtuous society by a malignant individual than a symptom of that society's own viciousness. Such a comedy would be the kind of intellectualized parody of melodramatic formulas represented by, for instance, the novels of Graham Greene. Next comes the ironic comedy directed at the melodramatic spirit itself, an astonishingly persistent tradition in all comedy in which there is a large ironic admixture. One notes a recurring tendency to be hankering after sentiment, solemnity, and the triumph of fidelity and approved moral standards. The arrogance of Jonson and Congreve, the mocking of bourgeois sentiment in Goldsmith, the parody of melodramatic situations in Wilde and Shaw, belong to a consistent tradition. Molière had to please his king, but was not temperamentally an exception. To comic drama one may add the ridicule of melodramatic romance in the novelists, from Fielding to Joyce.

Finally comes the comedy of manners, the portrayal of a chattering monkey society devoted to snobbery and slander. In this kind of irony the characters who are opposed to or excluded from the fictional society have the sympathy of the audience. Here we are close to a parody of tragic irony, as we can see in the appalling fate of the relatively harmless hero of Evelyn Waugh's *A Handful of Dust*. Or we may have a character who, with the sympathy of the author or audience, repudiates such a society to the point of deliberately walking out of it, becoming thereby a kind of *pharmakos* in reverse. This happens for instance at the conclusion of Aldous Huxley's *Those Barren Leaves*. It is more usual, however, for the artist to present an ironic deadlock in which the hero is regarded as a fool or worse by the fictional society, and yet impresses the real audience as having something more valuable than his society has. The obvious example, and certainly one of the greatest, is Dostoievsky's *The Idiot*, but there are many others. *The Good Soldier Schweik*, *Heaven's My Destination*, and *The Horse's Mouth* are instances that will give some idea of the range of the theme.

What we have said about the return of irony to myth in tragic modes thus holds equally well for comic ones. Even popular literature appears to be slowly shifting its centre of gravity from murder stories to science fiction – or at any rate a rapid growth of science fiction is certainly a fact about contemporary popular literature. Science fiction frequently tries to imagine what life would be like on a plane as far above us as we are above savagery; its setting is often of a kind that appears to us as technologically miraculous. It is thus a mode of romance with a strong inherent tendency to myth.

The conception of a sequence of fictional modes should do something, let us hope, to give us a more flexible meaning to some of our literary terms. The words "romantic" and "realistic," for instance, as ordinarily used, are relative or comparative terms: they illustrate tendencies in fiction, and cannot be used as simply descriptive adjectives with any sort of exactness. If we take the sequence *De Raptu Proserpinae*, *The Man of Law's Tale*, *Much Ado About Nothing*, *Pride and Prejudice*, *An American Tragedy*, it is clear that each work is "romantic" compared to its successors and "realistic" compared to its predecessors. On the other hand, the term "naturalism" shows up in its proper perspective as a phase of fiction which, rather like the detective story, though in a very different way, begins as an intensification of low mimetic, an attempt to describe life, exactly as it is, and ends, by the very logic of that attempt, in pure irony. Thus Zola's obsession with ironic formulas gave him a reputation as a detached recorder of the human scene.

The difference between the ironic *tone* that we may find in low mimetic or earlier modes and the ironic *structure* of the ironic model itself is not hard to sense in practice. When Dickens, for instance, uses irony the reader is invited to share in the irony, because certain standards of normality common to author and reader are assumed. Such assumptions are a mark of a relatively popular mode: as the example of Dickens indicates, the gap between serious and popular fiction is narrower in low mimetic than in ironic writing. The literary acceptance of relatively stable social norms is closely connected with the *reticence* of low mimetic as compared to ironic fiction. In low mimetic modes characters are usually presented as they appear to others, fully dressed and with a large section of both their physical lives and their inner monologue carefully excised. Such an approach is entirely consistent with the other conventions involved.

If we were to make this distinction the basis of a comparative value judgment, which would, of course, be a moral value judgment disguised as a critical one, we should be compelled either to attack low mimetic conventions for being prudish and hypocritical and leaving too much of life out, or to attack ironic conventions for not being wholesome, healthy, popular, reassuring, and sound, like the conventions of Dickens. As long as we are concerned simply to distinguish between the conventions, we need only remark that the low mimetic is one step more heroic than the ironic, and that low mimetic reticence has the effect of making its characters, on the average, more heroic, or at least more dignified, than the characters in ironic fiction.

We may also apply our scheme to the principles of selection on which a writer of fiction operates. Let us take, as a random example, the use of ghosts in fiction. In a true myth there can obviously be no consistent distinction between ghosts and living beings. In romance we have real human beings, and consequently ghosts are in a separate category, but in a romance a ghost as a rule is merely one more character: he causes little surprise because his appearance is no more marvellous than many other events. In high mimetic, where we are within the order of nature, a ghost is relatively easy to introduce because the plane of experience is above our own, but when he appears he is an awful and mysterious being from what is perceptibly another world. In low mimetic, ghosts have been, ever since Defoe, almost entirely confined to a separate category of "ghost stories." In ordinary low mimetic fiction they are inadmissible, "in complaisance to the scepticism of a reader," as Fielding puts it, a scepticism which extends only to low mimetic conventions. The few exceptions, such as *Wuthering Heights*, go a long way to prove the rule – that is, we recognize a strong influence of romance in *Wuthering Heights*. In some forms of ironic fiction, such as the later works of Henry James, the ghost begins to come back as a fragment of a disintegrating personality.

Once we have learned to distinguish the modes, however, we must then learn to recombine them. For while one mode constitutes the underlying tonality of a work of fiction, any or all of the other four may be simultaneously present. Much of our sense of the subtlety of great literature comes from this modal counterpoint. Chaucer is a medieval poet specializing mainly in romance, whether sacred or secular. Of his pilgrims, the knight and the parson clearly present the norms of the society in which he functions as a poet, and, as we have them, the *Canterbury Tales* are contained by these two figures, who open and close the series. But to overlook Chaucer's mastery of low mimetic and ironic techniques would be as wrong as to think of him as a modern novelist who got into the Middle Ages by mistake. The tonality of *Antony and Cleopatra* is high mimetic, the story of the fall of a great leader. But it is easy to look at Mark Antony ironically, as a man enslaved by passion; it is easy to recognize his common humanity with ourselves; it is easy to see in him a romantic adventurer of prodigious courage and endurance betrayed by a witch; there are even hints of a superhuman being whose legs bestride the ocean and whose downfall is a conspiracy of fate, explicable only to the soothsayer. To leave out any of these would oversimplify and belittle the play. Through such an analysis we may come to realize that the two essential facts about a work of art, that it is contemporary with its own time and that it is contemporary with ours, are not opposed by complementary facts.

Our survey of fictional modes has also shown us that the mimetic tendency itself, the tendency to verisimilitude and accuracy of description, is one of two poles of literature. At the other pole is something that seems to be connected both with Aristotle's word *mythos* and with the usual meaning of myth. That is, it is a tendency to tell a story which is in origin a story about characters who can do anything, and only gradually becomes attracted toward a tendency to tell a plausible or credible story. Myths of gods merge into legends of heroes; legends of heroes merge into plots of tragedies and comedies; plots of tragedies and comedies merge into plots of more or less realistic fiction. But these are change of social context rather than of literary form, and the constructive principles of storytelling remain constant through them, though of course they adapt to them. Tom Jones and Oliver Twist are typical enough as low mimetic

characters, but the birth-mystery plots in which they are involved are plausible adapta-
tions of fictional formulas that go back to Menander, and from Menander to Euripides'
Ion, and from Euripides to legends like those of Perseus and Moses. We note in passing
that imitation of nature in fiction produces, not truth or reality, but plausibility, and
plausibility varies in weight from a mere perfunctory concession in a myth or folk
tale to a kind of censor principle in a naturalistic novel. Reading forward in history,
therefore, we may think of our romantic, high mimetic, and low mimetic modes as a
series of *displaced* myths, *mythoi* or plot-formulas progressively moving over towards
the opposite pole of verisimilitude, and then, with irony, beginning to move back.

8. Jacques Derrida, 'From Restricted to General Economy: A Hegelianism without Reserve', from *Writing and Difference* (1967), translated by Alan Bass

To bear the self-evidence of Hegel, today, would mean this: one must, in every sense, go
through the "slumber of reason," the slumber that engenders monsters and then puts
them to sleep; this slumber must be effectively traversed so that awakening will not be
a ruse of dream. That is to say, again, a ruse of reason. The slumber of reason is not,
perhaps, reason put to sleep, but slumber in the form of reason, the vigilance of the
Hegelian logos. Reason keeps watch over a deep slumber in which it had an interest.
Now, if "evidence received in the slumber of reason loses or will lose the characteristics
of wakefulness" (ibid.), then it is necessary, in order to open our eyes (and did Bataille
ever want to do otherwise, correctly certain that he was thereby risking death: "the
condition in which I *would see* would be to die"), to have spent the night with reason,
to have kept watch and to have slept with her; and to have done so throughout the
night, until morning, until the other dawn which resembles, even to the point of being
taken for it – like daybreak for nightfall – the hour when the philosophical animal
can also finally open its eyes. That morning and none other. For at the far reaches of
this night something was contrived, blindly, I mean in a discourse, by means of which
philosophy, in completing itself, could both include within itself and anticipate all the
figures of its beyond, all the forms and resources of its exterior; and could do so in
order to keep these forms and resources close to itself by simply taking hold of their
enunciation. Except, perhaps, for a certain laughter. And yet.

   To laugh at philosophy (at Hegelianism) – such, in effect, is the form of the awakening
– henceforth calls for an entire "discipline", an entire "method of meditation" that
acknowledges the philosopher's byways, understands his techniques, makes use of his

ruses, manipulates his cards, lets him deploy his strategy, appropriates his texts. Then, thanks to this work which has prepared it – and philosophy is work *itself* according to Bataille – but quickly, furtively, and unforeseeably breaking with it, as betrayal or as detachment, drily, laughter bursts out. And yet, in privileged moments that are less moments than the always rapidly sketched movements of experience; rare, discreet and light movements, without triumphant stupidity, far from public view, very close to that at which laughter laughs: close to anguish, first of all, which must not even be called the negative of laughter for fear of once more being sucked in by Hegel's discourse. And one can already foresee, in this prelude, that the *impossible* mediated by Bataille will always have this form: how, after having exhausted the discourse of philosophy, can one inscribe in the lexicon and syntax of a language, our language, which was also the language of philosophy, that which nevertheless exceeds the oppositions of concepts governed by this communal logic? Necessary and impossible, this excess had to fold discourse into strange shapes. And, of course, constrain it to justify itself to Hegel indefinitely. Since more than a century of ruptures, of "surpassing" with or without "overtunings," rarely had a relation to Hegel has been so little definable: a complicity without reserve accompanied Hegelian discourse, "takes it seriously" up to the end, without an objection in philosophical form, while, however, a certain burst of laughter exceeds it and destroys its sense, or signals, in any event, the extreme point of "experience" which makes Hegelian discourse dislocate *itself*; and this can be done only through close scrutiny and full knowledge of what one is laughing at.

Bataille, thus, took Hegel seriously, and took absolute knowledge seriously. And to take such a system seriously, Bataille knew, was to prohibit oneself from extracting concepts from it, or from manipulating isolated propositions, drawing effects from them by transportation into a discourse foreign to them: "Hegel's thoughts are interdependent to the point of it being impossible to grasp their meaning, if not in the necessity of the movement which constitutes their coherence" (*EI*, p. 193). Bataille doubtless put into question the idea or meaning of the chain in Hegelian reason, but did so by thinking the chain as such, in its totality, without ignoring its internal rigor. One could describe as a scene, but we will not do so here, the history of Bataille's relations to Hegel's different faces: the one that assumed "absolute rending", the one who "thought he would go mad", the one who, between Wolff and Comte and "the clouds of professors" at the "village wedding" that is philosophy, asks himself no questions, while "alone, his head aching, Kierkegaard questions"; the one who "towards the end of his life," "no longer put the problem to himself," "repeated his courses and played cards"; the "portrait of the aged Hegel" before which, as "in reading the

Phenomenology of the Mind," "one cannot help being seized by freezing impression of completion." Finally, the Hegel of the "small comic recapitulation."

Burst of laughter from Bataille. Through a rise of life, that is, of reason, life has thus stayed alive. Another concept of life has been surreptitiously put in its place, to remain there, never to be exceeded, any more than reason is ever exceeded (for, says *L 'erotisme,* "by definition, the *excess* is outside reason"). This life is not natural life, the biological existence put at stake in lordship, but an essential life that is welded to the first one, holding it back, making it work for the constitution of self-consciousness, truth, and meaning. Such is the truth of life. Through this recourse to the *Aufhebung,* which conserves the stakes, remains in control of the play, limiting it and elaborating it by giving it form and meaning (*Die Arbeit* [...] *bildet*), this economy of life restricts itself to conservation, to circulation, and self-reproduction as the reproduction of meaning; henceforth, everything covered by the name lordship collapses into comedy. The independence of self-consciousness becomes laughable at the moment when it liberates itself by enslaving itself, when it starts to *work,* that is, when it enters into dialectics. Laughter alone exceeds dialectics and the dialectician: it bursts out only on the basis of an absolute renunciation of meaning, an absolute risking of death, what Hegel calls abstract negativity. A negativity that never takes place, that never *presents* itself, because in doing so it would start to work again. A laughter that literally never *appears,* because it exceeds phenomenality in general, the absolute possibility of meaning. And the word "laughter" itself must be read in a burst, as its nucleus of meaning bursts in the direction of the *system* of the sovereign operation ("drunkenness, erotic effusion, sacrificial effusion, poetic effusion, heroic behavior, anger, absurdity," etc., cf. *Méthode de méditation*). This burst of laughter makes the difference between lordship and sovereignty shine, without *showing* it however and, above all, without saying it. Sovereignty, as we shall verify, is more and less than lordship, more or less free than it, for example; and what we are saying about the predicate "freedom" can be extended to every characteristic of lordship. Simultaneously more and less a lordship and lordship, sovereignty is totally other. Bataille pulls it out of dialectics. He withdraws it from the horizon of meaning and knowledge. And does so to such a degree that, despite the characteristics that make it resemble lordship, sovereignty is no longer a figure in the continuous chain of phenomenology. Resembling a phenomenological figure, trait for trait, sovereignty is the absolute alteration of all of them. And this difference would not be produced if the analogy was limited to a given abstract characteristic. Far from being an abstract negativity, sovereignty (the absolute degree of putting at stake), rather, must make the seriousness of meaning appear as an abstraction inscribed in play. Laughter, which constitutes sovereignty in its relation to death, is not a negativity, as has been said. And it laughs at itself, a "major" laughter laughs at a "minor" laughter, for the sovereign operation also needs life – the life that welds the two lives together – in order to be in relation to itself in the pleasurable consumption of itself. Thus, it must simulate, after a fashion, the absolute risk, and it must laugh at this simulacrum. In the comedy that it thereby plays for itself, the burst of laughter is the almost-nothing into which meanings sinks, absolutely. "Philosophy" which "is work." Can do or say nothing about this laughter, for it should have "considered laughter *first*" (ibid.). This is why laughter is absent from the Hegelian system, and not in the manner of a negative of abstract side of it. "In the 'system' poetry, laughter, ecstasy are nothing. Hegel hastily gets rid of them: he knows no other aim than knowledge. To my eyes, his immense fatigue is linked to his horror of the blind spot" (*EI*, p. 142). What is laughable is the *submission* to the self-evidence of meaning, to force of this imperative, that there must be meaning, that nothing must be definitely lost in death, or further, that death should receive the signification of "abstract negativity," that a work must always be possible which, because it defers enjoyment, confers meaning, seriousness, and truth upon the "putting at stake." This submission is the essence and element of philosophy, of Hegelian ontologics. Absolute comicalness is the anguish experience when confronted by expenditure on lost funds, by the absolute sacrifice of meaning: a sacrifice without return and without reserves. The notion of *Aufhebung* (the speculative concept par excellent, says Hegel, the concept whose untranslatable privilege is wielded by the German language) is laughable in that it signifies the *busying* of a discourse losing its breath as it reappropriates all negativity for itself, as it works the "putting at stake" into an *investment*, as it *amortizes* absolute expenditure; and as it gives meaning to death, thereby simultaneously blinding itself to the baselessness of the nonmeaning from which the basis of meaning is drawn, and in which this basis of meaning is exhausted. To be indifferent to the comedy of the *Aufhebung*, as was Hegel, is to blind oneself to the experience of the scared, to the heedless sacrifice of presence and meaning. Thus is sketched out a figure of experience – but can one still use these two words? – irreducible to any phenomenology, a figure which finds itself *displaced* in phenomenology, like laughter in philosophy of the mind, and which mimes through sacrifice the absolute risk of death. Through this mime it simultaneously produces the risk of absolute death, the feint through which this risk can be lived, the impossibility of reading a sense or a truth in it, and the laughter which is confused, in the simulacrum, with the opening of the sacred. Describing this simulacrum, unthinkable for philosophy, philosophy's blind spot, Bataille must, of course, say it, feign to say it, in the Hegelian logos.

9. Mikhail Bakhtin, 'Rabelais in the History of Laughter', from *Rabelais and His World* (1965), translated by Helene Iswolsky

Rabelais, Cervantes, and Shakespeare represent an important turning point in the history of laughter. Nowhere else do we see so clearly marked the lines dividing the Renaissance from the seventeenth century and the period that followed.

The Renaissance conception of laughter can be roughly described as follows: Laughter has a deep philosophical meaning, it is one of the essential forms of the truth concerning the world as a whole, concerning history and man; it is a peculiar point of view relative to the world; the world is seen anew, no less (and perhaps more) profoundly than when seen from the serious standpoint. Therefore, laughter is just as admissible in great literature, posing universal problems, as seriousness. Certain essential aspects of the world are accessible only to laughter.

The attitude toward laughter of the seventeenth century and of the years that followed can be characterized thus. Laughter is not a universal, philosophical form. It can refer only to individual and individually typical phenomena of social life. That which is important and essential cannot be comical. Neither can history and persons representing it – kings, generals, heroes – be shown in a comic aspect. The sphere of the comic is narrow and specific in a comic aspect. The sphere of the comic is narrow and specific (private and social vices); the essential truth about the world and about man cannot be told in the language of laughter. Therefore the place of laughter in literature belongs only to the low genres, showing the life of private individuals and the inferior social levels. Laughter is a light amusement or a form of salutary social punishment of corrupt and low persons.

The Renaissance expressed its attitude toward laughter in the very practice of literary creation and appreciation. Neither was there any lack of theoretical opinion that justified laughter as a universal, philosophical form. This theory of laughter was built almost exclusively on antique sources. Rabelais himself developed it in the old and new prologue of the fourth book of his novel, based mostly on Hippocrates, whose role as the theorist of laughter was at the time important. Not only was his prestige founded on the comments contained in his medical treatise concerning the importance of a gay and cheerful mood on the part of the physician and patient fighting disease, but was also due to the "Hippocratic novel." This was an addendum to "Hippocrates' Aphorisms" (of course apocryphal) concerning the "madness" of Democritus had a philosophical character, being directed at the life of man and at all the vain fears and hopes related to the gods and to life after death. Democritus here made of his laughter a whole philosophy, a certain spiritual premise of the awakened man who has attained virility. Hippocrates finally agreed with him.

The teaching concerning the therapeutic power of laughter in the "Hippocratic novel" received special recognition and notoriety at the Montpellier Medical School where Rabelais studied and later taught. A member of this school, the famous physician Laurent Joubert, published in 1560 a special work under the characteristic title: *Traite du Ris, contenant son essence, ses causes et ses merverheus effeis, curieusement recherchés, raisonnes et observes par M. Laur. Joubert* ("a treatise on laughter, containing its essence, causes and wondrous effects curiously studied, discussed and observed by M. Laur. Joubert"). In 1579 Joubert published another treatise in Paris, entitled *La cause morale de Ris, de l'excellent et très renomme Démocrite, expliquée et témoignée par ce divin Hippocrate en ses Epîtres* ("The moral cause of laughter of the eminent and very famous Democritus explained and witnessed by the divine Hippocrates in his epistles"). This work was actually a French version of the last part of the "Hippocratic novel".

Although this treatise on the philosophy of laughter was published after Rabelais' death, it was a belated echo of the thoughts and discussions that were current in Montpellier at the time when Rabelais attended this school and that determined his concept of the therapeutic power of laughter and of the "gay physician."

The second source of this philosophy of laughter at the time of Rabelais was Aristotle's famous formula: "Of all living creatures only man is endowed with laughter." This formula enjoyed immense popularity and was given a broader interpretation: laughter was seen as man's highest spiritual privilege, inaccessible to other creatures.

[…]

According to Aristotle, a child does not begin to laugh before the fortieth day after his birth; only from that moment does it become a human being. Rabelais and his contemporaries were also familiar with the saying of Pliny that only one man, Zoroaster, began to laugh at the time of his birth; this was interpreted as an omen of his divine wisdom.

Finally, the third source of the Renaissance philosophy of laughter is Lucian, especially his image of Menippus laughing in the kingdom of the dead. Lucian's work "Menippus, of the Descent into Hades" had an essential influence on Rabelais, more precisely on the episode of Epistemon's journey to hell in *Pantagruel*. Another important influence was Lucian's "Dialogues."

Such are the three most popular antique sources of the Rabelaisian philosophy of laughter. They influenced not only Joubert's treatise but also the opinions current in literary and humanist circles concerning the meaning and virtue of laughter. All three sources define laughter as a universal philosophical principle that heals and regenerates; it is essentially linked to the ultimate philosophical questions concerning the "regulation of life" which Montaigne interprets in strictly serious tones.

Rabelais and his contemporaries were also familiar, of course, with the antique conception of laughter from other sources – from Athenaeus, Macrobius, and others. They knew Homer's famous words about the undestroyable, that is, eternal laughter of the gods, and they were familiar with the Roman tradition of the freedom of laughter during the Saturnalia and the role of laughter during the triumphal marches and the funeral rites of notables. Rabelais in particular makes frequent allusion to these sources.

Let us stress once more that for the Renaissance (as for the antique sources described above) the characteristic trait of laughter was precisely the recognition of its positive, regenerating, creative meaning. This clearly distinguishes it from the later theories of the philosophy of laugher, including Bergson's conception, which bring out mostly its negative functions.

In the Renaissance, laughter in its most radical, universal, and at the same time gay form emerged from the depths of folk culture; it emerged but once in the course of history, over a period of some fifty or sixty years (in various countries and at various times) and entered with its popular (vulgar) language the sphere of great literature and high ideology. It appeared to play an essential role in the creation of such masterpieces of world literature as Boccaccio's *Decameron*, the novels of Rabelais and Cervantes, Shakespeare's dramas and comedies, and others. The walls between official and nonofficial literature were inevitably to crumble, especially because in the most important ideological sectors these walls also served to separate languages – Latin from the vernacular. The adoption of the vernacular by literature and by certain ideological spheres was to sweep away or at least weaken these boundaries.

A number of other factors concerned with the disintegration of the feudal and theocratic order of the Middle Ages also contributed to the fusion of the official and nonofficial. The culture of folk humor that had been shaped during many centuries and that had defended the people's creativity in nonofficial forms, in verbal expression or spectacle, could not rise to the high level of literature and ideology and fertilize it. Later, in times of absolute monarchy and the formation of a new official order, folk humor descended to the lower level of the genre hierarchy. There it settled and broke away from its popular roots, becoming petty, narrow, and degenerate.

As we have said, laughter in the Middle Ages remained outside all official spheres of ideology and outside all official strict forms of social relations. Laughter was eliminated from religious cult, from feudal and state ceremonials, etiquette, and from all the genres of high speculation. An intolerant, one-sided tone of seriousness is characteristic of official medieval culture. The very contents of medieval ideology – asceticism, somber providentialism, sin, atonement, suffering, as well as the character of the feudal regime, with its oppression and intimidation – all these elements determined this tone of icy petrified seriousness. It was supposedly the only tone fit to express the true, the good, and all that was essential and meaningful. Fear, religious awe, humility, these were the overtones of this seriousness.

Early Christianity had already condemned laughter. Tertullian, Cyprian, and John Chrysostom preached against ancient spectacles, especially against the mime and the mime's jests and laughter. John Chrysostom declared that jests and laughter are not from God but from the devil. Only permanent seriousness, remorse, and sorrow for his sins befit the Christian. During the struggle against the Aryans, Christians were accused of introducing elements of the mime – song, gesticulation, laughter – into religious services.

At the same time certain religious cults inherited from antiquity were influenced by the East and in some cases by local pagan rites, especially by the rites of fertility. Rudiments of gaiety and laughter are present in these forms. They can be found in the liturgy and in funeral rites, as well as in the rites of baptism, of marriage, and in other religious services. But these rudiments are sublimated and toned down. If performed in a zone near a church, they had to be authorized. These rites of pure laughter were permitted as a parallel to the official cults.

Such were first of all the "feasts of fools" (*festa stultorum, fatuorum, follorum*) which were celebrated by schoolmen and lower clerics on the feast of St. Stephen, on New Year's Day, on the feast of the Holy Innocents, of the Epiphany, and of St. John. These celebrations were originally held in the churches and bore a fully legitimate character. Later they became only semilegal, and at the end of the Middle Ages were completely banned from the churches but continued to exist in the streets and in taverns, where they were absorbed into carnival merriment and amusements. The feast of fools showed a particular obstinacy and force of survival in France (*fête des fous*). This feast was actually a parody and travesty of the official cult, with masquerades and improper dances. These celebrations held by the lower clergy were especially boisterous on New Year's Day and on Epiphany.

Nearly all the rituals of the feast of fools are a grotesque degradation of various church rituals and symbols and their transfer to the material bodily level: gluttony and drunken orgies on the altar table, indecent gestures, disrobing. We shall later analyze some of these rituals.

Laughter at the feast of fools was not, of course, an abstract and purely negative mockery of the Christian ritual and the Church's hierarchy. The negative derisive element was deeply immersed in the triumphant theme of bodily regeneration and renewal. It was "man's second nature" that was laughing, the lower bodily stratum which could not express itself in official cult and ideology.

The curious apology quoted above belongs to the fifteenth century. But we find similar opinions expressed in earlier times. Rabanus Maurus, abbot of Fulda, an austere churchman of the ninth century, composed an abridged version of the *coena Cypriani*. He dedicated it to King Lothar II *ad jocunditatem*, that is, for amusement's sake. In his letter of dedication Maurus seeks to justify the gay and degrading tone of the *coena* by the following arguments: "Just as the Church contains good and bad men, so does this poem contains the latter's speeches." These "bad men" of the austere churchman correspond to men's "second foolish nature." Later Pope Leo XIII proposed a similar formula: "since the church is composed of the divine and the human element, the latter must be disclosed with complete sincerity, as it is said in the Book of Job."

In the early Middle Ages folk laughter penetrated not only into the middle classes but even in to the highest circles of the church. Rabanus Maurus was no exception. The attraction of folk humor was strong at all the levels of the young feudal hierarchy, both lay and ecclesiastical. This can be explained as follows:

1 The official ecclesiastical and feudal culture of the seventh, eighth, and ninth centuries was still weak and not completely formed.

2 Folk culture was strong and impossible to ignore; some of its elements had to be used for propaganda.

3 The tradition of the Roman Saturnalia and other forms of Roman legalized folk humor was still alive.

4 The Church adapted the time of Christian feasts to local pagan celebrations (in view of their Christianization), and these celebrations were linked to cults of laughter.

5 The young feudal system was still relatively progressive and therefore of a relatively popular nature.

For these reasons a tradition of a relatively tolerant attitude toward folk humor could be formed during that early period. This tradition continued to live, although suffering more and more restrictions. In the following periods (up to the seventeenth century) it became customary to found the defense of laughter on the authority of former churchmen and theologians.

The "feast of fools" and the "feast of the ass" are specific celebrations in which laughter plays the leading role. In this sense they are similar to their close relatives: carnival and charivari. But in all the other Church feasts of the Middle Ages, as we pointed out in our introduction, laughter also played a more or less important part, ordering the popular, marketplace aspect of the religious occasion. As a material bodily principle laughter has a fixed relation to the feast; it was preeminently a festive laughter. Let us first of all recall the *risus paschalis*. During the Easter season laughter and jokes were permitted even in church. The priest could tell us amusing stories and jokes from the pulpit. Following the days of Lenten sadness he could incite his congregation's gay laughter as a joyous regeneration. This is why it was called "Easter laughter." The jokes and stories concerned especially material bodily life, and were of a carnival type. Permission to laugh was granted simultaneously with the permission to eat meat and to resume sexual intercourse (forbidden during Lent). The tradition of *risus paschalis* was still alive in the sixteenth century, at the time of Rabelais.

Besides "Easter laughter" there was also "Christmas laughter." While paschal gaiety mostly featured amusing tales and anecdotes, Christmas laughter was expressed in gay songs. These songs of an extremely worldly content were heard in churches; some religious hymns were sung to worldly, even street tunes. For instance, a score of the *Magnificat* which has been preserved proves that this religious chant was sung to the tune of clownish street rigmaroles. This tradition was especially maintained in France. The spiritual content was combined with worldly tunes and with elements of material bodily degradation. The theme of birth of the new was organically linked with the theme of death of the old on a gay and degrading level, with the images of a clownish carnivalesque uncrowning. This is why the French *Noël* could later develop into one of the most popular genres of the revolutionary street song.

Laughter and the material bodily element, as a degrading and regenerating principle, played an essential role in other festivities held outside or near to the church, especially those which bore a local character. The latter absorbed elements of ancient pagan celebrations and represented a Christian substitute for them. Such were the rejoicings marking the consecration of a church (the first masses) and the feast of the patron saint. Local fairs were usually held at that time with their entire repertory of folk recreations, accompanied by unbridled gluttony and drunken orgies. Eating and drinking were also the main features of the commemoration of the dead. When honoring patrons and benefactors buried in the church, the clergy organized banquets and drank

to their memory the so-called *"poculum charitatis"* or *"charitas vini."* A record of the
Kvedlinburg Abbey openly states that the clergy's banquet feeds and pleases the dead:
plenius inde recreantur mortui. The Spanish Dominicans drank to the memory of their
deceased patrons, toasting them with the typical ambivalent words *viva el muerto.*
In these examples the gaiety and laughter have the character of a banquet and are
combined with the images of death and birth (renewal of life) in the complex unity of
the material bodily lower stratum.

Laughter's universal character is obvious in the parodies described above. Medieval
laughter is directed at the same object as medieval seriousness. Not only does laughter
make no exception for the upper stratum, but indeed it is usually directed toward it.
Futhermore, it is directed not at one part only, but at the whole. One might say that it
builds its own world versus the official world, its own church versus the official church,
its own state versus the official state. Laughter celebrates its masses, professes its faith,
celebrates marriages and funerals, writes its epitaphs, elects kings and bishops. Even
the smallest medieval parody is always built as part of a whole comic world.

This universal character of laughter was most clearly and consistently brought out
in the carnival rituals and spectacles and in the parodies they presented. But universality appears as well in all the other forms of medieval culture of humor: in the comic
elements of church drams, in the comic *dits* (fairy tales) and *débats* (debates), in animal
epics, *fabliaux* and *Schwanke.* The main traits of laughter and of the lower stratum
remain identical in all these genres.

It can be said that medieval culture of humor which accompanied the feasts was
a "satyric" drama, a fourth drama, after the "tragic trilogy" of official Christian cult
and theology to which it corresponded but was at the same time in opposition. Like
the antique "satyric" drama, so also the medieval culture of laughter was the drama
of bodily life (copulation, birth, growth, eating, drinking, defecation). But of course
it was not the drama of an individual body or of a private material way of life; it was
the drama of the great generic body of the people, and for this generic body birth
and death are not an absolute beginning and end but merely elements of continuous
growth and renewal. The great body of satyric drama cannot be separated from the
world; it is perfused with cosmic elements and with the earth which swallows up and
gives birth.

Next to the universality of medieval laughter we must stress another striking peculi-
arity: its indissoluble and essential relation to freedom. We have seen that this laughter
was absolutely unofficial but nevertheless legalized. The rights of the fool's cap were as
inviolable as those of the *pileus* (the clown's headgear of the Roman Saturnalias).

The feast was a temporary suspension of the entire official system with all its prohibitions and hierarchic barriers. For a short time life came out of its usual, legalized and consecrated furrows and entered the sphere of utopian freedom. The very brevity of this freedom increased its fantastic nature and utopian radicalism, born in the festive atmosphere of images.

The atmosphere of ephemeral freedom reigned in the public square as well as in the intimate feast in the home. The antique tradition of free, often improper, but at the same time philosophical table talk had been revived at the time of the Renaissance; it converged with the local tradition of festive meals which had common roots in folklore. This tradition of table talk was continued during the following centuries. We find similar traditions of bacchic prandial songs which combine universalism (problems of life and death) with the material bodily element (wine, food, carnal love), with awareness of the time element (youth, old age, the ephemeral nature of life, the changes of fortune); they express a peculiar utopian strain, the brotherhood of fellow-drinkers and of all men, the triumph of affluence, and the victory of reason.

The comic rituals of the feast of fools, the feast of the ass, and the various comic processions and ceremonies of other feasts enjoyed a certain legality. The diableries were legalized and the devils were allowed to run about freely in the streets and in the suburbs a few days before the show and to create a demonic and unbridled atmosphere. Entertainments in the marketplace were also legalized as well as carnival. Of course, this legalization was forced, incomplete, led to struggles and new prohibitions. During the entire medieval period the Church and state were obliged to make concessions, large and small, to satisfy the marketplace. Throughout the year there were small scattered islands of time, strictly limited by the dates of feasts, when the world was permitted to emerge from the official routine but exclusively under the camouflage of laughter. Barriers were raised, provided there was nothing but laughter.

Besides universalism and freedom, the third important trait of laughter was its relation to the people's unofficial truth.

The serious aspects of class culture are official and authoritarian; they are combined with violence, prohibitions, limitations and always contain an element of fear and intimidation. These elements prevailed in the Middle Ages. Laughter, on the contrary, overcomes fear, for it knows no inhibitions, no limitations. Its idiom is never used by violence and authority.

It was the victory of laughter over fear that most impresses medieval man. It was not only a victory over mystic terror of God, but also a victory over the awe inspired by the forces of nature, and most of all over the oppression and guilt related to all that was consecrated and forbidden ("mana" and "taboo"). It was the defeat of divine and human power, of authoritarian commandments and prohibitions, of death and punishment after death, hell and all that is more terrifying than the earth itself. Through this victory laughter clarified man's consciousness and gave him a new outlook on life. This truth was ephemeral; it was followed by the fears and oppressions of everyday life, but from these brief moments another unofficial truth emerged, truth about the world and man which prepared the new Renaissance conscience.

The acute awareness of victory over fear is an essential element of medieval laughter. This feeling is expressed in a number of characteristic medieval comic images. We always find in them the defeat of fear presented in a droll and monstrous form, the symbols of power and violence turned inside out, the comic images of death and bodies gaily rent asunder. All that was terrifying becomes grotesque. We have already mentioned that one of the indispensable accessories of carnival was the set called "hell." This "hell" was solemnly burned at the peak of the festivities. This grotesque image cannot be understood without appreciating the defeat of fear. The people play with terror cannot be understood without appreciating the defeat of fear. The people play with terror and laugh at it; the awesome becomes a "comic monster."

Neither can this grotesque image be understood if oversimplified and interpreted in the spirit of abstract rationalism. It is impossible to determine where the defeat of fear will end and where joyous recreation will begin. Carnival's hell represents the earth which swallows up and gives birth, it is often transformed into a cornucopia; the monster, death, becomes pregnant. Various deformities, such as protruding bellies, enormous noses, or humps, are symptoms of pregnancy or of procreative power. Victory over fear is not its abstract elimination; it is a simultaneous uncrowning and renewal, a gay transformation. Hell has burst and had poured forth abundance.

10. René Girard, 'Perilous Balance: a Comic Hypothesis' (1972)

Molière's *Bourgeois gentilhomme* is an avid seeker after culture. A wealthy man, he turns his house into his own private university. The whole affair is a professor's dream except for the tiresome presence of that good natured but incredible philistine, M. Jourdain, everybody's benefactor and only student.

At one point three teachers argue heatedly about the merits of their respective disciplines. According to the dancing master, music would not be much without dancing. According to the music master, dancing, without music, would not exist at all. According to the fencing master, even musicians and dancers need good fencing occasionally, in order not the cease to exist.

In the midst of the fracas, a fourth man appears, the philosopher in residence. The sorry spectacle presented by this interdisciplinary committee moved him to philosophical grief. With a learned reference to Seneca's treatise on Anger, he steps into the midst of the quarrel to put an end to it.

He is sure to succeed because all the arguments in his view are equally inane. All three crafts are really on a par, at the bottom of the scale of learning, the top of which philosophy alone is worthy to occupy.

This word from above is rejected with indignation. Now blind with rage, the philosopher comes to blows with his three colleagues. Thus, the attempted mediation turns the three-cornered dispute into a four-cornered battle, with the would be mediator as one more participant.

I am always impressed by the similarity between this scene, so typical of a certain type of comedy, and what might be called the dynamics of tragedy, in no other play than *Oedipus Rex*.

All three masculine characters in that play, Oedipus, Creon, Tiresias, are invited to turn to master a situation which is vaguely described as "the plague" and which we may assume to be conflictual in character.

Oedipus comes first; he has solved the riddle of the sphinx: no problem is too difficult for him. More modest outwardly, Creon feels no less complacent underneath. He is just back from Delphi and he brings back an oracle which cannot fail to set everything right.

As for Tiresias, his resemblance to the philosopher in Molière is the most striking of all. By the time he appears the Theban plague is truly revealed as a situation of internal dissension, notably between Creon and Oedipus himself. Tiresias is so great a prophet that he will not respond to the call unless things get completely out of hand. As he enters, the chorus chants: "Here comes the only man who carries truth in his bosom." No wonder he sounds a little pompous.

Oedipus immediately flies into a rage. He always behaves that way, we are told, when things do not come out exactly the way he wants. But the other two also fly into a rage and they are not supposed to be prone to anger.

Not one, this time, but three would-be mediators are literally sucked into the conflict they presume to mediate. Discord seems to have a power of its own which will assert itself especially against those who foolishly assume they can dominate its violence.

Comedy and tragedy, in these two examples, are very close to each other. The basic pattern of a presumption which rebounds against the presumptuous is constantly repeated. If this closeness is real, why are the effects of tragedy so different from the effects of comedy?

[...]

Going back to laughter, now, we will note that it includes tears as an integral part of itself. That fact is often minimized or brushed aside. Our desire to oppose laughter and tears as two contraries make us emphasize only those aspects of laughter which appear to differentiate the two. Academic considerations are less important here than what we might call the modern *praxis* of laughter. Modern man is constantly pretending to laugh when he has really nothing to laugh about. Laughter is the only socially acceptable form of *katharsis*. As a result, there is a lot that passes for laughter which is not laughter at all; polite laughter, sophisticated laughter, public-relations laughter. All that false laughter often increases the tension it is supposed to relieve and it naturally includes no genuine, involuntary physical reactions, notably tears.

Many physical symptoms of laughter are easier to mimic than tears but they also become involuntary and compulsive when real laughter is present. The entire body is shaking convulsively; the air is rapidly expelled from the respiratory track through reflex motions analogous to coughing and sneezing. All these reactions have functions similar to crying. Here again the body acts *as if* there were physical objects to expel. The only difference is that more organs are involved.

The closest thing to a purely natural and physical laughter must be our body's response to a tickling sensation. In terms of sheer intensity, this response seems out of proportion with the feebleness of the stimulus, but it may well be appropriate to the real nature of the yet unidentified threat. In conditions of natural hostility, an urgent and deadly menace, a snake bite, for instance, might very well be preceded by no warning at all except for a little tickle. The fact that the stimulus is unknown and that it cannot be located with precision, at least immediately, increases the intensity of the reaction.

The protective nature of this reaction is also revealed by the extreme sensitivity to tickling of those parts of the body which are particularly vulnerable and/or usually protected, either by other parts of the body, like the armpits, or the inside of the thighs, or by clothing, or by a combination of both, like the soles of our feet, often especially ticklish among people used to wearing shoes and socks.

Laughter, in other words, especially in its least "cultural" forms, seems to be asserting, exactly like tears, that it must get rid of something; there is more of that something, and laughter must get rid of it more promptly than mere crying. If the body is the orchestra, more instruments have joined in the accompaniment of the invisible and inaudible soloist.

We may also note that when crying becomes intense, it turns into sobbing and, as such, it resembles laughter more and more. Someone whose laughter is beyond control, who is really laughing, therefore, and no longer pretending, is said to be sobbing with laughter.

Between tears and laughter, therefore, the difference is not in nature but in degree. And the real paradox is really in the way the pluses and minuses are distributed. Contrary to the commonsense view, the crisis element is more acute in laughter than in tears. Laughter seems closer to tears to a paroxysm which would turn it into actual convulsions, to a climactic experience of rejection and expulsion. Laughter is further along towards a total negative response to a threat considered overwhelming.

What kind of threat are both tragedy and comedy trying to ward off? What is it they are trying to expel? There are some famous answers to that question but I will look for my own in my twin reading of *Le Bourgeois gentilhomme* and *Oedipus Rex*.

In that reading, practically no difference remains between the comedy and tragedy. Why? We emphasized a pattern which keeps recurring at the beginning of the play. We cannot do that without minimizing the differences between the characters. We can do that only at the expense of individual features which critics usually consider important. In that reading, Oedipus, Creon, and Tiresias turn out to be more or less identical just as, in *Le Bourgeois gentilhomme,* the philosopher turns out to be more or less identical to his three colleagues.

This emphasis upon recurring patterns gives *Oedipus Rex* a slightly parodic flavor and immediately tragedy evaporates. Tragedy demands that we take the individuality of individual heroes seriously. Even though their "destinies" may be in the hands of the gods and their "freedom" curtailed, the individual heroes do remain the true center of reference. This is no longer so in comedy where recurrence and other structural effects are emphasized. The vengeance of the gods, the meanness of destiny, and the malice of the "human condition" may well crush the individual but not to the extent they do in the case of comic patterns which are truly "structural" in the sense that they dominate individual reactions ably thwarted by these same patterns and individual thinking is unable to take them into account. The structural patterns of the comic, therefore, deny the sovereignty of the individual more radically than either god or destiny. As they begin to emerge, audience interest in the hero must necessarily weaken as it shifts to the pattern itself.

Is the pattern really there, in tragedy as well as in comedy? The pattern is really there; it is already there in the myths which are the common source of both tragedy and comedy. Certain myths have always been considered appropriate both to tragedy and comedy. There were comic and tragic *Amphytrions,* for instance. Many of Shakespeare's comedies play openly with patterns which are present but less visible in tragedies. Good literary criticism is often a little comic, because only half visible patterns become fully visible in it. Great writers, great novelists in particular, often become their own parodists in their later words, and they develop a comic vein because they are their own best critics; they bring out more fully the patterns of earlier work; they express their obsessions more completely as Charles Mauron had so well shown.

Racine's tragedies deal mostly with passion. As soon as it is suggested that the lack of reciprocity in the love relationship is too constant to be due to "destiny" or to the mystery of personal choice, as soon as it appears that a law is at work, psychological or whatever, tragedy is annihilated. It is almost impossible to summarize *Andromaque* without satirical effect. The simplest enunciation of the relationship between the four major characters reveals a structural pattern. Orestes loves Hermione who does not love him. Hermione loves Pyrrhus who does not love her. Pyrrhus loves Andromaque who does not love him. Andromaque loves Hector who cannot love anymore, being dead. Were it not for that death, the chain of non-reciprocal passion might go on *ad infinitum.* And it does go on, as a matter of fact, but in the other plays of Racine.

If we convince ourselves that Racine's heroes, for whatever reason, cannot experience what they call passion unless their desire is thwarted, if we see in them the dupes of some hidden mechanism, we can no longer take these passions seriously *as passions.* For one thing, all these passions have become identical; they cannot be read as the exceptional, unique sentiments that tragedy demands.

An individual is trying to assert upon his environment what he takes to be his own individual rule. We laugh when this pretention is suddenly and spectacularly shattered. Impersonal forces are taking over. In the crudest forms of comic, these impersonal forces may simply be those of gravity. The man who loses his balance on the ice is comic in proportion either to his self-assurance or to his prudence, neither of which, however extreme, succeeds in preserving *son équilibre avec sa dignité.*

There are worse obstacles than gravity to our satisfactory handling of the world. Other human beings and we, ourselves, constitute a more formidable stumbling block, the more stubborn as a matter of fact, when it appears to have been cleared, when the road to complete mastery and graceful triumph seems to lie wide open in front of us. The Racinian heroes, for instance, may appear in a comic light. They, too, are the victims of impersonal forces which they do not perceive even though they are one with their desires. The three wise men of *Oedipus Rex* and the philosopher in Molière also fall prey to impersonal forces which, paradoxically enough, are the forces of human relations.

What does happen to all these people? We cannot attribute their downfall to a purely personal presumption. They all do the same thing. There should be an interpretation valid for all of them. We cannot talk about a "tragic flaw" in the case of Oedipus and laugh at the philosopher on the grounds that he is only acting "true to type," that he conforms to the natural pomposity of his breed.

When all our characters arrive on the stage, something already is going on, which is in the nature of a conflict, the plague in *Oedipus Rex*, the dispute of the three teachers in *Le Bourgeois gentilhomme*. Eagerness to arbitrate the conflict is rooted in the illusion of superiority created by a pure spectator status.

The philosopher is exposed to ridicule because of this late arrival. We must not even think of him as a philosopher first and as a late-comer second. His status as a philosopher is rooted in his status as a spectator. The philosophical attitude depends entirely on the type of observation which a late appearance makes possible. Hegel compares philosophy to an owl that begins to fly at dusk. As he contemplates the wreckage left by his predecessors, the philosopher cannot help feeling superior.

The spectator's position is both one of austere moral pessimism and satiric glee over human foibles. The spectacle of human frailty has an exhilarating as well as a depressing effect upon the moralist. Even after the battle, the philosopher wants to think of his colleagues as primarily comic characters; as a vengeance against them, he plans to write a comic work, a satire "in the style of Juvenal."

This spectator's position is not his only, but our own as well since we are the spectators of the play. When we laugh at the dispute of the first three men, the philosopher is with us and we are with him; our reading of the scene is exactly the same as his.

The only difference is that our spectator status is a permanent one. We cannot step foolishly into the battle, as the three teachers have done before, as the philosopher is now doing. We are protected not by some innate superiority but by the fact we are only watching a play. Our own illusions can never be revealed for what they are, as one more lie, as another incitement to feel "above the battle" and to volunteer as an arbitrator. We will never know if we would resist that insidious temptation because the stage is only a stage.

We are really laughing at something which could and, in a sense, which should happen to anyone who laughs, not excluding ourselves. This, I believe, clearly shows the nature of the threat, unperceived yet present, which laughter is always warding off, the still unidentified object it has to expel. The man who laughs is just about to be enveloped into the pattern of which his victim is already a part; as he laughs he both welcomes and rejects the perception of the structure into which the object of his laughter is already caught; he welcomes it insofar as it is someone else who is caught in it and he tries to keep it away from himself. The pattern is never an individual one and it tends to close in upon the man who laughs. We understand, now, why laughter is more of a crisis than tears; the pattern is much more visible in the comic than in the tragic; the threat to the autonomy of the spectator is more urgent and serious.

We understand, too, why the inclusion of a laughing spectator is a major procédé of comic writers. As this spectator laughs, he falls into the very trap which has already swallowed his victim and he becomes laughable in his turn.

The loss of autonomy and self-possession which is present in all forms of comedy must be present, somehow, in laughter itself. Laughter, in other words, must never be very different from whatever causes it. Scenes in which the laughing spectator is included are invariably circular. The culprit is getting his just deserts. This retributive justice is no idealist illusion; it is the reality of the structure. He who laughs last laughs best. The simplest forms of comedy show clearly this equalizing effect of laughter which never fails to be present whenever he who is laughed at and he who laughs are not separated by some artificial barrier like the barrier between the stage and the audience in a theater.

A man falls on the ice; also on the ice is another man who laughs so hard that he loses his balance and brings about his own fall. The second man is funnier than the first. A third one might be funnier still, unless of course, it is myself. As the scene keeps being repeated it reveals a strange and remarkable continuity between the essence of the comic and laughter itself. All the scenes we have mentioned so far are scenes in which the comic possibilities of laughter are already exploited, as in Molière, or readily exploitable, as in Sophocles.

We found earlier that physical laughter is intended to repulse an aggression from the outside, to shut off the body against a possible invasion. But the near convulsions of laughter, if they continue for a while, will ultimately result in a disintegration of that self-control they are supposed to preserve. Real laughter makes us physically weak; it reduces us to near impotence.

As an assertion of superiority, in the more intellectual forms of the comic, laughter really means a denial of reciprocity. The man who makes me laugh has already tried and failed to deny reciprocity between himself and others. As I laugh, I mimic and repeat the whole process I have been watching, both the attempt to establish mastery and its failure, both the dizzy feeling of superiority and the loss of balance which comes with the dizziness, the disintegration of self-control which is always creeping upon us in the wild reactions and uncontrolled convulsions of laughter itself.

Reciprocity is reestablished through the very actions which are meant to undo it. Laughter becomes a part of the process; that is why, in itself, it can be funny. There comes a point when we no longer know if we laugh "with" or "against" the man who is already laughing. We only say, at that stage, that laughter is "infectious."

Bergson, in *Le Rire*, defined the comic as "du mécanique plaqué sur du vivant," as a mechanical overlay upon the fluidity and continuity of "life," as something jerky, discontinuous, and maladjusted being substituted for the perfect mobility and grace of what he called "élan vital." Bergson, of course, was the philosopher of this "élan vital." Thus, all philosophies appeared a little funny to him, except his own. Such is the case, assuredly, with most philosophers.

The Bergsonian definition of "le mécanique" included many aspects of what had been called here "structural." What is missing, in my view, from Bergson's analysis is not a word, which has no importance whatever but a full realization of "le mécanique" as something more than an individual or even a collective disgrace. In its major manifestations, "le mécanique" is only the outward consequence, esthetic or intellectual, of a formidable "problem" which the philosopher never really tackles. Living as he does in an age of "individualism," Bergson cannot see that the comic is rooted in the ultimate failure of all individualism, at least at a certain level. There is an element of reciprocity, in human relations, which will keep reasserting itself regardless of what we do; reciprocity will be there whether we welcome or reject it for the rejection itself will be reciprocated. The reciprocity which is not welcome is the reciprocity of conflict, the *unexpected* reciprocity which will always have both in its physical and intellectual manifestations, that jerky, discontinuous, and disharmonious quality which Bergson so aptly recognized in the comic.

Bergson, most of the time, seems to place the man who laughs squarely on the side of the "élan vital," on the side of the gods, in other words. But laughter itself, about which Bergson says very little, in spite of the title of his book, is no less mechanical and convulsive than its own cause. The point had already been made by Baudelaire who compares the man who laughs to a jack-in-the-box. In his few admirable pages on *De l'essence du rire*, Baudelaire clearly perceives the difference between the mocker and the mocked as a disintegrating and vanishing difference, as creeping identity.

"What could be more deplorable, he writes, than weakness rejoicing at weakness?"

As we try to assert our independence through laughter, that laughter becomes uncontrollable and independence is already slipping away from us. This ambiguous nature accounts for the very diverse roles that laughter can play with diverse people at diverse moments in their lives. Laughter can be almost unbelievably intelligent and sensitive as well as unbelievably cruel and stupid.

Most laughter, of course, is safely ensconced in a well-protected illusion of superiority, but the slippery nature of this bizarre affection, its shaky and shaken superiority, can make it serve very different ends. It can weaken as well as strengthen the barriers which separate each of us from the others. Laughter will erupt when we see our long cherished prejudices confirmed and also when we see them, finally, crumble into the dust. Baudelaire is often accused of entertaining too pessimistic a view of laughter, but he is among the few who recognize the existence of a truly superior laughter, the one which welcomes its own downfall. Unlike so many of our peevish "demystifiers," he was not building intellectual cages in which to imprison everyone but himself. He read laughter in a Pascalian light, as a sign of contradiction pointing both to the "infinite misery" and the "infinite greatness" of man.

The fact remains, however, that most people, or rather man in general, if we can still use the phrase, have very little to laugh about. If laughter is really the slippery affair we describe, if we enjoy in it our last dizzy instant of illusion before disaster strikes, why do we keep laughing as we do, why do we like laughter, why is it pleasurable?

One reason, of course, must be that we are ambivalent toward everything we call our "self," our "ego," our "identity," our "superiority." All this is both the ultimate prize we are trying to win, the most precious treasure to which we keep adding tirelessly, like busy ants, and a most frightful burden we are desperately eager to unload, preferably on the back of someone else.

Since we can never unload that burden permanently, we are constantly looking for temporary release; laughter provides some. In laughter, for a few brief moments, we seem to have the best of two incompatible worlds. Our feeling of control and autonomy is increased as we see others lose theirs and slip into the pattern. And as we, ourselves, begin to "come loose," the feeling of rigidity and tension which goes with self-control is relaxed.

Laughter can be compared to a drug, and notably to alcohol, which gives us at first a feeling of heightened control, of easy triumph over insuperable obstacles. A slight tipsiness is pleasurable; a little drinking will make us laugh; more will bring vertigo and nausea.

Why do we rarely if ever get that feeling of nausea and sickness even when our laughter seems to go on forever? How can we have a "good laugh" and come out unscathed? The reason, obviously, is that our laughter is in the hands of entrepreneurs, working as amateurs or as professionals, who make it their business to make us laugh. These people provide us with exactly the right amount of the drug, neither too much nor too little. They see to it, in other words, that the exact conditions are fulfilled which make laughter possible. If there were no such entrepreneurs we would laugh very little and only very briefly.

What are these conditions? A man will not laugh, we found out, unless there is an actual threat to his ability to control his environment and the people in it, even his own thoughts and his own desires. A man will not laugh, however, if that threat becomes too real. The conditions necessary for laughter are therefore contradictory. The threat must be both overwhelming and nil; the danger of being absorbed into the pattern which has already devoured the victims of our laughter must be both immediate and nonexistent. In order to "have a good laugh," we must always come out "on top" even as we are constantly threatened to "go under."

The main recipe, of course, for fulfilling these two contradictory conditions is to provide us with real sacrificial victims. Any clown or comedian who knows something about his profession is fully aware that people will laugh only at his own expense or at the expense of a third party.

But this is not enough. We discovered earlier that, in order to laugh freely, the audience must be completely cut off from the object of its laughter. If I, myself, am standing on the ice, I will not laugh freely at the man who falls on it. The isolation of the stage is only one of the protective devices which give us that pure spectator status necessary to produce laughter. The distance which separates us from foreign customs or from the distant past also makes it possible for us to laugh with impunity, therefore to laugh with abandonment.

This is not yet enough. In a culture where people have a good deal of imagination, where they "put themselves" easily in the place of others, they will not laugh unless the cancellation of personal will by impersonal forces is limited to rather minor consequences. The victim must suffer only unpleasantness; if a major catastrophe is involved, people will no laugh anymore, especially if the victim is felt to be "close."

The conditions of laughter are so complex and difficult that they would rarely be met if they were not met artificially. There are people who make it their business to meet them, sometimes through means so complex and so technical that the reality of the two contradictory conditions we have just defined becomes obvious.

This fact can be verified easily in those cases where there is no sacrificial victim to spark our laughter and put the necessary distance between ourselves and the impersonal forces which are taking over, when we, ourselves, or rather our bodies, are the prime object of our amusement.

What I have in mind, here, is a particular kind of chiefly physical laughter, the one which is derived from dangers narrowly avoided, from accidents barely missed, from hairpin turns taken at speeds greater than prudence allows. All this brings joy to some people; more people, however, will enjoy such experiences only when they are simulated, in carnival rides for instance, when they are duplicated, with a great degree of realism and a reasonable degree of safety. Only when physical risks are really minimal, even though they appear very great, will the fact of being violently shaken and thrown in all directions not only bring pleasure to some people but provoke their actual laughter.

We can see very clearly, here, that the production of laughter demands a threat which is both massive and nil. Thus, the two contradictory prerequisites of laughter are present both in the crudest and in the more intellectual forms of laughter. The only difference is that, in the first case, the impersonal forces which threaten the autonomy of man are purely natural and physical, whereas, in the second case, they stem from human relations themselves; they spell the inability of any individual to control these relations completely.

In tickling, which I have described earlier as one of the most primitive, if not the most primitive form of laughter, we may discover yet another indication that the two contradictory conditions of laughter defined above may be universal. An interesting fact about tickling is that, like other forms of laughter, it can be artificially induced. When tickling is, so to speak, engineered by another human being, it produces a reaction much stronger than in natural tickling and much closer to real laughter.

There is a strategy to artificial tickling which resembles closely the strategy of offensive warfare. One must not aim solely at a well-defined area of the body, however ticklish it may be. A precise aim would make it too easy for the tickled individual to locate the threat and to protect himself. In order to tickle efficiently, one must move rapidly from one area to the next, shifting targets constantly so that protection becomes impossible. In military warfare, similarly, success will go to the side that had enough mobility to multiply its strikes and makes them so rapid and so distant from each other that they cannot be countered.

There is a major difference, however. In tickling, no real aggressive action or intention is present. If such an intention is even suspected, laughter will not result. The threat to the body must be many sided, the assault must be vigorous, even overwhelming but, at the same time, there must be no threat at all, there must be no assault at all. Tickling is mock total warfare on the other's body.

The prohibition which the tickler must never transgress will usually include overtly sexual gestures but it is not primarily sexual. It bears essentially on the *real* violence which tickling constantly mimics but never practices.

The tickling reaction is not as easy a prey for Freudian imperialism as it superficially appears. There is something definitively nonsexual about tickling, even anti-sexual. The sexual organs, even though they are usually protected and vulnerable, are not particularly ticklish and properly so. Feeling tickled in response to an openly sexual initiative is normally resented, being interpreted as a form of rejection, the more deep seated for being involuntary.

Tickling a potential partner for sexual purposes is, of course, a common practice. It makes it possible to break down physical resistance without incurring hostility. The non-sexual connotations of tickling make it particularly serviceable as a means of sexual seduction. Tickling will permit bodily contacts which, in spite of their intimacy, deny up to a point any immediate sexual intention on the part of the assailant.

I hope I will not be misinterpreted if I say that comedy is intellectual tickling; more than any other type of esthetic representation it deprives us of the autonomy to which we cling and yet it does not deprive us of anything at all. When offensive thrusts are not neutralized through one device or another, they are never pursued to the bitter end. We would not laugh if we did not feel that whatever makes us laugh can be shrugged off at any time, that we can always laugh it off.

A great comic writer does not avoid "ticklish" subjects, he will not stay away from "touchy" problems. He knows, however, like the tickler, that he must "use the light touch" and he alone knows how to use it. He knows where he must stop; he alone can give the rug on which we stand a tug strong enough to startle us into laughter without really pulling it from under our feet and sending us head over heels.

There is something profoundly subversive in all true comedy. One might say that Molière's laughter is anti-cartesian, because it reveals as false the pretentions of Descartes' *cogito*. No philosophy in the classical sense can understand laughter or account for it since philosophy tries to establish our mastery, as human being or individuals on unshakable ground.

Today we live in an entirely different world. The great prophets of the modern world always have the same message in slightly different forms. Our actions, our thoughts, our desires are entirely dominated by patterns not of our own making and which we never read correctly.

This is true of the natural scientist, this is true of the social scientist, this is true of thinkers like Marx, Nietzsche, or Freud. These last three, in particular, work in areas from which earlier comic writers drew much of their material. Before the XIXth century, the relations between people of various cultures, or different social and economic levels, the relations between servants and masters, for instance, were a staple of comedy. So were the sexual fumblings of younger and older people. Marx, Nietzsche, and Freud have certainly tried and often succeeded in taking the fun out of all that.

Nous avons changé tout cela. Freud, in particular, has introduced his fateful *slip* into former puns, jokes, *calembours*, and other *mots d'esprit*; he has turned the whole domain of wit into the object of a grave and continuous debate.

To say that this state of affairs is not "funny" does not suffice; this world attempts to take away from us all future possibilities of laughter. No illusions of human autonomy can be shattered since none is supposed to remain. But this one-sided interpretation may well be another egotistical illusion.

Modern man's extreme humility is strangely coupled with the greatest pride of all times. As we discover the unknown forces which shape our destinies, they are supposed to come at least partly under our control. Every new discovery gives us new manipulative powers over our environment and our fellow men. We are constantly told, therefore, on the one hand that we are absolute nonentities, on the other that a world is being created which will be entirely dominated by human will.

One fact is always left out of account in these predictions, the fact that there is no such thing as a unified human will. Men are no more able to dominate their own relationships than they ever were. The formidable ambitions and realizations of modern man, thus, are extremely fragile; they are at the mercy not of nature or destiny but of those same "impersonal forces" which turn all the characters in *Le Bourgeois gentilhomme* into puppets with no one to pull the strings.

In a sense, therefore, possibilities for comedy have never been greater. The stakes, however, are so high, and the uncertainties so great that our laughter cannot be as complacent and secure as it once was. Never before has the precarious, unstable, and "nervous" nature of laughter been so much in evidence. When we consider the type of comic we have in our contemporary world, we may well think that this age is adding, or rather revealing, a new dimension to Molière's famous words about laughter and the creation of comedy:

C'est une étrange entreprise que de faire rire les honnêtes gens.

11. Gerald Mast, 'Comic Films – Categories and Definitions', from *The Comic Mind: Comedy and the Movies* (1973)

Inevitably, the comic film "says" something about the relation of man to society. The comedy either (*a*) upholds the values and assumptions of society, urging the comic character to reform his ways and conform to the societal expectations; or, (*b*) maintains that the antisocial behavior of the comic character is superior to society's norms. The former function of comedy underlies most pre-twentieth-century theory (and practice). Jonson, for example, presented characters of "humours," whose overzealous preoccupation with a single need or desire was an offense against both nature and society. Jonson's plays and prologues urge the offender to purge the "humour" and return to balance. Bergson similarly finds laughter a social cure (even the metaphor parallels Jonson's) for the disease of "mechanical inelasticity"; when the comic figure fails to exhibit the elasticity that social life demands, our laughter serves to turn the human machine back into malleable flesh and soul.

Underlying such a definition of comedy is an assumption about the relationship between nature and society. Although Jonson and other Renaissance thinkers may have been engaged in a "nature-nurture controversy," Jonson seems to avoid the dilemma by implying that the demands of society and of nature are allied, that it is inherent in *human* nature to live socially (hence his use of animal names for antisocial behavior in *Volpone*). Bergson similarly equates social behavior and natural behavior, as opposed to antisocial behavior and unnatural ("mechanical") behavior.

Modern thought, however, makes very different assumptions; rather than allying nature and society, the twentieth-century thinker sees the two as antithetical. The hero of modern comedy is the natural rebel who, intentionally or unconsciously, exposes the shams of society. [...] In such comic works, the central figure's errors in society's eyes are his virtues in the eyes of his creator. Even anti-heroism is a virtue in a world in which heroism either does not exist or has no value. In Bergsonian terms, one might say that in modern comedy, society and its representatives have become encrusted with the mechanical, rather than the comic protagonist with a comic flaw. Only he, because of that "flaw," is elastic enough to expose society's petrifaction.

In this same tradition, the most thoughtful film comedies are iconoclastic. The movies throw a custard pie (sometimes literally) in the face of social forms and assumptions. The greatest film comedians are antisocial, but in this antagonism they reveal a higher morality. Ironically, these iconoclastic comedies are products of a commercial system that depended on the support of mass audiences composed of anything but iconoclasts. [...] Many other film comedies—often very entertaining ones—do not confront the mores of the status quo. Some avoid any appearance of a social or a moral issue by basing the action and the characters' motivations on literary formulas and moral platitudes: rich people are invariably unhappy; man must work to be happy; self-indulgence is necessarily self-abuse; fate inevitably rewards the virtuous and punishes the vicious. Such comedies cannot be said to be "thinking" at all, since their value systems defy serious reflection and since an audience accepts such systems (if at all) solely because they are the hackneyed descendants of so many other books, plays, films, and political speeches. [...] But the comedies that look best today are those which challenge society's ability to make human experience meaningful. That also implies something about today.

One distinction, then, among "serious" comedies is whether they are iconoclastic or apologetic. Another is whether the film transmits its values exclusively by comic devices or by serious sections interspersed with comic ones. [...]

Chaplin's great gift was his ability to convey moral attitudes without moralizing. A one-second piece of comic business could reveal a whole philosophy of human experience. [...]

The greatest film comedies communicate serious values through the comedy itself; they do not serve a comic *digestif* between the serious courses. [...] As a result, the most effective film comedies—as well as the most thought-provoking ones—are mimetic rather than didactic, descriptive rather than prescriptive. [...] The human problems depicted in *Modern Times, The Rules of Game, Trouble in Paradise, The General, The Italian Straw Hat, Mr. Hulot's Holiday,* and *Smiles of a Summer Night* do not admit easy solutions. Often when the comic filmmaker does provide one—the utopian idyll at the end of À Nous la liberté, the reformation of all the crooks and the eradication of poverty at the end of *Easy Street*—it deliberately shows the ridiculousness of expecting easy solutions.

Not only does the effective comic film present its serious values through the means of comedy itself, but its comic and serious matter are inseparable. Indeed, the film's view of human experience is a function of its comic technique, and its comic technique is a function of its view of human experience. Keaton and Chaplin films "say" different things about human experience because Keaton and Chaplin have different comic styles, find different things funny, use different comic principles. [...] Cinematic style is a function of comic style is a function of philosophic vision is a function of cinematic style and so forth around the perfect and unbreakable circle.

Silence and sound

The great silent comedies revolve about the body and personality of its owner; the great sound comedies revolve about structure and style—what happens, how it happens, and the way those happenings are depicted. Film comedy, as well as film art in general, was born from delight in physical movement. The essence of early filmmaking was to take some object (animate or inanimate) and simply watch it move. The essential comic object was the human body, and its most interesting movements were running, jumping, riding, colliding, falling, staggering, leaping, twirling, and flying. The early comic filmmakers [...] needed athletes, not wits; men who could turn in the air and take a fall, not turn a phrase. The university for such athletes was not the legitimate stage but vaudeville, burlesque, the music hall, and the circus.

[...]

The sound comedy is far more literary. Given the opportunity to use the essential tool of literature, words, as an intrinsic part of the film's conception, the filmmaker did not hesitate to do so. In silent films, the use of words in titles was intrusive, a deliberate interruption of the cinematic medium and a substitution of the literary one. We stop looking and start reading. But the sound film provided the means to watch the action and listen to the words at the same time. [...]

Another difference is that because he could talk, the sound performer was more like an ordinary human being in society than a specially gifted comic-athlete-dancer-gymnast-clown. Further, the visual interest in sound films was not the physical motion of the performer but the visual juxtaposition of the people with their social and physical milieu. Images and imagery replaced movement. All such shifts were in what can be termed a "literary" direction, making the film far more like a play or novel.

The art that conceals art

Finally, a word must be said about one of the most difficult aesthetic questions about comedy, a question so closely related to personal taste and audience psychology that aestheticians usually avoid it altogether. When is a film (or gag, or line, or character) that is intended to be funny truly funny? What is the difference between meaning to be funny and being funny?

Imprecise as it may be, the only answer seems to be this: A film (or gag, or line, or character) is truly funny when the audience is not conscious that it intends to be funny. As soon as one becomes aware of artifice and fakery (not the kind that often functions as an integral part of the comic climate), comedy disintegrates into banal and obnoxious posturing. Although intellectual detachment is crucially related to the experience of successful comedy, when the detachment becomes so great that the mind is no longer amused and engaged but notes the gap between intention and accomplishment, conception and execution, the comedy fails to amuse and entertain.

Perhaps the only term for describing the successful marriage between comic intention and execution is one of the key concepts of the Renaissance—*sprezzatura*. *Sprezzatura* might be defined as the art that conceals art, the supremely artificial that strikes us as supremely natural. The great comedy endows the most contrived and artificial situations (comedy has always depended on artifice) with the impression of spontaneity.

12. Stanley Cavell, *Pursuits of Happiness: The Hollywood Comedy of Remarriage* (1981)

Introduction: words for a conversation

[T]he genre of remarriage is an inheritor of the preoccupations and discoveries of Shakespearean romantic comedy, especially as that work has been studied by, first among others, Northrop Frye. In his early "The Argument of Comedy," Frye follows a long tradition of critics in distinguishing between Old and New Comedy. [...] New Comedy stresses the young man's efforts to overcome obstacles posed by an older man (a senex figure) to his winning of the young woman of his choice, whereas Old Comedy puts particular stress on the heroine, who may hold the key to the successful conclusion of the plot, who may be disguised as a boy, and who may undergo something like death and restoration. What I am calling the comedy of remarriage is, because of its emphasis on the heroine, more intimately related to Old Comedy than to New, but it is significantly different from either, indeed it seems to transgress an important feature of both, in casting as its heroine a married woman; and the drive of the plot is not to get the central pair together, but to get them *back* together, together *again*. Hence the fact of marriage in it is subjected to the fact or the threat of divorce.

[...]

The achievement of human happiness requires not the perennial and fuller satisfaction of our needs as they stand but the examination and transformation of those needs. [...] It applies only in contexts in which there is satisfaction enough, in which something like luxury and leisure, something beyond the bare necessities, is an issue. This is why our films must on the whole take settings of unmistakable wealth; the people in them have the leisure to talk about human happiness, hence the time to deprive themselves of it unnecessarily. [...] The economic issues in these films, with their ambivalence and irresolution, are invariably tropes for spiritual issues. (Which is not to deny that they can be interpreted the other way around too, the spiritual conflicts as tropes for the economic. These conflicts are bound up with the conflict over the direction of interpretation, the question, say, of what money, and how you get it, can make you do.)

[...]

Our films may be understood as parables of a phase of the development of consciousness at which the struggle is for the reciprocity or equality of consciousness between a woman and a man, a study of the conditions under which this fight for recognition (as Hegel put it) or demand for acknowledgement (as I have put it) is a struggle for mutual freedom, especially of the views each holds of the other. This gives the films of our genre a Utopian cast. They harbor a vision which they know cannot fully be domesticated, inhabited, in the world we know. They are romances. Showing us our fantasies, they express the inner agenda of a nation that conceives Utopian longings and commitments for itself.

[...]

The conversation of what I call the genre of remarriage is, judging from the films I take to define it, of a sort that leads to acknowledgement; to the reconciliation of a genuine forgiveness; a reconciliation so profound as to require the metamorphosis of death and revival, the achievement of a new perspective on existence; a perspective that presents itself as a place, one removed from the city of confusion and divorce. [...] I find a precedent for the structure of remarriage, as said, in Shakespearean romance, and centrally in *The Winter's Tale*. This was one of the earliest and, while encouraging, most puzzling discoveries I made as I became involved in thoughts about the set of films in question here. Two puzzles immediately presented themselves. First, since Shakespearean romantic comedy did not remain a viable form of comedy for the English stage, compared with a Jonsonian comedy of manners, what is it about film that makes its occurrence there viable? This goes into the question of why it was only in 1934, and in America of all places, that the Shakespearean structure surfaced again, if not quite on the stage. [...] Nineteen thirty-four—half a dozen years after the advent of sound—was about the earliest date by which the sound film could reasonably be expected to have found itself artistically. And it happens that at the same date there was a group of women of an age and a temperament to make possible the definitive realization of the genre that answered the Shakespearean description, a date at which a phase of human history, namely, a phase of feminism, and requirements of a genre inherititing a remarriage structure from Shakespeare, and the nature of film's transformation of its human subjects, met together on the issue of the new creation of a woman. No doubt this meeting of interests is part of America's special involvement in film, from the talent drawn to Hollywood in making them to the participation of society as a whole in viewing them, and especially America's pre-eminence in film comedy.

The second puzzle about the Shakespearean precedent is why the film comedies of remarriage took as their Shakespearean equivalent, so to speak, the topic of divorce, which raises in a particular form the question of the legitimacy of marriage. Since I am saying that the comedy of remarriage does not look upon marriage as does either French farce or Restoration comedy, I had thought in vain about a comedic precedent for the remarriage form more specific than the Shakespearean. It finally dawned on me that the precedent need not be found in the history of comedy but in any genre into which the film comedies in question can be shown to have an exact conceptual relation. This thought permitted me to find an instance of what I was looking for in the most obvious place in the world I know of drama, in Ibsen, and particularly, it turns out, in *A Doll's House.* [...] In *A Doll's House* a woman climactically discovers that her eminently legal marriage is not comprehensible as a marriage, and therefore, before her own conscience, that she is dishonored. [...] I have described the genre of remarriage in effect as undertaking to show how the miracle of change may be brought about and hence life together between a pair seeking divorce becomes a marriage. *A Doll's House* thus establishes a problematic to which the genre of remarriage constitutes a particular direction of response, for which it establishes the condition or costs of a solution.

[...]

Having located certain causes for the genre's beginning when it does, I ought to have some speculations about why it ends when it does. It would be an answer to say that it ends when the small set of women who made it possible are no longer of an age to play its leads. Yet one feels that if the genre has not exhausted its possibilities and if the culture needs them sufficiently, people will be found. And indeed it is not clear that the genre has yielded itself up completely. [...] My thought is that a genre emerges full-blown, in a particular instance first (or set of them if they are simultaneous), and then works out its internal consequences in further instances. So that, as I would like to put it, it has no history, only a birth and a logic (or a biology). It has a, let us say, prehistory, a setting up of the conditions it requires for viability. [...] But if the genre emerges full-blown, how can later members of the genre *add* anything to it?

This question is prompted by a picture of a genre as a form characterized by features, an object by its properties; accordingly to emerge full-blown must mean to emerge possessing all its features. The answer to the question is that later members can "add" something to the genre because there is no such thing as "all its features." [...] [A] narrative or dramatic genre might be thought of as a medium in the visual arts might be thought of, or a "form" in music. [...] It may be helpful to say that a new member gets its distinction by investigating a particular set of features in a way that makes them, or their relation, more explicit than in its companions. [...] Let us think of the common inheritance of the members of a genre as a story, call it a myth. The members of a genre will be interpretations of it. [...]

[...]

[In comedies of remarriage, [a] criterion is being proposed for the success or happiness of a society, namely that it is happy to the extent that it provides conditions that permit conversations of this character, or a moral equivalent of them, between its citizens. [...]

13. Mahadev L. Apte, 'Sexual Inequality in Humor', from *Humor and Laughter: An Anthropological Approach* (1984)

In this chapter, I aim to study the sex-related differences in the nature, dissemination, use, and appreciation of humor across cultures and to explore and generalize regarding the many factors likely to be responsible for these differences. Such an endeavor is timely and significant in view of social scientists' growing interest in exploring similarities and differences between the sexes in both human and nonhuman social groups. Anthropologists interested in humor should also find useful the opportunity to develop a better general understanding of humor's relationship to social organization.

Social scientists interested in sex roles have investigated anatomical and physiological differences between the sexes, sexual division of labor, role models available to children in the enculturation and socialization process, and social-structural variables responsible for differential status and behavior. Anthropologists have contributed substantially to this research by providing ethnographic material, thus adding a cross-cultural perspective. There are, however, no anthropological analyses of humor as it relates to sexual differences. The discussion of humor, when it occurs in the context of sexual differences, is brief, cursory, and often marginal with respect to other empirical and analytical issues. On the other hand, psychologists have begun to study sex-related humor in earnest, as indicated by recent experimental research and publications. Although the psychological studies, based on empirical data and rigorous method-ology, are interesting, their samples are mostly limited to Western societies, especially Anglo-American ones. Such studies are also primarily oriented toward exploring sexual differences in the appreciation and evaluation of humor and lack analyses of its content and techniques. Such studies are important, however, not only because of their methodological contributions but also because of their attempts to relate their findings to socio-cultural phenomena. In this respect the psychological research complements anthropological investigations.

Keeping this background in mind, we should ask the following crucial questions. Are there differences between men's and women's humor? If so, then what is the nature of these differences? To what extent are these differences related to societal attitudes toward sex-role models and to normative behavioral patterns concerning women? And finally, under what circumstances and in what manner are these differ-ences minimized, if at all? The extent to which biological differences between the sexes influence the personality development of men and women is a complex issue that remains unresolved. It is readily apparent from ethnographic data that generally, but not universally, men and women have different social status, and women on the whole seem to have lower social status than men, especially in the public domain.

[...]

Basic premises

I wish to put forward three basic premises concerning sex-related aspects of humor. First, women's humor reflects the existing inequality between the sexes not so much in its substance as in the constraints imposed on its occurrence, on the techniques used, on the social settings in which it occurs, and on the kind of audience that appreciates it. Second, these constraints generally, but not necessarily universally, stem from the prevalent cultural values that emphasize male superiority and dominance together with female passivity and create role models for women in keeping with such values and attitudes. Finally, certain social factors such as marriage, advanced age, and the greater freedom enjoyed by women in groups remove some of the constraints ordinarily imposed on them and reduce the differences between men's and women's humor. These hypotheses primarily indicate existing cross-cultural trends suggested by available ethnographic data and should not be considered absolutely universal. It is also important to realize that men's capacity for humor is not superior to women's. Rather, both the prevalent cultural values and the resultant constraints prevent women from fully using their talents.

Attributes and varieties absent from women's humor in the public domain

A major consequence of the behavioral, expressive, and other sociocultural constraints imposed on women is that many common attributes of men's humor seem to be much less evident or even absent in women's humor. In public domains women seem generally not to engage in: verbal duels, ritual insults, practical jokes, and pranks, all of which reflect the competitive spirit, and the aggressive and hostile quality, of men's humor; slapstick; institutionalized clowning; and institutionalized joking relationships with female kin.

Women's humor generally lacks the aggressive and hostile quality of men's humor. The use of humor to compete with or to belittle others, thereby enhancing a person's own status, or to humiliate others either psychologically or physically, seems generally absent among women. Thus the most commonly institutionalized way of engaging in such humor, namely, verbal duels, ritual insults, and practical jokes and pranks, are rarely reported for women. Ethnographic data from many cultures show, for example, that adolescent boys and men engage in ritual insults. In such verbal duels the participants hurl all sorts of obscenities and insults at each other – often at the expense of their female relatives – to the amusement of the audience. These verbal duels and ritual insults are well institutionalized, the rules of performances are known to contestants and spectators alike, and the goal is one-upmanship on the basis of quick repartee until one contestant either gives up or resorts to physical violence. Such accounts of verbal dueling and ritual insults among women contestants have generally not been reported. The only example I have found is that of Mitchell-Kernan (1972), who reported her own participation in such a contest with a male opponent. Although in some cultures it is believed that women play their own verbal duels, neither female nor male ethnographers have substantiated the report. Gossen (1976:127–8) claims that such is the case among the Chamula Indians in Mexico, but also states that young girls are not supposed to hear men's verbal duels and that girls who do cannot giggle or otherwise acknowledge the exchanges because to do so would suggest that they are sexually available.

Ethnographic accounts of women playing practical jokes or pranks on each other or on men in everyday social interactions seem almost nonexistent. On the other hand, men seem to play practical jokes not only on other men, but also on women.

Among the Hupa Indians of North America, men prefer playing practical jokes, while women show a lack of interest in this type of humor (W.J. Wallace 1953). The Trumai Indians of Central Brazil often frightened women by playing practical jokes on them. Interestingly, women played an active role, pretending fright when they were the victims of such pranks (Murphy and Quain 1955:92–93). The folklore and mythologies of many cultures present additional evidence that aggressiveness and pranks are absent from women's humor. While no female trickster or clown figures are to be found in the prose narratives of any culture, there is a preponderance of male tricksters and clowns. Even when the trickster figures are animals, they are either specifically identified as males, as in the case of the Raven in the Tlingit Indian myths (Radin 1956/1969), and Ture, the spider, in Zande tales (Evans-Pritchard 1967), or references to their physical features, especially the penis, leave no doubt about their male identity. Sometimes the events in the various episodes of the trickster cycles of myth clearly suggest the maleness of the character, as evidenced by the Assiniboine trickster myths (Radin 1956/1967: 97–103).

Occasionally, oral literature indicates that a society prefers men to be tricky and clever in their humor. While examining humorous situations in the myths of Clackamas Chinook Indians for the purpose of classifying fun-generating stimuli, for instance, Jacobs (1960) found that trickery and cleverness in men and children, but not in women, was a stimulus for humor and laughter. "In their myths Chinook did not indicate that a woman before menopause would ever display so masculine a virtue as canniness" (p. 186).

Slapstick

Just as verbal aggressive humor and practical jokes seem much less prevalent among women, there is little ethnographic evidence to suggest that women individually participate in slapstick or in other similar kinds of humor in which physical rough-housing or horseplay are involved. In a cross-cultural study of sex difference in the behavior of children aged three through eleven (Whiting and Edwards 1973), it was found that boys engaged in more rough-and-tumble play and verbal aggression than girls. Boys were also more likely to counterattack physically or verbally if someone took aggression against them. Girls showed an overall tendency to withdraw in the face of aggression. Aversion to physical and aggressive action thus appears to be inculcated quite early in women, and this perhaps explains the near absence among them of humor that involves slapstick, physical roughhousing, and horseplay. Almost no account of rough physical games among women in non-Western cultures is to be found. Even in Western societies women have generally not participated in the rougher physical games, and although women in recent years have increasingly done so, they are still quite few compared with men. In this connection Tiger remarks that "a cursory survey of the world's major sports must lead to the conclusion that they are very much male-dominated – almost entirely so for sports involving teams of more than two persons" (1969/1970: 149).

Institutionalized clowning

In general, women individually do not clown for humorous effect, especially in social situations that are public. Ethnographic accounts of secular and ritual clowning indicate that in very few cultures are there female clowns. Court jesters and clowns, whether they appear in classical Sanskrit plays of ancient India (Bhat 1959) or in Shakespearean plays, are generally males. Historical and analytical studies of the development of court jesters, clowns, buffoons, and fools (Swain 1932; Towsen 1976; Welsford 1935; Willeford 1969) show that women rarely, if ever, played such roles. Ethnographic accounts of festivals and/or rituals indicate that women rarely act as clowns, either by themselves or in cooperation with men, and some scholars (King 1979; Makarius 1970) have offered explanations. In Western societies, the occasional woman clown in theaters and circuses, the most conventional arenas for clowning, merits feature stories in newspapers and magazines. Even in ordinary social relation-ships and interpersonal interactions, especially in the public domain, women develop humor by clowning much less frequently than men.

One possible explanation for the relative absence of clowning among women is that norms of propriety in many societies do not permit women to be totally uninhibited. Fox wrote of a "normative restriction" applied to women, and a kind of "social control over women's social behavior is embodied in such value constructs as 'good girl', 'lady', or 'nice girl.' As a value construct the latter term connotes chaste, gentle, gracious, ingenuous, good, clean, kind, virtuous, noncontroversial, and above suspicion and reproach" (1977: 807). Yet freedom of behavior and freedom from social sanctions are a major aspect of any kind of clowning. Thus women feel more constrained in social interaction in the public domain that involve individuals of both sexes and of diverse ages and occupations. In social interactions involving only women, however, clowning does occur, as I shall show later.

In cultures where institutionalized clowning is an integral part of rituals, women often either are excluded from participation in the ritual or may function only on the periphery and therefore cannot be clowns. In societies where ritual clowning is

a well-established institution, clowns have a high social status and important duties
to perform (Spicer 1940: 125). In some American Indian communities in the south-
western United States and Mexico, men must be apprentices for some time before they
can act as clowns (Bricker 1973: 70, 155–6). The leaders of the ritual clowns usually
acquire extensive experience over a long period of time (Spicer 1954: 91). The longer
a person acts as a clown at a religious function, the higher his prestige. Within the
framework of the ritual itself, clowns can burlesque and mock with total impunity
anybody and everybody, including the priests and the officials at the ceremonies
(Crumrine 1969; Parsons and Beals 1934; Spicer 1954: 173–4). Among the Rio Grande
Pueblos, clown societies exist, but only males become members (Dozier 1961: 115–16).
In religious contexts clowning manifests high social status. The absence of women
clowns therefore suggests that their status relative to that of men in community rituals
and ceremonials is inferior overall.

Institutionalized joking relationships

Also absent from women's humor is an institutionalized joking relationship between
female kin. Although many societies have well-established joking relationships among
various kin, these appear to be primarily between males or between a male and a
female. I found only two examples of structured joking involving female relatives in
my survey of the extensive ethnographic literature on the subject, which I discussed in
Chapter 1. Among the Tallensi there is a mutual joking relationship between a woman
and her brother's wife (Fortes 1949: 94, 120), and grandmothers and granddaughters
have a joking relationship among the Tarahumara Indians of Mexico (Kennedy 1970).

My discussion suggests that several points should be noted. Women seem not to
engage in the development of certain categories of humor because they do not have the
same degree of freedom that men do. Sociocultural reality in many societies means in
part that men's activities usually take place in public arenas, while women's activities
occur in more private ones (Farrer 1975: ix). Women's relative lack of freedom to
engage in certain types of activities in the public domain seems closely related to their
socially inferior status in that domain (Sanday 1974: 205) and to the emphasis that
many societies place on such cultural values as modesty, politeness, and passivity in
the context of female sex roles.

It could be argued that the lack of ethnographic data on humor as part of women's
expressive behavior is due to difficulties in obtaining such data. Male ethnographers
may not have easy access to women's activities that provide a setting for humor (Farrer
1975: ix). This view, however, does not take into account the fact that it is in the public

domain of social interaction, which is generally accessible to ethnographers of both sexes, that certain humor-generating activities are not undertaken by women individually. A more plausible argument may be that bias on the part of anthropologists and folklorists may result either in a lack of interest in women's activities, especially their expressive behavior, or in attempts to force women's verbal creations into preexisting culture (Farrer 1975: viff.). Such a lack of interest in women's activities may reflect the belied that they are insignificant, a view that seems to have been accepted until recently even by women's scholars. A greater awareness of the relevance of women's roles and activities to cultural systems should lead to extensive research on women's humor in the future. Such research may indicate that the varieties of humor discussed above do occur among women, and possibly women have developed certain types and attitudes of humor generally not found among men.

The cultural values of modesty and passivity for females that are found in many societies mean that girls receive differential treatment. The purpose of such treatment is to inculcate in girls from early childhood the value of ideal female sex roles. There is generally stricter control over girls than over boys with respect to overall behavior, but especially sexual conduct, personal attire, appearance and posture, work load, expressive behavior, and the appropriate share of responsibilities. While the degree of control over girls may vary cross-culturally, in almost no societies is boys' overall behavior regulated more strictly than girls. Whiting and Edwards (1973) found cross-culturally that girls from ages seven to eleven were significantly more compliant with respect to their mother's demands than were boys, a finding that echoes the results of an earlier cross-cultural study (Barry, Bacon, and Child 1957), which concluded that girls were under more pressure to be nurturant, obedient, and responsible, while boys were under more pressure to achieve and to be self-reliant.

Girls are instructed from an early age to sit so as not to expose themselves, and they generally start wearing clothes sooner than boys. Girls are also given household tasks earlier than boys, so that their play activities are restricted sooner. In their cross-cultural study of sexual patterns, Ford and Beach (1951) found that, in societies that treat boys and girls differently, the sexual activities of girls are more carefully controlled. Similarly, Ford and Beach concluded that, in societies that practiced segregation and chaperonage to control the sexual behavior of adolescents, boys were less carefully watched than girls. The restrictions on women's behavior are manifested in other ways as well. In many cultures norms of modesty cause women who laugh freely and openly in public to be viewed as loose, sexually promiscuous, and lacking in self-discipline. Such restrictions are found among the Mundurucu Indians in South

America, the Sarakatsani shepherds of Greece, people in rural India and the Middle East, and other groups.

Another reason for the absence of certain varieties in women's humor is their lack of opportunities for "performance" in public. It is commonly recognized by folklorists that performance is a crucial and indispensable factor in the realization of humor in prose narratives and other genres, especially in preindustrial societies (Bascom 1955; Finnegan 1970: 2–7, 319–32). In many societies boys are actively encouraged from an early age to develop rhetorical and linguistic skills, because good orators and story-tellers acquire public recognition; storytelling is a significant event for amusement and entertainment. Women, however, are not encouraged to develop the linguistic skills necessary for such performances. Among the Limba in Africa, for instance, women generally do not tell stories because it is believed that speaking well, using rhetoric, parable, or illustration effectively, is a specifically masculine activity: women are mostly expected to listen (Finnegan 1967: 69–70).

Such differential attitudes and consequent behavior with respect to linguistic skills are by no means characteristic of only preindustrial societies. In discussing the charac-teristic features of American women's language, Lakoff (1975: 56) claims that women generally do not tell jokes in social situations because such behavior is not in keeping with the politeness expected of them. According to a folk belief in American culture that is shared by both men and women, women cannot tell stories or jokes correctly. The persistence of such beliefs and the resulting attitudes may explain why a woman folklorist (Kalcik 1975: 5, 7) found that, even in women's rap sessions, women "consist-ently began and ended with apologies: for speaking, for the content of their speech, for speaking too long," and so forth. Such behavior indicates that middle-class American women do not feel that they have the same freedom and choice of speech that men do.

Factors that reduce sex-related differences

I do not mean to create the impression that women's humor and other modes of expressive behavior are totally constrained. First, constraints are viewed as necessary for an ideal female sex role, and not all women necessarily conform to such expecta-tions. When the norms are broken, the nature of sanctions carries across cultures, from the strongest (such as a gang rape among the Mundurucu Indians in South America) to mere whispered gossip. Several factors also alleviate the sociocultural restraints on women, allowing them to engage occasionally in humorous activities comparable to those of men. In addition, women use certain strategies to circumvent the sociocul-tural restraints.

Women's humor among women

Some varieties of humor that are usually absent from women's expressive behavior in the public domain are present in the private domain, where the audience generally includes only women. In many preindustrial societies humor created by women individually seems confined to social situations in which only women are present; in an all-female audience women behave more freely and creatively. Common topics for humor development in such gatherings include men's physical appearance, their social behavior, their idiosyncrasies, their sexuality, their status-seeking activities, and their religious rites. These characteristics are genereally presented in an exaggerated and mocking fashion.

Elizabeth Fernea (1965/69) reports that the chief entertainment among women of the Iraqi village where she lived consisted of mock imitation of men. The women felt free to do these mock imitations because the audience was exclusively female. The men never knew about these activities, because there was almost total segregation of the sexes; few social interactions involved participation of both men and women, even within kinship and household groups. [...]

In Sicily, ribaldry as a form of humor occurs frequently among women's groups. "There are women who function in the role of comedians or social satirists, always in an explicitly sexual context" (Cronin 1977: 85–6). Such women become famous for their expertise in satire, teasing, joking, ridicule, and impersonation. Men are never permitted to participate in the humor-creating activities of these women but know of them and are afraid of becoming the subject of such "female dramas" (ibid.).

Mock imitations of men by women may occasionally become obscene. It appears, however, that obscene elements are introduced only by married women, and unmarried women and young people generally do not participate. Among the Magars, a tribe in Nepal, weddings provide opportunities for mock imitations. In a groom's village, when all adult men leave to accompany the groom, the married women gather at the groom's house. Some dress in their husbands' clothing, especially military uniforms, and one or two tie large phalli to themselves. These women sing erotic songs. Some dance, and those with phalli chase the dancers and pretend to force them to have sexual intercourse. "The women who take the part of the men are the focal figures, and their rendition of the sexually aroused male is satirical and immensely amusing to the group" (Hitchcock 1966: 46).

The case of the Magars and similar practices among other groups suggest that standards of modesty, which is considered an essential aspect of women's behavior and personality in many cultures, are observed more stringently for single women than for married women. In many societies, especially those in which segregation of the sexes is quite rigid and those in which notions of honor and shame are intimately related to women's sexuality (Fox 1977: 807–8; Peristiany 1966), unmarried women are strictly guarded, are expected to behave passively, and are not supposed even indirectly to encourage males in any form of sexual encounter. In some cultures, unmarried women are not supposed to have a knowledge of sexual activity. Married women, on the other hand, have a somewhat higher status than unmarried ones. Because they are supposed to have had sexual experiences, they are considered knowledgeable about male sexuality. Nevertheless, married women are more likely to imitate male sexuality for an all-female audience than for a mixed audience except on special ceremonial occasions when such imitation may be carried out by women collectively.

Women's collective engagement in humor

When women act collectively, many of the behavioral constraints that they must observe as individuals can be disregarded. This is especially the case in rituals involving female rites of passage, especially women's puberty rites (B. B. Whiting 1963: 189). Marriage also seems to be a rite of passage that frees women from social restraints with respect to humor. One collective humorous activity of women involves singing songs that ridicule male sexual activity, especially at rites of passage. Women seem to derive much amusement from such songs, and in some cases the practice has developed into a social institution. The mock imitations of men by Magar and Gusii women are also accompanied by singing activities. In North India women from the bride's side collectively sing obscene songs at weddings, deriding and ridiculing the bridegroom about his lack of sexual powers (E. O. Henry 1975; Jacobson 1977). Jacobson reports having seen women from a bride's party dashing potfuls of scarlet and indigo dye into the faces of the men who accompanied the groom. The women smeared the bright goo into the ears and noses of their unprotesting victims and, after tying a cowbell around the neck of the groom's father, began to sing "raucous and risqué" songs.

The burlesquing and ridiculing of men's ritual and status-seeking activities form another collective humorous activity of women. Among the Kwakiutl Indians of the northwestern United States, the potlatch ceremony was very important to men, because the prestige and status of chiefs depended on their generosity at such events. Yet Kwakiutl women have reportedly performed mock potlatch ceremonies (Codere 1956: 343). Gusii women seem to treat men's rituals lightly and occasionally try to be amusing by mocking various acts or by creating a recreational atmosphere inconsistent with the seriousness of such ceremonies (B. B. Whiting 1963: 82). Hopi Indian women mock men's kachina dances and sing obscene and humorous sings about men during the Marau ceremony (Schlegel 1977: 257).

Among the people of Alor, boys around the age of sixteen grow their hair long and start to borrow male accoutrements such as a sword, front and back shields, a bow, a wide belt of woven rattan, and other similar objects. Boys rarely succeed in acquiring all of them but try to get as many as possible. The boys will walk about, wearing the emblems to show off and to proclaim adulthood. On such occasions, they are often subjected to the half-admiring, half-derisive comments of old women and girls. There is even a special expression for the type of laughter women direct toward such young men, which anthropologist DuBois translates by the word "hoot." The character of this laughter "is as unmistakable as the laughter that accompanies the telling of smutty jokes in our culture" (DuBois 1944/60: 81). A boy among the Blackfoot and Cree Indians setting out on his first war party – an important event – is given a derogatory name, which sticks with him until he has won honor in war by stealing a horse, killing an enemy, or performing some other heroic deed. Women, including the fiancées of such young men, take a special part in ridiculing and making fun of them (Driver 1969: 384).

The effects of advanced age and altered body state

Age and the resultant changes in a woman's body seem to be other important variables affecting humor. Ethnographic evidence suggests that as women age and reach menopause, they seem to grow bolder, start competing with men openly and freely in all types of humor, and often prove their equals. In many societies men seem to accept this change in elderly women, perhaps because such women no longer bear children and the sex-specific norms of behavior are relaxed for them. Even in societies with strict segregation of the sexes and the practice of purdah, elderly women are much less restrained than younger ones (Fox 1977).

Elderly women's relative freedom of speech and behavior has been noted in many ethnographies. Osgood (1951: 114) reports that, among the Koreans, a woman beyond menopause is considered to be sexless in the eyes of the people and can therefore do pretty well as she pleased. In Bali, where "modesty of speech and action is enjoined on women, such behavior may no longer be asked from the older women, who may use obscene language as freely as or more freely than any man" (Mead 1949: 180). Elderly women participate in supposedly exclusive male activities such as political deliberations, drinking and smoking, and decision making. Their freedom to indulge in obscene speech also offers them opportunities to compete with men in humor.

Devereux reported of his old female informant thus: "My aged informant, Tcatc, because of her age, felt free to speak up in the tribal council. 'Because of her age' she was also quite ready to engage in sexual banter, obscene even by the standards of the Mohave man" (1947: 532).

In Chinese villages old women, in addition to smoking and attending meetings normally reserved for males, also talk "dirty" and act as teasers. When an old woman in a social group clears her throat, preparing to speak, other people stop talking and listen intently, expecting to be amused. Barnett (1970), who made these observations, narrates the following incident, in which he himself became the target of their teasing: "I was sitting in front of the village store in a group one day while four married girls were washing clothing across the street in a bent-over position. A women of eighty nudged me and in a loud voice exclaimed 'That girl over there is waving it at you. Go over and stick her!' She and the other older women laughed loudly as several men smiled" (Barnett 1970: 450).

In Okinawan villages men and women are entertained at festivals by drinking, dancing, and joking. While young women do not drink sake at these celebrations and show much inhibition and restrained behavior, old women consume sake as men do and have few inhibitions. Dances simulating sexual behavior performed by an old woman and a young man appear to be funnier and more humorous than similar dances performed by other pairs (B. B. Whiting 1963: 452).

The relaxation of sociocultural norms for older women and their active participation in humor in the public domain characterize not only preindustrial but also industrial societies. In a study of joking relationships among male and female workers in a Glasgow factory by Sykes (1966), it was observed that old women often initiated sexual banter when interacting with young men in front of other people. Young women rarely initiated such encounters, either with old men or with young women. Although sexual encounters occurred between young men and women in isolated areas of the factory, the convention that young women should be modest in their behavior and speech in public was retained, and hence they did not take the initiative in joking exchanges.

Theoretical propositions

The general discussion in this chapter permits the formulation of several theoretical propositions.

Men and women appear to have unequal status across cultures. By restricting the freedom of women to engage in and to respond to humor in the public domain, men emphasize their need for superiority. Men justify such restrictions by creating ideal role models for women that emphasize modesty, virtue, and passivity.

Restrictions on the kinds of humor in which women can engage offer an important avenue to social culture that has been generally ignored in anthropological research.

A sexual distinction that transcends gender constitutes the basis of competition and tension between men and women for sociocultural dominance. This distinction emphasizes women's ability to engage in sexual intercourse, to conceive, and to give birth, while the gender aspects imply merely the anatomical differences. Men seem intimidated by the idea of sexual freedom for women because they fear that it might make women more like men: aggressive and promiscuous. They also fear that such freedom may disrupt social order, hence their desire to control women's sexuality at least in the public domain.

Women's relative freedom to engage in humor in the public domain is related to their position in the life cycle. As they advance through it, the restrictions are relaxed, and women publicly engage in humor to greater degrees, eventually competing with men.

14. Linda Hutcheon, *A Theory of Parody* (1985)

Modern parody, however, teaches us that it has many more uses than traditional definitions of the genre are willing to consider. Nevertheless, many still feel that parody that does anything short of ridiculing its "target" is false parody. One logical conclusion of this sort of reason is that mock epics that do not discredit the epic cannot be so labeled (Morson 1981: 117). To argue this, of course, is to go against the entire tradition of the term's usage. I would like to argue that the same is true of parody in general, despite its long tradition—dating back to Quintilian (1922: 395), at least—that demands that parody be considered pejorative in intent and ridiculing in its ethos or intended response. The traditional range allowed seem to be "amusement, derision, and sometimes scorn" (Highest 1962: 69). Most theorists implicitly agree with Gary Saul Morson's (1981: 110, 113, 142) view that a parody is intended to have higher semantic authority than its original and that the decoder is always sure of which voice he or she is expected to agree with. While the latter might be true, we have seen that the "target" of parody is not always the parodied text at all, especially in twentieth-century art forms.

Theodor Verweyen (1979) has separated theories of parody into two categories: those that define it in terms of its comic nature and those that prefer to stress its critical function. What is common to both views, however, is the concept of ridicule. As a subgenre of the comic, parody makes its model ludicrous: this is one tradition. But even as a "departure of pure criticism" (Owen Seamen, cited in Kitchin 1931: xix) parody exercises a conservative function, and does so through ridicule, once again. The majority of theorists want to include humor or derision in the very definition of parody (see, for example, Dane 1980; Eidson 1970; Falk 1955; Macdonald 1960; Postma 1926; Stone 1914). This is probably why Max Beerbohm thought parody the speciality of youth rather than mature wisdom (1970: 66).

For others, however, parody is a form of serious art criticism, though its bite is still achieved through ridicule. Admittedly, as a form of criticism, parody has the advantage of being both a re-creation and a creation, making criticism into a kind of active exploration of form. Unlike most criticism, parody is more synthetic than analytic in its economical "trans-contextualizing" of backgrounded material (Riewald 1966: 130). Among those who argue for this function of parody (see Davis 1951; Leacock 1937; Lelièvre 1958; Litz 1965), W. H. Auden perhaps articulated it most memorably. In his "daydream College for bards" the library would contain no works of literary criticism and "the only critical exercise required of students would be the writing of parodies" (1968: 77). This more serious function of parody has the potential to allow for a wider pragmatic range besides ridicule, yet few chose to extend it in that direction; "critical ridicule" (Householder 1944: 3) remains the most commonly cited purpose of parody.

There have, however, been important oppositions to this limitation of the parodic ethos to one of mockery. Fred Householder (1944: 8) has pointed out that, in classical uses of the word parody, humor and ridicule were not considered part of its meaning; in fact, another word was added when ridicule was intended. In examining the *OED* history of the usage of the word parody in English from 1696 on, Howard Weinbrot (1964, 131) argued that ridicule or burlesque were certainly not the only meanings of the term, especially in the eighteenth-century mock epic, as we too have seen. Yet that century did mark both a valuing of wit and an almost paradigmatic mixing of parody and satire, one that tended to dominate in subsequent attempts to develop a theory of parody; from then on, parody had to be funny and pejorative, as the Abbé de Sallier decreed in 1733. But, if we no longer accept the limitation of the form of parody to a verse composition of a certain kind, why should we accept an outdated limitation of ethos? Within a pragmatic perspective too, there again appears to be no transhistoric definition of parody: nothing is perhaps more culture-dependent than ethos. Why must Sallier's model (which presents the attitude of the parodist to the "target" as one of aggression and ridiculing criticism) necessarily still be relevant today—especially since modern parodic texts from Eliot to Warhol suggest the contrary? Yet, as Wolfgang Karrer (1977: 27) has documented so extensively, most work on parody today still accepts this limitation.

There are a few exceptions to this finding. One critic makes a useful distinction between parodies that use the parodied text as a target and those that use it as a weapon (Yunck 1963). The latter is closer to the truth of modern, extended, ironic parody. Another similar distinction is Markiewicz's (1967: 1271) differentiation between parody "sensu largo," which is imitative recasting, and parody "sensu stricto," which ridicules its model. But both depend, once again, upon the *comic*, instead of upon, as I prefer, the *ironic*. The marking of difference through irony is one way of dealing with what I call the range of parodic ethos, or what others have called its ambivalence (Alleman 1956: 24; Rotermund 1963: 27).

At the end of Chapter 2 I suggested that one of the reasons for the confusion in terminology between satire and parody lay in their common use of irony as a rhetorical strategy. Critics have helped confuse us by announcing that "satire must parody man" (Morton 1971: 35) and that the "hidden irony and satire against the parodied text" is a necessary part of the parodic effect of a work (Rose 1979: 27). As the last quotation suggests, irony does seem to play its role in this taxonomic muddle. As a trope, irony is central to the functioning of both parody and satire, but not necessarily in the same way. The important difference stems from the fact that irony has both a semantic and a pragmatic specificity (Kebrat-Orecchioni 1980). Therefore, as we found with parody, irony must be examined from a pragmatic perspective as well as from the usual formal (antiphrastic) one. A pragmatic approach that concentrates on the practical effects of signs is particularly relevant to the study of the interaction of verbal irony with parody and satire, because what is required in such a study is an account of the conditions and characteristics of the utilization of the particular system of communication which irony establishes within each genre. In both, the presence of the trope underlies the necessary postulating of both inferred encoded intent and decoder recognition in order for the parody or satire even to exist as such.

There is little disagreement among critics that the interpretation of irony does involve going beyond the text itself (the text as semantic or syntactic entity) to decoding the ironic intent of the encoding agent. Recent work in pragmatics (Warning 1979; Wunderlich 1971) has attempted to define the act of language as a "situated" one, moving beyond Jakobson's (1960) more static model into a wider frame of reference. This kind of "situating" is of obvious interest to a discussion of the contextual usage of irony in parody. Because verbal irony is more than a semantic phenomenon, its pragmatic value is of equal importance and ought to be incorporated as an autonomous ingredient, not just in definitions, but in analyses involving the trope. [...] This semantic contrast between what is stated and what is meant is not the only function of irony. Its other major role—on a pragmatic level—is often treated as if it were too obvious to warrant discussion: irony judges. Yet in this lack of differentiation between the two functions appears to me to lie another key to the taxonomic confusion between parody and satire.

The pragmatic function of irony, then, is one of signaling evaluation, most frequently of a pejorative nature. Its mockery can, but need not, take the usual form of laudatory expressions employed to imply a negative judgment; on a semantic level, this involves the deployment of manifest praise to hide latent mocking blame. Both of these functions—semantic inversion and pragmatic evaluation—are implied in the Greek root, *eironeia*, which suggests dissimulation and interrogation: there is both a division or contrast of meanings, and also a questioning, a judging. Irony functions, therefore, as both antiphrasis and as an evaluative strategy that implies an attitude of the encoding agent towards the text itself, an attitude which, in turn, allows and demands the decoder's interpretation and evaluation. Like parody, then, irony too is one of Eco's "inferential walks" (1979, 32), a controlled interpretive act elicited by the text. Both, therefore, must be dealt with both pragmatically and formally.

[...]

Although parody is by no means always satirical (Clark and Motto 1973: 44; Riewald 1966: 128–9), satire frequently uses parody as a vehicle for ridiculing the vices or follies of humanity, with an eye to their correction. This very definition orients satire toward the negative evaluation and a corrective intent. Modern parody, on the other hand, rarely has such an evaluative or intentional limitation. The work of Sylvia Plath has been seen as a feminist reworking (or parody) of the models of male modernism which she inherited. Her competitive spirit could drive her to oppose that heritage, but she could also draw upon it for strength (Gilbert 1983). The other major difference between the two genres, of course, is that of the nature—intra- or extramural—of their "targets."

Let us return now to the two functions of irony: the semantic, contrasting one and the pragmatic, evaluating one. On the semantic level, irony can be defined as a marking of difference in meaning or, simply, as antiphrasis. As such, paradoxically, it is brought about, in structural terms, by the superimposition of semantic contexts (what is stated/what is intended). There is one signifier and two signifieds, in other words.

Given the formal structure of parody, as described in the previous chapter, irony can be seen to operate on a microcosmic (semantic) level in the same way that parody does on a macrocosmic (textual) level, because parody too is a marking of difference, also by means of superimposition (this time, of textual rather than of semantic contexts). Both trope and genre, therefore, combine difference and synthesis, otherness and incorporation. Because of this structural similarity, I should like to argue, parody can use irony easily and naturally as a preferred, even privileged, rhetorical mechanism. Irony's patent refusal of semantic univocally matches parody's refusal of structural unitextuality.

15. Henry Jenkins, 'Agee, Mast, and the Classical Tradition' and 'Early Sound Comedy and the Vaudeville Aesthetic', from *What Made Pistachio Nuts?: Early Sound Comedy and the Vaudeville Aesthetic* (1992)

What Made Pistachio Nuts? examines representative works drawn from a body of comedian-centered comedies produced within the Hollywood studio system during the late 1920s and early 1930s. The films constitute a particular chapter in the larger generic history of the comedian comedy tradition. Such films are characterized by a subordination of visual and aural style, narrative structure and character development to foregrounded comic performance; they are marked by general questioning of social norms. In short, these comedies are recognizable through their difference from or opposition to dominant film practice. [...]

Consequently, I have adopted the term *anarchistic comedy* to refer to this particular group of films. *Anarchistic comedy* is a doubly appropriate label. First, these comedies are anarchistic in that they press against traditional film practice, moving from the classical Hollywood cinema's emphasis upon linearity and causality toward a more fragmented and episodic narrative. If a dominant tendency of classical narrative is its push to unify its materials into a coherent story, the tendency of anarchistic comedy is toward heterogeneity, even at the risk of disunity and incoherence. Second, these films are anarchistic in that they often celebrate the collapse of social order and the liberation of the creativity and impulsiveness of their protagonist. These comedies are anarchistic in both form and content, though the relationship between these formal and thematic conventions is more complex than most previous accounts have acknowledged. I prefer the term anarchistic comedy to the alternative form, *anarchic comedy*, for two reasons: first, my chosen term preserves a sense of process in the texts, a movement from order to disorder, while *anarchic comedy* might suggest a consistent state of anarchy; second, *anarchistic comedy* foregrounds the active and central role of the clowns as bringers of anarchy.

[...]

My central claim will be that anarchistic comedy emerged from the classical Hollywood cinema's attempt to assimilate the vaudeville aesthetic, an alternative set of social and artistic norms that enjoyed an uneasy relationship with dominant film practice in the early 1930s. Neither fully contained within the classical Hollywood cinema nor fully free of its norms, these films represent a succession of uneasy compromises, painstakingly negotiated during the production process, between two competing aesthetic systems, one governed by a demand for character consistency, causal logic, and narrative coherence, the other by an emphasis upon performance, affective immediacy and atomistic spectacle. Probably no two films resolved these formal problems in precisely the same way. During this transitional period, various strategies for constructing comic texts were tested. [...] These films cannot be fully explained through reference either to classical Hollywood norms or the vaudeville aesthetic but represent some overlap between the two formal systems. These films were, after all, produced within the mainstream commercial cinema and were answerable to the same institutional constrains as any other Hollywood movie. If these films are transgressive, it is because the Hollywood studios that financed, produced, and released them allowed and even encouraged those transgressions. For the most part, even these films conform to classical Hollywood norms. They are narratives. They have goal-centered protagonists. They maintain spatial and temporal coherence. They provide at least a minimal degree of causal integration. At the same time, they contain elements that transgress classical expectations about how stories should be told and how characters should be constructed.

The history of anarchistic comedy is the history of Hollywood's attempts to absorb those aspects of the vaudeville tradition most compatible with its norms, to make its devices functional within the pre-existing logic of the narrative film, and to jettison those elements that proved irreconcilable with classical conventions. [...] This study has the intention of providing a theoretical and historical framework within which additional studies of the comic genre might be constructed. It strives to displace auteur-dominated studies and the ahistorical comedian comedy model with an account of the comic film that is grounded in "historical poetics" and attentive to the politics of taste.

16. Simon Critchley, *On Humour* (2002)

Comic Timing

Mention of the suddenness of the bathetic shift that produces humour brings attention to the peculiar *temporal* dimension of jokes. As any comedian will readily admit, timing is everything, and a mastery of comic forms involves a careful control of pauses, hesitations and silences, of knowing exactly when to detonate the little dynamite of the joke. In this sense, jokes involve a shared knowledge of two temporal dimensions: *duration* and the *instant*. What I mean is that when we give ourselves up to being told a joke, we undergo a peculiar and quite deliberate distention of time, where the practice of joking often involves cumulative repetition and wonderfully needless circumlocution. [...] In being told a joke, we undergo a particular experience of duration through repetition and digression, of time literally being stretched out like an elastic band. We know that the band will snap, we just do not know when, and we find that anticipation rather pleasurable. It snaps with the punchline, which is a sudden acceleration of time, where the digressive stretching of the joke suddenly contracts into a heightened experience of the instant. We laugh. Viewed temporally, humorous pleasure would seem to be produced by the disjunction between duration and the instant, where we experience with renewed intensity both the slow passing of time and its sheer evanescence.

Laughter as an Explosion Expressed with the Body

It is important to recall that the success of tension by relief in humour is an essentially bodily affair. That is, the joke invites a corporeal response, from a chuckle, through a giggle to a guffaw. Laughter is a muscular phenomenon, consisting of spasmodic contraction and relaxation of the facial muscles with corresponding movements in the diaphragm. The associated contractions of the larynx and epiglottis interrupt the pattern of breathing and emit sound. [...] It is just this interruption of breath that distinguishes laughter from smiling, a revealing distinction. [...] Picking up on a word employed by Descartes, and used by a whole tradition extending to Charles Baudelaire, André Breton and Plessner, laughter is an *explosion* expressed with the body. [...] When I laugh vigorously, I literally experience an oscillation or vibration of the organs, which is why it can hurt when you laugh, if you engage in it a little too enthusiastically. [...] It is this link to the body that was the reason for the Christian condemnation of laughter in the early Middle Ages, its careful codification in the later Middle Ages, before the explosion of laughter in the early Renaissance, in the work of Rabelais and Erasmus.

Changing the Situation

[H]umour is not just comic relief, a transient corporeal affect induced by the raising and extinguishing of tension, of as little social consequence as masturbation, although slightly more acceptable to perform in public. I rather want to claim that what goes on in humour is a form of liberation or elevation that expresses something essential to what Plessner calls 'the humanity of the human'. [...] A true joke, a comedian's joke, suddenly and explosively lets us see the familiar defamiliarized, the ordinary made extraordinary and the real rendered surreal. [...] Humour brings about a change of situation, a surrealization of the real which is why someone like the great surrealist André Breton was so interested in humour. [...]

This idea of a change of situation can be caught in Mary Douglas's claim that, 'A joke is a play upon form that affords an opportunity for realising that an accepted pattern has no necessity'. Thus, jokes are a play upon form, where what is played with are the accepted practices of a given society. The incongruities of humour both speak out of a massive congruence between joke structure and social structure, and speak against those structures by showing that they have no necessity. The anti-rite of the joke shows the sheer contingency or arbitrariness of the social rites in which we engage. By producing a consciousness of contingency, humour can change the situation in which we find ourselves, and can even have a *critical* function with respect to society.

Reactionary humour

But before we get carried away, it is important to recognize that not all humour is of this type, and most of the best jokes are fairly reactionary or, at best, simply serve to reinforce social consensus. [...]

Most humour, in particular the comedy of recognition—and most humour *is* comedy of recognition—simply seeks to reinforce consensus and in no way seeks to criticize the established order or change the situation in which we find ourselves. [...]

Is humour human?

Humour is human. Why? Well, because the philosopher, Aristotle, says so. In *On the Parts of the Animals*, he writes, 'no animal laughs save Man'. [...] Now if laughter is proper to the human being, then the human being who does not laugh invites the charge of inhumanity.

[...]

One need only observe the behavior of chimpanzees and dogs to see that animals certainly play, and they do get frisky, but the question is: do they laugh? [...] [I]n her 1971 paper, 'Do Dogs Laugh?', Mary Douglas sets out to trouble the assumption that we can divide human from animal along the faultline of laughter. [...] We are not going to be able to decide the issue here and animals are full of surprises. So, whilst we cannot say with any certainty whether dogs laugh or not, we can, I think, grant that humour is an anthropological constant, is universal and common to all cultures. There has been no society thus far discovered that did not have humour, whether it is expressed as convulsive, bodily gaiety or with a laconic smile. Thus, humour is a key element in the distinction of the human from the animal; it is a consequence of culture, and indeed of civilization. [...] As Plessner puts it, laughter confirms the eccentric (*exzentrisch*) position of the human being in the world of nature. [...]

17. Glenda R. Carpio, *Black Humor in the Fictions of Slavery* (2008)

Black humor began as a wrested freedom, the freedom to laugh at that which was unjust and cruel in order to create distance from what would otherwise obliterate a sense of self and community. Until well into the twentieth century, it had to be cloaked in secrecy lest it be read as transgressive and punished by violence. Hence the popular slave aphorism "Got one mind for white folk to see / 'Nother for what I know is me."[9] In the tale just cited, the slave was likely "puttin' on Massa," catering to whites' beliefs in the inferiority of blacks in order to mask the aggressive message of his retort. Despite the life-threatening injunctions against black laughter, African American humor flourished, at first under the mask of allegory and increasingly in more direct forms. It developed a Janus-faced identity: on the one hand, it was a fairly nonthreatening form that catered to whites' belief in the inferiority of blacks but that usually masked aggression; on the other, it was a more assertive and acerbic humor that often targeted racial injustice but that was generally reserved for in-group interactions. For black Americans, humor has often functioned as a way of affirming their humanity in the face of its violent denial.

By most accounts, African American humor, like other humor that arises from oppression, has provided a balm, a release of anger and aggression, a way of coping with the painful consequences of racism. In this way, it has been linked to one of the

---

[9] This folk saying appears in numerous sources, including slave songs and blues lyrics. It is reprinted in Watkins, *On the Real Side*, 32.

three major theories on humor: the relief-theory made popular by Freud, which posits that we laugh as a way to release pent-up aggression. Freud claimed that "tendentious jokes," of which he identified two main kinds, the obscene and the hostile, allow the joker and his or her audience to release energy used for the purposes of inhibition. Much, but certainly not all, African American humor can be understood as a kind of relief-inducing humor. Indeed, under the violent restrictions of slavery and segregation, African Americans developed the art of tendentious jokes so well, in particular those that mask aggression, that often they left whites "with the baffled general feeling that [they had] been lampooned [before their very eyes] without quite knowing how."[10] Among themselves, however, African Americans have expressed aggression against their oppressors much more openly. For instance, in a tale that became popular during the postbellum period, when slavery was often portrayed in the public sphere in mythic and picturesque modes (full of paternalistic masters, benevolent mistresses, and happy, loyal 'darkies'), a slave owner bids a sentimental farewell to his slave, Uncle Tom, soon after emancipation. "Ah, dear, faithful, loyal Uncle Tom!" the master says. "Lincoln has forced you to accept freedom—against my wishes, and, I am sure against yours. Dear old friend and servant, you need not leave this plantation. Stay here with us." To which Uncle Tom replies, "Thank you, deah, kine, lovin', gen'rous Massa. I reckon I'll leave. But befo' I go I wants you to know I will allus 'membuh you ez de son uv a bitch you is an' allus wuz!"[11]

While African American humor addresses many topics other than black and white relations, it frequently marks the multifaceted nature of those relations, both how much they have changed and how much they have stayed the same over time. Thus, in another well-known tale, a black man gets off in a strange town in Mississippi sometime in the early twentieth century. Seeing no members of his race, he asks a white man, "Where do the colored folks hang out here?" Pointing to a large tree in the public square, the white man replies, "Do you see that limb?" Jokes about lynching and other forms of racial violence in the aftermath of slavery attest to the perversion of freedom. At the same time, they express the quintessential quality of gallows humor, which Freud called the "triumph of narcissism" because it asserts the ego's invulnerability in the face of death.[12]

African American humor is also, although less commonly, linked to a second major theory of humor, the superiority theory, which posits that we laugh at other people's

---

[10] Dollard, *Caste and Class in a Southern Town*, 309–10, as quoted in Levine, *Black Culture and Black Consciousness*, 313.

[11] As quoted in Watkins, *On the Real Side*, 79.

[12] Freud, "Humour."

misfortunes. In some ways, the tradition of signifyin', including the play of the dozens, of boasting and toasting, belongs to this kind of humor, although the verbal battle of capping and "you mamma" jokes savor verbal wit over any mean-spirited competition or put-down. The signifying tradition is generally known as mother wit and departs significantly from the Freudian model of humor, which stresses sublimation, in that it relishes exposure and does not depend on the joke form. Instead, it is mainly visual and depends on the verbal dexterity of the dozens, the toasts (long, metrically and rhythmically complex compositions), and the telling of "lies," or stories. Signifying remained largely segregated until Richard Pryor broke out of his original image as a slim, mild-mannered comedian who, believe it or not, never cursed and usually told charming jokes patterned after Bill Cosby's material. But Pryor began performing revolutionary acts for mixed audiences in the late 1960s and thus was largely responsible for desegregating African American humor. Black comedians before Pryor, most notably Moms Mabley, Dick Gregory, Godfrey Cambridge, Flip Wilson, Redd Foxx, and Bill Cosby, had introduced aspects of black humor to mixed audiences, but it was Pryor, after a remarkable self-transformation, who brought all aspects of black humor to the stage. In a sense, he "outed" black humor from the closely guarded circles within which black folk had kept it since slavery.

Rarely is black humor connected to a third and, for me, the most interesting theory on humor: the incongruity theory. Simply put, this theory suggests that we laugh when our expectations are somehow disturbed. Such a simple definition hardly argues for why I am interested in this theory, so allow me to explain. The humor of incongruity generally entails the playing of "what if" games that suspend normativity. They are games that momentarily reconfigure habits of mind and language and that can lead to what Ralph Ellison calls "perspective by incongruity" (after Kenneth Burke).[13] At its best, the humor of incongruity allows us to see the world inverted, to consider transpositions of time and place and to get us, especially when the humor is hot enough to push our buttons, to question the habits of mind that we may fall into as we critique race. The kind of humor that I am invoking is not the kind that has been romanticized and thus normalized, as in some interpretations of Mikhail Bakhtin and his theories of carnival. In the context of African American expressive culture, and particularly in the hands of writers and artists that I have selected, the humor of incongruity allows us to appreciate the fact that, far from being *only* a coping mechanism, or a means of "redress," African American humor has been and

---

[13] Ellison, *Going to the Territory*, 193–4.

continues to be both a bountiful source of creativity and pleasure and an energetic mode of social and political critique.

18. Michael North, *Machine-Age Comedy* (2009)

Early in the 1920s, Viktor Shklovsky [...] suggested that the essence of Chaplin's humor is to be found in its mechanical quality, but he could not decide any more than Benjamin, why this should be so.[14] The situation is puzzling in part because comedy has traditionally been associated with the spontaneous, the illogical, the organic, and the primitive, so that a comic style that arises from repetitive, machinelike movements seems almost a contradiction in terms. The theory of Henri Bergson, though it derives comedy from the mechanical, changes rather little in this respect because it depends on the notion that laughter is an expression of the natural hostility of organic life to the machine. Bergson's theory was thus of little use to critics of a revolutionary persuasion, wondering at what seemed like the genuine delight of the masses in comic routines that embodied modern mechanization. [...] Chaplin's peculiar way of moving on-screen is only a minor revelatory example of a much larger problem, that of accounting for mass-produced comedy in general. Comedy has been traditionally thought to depend for much of its effect on surprise. What happens to this valuable comic resource when the same routines can be seen in exact repetition dozens of times. [...] In Chaplin's routines [...] the reproducible quality of the comedy is not just suffered but actually embraced, since the repetitious bits of comic shtick, the cookie-cutter motions that so intrigued Benjamin, are simply inten-sified reflex versions of the repetition intrinsic to film. Rather than trying to modify this quality, Chaplin makes it the essence of his performance, turning himself into a "walking trademark," as Benjamin puts it. [...] Later, radio and television would make this peculiar kind of amusement their stock-in-trade. When Jack Benny faces a holdup man in one celebrated radio routine, the audience laughs because it knows, without Benny having to say a word, that the question "Your money or your life?" is one he simply cannot answer. Dick Van Dyke gets laugh after laugh out of the same ottoman because the audience expects he will fall over it yet again. To wonder at this to ask why the purely repetitive aspects of a comic performance should be just as funny as the novel parts, is to pose Benjamin's question about Chaplin in a different and larger context. It is to wonder whether there might be something potentially

---

[14] Viktor Shklovsky, "Literature and Cinema," in *The Film Factory: Russian and Soviet Cinema in Documents*, ed. Richard Taylor (Cambridge, Mass.: Harvard University Press, 1988), 98.

comic in mechanical reproductions itself. [...] Thus the machine age seems to have brought, along with all its other dislocation, a new motive for laughter and perhaps a new form of comedy. Entertaining this possibility [...] may tell us something as well about the relation between modernism and modernity, which is governed so largely by the variable ratio between mechanical repetition and incessant novelty. If there is something inherently funny in mechanical reproduction, then it is also possible that modernity itself is governed by a comic rhythm, even when it is not particularly amusing.

Far more than any other literary or artistic form, comedy is thought to be unchanging and thus to lack a history, except in the most trivial sense. "In the millennia since Susarion," as Erich Segal puts it, "none of the stimuli that arouse laughter have changed."[15] Of course, establishing perfection at the very outset does mean that any development will be a decline, so it is not odd that Segal believes that "after reaching its apogee with Figaro, comedy had nowhere to go but down." [...] However, the inability of this theory founded on classical precedents to cope at all with any comedy after 1896 suggests another possibility: that Segal's original premise is wrong and that the sources of laughter change over time just as they vary from place to place.

For the Romantics, in fact, there was an implicit association of comedy with freedom that made it quintessentially modern, not ancient. Schiller, for example, took the view that comedy is human, expansive, and unconstraining, in utter contrast to an older view, most often associated with Hobbes, that comic spite is one of the chief ways in which society punishes difference.[16] In Hegel's *Phenomenology of Spirit*, comedy stands at the culmination of the process of spirit's self-conscious realization, in which the abstract and alien are revealed as mere aspects of self-consciousness. The resulting "self-certainty" is, according to Hegel "a state of spiritual well-being and of repose therein, such as is not to be found anywhere outside of this Comedy."[17] In this view, comedy is to be found not at the dawn but very close to the end of history, as one of spirit's freest and highest expressions.

From the Restoration on, the English often congratulated themselves on their comic spirit, which could not have developed, they felt, without a long history of humane tolerance and political freedom. In the Victorian period, however, comedy seems

---

[15] Erich Segal, *The Death of Comedy* (Cambridge, Mass.: Harvard University Press, 2001), 31.

[16] T. G. A. Nelson, *Comedy: An Introduction to Comedy in Literature, Drama, and Cinema* (Oxford: Oxford University Press, 1990), 5, 174; McFadden, 7–18.

[17] G. W. F. Hegel, *Phenomenology of Spirit*, trans. A. V. C. Miller (Oxford: Clarendon Press, 1977), 453.

almost to have disappeared from the English stage. [...] For the Victorians, comedy, like so many other things, was held to be fine in moderation, but it was not to be enjoyed for its own sake alone. Thus Victorian comic theory emphasized the necessity of constraining comedy within a formal balance and timing it with a strong sense of realism. [...] By the end of the century, in the English-speaking countries at any rate, comedy had been firmly tucked into place as a pleasant recreation, a mild reminder of dreams of freedom now subordinated to a higher responsibility. On the Continent, however, comedy enjoyed for its own sake, to the very point of anarchy, had become the stock-in-trade of a particular branch of the avant-garde. [...]

Perhaps because their work seemed so different from the comedy of the past, these groups coined or adapted a whole series of new terms for it, the most common and enduring of which was *fumisme*. Essentially undefinable, *fumisme* could be discerned mainly in its opposition to common artistic requirements of balance, consequence, and realism, which it answered with extravagance, incoherence, and nonsense.[18] [...] [E]xtending from the cabarets of Montmartre to the film studios of New Jersey, was a particular kind of humor, developed out of *fumisme* and displayed to its fullest in animated cartoons.

This comic technique, born as the in-joke of the avant-garde salon, worked just as well in cartoons generated for a mass American audience in part because roughly similar changes had been taking place, on both sides of the Atlantic, in popular humor. [...] Sober critics were concerned simply by an apparent increase in the sheer amount of humor, which raised the alarming possibility that Americans would "become a laughing nation, a country of frivolous and hyperglasts, a culture dangerously out of control." But it was also the quality of this humor that raised concern. The New Humor was associated with the new mass-market publications coming into prominence at this time. [...] [T]he New Humor also came to be associated with vaudeville and thus with audiences, performers, and performance styles that were inevitably, if not always accurately, linked to recent increases in immigration. [...]

[T]he machine age had begun to affect comedy even before very much of it was mechanically reproduced. [...] [T]he new humorists favored gags and stunts, nonsensical routines that amuse because of their inconsequence, and repetitive, stereotyped buts of shtick that spark a laugh of recognition, as well as surprise. In accepting and

---

[18] *Spirit of Montmartre*, 23–254; Jeffrey Weiss, *The Popular Culture of Modern Art: Picasso, Duchamp and Avant-Gardism* (New Haven: Yale University Press, 194), 143–4. According to Weiss, the *fumiste* was originally a chimney sweep, depicted in mid-nineteenth-century vaudeville as a dry jokester.

advancing these changes, comics were embracing an aspect of modern experience, the way that so much of it seemed to be mechanically organized, that was otherwise causing widespread dismay. Critics reacted so harshly to the New Humor not just because it was ill-mannered but also because it was creating laughter from the very aspects of modern life that well-intentioned people were supposed to fear and dislike. [...] They were tinkerers, whose interest in expanding and refining the possibilities of machine-produced art was communicated to their audiences, who were often amused simply by the processes of mechanical reproduction. [...] Bringing the previously inanimate world of pictures to life looked a lot like bringing the inanimate itself to life, which is what the animated cartoon did on a more basic level. [...] In short, it is no simple coincidence that the vast majority of all animated cartoons are comedies; this fact simply reflects the humor inherent in film movement itself. [...] The comedy is not imposed on the industrial process, or invented in defiance of it, but is derived from its workings.

[...]

When the stolid objects of everyday life acquire their own motive and transformative powers, the result is a kind of exhilarating comic nonsense that is nothing more than a reflect of the manufacturing process that makes new objects out of old ones all the time.

Some of the most famous film comedians got their laughs by exploiting the uncanny power that industrialization had invested in ordinary objects. The many instances, typified perhaps by Chaplin's *Modern Times*, in which the silent film hero is victimized by mindless and seemingly malevolent machinery are universally familiar. A little less obvious is the fact that the seemingly hapless comedian needs exquisite mechanical skills and intimate familiarity with his apparent antagonist in order to make the comic routine function. In a sense, the median needs to become part of the machine in order to extract its comic possibilities. [...] Silent comedies are almost always marred by this inversion: the more helpless the comedian is in the role of dramatic hero, the more skillful he has had to be in handling the technical demands of filmmaking. [...] [Buster] Keaton's success with machines suggested that the whole process of industrialization, as inhuman as it may have seemed, was at least twofold: the same process that seemed to rob human beings of so much of their freedom also fostered the imaginative powers necessary for people to manipulate it. In other words, the great Keaton films slowly and carefully defetishize the huge industrial objects on which they are based. [...] With every step he takes, Chaplin rocks back and forth on a similar dichotomy.

As a human being, he is rigid and absurd, but as a machine that moves he is a living allegory of the peculiar abandonment of sense that machines can bring to the human situation.

III

Very early in modern history, comic theory began to reflect the influence of mechanical reproduction, though this may not be immediately obvious from a first reading of any of the relevant texts. The main difficulty facing comic theory, as Umberto Eco has complained, is that there are simply too many different things that make people laugh.[19] Rather than admit the fearsome possibility that what we call comedy might not be a unitary phenomenon at all, critics usually try to reduce this wide range of behaviors, linguistic habits, and artistic devices to its simplest forms, like the joke or the pratfall. This search for a common factor is intrinsically ahistorical, and it tends to produce predictably circular conclusions that comedy itself does not change over time. [...] Since it is clear to everyone that comedy depends very strictly on context, so that the same fall might promote real concern or vicious laughter, depending on the situation, it should be easy to see that the meaning of laughter may change with context, and with time. [...]

One of the most intractable debates in modern comic theory pivots on the opposition between release and combination. For one side, comedy looks anarchic and even revolutionary, since it frees its subjects from the reign of sense, while for the other side this release is illusory or contradictory, given the power of humor to punish those who deviate from the dominant norm. The choice itself seems a product of the expectation that comedy should have an essence, with all the variety in the form hammered down into one of two pigeonholes. But the indecision between the possibilities may be historically revealing, especially since they have an odd tendency, particularly in the most sophisticated thinkers on the subject, to turn into one another.

Freud's *Jokes and Their Relation to the Unconscious*, for example, is basically a theory of release. [...] As it happens, though, the situation is not quite as straightforward as it sounds. It is not so much that a joke simply opens the floodgates, allowing pent-up emotions to escape, as it is that the joke frees a certain quantum of psychic energy that had been used to keep the floodgates in place.

[...]

---

[19] Cited in Nelson, 22.

Freud's theory converges from an unexpected direction on that of another noted theorist: Henri Bergson. In very general terms, Bergson's theory continues the Romantic tradition in which comedy expresses all that is flexible, free, organic, and spontaneous in the human condition. And yet, humor as Bergson describes it is really a pretty grim affair. Laughter, in his opinion, is, above all, a corrective. Being intended to humiliate, it must make a painful impression on the person against whom it is directed. By laughter, society avenges itself for the liberties taken with it. It would fail in its object if it bore the stamp of sympathy or kindness."[20] Thus, Bergson enclosed within a generally Romantic value system a definition of comedy that is more or less that of Hobbes, who saw it, from an older perspective, as a means of domination.

In actuality, though, Bergson's theory turns out to emphasize both release and domination, almost as if it had been composed so as to confuse these two diametrically opposed ways of looking at comedy. As he explains it, comedy dominates only on behalf of human freedom. [...] Comedy thus finds itself in the rather strange position of punishing people in order to make them free, lashing them out of their rigid automatism and into an enforced spontaneity.

The full complexity of this situation emerges as Bergson elaborates his most famous claim, which defines comedy itself as "*something mechanical encrusted on the living.*" The butt of all humor, as Bergson sees it, is "*a certain mechanical inelasticity,*" and human beings are laughable insofar as they remind others "*of a mere machine.*" But it is also true in Bergson that laugher is itself mechanical, at least metaphorically, so that he, like Freud, can speak of the "inner mechanism" that drives a joke. [...] On one level, Bergson means that people laugh at automatism, but he also means to say that laughter itself is a kind of automatism.[21] [...]

Like Freud, Bergson sometimes sees this process as a very specific, very modern kind of machine. [...] [T]he relationship between the mechanical and living is a circuit and not a simple opposition. If a correctly humane point of view can arise from so automatic a reaction as laughter, then it seems that the living can sometimes be found encrusted, as it were, on the mechanical. It somehow becomes possible for automatism to yield the very spontaneity it seems to cancel out. [...]

This tangled relationship between freedom and domination, the human and the mechanical, was the problem Benjamin tried to resolve in his critique of mechanical reproduction. [...]

---

[20] Henri Bergson, *Laughter: An Essay on the Meaning of the Comic*, trans. Cloudsley Brereton and Fred Rothwell (New York: Macmillan, 1911), 197. [...]
[21] See Nelson, 183–5, and McFadden, 112–15.

Once a secondary and specialized form, one so minor it received no particular attention from Freud or Bergson, mechanically reproduced comedy became the dominant form, affecting even the ancient humor of jokes and pratfalls. The effect of that change can be seen throughout the art and literature of the twentieth century.

IV

[...]

On what level, then, is the humor being enjoyed, in defiance of the mechanical or in mimicry of it? The reappearance of this indecision in theory and in practice suggests that it reveals some fundamental tension, brought about by the new interference of machines with art, that is characteristic of the humor of this time. [...]

In fact, the affinity between modern art and popular comic forms of various kinds was apparent from the beginning of the twentieth century.

[...]

Somehow, though, the similarities are so striking between the humor directed at society by the avant-garde and that directed back at the avant-garde by society as to suggest that this apparently fundamental distinction between revolutionary and conservative comedy has been rendered obsolete. [...] Something seems to have been unbalanced in the time-honored comic opposition of a stable society and its eccentric outlaws, something clearly having to do with the establishment of incessant progress as a societal norm. The avant-garde is often treated as a joke because it seems to be manufacturing empty innovations, which is pretty much exactly what the avant-garde seems to have been mocking in society itself. [...] The avant-garde and the bourgeoisie are really telling the same joke, which is all about the way that mechanical regularity and incessant innovation have collapsed into one another, and shock is no longer distinguishable from routine.

Bergson is obviously on the right track, then, when he finds the source of all humor in the mechanical encrusted on the living, not because comedy aims to distinguish those categories but rather because so much modern comedy derives from their confusion. [...] One of the products that industrial society manufactures [...] is comedy, which it makes out of the imbalanced mixture of the unique and the reproduced, the new and the repetitive, the human and the mechanical.

Comedy may be an especially significant form in the twentieth century because it shows the realities of modern life at work in popular culture, art, literature and philosophy, more or less simultaneously.

19. Ruth Wisse, *No Joke: Making Jewish Humor* (2013)

[S]tereotypes are a regular feature of joking, which depends for its effect on brevity. With no time for elucidation, jokes often designate people by a single characteristic. Is it fair that Poles or "Newfies" (Newfoundlanders) get labelled as dumb? Are all Scots stingy? Are all mothers-in-law hateful?

[…]

I cheerfully confess that theories about humor interest me less than evidence they offer of folk creativity—jokes being the only surviving form of "folklore" that is not protectable by copyright. From the late eighteenth century onward, we have some record of the Jewish humor that bubbled up from below as well as whatever came from writers and intellectuals. Of all the arts, humor depends the most on its immediate context, which makes it hard to generalize about this body of wit shaped variously by different surroundings and circumstances. Getting jokes is usually the hardest stage of acculturation, and the languages in which they joked separates as much as they united Jews in modern times.

In place of a general theory, I therefore intend to offer a descriptive map of some of the centers where Jewish humor thrived and where it still prospers, drawing examples from literature and mass culture that acted on one another. These comparative instances of Jewish humor in various languages should caution against overly facile generalizations about its provenance and nature. Laughter may be universal, but we will benefit from looking at some of the market conditions governing its production and consumption.

[…]

This book's inquiry into the varieties of Jewish humor in different languages and under diverse conditions hopes to advance our understanding of its various parts along with our appreciation of the whole. There is no denying that humor, the consummate insider's sport, has flourished among Jews, prompting us to ask why this activity should enjoy such a widespread popularity. The subject begins to interest us at the point that humor is identified by others and Jews themselves as a Jewish speciality, a pursuit disproportionately associated with Jews. That this occurs only at certain points of intersection between tradition and modernity helps us to arbitrate the dispute between those who want to trace its origins back to biblical times, and others who insist on its contemporaneity. Jewish humor obviously derives from Jewish civilization, but Jews became known for their humor only starting with the Enlightenment. As this book will show, it responds to conditions of Jewish life, but only where it becomes the response of choice.

This focus on Jewish humor at the point that the phrase begins to trip off the tongue accounts for what some readers may resent as the Eurocentrism of this book. Comedy and laughter are common to all cultures, and for most of Jewish history, humor was no more observably associated with Jews than with other religious or ethnic groups. In some parts of the Jewish world, this remains the case. The Ladino folktales of the Jewish trickster Joha bear a close resemblance to the Arabic ones of the Muslim trickster Juha and his Turkish counterpart Nasreddin, but recent collectors of these tales do not claim they were any more prominent among Jews than their analogous versions among other peoples of Yemen, Iran, Egypt, Turkey, or Morocco. Jewish humor in Judeo-Persian, Judeo-Arabic, and Judeo-Spanish, or Judezmo (Ladino), generated no treatises about the schlemiel or schlimazel, and no theories about parody as compensation for power-lessness. Jews laughed in Casablanca as they did in Kraków, and maybe at some of the same things, but though there are scarcely five hundred Jews left in Kraków, its bookstores still carry Polish collections of Jewish humor, whereas today's Casablanca, with more than ten times as many Jews, has no such Arabic equivalent. Jews of Arab lands appeared to have acquired no comparable reputation for humor.

The Yiddish expression *mit vos est men es*? (With what does one eat this?) means something like, "Please explain to me why this matters?" or, "How does this apply?" That Jewish humor becomes prominent at a certain point does not yet address its significance or functions. How and why does it explode at the point when ghetto doors are breached, and as Jews begin mingling with fellow Europeans who also are being granted new rights and freedoms? Suppose we establish that it gains momentum among Jews who lose divine justification for their exceptionalism and now face the world stripped of the authority of the covenant in whose name they were Jews. Suppose we see its escalation in times of threat—which are nothing new in a history replete with massacres, expulsions, and inquisitions, but are now experienced for the first time without the perceived protection of God in whose name Jews are being threatened. Suppose we can demonstrate that Jewish humor erupts at moments of epistemological and political crisis, and intensifies when Jews need new ways of responding to pressure. Does this mean that humor compensates them for the absent security? Does it work to their benefit or detriment? Does it become a secular expression of their identity? And what do these findings tell us about the universal significance and functions of humor?

To be sure [...] not everyone savored Jewish humor to the same degree. Observant Jews who kept their cultural distance from Gentile society, whether in Christian or Muslim lands, did not all take up the Jewish sport with the same enthusiasm as those who relished contradictions between the foundational idea of Jewish *chosenness* and the historical record of persecution. At the other end of the religious spectrum, young people dedicated to socialist or nationalist political action did not appreciate ridicule of their goals. "How many feminists does it take to change a lightbulb?" "That's not funny!" Ideologues do not welcome levity. Joking flourishes among those who sustain contrarieties, tolerate suspense, and perhaps even relish insecurity. Many writers featured in this book are situated—none put it better than Franz Kafka—with their posterior legs still glued to their father's Jewishness, and their waving anterior legs finding no new ground. But other Jews preferred to seek out steady, level land.

As for Jewish humor's genealogy, scholars are certainly justified in tracing its roots to its sources in the Bible and Talmud. One might locate the seeds of Jewish skepticism in Sarah's laughter when she is informed in Genesis 18.12 that she and Abraham, at their very advanced age, will conceive a child. "Therefore Sarah laughed within herself, saying 'After I have grown old shall I have pleasure, my lord being old also?'" Joking frequently exposes unauthorized truths, and Sarah's trust in biological probability over divine prophecy is an early example of the cognitive independence that Judaism encourages. Biblical challengers to authority often outdid even the boldest of moderns in daring, and the Talmudic record of disputation supplies incontrovertible proof that Abraham and Job invited emulation of the part of generations of rabbis. Yet the Bible confirms that Sarah *did* bear Isaac, and duly named her son *Yitzhak*, signifying a laughter of joy more than cynicism: Abraham's challenge to God over his intention of destroying Sodom is finally quashed by the wickedness of that condemned city. In each case, the Bible's claim of divine authorship guarantees the predominance of the Lord's point of view. Modern humorists, in contrast, challenge authority without conceding its supreme authority.

Similarly, while Jewish tradition offers occasions of merriment and templates for humor, these are part of an ultimately, if not at all times, well-ordered universe. Jews everywhere celebrated the feast of Purim that recorded the improbably political victory of their ancestors Esther and Mordecai over their archenemy Haman in Persia. On that day of merrymaking, the Talmud encourages drinking to the point that one can no longer distinguish "cursed be Haman" from "blessed be Mordecai." Some communities of eastern Europe got into the spirit of inversion by appointing a Purim rabbi to upend homiletics for a day. But in the 1930s, as we will see, a Yiddish writer forging his own rendition of the Purim story felt it necessary to add a jilted lover and a failed assassin to the cast of characters to represent the disastrous realities of Jewish politics that stood in ironic contrast to the victory recorded in the Book of Esther. Rather than celebrating the exception, he reintroduced the more likely failure, reversing the reversal, recording what the Jews of Europe were actually experiencing in his time.

Modern Yiddish "proverbs" did the same with the liturgy: "Thou hast chosen us from among the nations—why did you have to pick on the Jews?" "God will provide—if only He would provide until He provides." "Pray to the Lord—and talk to the wall." Whereas religion reinforced God's promise, modern humor questions His constancy. True, modern scholarship has found commonalities in the language play of the midrash and Marx Brothers. [...] But it was only in the modern period that humor became the *aim* of such entrainment as opposed to a delightful by-product of otherwise earnest interpretation.

[...]

An association with humor would seem to have benefited Jews, since physiologists nowadays confirm the advantages of joking, long since touted by philosophers. [...] Yet I am obliged to ask whether an excess of laughter might exacerbate the tensions it is meant to alleviate. Can a surfeit of comedy be unhealthy? Is there a point at which too much joking could cause someone harm?

20. Magda Romanska, 'Disability in Tragic and Comic Frame' (2015)

The connection between humor and disability is perhaps one of the most challenging, and underresearched, aspects of comic theory. Modern theorists of humor and comedy generally pursue two lines of inquiry: along one they analyze how, historically, humor at the expense of the disabled has created and reestablished discriminatory and alienating comic conventions (these critics also argue about whether we've experienced the emergence of a taboo on such humor—or the continued lack of such a taboo); along the other line of inquiry theorists investigate different comic strategies used by the disabled to avert and displace comic insults (including black humor, ironic detachment, and self-deprecation). Disability and humor studies share a number of salient critical points, among them a focus on incongruity theory, which traces the source of humor to disjunction between normative and non-normative appearances and behaviors. We can even argue that it is, in fact, the comic frame that has structured the very experience of disability across the world.

In the historical context of disability (as a socially constructed category connected to but not convergent with impairment—like gender and sex, for example), the very foundation of comic theory (as established by Plato and Aristotle) involves positioning oneself ethically and aesthetically towards the disabled. Plato makes an argument that the comic impulse is fundamentally a flaw of character because it involves laughing at others' misfortune. In turn, Aristotle argues that comedy should in fact mock "a species of the ugly." These two approaches to comedy, Plato's and Aristotle's, set up a theoretical framework that continues to be at the crux of humor and disability studies: how is it appropriate or not appropriate to laugh at disability (or, for that matter, any non-normative body and behavior), and at whom or what?

Existentially, disability is simultaneously an extremely alien experience to the non-disabled and an extremely familiar experience of the body-in-waiting (every-one's body will eventually fall apart, and disability often functions as both a reminder of that fact and a certain relief at a not-yet-reached future). Thus, most historical and contemporary tragic narratives dealing with disability revolve around two extreme notions: on one hand, the disabled character is an "inspirational" figure (often sacrificed in melodramatic plots of suffering and redemption); on the other, he or she is an embodiment of "evil" (as defined by Freud's ['Some character-types met with in psycho-analytic work', 1916] analysis of Shakespeare's Richard III as an archetypal model of the disabled who exhibits, according to Freud, an "obvious" correlation between physical disability and "deformities of character"). The two extreme tragic narratives are translated into comic formulas through two strategies: (1) the disabled character—though the comic trope of self-deprecation—somehow manages to acquire the status of the "human" (and, thus, is no longer an alien object of mockery but in some way is "in on the joke" with the audience. He becomes, alternatively, inspiring and endearing); (2) the disabled character's "evil" impulses are so farfetched that they become grotesque: his ambitions are at once unrealistic and delusional (he becomes alternatively more and less than human, super threatening and super weak). These two comic formulas have persisted more or less unchanged, and they have remained mostly uncontested in both theoretical and comic writings and performance.

Starting in antiquity, it was quite common and appropriate to laugh at the disabled. As a result, throughout the centuries, more often than not, they would perform either in circuses or as court jesters. In medieval and Renaissance Europe, in fact, dwarf jesters were so popular that the practice of kidnapping and artificially stunting children became common to keep up with demand. In Shakespeare's *A Midsummer Night's Dream* (1600), Lysander insults Hermia by calling her an artificially, "knot-grass made" dwarf: "Get you gone, you dwarf; / You minimus, of hindering knot-grass made; / You bead, you accord!" The desire to keep dwarfs and other "freaks" at court was almost universally viewed as a way to contain their magical capacity for evil. It was also believed that the touch of a dwarf could cure and fend off illness, and his stinging wit could "purge ill humour." Some court jesters were developmentally challenged, with Down syndrome, Asperger, or autism, and they too were used for amusement, as their antics were considered a great source of entertainment.

Although some court jesters were killed in revenge for their biting humor; many others, ironically, found shelter in the safety of the court. The body of the disabled court jester, his ambivalent—if also precarious—position as both a prized possession and the object of ridicule, illustrates well the uneasy connection between disability and the tragic and comic frames. Paradoxically, disability can embody both of them simultaneously, depending on our degree of identification with the object. As Trissino (1529) aptly put it: "if we have like sufferings, the sight of them in others does not move us to laughter." If the wounds and suffering are "deadly and painful [...] they do not move laughter, but rather pity through fear that similar ills may come to ourselves." The disabled body can at once be an object of mockery and object of pity. This paradoxical position of the disabled body as both tragic and comic is intimately intertwined in our sense of human dignity, both as a narrative trope (the way its loss functions in Arthur Miller's definition of modern tragedy, and the way its loss functions in Aristotle's definition of comedy) and as the essential precondition to humanist ethics.

In his famous essay "Tragedy and the Common Man" (1949), Arthur Miller modifies the Aristotelian definition of tragedy (as based on a "tragic flaw") and argues that "the tragic feeling is evoked in us when we are in the presence of a character who is ready to lay down his life, if need be, to secure one thing—his sense of personal dignity." Tragedy then, Miller writes "automatically demonstrates the indestructible will of man to achieve his humanity." The concept of human dignity, like the concept of "humanity," can be considered a historical and exclusionary concept that defines an exclusionary category (since not everyone is automatically granted the status of 'human'). The disabled characters and their narrative journeys towards humanity and human dignity (e.g., *Elephant Man* narratives) are at the core of Miller's understanding of tragedy. Their narrative journeys are very much rooted in this narrative model of a quest towards human dignity. In tragic narratives, this quest succeeds (through the pathos of suffering, sacrifice and self-sacrifice, and eventual redemption). In comic narratives, this quest can either fail or succeed. It succeeds in inspirational, "heroic" narratives that employ humor to make the quest and heroism of the character more palpable for non-disabled audience members. However, it fails in grotesque and farcical narratives where the disabled character is either demonically "evil" or a surreal fantasy creature (outside of the category of "human").

Like all other marginalized groups, the disabled have also found recourse in humor as a coping strategy. Since most of that type of coping humor involves some form of self-deprecation, like other critics the theorists of disability and humor studies have wondered whether such humor indeed has liberatory potential or whether it reinforces and codifies the marginalization of non-normative bodies. In her book on Jewish humor, Ruth R. Wisse (2013) asks whether Jews can ever "overdose" on the self-deprecating humor: can a group of people who have been threatened with violence and extinction time and time again really afford to perpetuate the kind of humor that further self-marginalizes them? In a similar vein, the theorists of African American humor have wondered to what degree the self-deprecating humor "engendered by the slavery experience and codified during the relatively extended and popular run of blackface entertainment endured" backfired on the African American community by confirming and perpetuating some of the worst stereotypes of the era (Watkins 39). Today's self-deprecating Jewish, African American, or feminist humor often involves the element of meta-irony, and critics continue to argue about how effective such comic strategies are. Some disabled stand-up (or stand-down) comics, like Stella Young or Maysoon Zayid used the reversed gaze humor as a way to reframe the narrative language around their disabilities.

Like with every other marginalized group, the humor of the disabled has an inside and an outside audience. The humor directed at the outside audience is often performed at the expense of the marginalized group (with awareness of that group's marginal status and its relationship to the mainstream audience). The inside humor, on the other hand, returns a comic gaze, often poking fun not so much at the marginal group but at the mainstream that marginalizes it. In one of her 1950s interviews, Lorraine Hansberry noted that "The intimacy of knowledge which the Negro may culturally have of white Americans does not exist in the reverse." The rights of the disabled lag significantly behind those of every other minority group, and Hansberry's statement captures well the current state of the relationship between the disabled and non-disabled groups:

the intimacy of knowledge that the disabled have of the non-disabled community does not exist in the reverse. Susan Wendell (1997) noted that "if disabled people were truly heard, an explosion of knowledge of the human body and psyche would take place" (274). Perhaps the same can also be said of our humor?

Permissions Acknowledgements

Chapter 1

Plato, tr. J. Rusten (2011), 'Philebus', in Plato, *Philebus*, 48a–50b, reprinted by kind permission of the translator.

Aristotle, tr. J. Rusten (2011), 'Poetics', in Aristotle, *Poetics*, reprinted by kind permission of the translator.

Aristotle, tr. J. Rusten (2016), 'Wittiness, Buffoonery, and Boorishness' taken from Aristotle, *Nichomachean Ethics*, 107–8, reprinted by kind permission of the translator.

Aristotle, tr. J. Rusten (1999), 'On the Qualities of Character that Are Moderate', in Aristotle, *Nichomachean Ethics*, reprinted by kind permission of the translator.

Aristotle, tr. J. Rusten (2011), 'Tractatus Coislinianus', in Aristotle, *Tractatus Coislinianus*, 48a–50b, reprinted by kind permission of the translator.

Horace, tr. J. Rusten (2011), 'Remarks on comedy', in Horace, *Epistles, Satires*, reprinted by kind permission of the translator.

Quintilian, tr. J. Selby Watson (2008), 'Institutio Oratoria (A.D. 95) Quintilian', in Honeycutt, L. (ed.), *Institutes of Oratory*, reprinted by kind permission of Lee Honeycutt.

Evanthius (1974), 'On Drama', in Alex Preminger, O. B. Hardison, Jr., and Kevin Kerrane (eds), *Classical and Medieval Literary Criticism: Translations and Interpretations*, 301–5, New York: Frederick Ungar Publishing.

Donatus, tr. S. G. Nugent (1974), 'On Comedy', in Alex Preminger, O. B. Hardison, Jr. and Kevin Kerrane (eds), *Classical and Medieval Literary Criticism: Translations and Interpretations*, 305–9, New York: Frederick Ungar Publishing.

Hrotsvita of Gandersheim, tr. Christopher St. John (1966), Prologue to the Comedies, in *The Plays of Roswitha*, New York: Benjamin Bloom.

Dante Alighieri, tr. S. Botterill (1996), *De Vulgari Eloquentia* ('On Eloquence in the Vernacular') in Steven Botterill (ed., tr.) *De Vulgari Eloquentia* (*On Eloquence in the Vernacular*), © Cambridge University Press 1996, reproduced with permission. Reprinted by kind permission of the translator.

Rusten, J. (2011), 'Definitions of Comedy' in John of Garland, Dante, John Lydgate, *Definitions of Comedy*, reprinted by kind permission of the translator.

Rusten, J. (2011), 'Attitudes to the Comic Theater', in John of Salisbury, Honorius of Autun, Liuprand of Cremona, *Attitudes to the Comic Theater*, reprinted by kind permission of the translator.

Chapter 2

Erasmus, from the *Collected Works of Erasmus*, Volume 24: *Literary and Educational Writings 2: De Copia/De Ratione Studii*, edited by Craig R. Thompson © University of Toronto Press 1978, 584–690. Reprinted with permission of the publisher.

Trissino, G. G., 'Division VI: Comedy', 224–32, reprinted from *Literary Criticism: Plato to Dryden*, edited by Allen H. Gilbert. © 1962 Wayne State University Press, with the permission of Wayne State University Press.

Battista, G., 'Compendium of Tragicomic Poetry', 507–9, 511–14, 521–5, reprinted from *Literary Criticism: Plato to Dryden* edited by Allen H. Gilbert. Copyright © 1962 Wayne State University Press, with the permission of Wayne State University Press.

Chapter 3

Molière, tr. P. Lauter, Excerpt: 'Preface to Tartuffe', 155–61, from *Theories of Comedy* by Paul Lauter, translation copyright © 1964 by Paul Lauter. Used by permission of Doubleday, an imprint of the Knopf Doubleday Publishing Group, a division of Penguin Random House LLC. All rights reserved. Any third party use of this material, outside of this publication, is prohibited. Interested parties must apply directly to Penguin Random House LLC for permission.

Chapter 4

Chapter 5

excerpt of approximately 1,424 words, 20–6, Reproduced by permission of the University of Chicago Press.

Cavell, S., Selections from pp. 1–33, *Pursuits of Happiness: The Hollywood Comedy of Remarriage*, by Stanley Cavell, © 1981 by the President and Fellows of Harvard College.

Apte, M. L. (1984), 'Sexual Inequality in Humor' (67–81), from *Humor and Laughter: An Anthropological Approach*.

Hutcheon, L. (1985), Extract from *A Theory of Parody*. Reprinted with the kind permission of the author.

Jenkins, H. 'Agee, Mast, and the Classical Tradition' and 'Early Sound Comedy and the Vaudeville Aesthetic' (22–5), from *What Made Pistachio Nuts?: Early Sound Comedy and the Vaudeville Aesthetic*, published by Columbia University Press, 1992.

Critchley, S., Extracts (6–11, 25–9) from *On Humour* by Simon Critchley. Published by Routledge, 2002. Reproduced by permission of Taylor & Francis Books UK.

Carpio, G., 'Laughing Fit to Kill', *Black Humor in the Fictions of Slavery* by Glenda Carpio (2008): 1,231w (4–7). Reprinted with permission from Oxford University Press.

North, M., *Machine-age Comedy* by Michael North (2009): 3,130w (4–23). Reprinted with permission from Oxford University Press.

Wisse, R., Extracts (2, 13–14, 19–24, 28, selections) from *No Joke: Making Jewish Humor* (Princeton University Press, 2013). Reprinted with permission.

Romanska, M., 'Disability in Tragic and Comic Frame'. © by Magda Romanska. Reprinted with the kind permission of the author.

Index